CHINA BUSINESS:
CHALLENGES IN THE 21ST CENTURY

China Business:
Challenges in the 21st Century

Edited by

Oliver H. M. Yau and Henry C. Steele

The Chinese University Press

China Business: Challenges in the 21st Century
Edited by Oliver H. M. Yau and Henry C. Steele

© **The Chinese University of Hong Kong,** 2000

ISBN 962–201–853–X

First edition   2000
Second printing 2001
Third printing   2004

THE CHINESE UNIVERSITY PRESS
The Chinese University of Hong Kong
SHA TIN, N.T., HONG KONG
Fax: +852 2603 6692
      +852 2603 7355
E-mail: cup@cuhk.edu.hk
Web-site: www.chineseupress.com

Printed in Hong Kong

Contents

Preface

As we approach the 21st century, China is emerging from self-imposed isolation to become one of the world's largest economies. Despite economic downturn in the region from 1997, China's economy has continued to show a high rate of growth helped by the large amount of foreign investment received in the years following the open-door policy begun in 1979. China's experience is unique, has required many changes and included some experiments as it tries to build an internationally acceptable framework for doing business. At the same time, there is the formidable political task to maintain unity of a vast, populous and surprisingly diverse country. All this at a time when dramatic, social, economic and political changes are taking place. China's path to internationalization is not easy. The process is fraught with pitfalls. Reforms to both the banking system and state-owned enterprises (SOEs) pose more immediate issues still to be resolved.

For foreign business to succeed the need is to be better informed of the challenges that China presents — it is a harsh business environment. China has a lot of catching up to do for the lost years when there was no business education, a lack of legal and regulatory frameworks and a lack of any opportunity to gain management experience. China is making up for lost time with unequalled energy and determination. Contributors in this book address a wide range of business issues through their research and present a glimpse of China in the late 1990s. It is further anticipated that in so doing a benchmark of continuing progress and change will be provided and from this can be extrapolated the challenges that are being faced both by managers and businesses, whether indigenous or international.

China is undergoing a quiet revolution, the greatest free market reforms ever seen. Looking in from the outside is not easy, there remain restrictions on access to information, questions remain about the reliability of published statistics so as editors of this collection of research-based essays an objective assessment is given of a selection of topics that will be of interest to those with concern in the development of China. The topics have been chosen for their representation of a broad range of emerging issues. They are presented by the authors in such a way that they are both accessible and interesting appealing to the business person who are involved in China trade and students alike.

For the more serious researchers they should find materials that are illuminating and provoking. The book is comprised of four parts each with a theme: business environment, management, marketing and international business. Contributions are from business people and researchers who have extensive knowledge, experience and contact with the People's Republic of China and who have witnessed not only progress but also some of the pain that has accompanied the path to a market economy. Much may go un-recorded, or become forgotten so it is important that the results of research in China are given a permanent record and that they are made available to a wider audience. An extensive bibliography is provided at the end of the text which, for serious readers and researchers, should make further recording and investigation both more practical and rewarding.

The editors only provide a guide to recent developments in China and the contents are selective, rather than comprehensive, but include a variety of insights, often into areas or aspects which have rarely been investigated or presented previously. To this extent there is a contribution to our knowledge, albeit a fleeting one, at a point in time. For this insight, we must thank all the contributors. We recognize all the time and effort devoted to the research that made possible the contributions that make up this book. It is difficult to acknowledge them individually, so only a general acknow-ledgement of our indebtedness to them is made here. However, a special mention must be given to Raymond P. M. Chow for his contribution in preparing the drafts for publication, and to the editorial board of the Chinese University Press in publishing this timely book, which is unique in its content and wide in its coverage. In particular, we would also like to thank solemnly Dr. H. L. Chan, the contributor of Chapters 8 and 9 of this book, who passed away early this year, in his sincere endeavour of expand-ing the knowledge of Chinese management.

It is in the interests of sharing experience, and in fostering knowledge that we seek reward for our efforts. We would like our readers to share, and to reflect on, the contributions that we have included. China business faces many challenges as we enter the 21st century.

Oliver H. M. Yau
Henry C. Steele

Introduction

1

China Business: Challenges in the 21st Century

Oliver H. M. Yau and Henry C. Steele

This introduction chapter has two objectives: first, to provide readers with a road map for this book, detailing its structure, and second, to serve as a guideline for recent developments in the business environment, marketing, management and international business in China. This chapter thus provides a perspective for the book as a whole, underlining its novelty and innovative aspects in terms of problems and challenges emerging as a result of recent economic reforms.

This book is divided into four sections: environment, management, marketing and international business. We will give a brief account of each section as follows.

Section I. Business Environment in China

Section I of this book includes six chapters examining the development of economic and financial environments, the reform of accounting standards and its implications for foreign investors, the legal reform and its impact on business enterprises, the changes of societal and cultural environments in the recent business setting. These chapters provide a sound foundation for readers who do not have a good knowledge of what has been happening in the People's Republic of China (PRC).

In Chapter 2, K. W. Li gives an account of the Chinese economy since the beginning of reform in 1978. China has experienced a positive and strong growth of about 8.87% per annum from 1979 until 1997 and is the only economy whose growth rate has kept at a two-digit level throughout the period of reform until now (1997), especially when compared with those of Western countries. Since 1978, economic reform in China can be classified into the following four stages:

1st stage: Rural Reform (1978–1984) in which the "family responsibility system" was implemented;

2nd stage: Urban Reform (1985–1988) in which the two pricing systems and enterprise autonomy were introduced;

3rd stage: Preparatory effort for Deepening Reform (1989–1992);

4th stage: Deepening Reform (1992–present), which was signified by Deng Xiaoping's tour to the southern part of China.

As a consequence of the economic reforms, China has achieved laudable macroeconomic performances in a range of important areas. Firstly, the growth of nominal income since 1980 has experienced double-digit growth, rates, which in three years peaked at 24% (1984–85), 24.8% (1988) and 30% (1994) respectively. This rapid growth of income has brought about the deterioration in income equality between the richer, mostly coastal, regions and the poorer, mostly interior regions.

Accompanying the income growth, inflation rates have increased since 1978, reaching the first peak of 18.8% in 1988 and a second peak of 21.7% in 1994. The first peak was due to households trying to get rid of their surplus cash and hoarding commodities as the inflation rate went up and to enterprises' accumulating raw materials, expecting to sell at a higher price. The inflation rate fell as a result of political unrest in 1989. The second peak was curbed by a tight monetary policy in 1993, which became effective in 1995.

Industrial output and agricultural output have both reached new heights in 1995. Interestingly, with more or less the same output in 1978, industrial output has exceeded agricultural output by almost fivefold, indicating the emerging significance of the industrial sector.

Superficially, unemployment in China is low at 3%. However, there are two main sources of potential unemployment, one in the rural sector, and the other from loss-making state-owned enterprises which are about to close down. Hence, the agenda for reform in 1996 was to rejuvenate the state-owned enterprises.

In money and banking, China has experienced several concerns. Firstly, it has a dual interest rate system: the official rate and the market rate, which has not been effectively used for economic reasons. Secondly, the issue of triangular debts that have been prevailing amounted to RMB700 billion in 1995. Thirdly, the functions of policy banks, commercial and corporate banks were not clear. As a result, the most prominent reform in the banking sector was the introduction of the Banking Law in 1995, which declared the responsibility of various types of banks and called for establishing a central bank to oversee the activities of other banks. It was anticipated that the monetary policy in China would continue to be tight in the next five-year plan.

Regarding fiscal policy and reform, China's budget has been in deficit for several years. On one side, the two largest items of government expenditure are subsidies to loss-making enterprises and price subsidies. On the other side, China is suffering from a low tax base and the extent of taxability. Given these shortcomings, several measures were introduced. First, the introduction of a value added tax (VAT) to replace the product tax and also a business tax, which has replaced the consolidated industrial and commercial tax previously applied to foreign enterprises. Second, the tax structure was further simplified. Last, a new "tax sharing system" was introduced to solve the issue of the "central-local" relationship. Since 1978, several measures have been introduced to attract foreign capital and investments. These include the establishment of five Special Economic Zones (Shenzhen, Zhuhai, Shantou, Xiamen and Hainan) and the opening of fourteen coastal cities, followed by New Pudong Area in Shanghai. The special nature of these coastal Economic Zones was challenged in 1995 and special treatments such as duty-free privilege and tax holidays enjoyed by some of these cities were removed.

Among other forms of foreign capital, foreign direct investments remain the largest and have increased tremendously over the years. Guangdong, Jiangsu, Fujian, Shandong and Shanghai were the top five recipients of foreign investments. In value terms, the industry sector and real estates were ranked at the top while the manufacturing industry had encountered a sharp decline in foreign investments.

The reform of state-owned enterprises has emerged as an important agenda item over the years. These enterprises have accumulated huge debt as a result of wastage in welfare and wage expenses and unproductive investments. The concerns the Chinese authority now are to set an appropriate timetable for individual enterprises in their pursuit of economic independence, to clean up corruption among officials, and to reduce the divergence of political interests between the localities and the central government.

In Chapter 3, John D. S. Ho examines the legal environment of Chinese business enterprises since 1978. In this chapter, Professor Ho traces the reconstruction of the legal environment after years of neglect, examining the legislation that aimed at building a "socialist market economy" and investigating the formation, capitalization, operation, and bankruptcy of the modern Chinese enterprises under the Company Law and the Bankruptcy Law.

The legal reform of enterprise came in the form of the Company Law enacted on 29 December 1993. The new law, making the corporation the most important form of Chinese enterprises, provides for the restructuring of the organization and management of state-owned enterprises, private enterprises, and branches of foreign companies. It embraces several new legal concepts such as legal person status of a company, private minority of state enterprises, the provision of private enterprises, limited liability, the limited company, the joint stock company, the shareholders' meeting, the board of directors and the legal representative, etc.

The trend in the law towards greater autonomy for state enterprises has sometimes resulted in managerial abuses. Some enterprises have made use of the autonomy to issue bonuses and increase fringe benefits despite substantial losses. These losses were then written off through state budget appropriations or administrative measures against the enterprises by closing, merging or changing their business operations. The Law of the People's Republic of China on Bankruptcy of Enterprises became effective as of 1 November 1988. However, the government is very much concerned about the possible social and economic implications of bankruptcies of state enterprises as they are the providers of social welfare such as preschool childcare and hospitals. Unpaid bank loans by bankrupted state-owned enterprises could also bring destabilizing losses to loan providing banks.

The Civil Procedure Law governs the bankruptcy of non-state-owned enterprises with legal status was in force in 1991. With this regard, the government is more concerned with protecting the creditors than those bankrupted enterprises.

The author identifies several challenges given the changes in the legal environment. He warns that one of the real challenges is to build a viable legal system in a socialist market economy and not in a capitalist one as many people wish to. This is not easy to achieve. The second challenge, as he indicates, is to perfect the legal environment. This can only be achieved gradually and cautiously.

In this first section, there are two chapters regarding the financial environment of China. In Chapter 4, David Y. K. Chan provides us with a picture of the development of stock markets in China. There are two stock exchanges in China, the Shanghai Stock Exchange formed in 1990 and the Shenzhen Stock Exchange established in 1991. Recently, the China stock market has become internationalized. A huge amount of capital has come from foreign investors, most of which is invested in the B shares market which is available to overseas investors only, whereas local individual investors can only purchase A shares. Chinese enterprises can use five different types of ordinary shares: A shares, B shares, C shares, H shares and N shares, to raise capital. Professor Chan found that the China stock market has several distinctive characteristics.

> *Turnover and Market Liquidity:* The two stock exchanges have exhibited that the B shares market was thinner than A shares market with very low turnover. Further, the A shares market has a higher liquidity than B shares market on the two exchanges.
> *Concentration:* Trading was concentrated among a small number of members.
> *Sectoral Composition:* Most of the shares listed are industrial companies.
> *Clearance and Settlement:* A shares have a shorter settlement time.
> *Transaction Cost:* Buyers and sellers are subject to commissions, fees and stamp duties.
> *Taxation and Dividend Payment:* There are no capital gains and dividend taxes on trades.

Given the above characteristics, it was found that the stock exchanges are inefficient in the new share issues process due to some possible reasons such as (1) high degree of investors uncertainty, (2) speculation as a result of not knowing the allocation mechanism adopted for the new share issues, and (3) the monopolistic nature of local underwriters and their inexperience.

In terms of stock price volatility, it was also discovered that A shares markets in both Shanghai and Shenzhen were greater than B shares markets. Volatility patterns indicated that A shares and B shares markets were thin and inefficient as information was dispersed slowly to investors; and large daily jumps in volatility were found.

The above phenomena could be largely attributed to problems in converting RMB to other currencies in the foreign exchange market, government intervention and the lack of an appropriate legal framework, an adequate amount of professional practitioners and a supporting infrastructure. To improve the efficiency of the equity market, it is proposed to cross-list shares of the two exchanges. Given the complex financial environment in China, it is necessary to forecast RMB exchange rate. K. C. Mun, in Chapter 5, gives a detailed description of the technique of forecasting RMB exchange rate.

Chapters 6 and 7 of this book deal with cultural and consumer values. Chapter 6 provides a detailed description of the Chinese cultural values that are regarded as the foundation of understanding how Chinese business operates and Chinese consumers behave. Although there exist a few cultural dimensions as proposed by Rokeach (1973), Hofstede (1982), and Hofstede and Bond (1988) in the literature, their works are not deemed as appropriate to accurately and comprehensively describe Chinese cultural values. Highly regarded, Rokeach's values suffer more from their measurement than from their content. Hofstede's classification is lacking in content validity, not to mention the serious sampling problem in the survey on which the classification was based. By no means are the four dimensions he suggested suitable for measuring cultural values of the Chinese. Bond's classification, based on a factor analysis of 40 abstract nouns, was another disappointment in classifying Chinese cultural values. The abstract nouns used were written in classical Chinese and they could be interpreted differently by people with various backgrounds. Further, Hofstede's classification also suffers from content validity as the numbers of dimensions are regarded as insufficient. Hence, in this chapter, Oliver H. M. Yau makes use of the five cultural orientations classification suggested by Kluckhohn and Strodbeck (1961): man-to-nature orientation, man-to-himself orientation, relational orientation, time orientation and personal activity orientation. He then further divide them into a total of twelve Chinese cultural values:

Man-to-Nature Orientation
 1. Harmony with the nature
 2. *Yuarn*
Man-to-Himself Orientation
 3. Abasement
 4. Situation-orientation
Relational Orientation
 5. Respect for authority
 6. Interdependence
 7. Group-orientation
 8. Face
Time Orientation
 9. Continuity
 10. Past-time Orientation
Personal Activity Orientation
 11. The Doctrine of the Mean
 12. Harmony with Others

The man-to-nature orientation shows that the Chinese do not prefer to overcome and master nature but to adapt to it so as to reach harmony. Hence, the Chinese usually attribute failure of products or services to fate rather than to the company from whom the products or services were purchased, or even the manufacturer. The man-to-himself orientation indicates the flexible behaviour and the moderate nature of the Chinese. The importance of this orientation emphasizes the values of both situational orientation in decision making and abasement in sales force management. A look at the relational aspect shows off-duty personal behaviour is highly important to the firm's image and its effectiveness. Firms also need to keep in mind the informal channels of communication in Chinese society, the brand loyalty, the small social circles, and the importance of the extended family. The time orientation reemphasizes the values of continuity and past-time orientation that tend to make the Chinese so brand loyal. Finally, the personal activity orientation involves not complaining about products or services, slowly accepting new fashions or technology, and being risk averse.

Many of the values were overlooked and not covered by Rokeach, Hofstede and Bond. This is the main reason why their values were found either not appropriate or inadequate in explaining Chinese behaviour. In reality, readers will find these values not only important to marketers, but also to managers who deal with human resources.

In Chapter 7, Stephen S. L. Lau disagrees with Oliver Yau's emphasis on traditional cultural values. He argues that traditional cultural values have been contaminated by the communist ideology since 1949, especially during the Cultural Revolution from 1966 to 1976. The chapter begins by comparing China's present socioeconomic environment with those of the newly industrialized economies. As a result, diversity exists in terms of population growth rate, infant mortality, life expectancy, literacy rate, people per TV, and people per telephone. He then looks into a number of consumption related issues and concludes that consumption habits are changing, to a great extent, in a direction closely to those of Western societies as traditional Chinese cultural values are further corrupted.

In this chapter the distinction between "modern" and "western" is not made. Some directions are needed to show how traditional (consumption) values that we discussed can be modernized, but not Westernized.

Section II. Business Management in China

In the section on Business Management in China, there are contributions in four aspects relating to dimensions of management issues. The first examines Confucian beliefs and values and shows the implications for management in China. From a historical perspective, the evolution of Confucianism is shown, and the way that these values are important today as China undergoes rapid economic and social changes. This is followed by a chapter to review political risk, illustrating the management environment faced by firms entering and doing business in China. As the reader will be able to see the philosophical foundations of Chinese Society are still significant influences in management issues, but are further modified by exposure to a variety of regimes in a short time frame, with the most recent changes designed to bring about China's modernization and to encompass a socialist market economy. The following chapters give an overview of two major areas of influence on management in China. Two writings showing the trends and current position for the international banking sector and the transfer of international technology and its management by firms in China for new product development complete this section.

In chapter 8, H. L. Chan, Anthony Ko and Eddie Yu emphasize that Confucianism and its thoughts and beliefs are generally seen as part of the influence on current Chinese attitudes and behaviour and an influence on management, thought and style. Although Confucianism is subject to continuous reinterpretation, the fundamental philosophical elements remain strong motivators of behaviour. The foundation of Confucianism was in a population based in the countryside, engaged in subsistence agriculture. Here limited resources could be distributed according to a prescribed hierarchical political and social order with the origins of the deemphasization of commerce as merely "the branch" whereas agrarian production provided "the root." Much of both life and economy was based on natural rhythms, the farming year was marked by the seasons. No change was desired, invention or discoveries were therefore, often discouraged. Living and working on the land tied everyone to their family and community in a particular place. Mutual dependence made harmony a necessary virtue. Confucianism resulted from a theoretical expression of this social system, and the Chinese social system was characterized by the "family state," which is both autocratic and hierarchical. In the West, emphasis is placed on the intrinsic value of a human being as a free and independent individual, whereas in China what is important is the relationship with fellow men and through these relationships, an individual's potential is realized.

Explained are the five constant virtues, and these virtues form the basis of harmony in society. Three out of the five cardinal human relationships belong to the family. Unlike relationships in the West, they are not contractual, but are personalistic and particularistic, being defined in Confucianism in terms of duties or rules within the social hierarchy. It is one's status in the social hierarchy that determines duty to others, age is important in conferring status in this hierarchy. *Wu lun* (five constant virtues) are the relationship between father and son, or sovereign and subject. The father can never be wrong and commands unconditional respect, and in return the father will take care of his son. This basic hierarchical relationship between father and son is a model for extension to other social relationships. As a result, everyone in Chinese society knows his or her rank, and behaves in accordance with the roles and duties prescribed by that rank. The result is a long time harmonious and stable society.

For an understanding of management in China in the 21st century, it is necessary to appreciate the nature of Confucianism and its long-term influence. Although the modernization of China has been achieved largely by Western investment bringing Western management to joint ventures and wholly-owned foreign enterprises (WOFEs), underlying Confucian beliefs remain, something which can make the managerial task based on organizational achievement and performance a difficult balancing act. The need for efficiency and bottom line results can be helped by harnessing the values of traditional Confucianism. To some extent, recent history and turmoil in China has weakened Confucian values, but their reemergence can give strength to Chinese organization if they can be utilized into the 21st century. Confucianism has important implications for future management in China. The morality orientation in management, the importance of motives and the sprit of self-cultivation leading to achievement orientation characterized by hard work, thrift and perseverance. It is evident that given an appropriate business environment, Chinese are generally high in achievement orientated behaviour. There is great emphasis on the virtue of the leader who sets the moral example. In so doing, this produces a situation in which clear and comprehensive systems with formal regulations are perceived as relatively unimportant.

It is hoped that through the traditional Chinese value and belief system a paradigm of Chinese management can be established and can eventually borrow from both the West and Japan to meet the demands of organizations in the coming millennium.

In Chapter 9, H. L. Chan identifies two separate issues, the attractiveness of financial opportunity and political risks. Investment decisions will be made by making trades between risks and opportunities. More attractive investment opportunities will result in a willingness to be exposed to higher political risk. A systematic examination is made of the risks associated with China's modernization programme, and the likely sources of political risks for businesses are traced and suggestions made for ways in which these risks can be managed. The progress of economic reform has followed a variable path with sudden changes of direction and consequent effects on economic growth, and unemployment and fostering labour unrest. Economic performance is recognized as the means by which potential power can remain in the hands of the Chinese Communist Party (CCP). There are increasing disparities in wealth as market forces take hold, and rapid industrialisation in the cities leaves rural communities impoverished. Coastal provinces have prospered as modernization policies have been initiated, and interior provinces have become relatively disadvantaged. An increasing decentralisation of economic decisions away from Beijing to provinces, cities and local authorities is manifested in local policies and smooth progress may be assisted by corruption. The central government is unable to monitor and control compliance with regulations and the further away from Beijing the greater is the feeling of local freedom and less need for compliance.

Sources of political risk identified are ideological conflicts, loss of control and income disparity. Managerial decisions are evaluated in relation to financial opportunity, political risks and investable resources, emanating in a number of possible strategies, risk avoidance, transfer, or control, diversification, good corporate citizen profile and alliances. The economic reforms have been viewed widely as successful in achieving sustained high levels of economic growth bringing a general increase in the standard of living. At the same time, such drastic change that has occurred in Chinese society within a short time period cannot avoid arousing social discontent among those groups. These groups perceive their economic well-being threatened by the changes or have become relatively disadvantaged as others have become rich not necessarily from their own endeavours but as a result of local political support or worse still beneficiaries of crime or corruption. Avoiding exposure to political risk in China will mean missing out on a potential market. A decision model for political risk management strategies is suggested. For the foreseeable future there is a need to be alert and flexible as government policies are subject to unpredictable changes of direction and the situation at local level remains fluid. The days of tight central control are not likely to return as economic reforms progress apace to make up for the lost years of previous decades.

In the process of the opening up of China to foreign companies and investment, it is more recently that there are opportunities for service industries to become established and this is a process that is still continuing. Banks have been permitted to establish representative offices and branches which can engage in limited banking activities but have by no means been permitted to offer their full range of services including local currency transactions and retail banking. At present, banks are limited to serving foreign investors, foreign invested enterprises and state-owned corporations and authorities. The regulations and laws are being introduced and are constantly changing. They are, as yet, incomplete and less than adequate with a certain degree of opaqueness. When transgressions occur there is no standard legal recourse. As an illustration of the entry strategy of multinational transaction services firms in China, Abby Sin and Thamis W. C. Lo in Chapter 10 have chosen the example of Japanese banks. Among the international banks that have a presence in China, the Japanese banks are the largest in terms of both numbers of representative offices and branches. They are the largest lenders accounting for 60% of all private lending to China. Japanese banks have had the benefits of the Overseas Development Aid Programme of the Japanese government and the special benefits of a double taxation treaty that has enabled the banks to provide loans at low cost. Given the structure of Japanese banking and the inter-relationships between the banks and their customers, dealing with Chinese state-owned enterprises has been acceptable without the normal full disclosure required by Western banks. The Japanese banks have been aggressive in offering competitive pricing and low interest rates, and the Chinese customers have been more willing to approach the Japanese banks, knowing that little financial information will need to be disclosed. Japanese banks have sacrificed margins as part of long-term market penetration strategy for which profitability is trimmed but growth is extremely important.

China will continue to introduce new laws and regulations and improve on existing ones. Given the pace of economic development, the banking industry will grow and multinational banks will play a greater role in the future as restrictions on foreign service industries are relaxed. For most multinational service firms, the pay-off is seen in the long term. The multitude of problems faced in establishing a base in the China market is a part of the strategy of building up a presence in the market, gaining knowledge and understanding, being in proactive position to combat competitors, and having a long-term commitment which is seen as bringing eventual rewards, namely profitability in the long term.

In meeting the requirements for membership of World Trade Organization (WTO) more open access will need to be given to foreign owned service industries and continuing moves in this direction can be expected, giving a widening scope of banking services, and allowing other service industries some degree of access to the China market. Moves are now taking place to reform the insurance industry in China by allowing limited foreign participation.

Section III. Marketing in China

Section III of this book consists of four chapters on marketing in China. The first two chapters are related to the development of the distribution system while the last one focuses on how time is used by consumers in retail services.

In Chapter 11, Oliver H. M. Yau and Y. J. Li give an account of the recent development of the distribution system in China. They classify the recent development into three stages: the initial reform stage (1979–1984), the comprehensive reform and development stage (1985–1991), and the in-depth reform stage (1992–present). At each stage of the development, the distribution system has made tremendous progress as it evolved towards the next stage and disentangled itself from the centrally planned economy. Having said that, the current distribution system is still remaining socialist in nature although various levels of wholesaling stations and retailers seem to enjoy economic freedom in their operations. They also compare the distribution systems between the first and the third stages, indicating the changes in the reorganization of the government structure, the availability of new intermediary institutions, and the introduction of the agency arrangement which replaced the purchasing system through the Ministry of Foreign Trade & Economic Cooperation. Finally, they also provide insights into stumbling blocks that hinder China from developing an effective and efficient system. These blocks include (1) the confounding functions of enterprises as both political organs, social welfare units and enterprises in pragmatic terms, (2) unsuccessful price reform leading to a dual price system (state-set-prices and market-adjusted prices) and inflation and (3) serious regionalism and (4) disorder of the market place.

Following similar lines, Chapter 12 focuses on the development, problems and prospects of chain stores that are an emerging form of retailing in the distribution system of China. Three distinctive stages of chain store development in China are examined by Z. Q. Sha and his associates. The way these stages are categorized differs from those of the distribution system. In the embryonic stage, the authors attributed that retailing in the form of chain stores started much earlier than those counterparts in the USA. The second stage is the period when chain stores were operated under the centrally planned economy. In this stage, chain stores were all owned by the state and sold similar merchandise.

The third stage, named as "upsurge of the modern chain store — The 'Entry Stage,'" began in 1979 and ended in 1997. They regard this stage as the period of transition from entry to growth stage using the product life cycle concept. Consistent with the progressive development of chain stores in Western societies, the implication is that chain stores in China still have a long way to go before they eventually reach the decline stage.

In the same vein, C. S. Tseng tells us how foreign investors feel their way when entering the retail industry in China. As mentioned in Chapter 11, retail distribution remains a state monopoly with a three-tier structure and a degree of regional protectionism. Flexibility and competition has been introduced since the mid 1990s and different types of companies have become involved in distribution, including state-owned enterprises which have set up subsidiaries to make use of excess staff and workers.

In Chapter 13, the historical development of foreign participation in retailing is charted and the current ways in which an overseas company can gain access to sell products to the consumers are identified. It is evident that there is a range of methods but gaining widespread distribution and availability of foreign products is not easy and it is fraught by bureaucracy, restrictions, regional differences and an element of political interference. For the smaller scale retail operation, local government can give approval to joint venture retailing projects but without conferring any import rights. A rapid development of supermarkets and chain stores is being witnessed in major cities throughout China using the legally permitted methods of foreign involvement, namely equity or contractual joint venture or licensing.

As franchising is not a recognized form of market entry in China, it is not generally accepted that payment be made for "soft technologies" such as store management and marketing expertise when many international fast food groups use one of the above means of entry. Sometimes the Western companies franchise to Hong Kong or Taiwanese companies eventually handle the problem of payment for soft technologies.

A number of issues relating to current practices and associated problems are discussed, including difficulties in obtaining payment, geographical differences, limited market information, shortcomings in the transport and distribution infrastructure and the ever present problem of training and keeping good quality personnel. It is evident that further opening up to foreign investment is going to be seen in retailing. There is already a preference for Western department stores and their more advanced technology to be attracted to China as all existing licensees have attracted Asian partners. Major changes are taking place in consumer attitudes and behaviour in shopping patterns and preferences, and the retailer and distribution sectors of the economy will become more flexible, more open to market forces and a rapid transformation can be expected, at least in the cities.

In chapter 14, though relating to retail services, Henry Steele emphasizes the use of time by consumers. People experience time in different ways. Attitudes towards the use of time and time at work and at leisure are important in gaining an understanding of Chinese consumer behaviour. With increasing emphasis on globalization of firms there is a need to be cognisant of foreign market needs. Superficially similar cultures may have different temporal characteristics. In this chapter, a survey was conducted to compare how time is used in retail services between consumers in Hong Kong, Guangzhou and Beijing. The framework of social time was used. Findings indicate that consumers of similar cultures have significant differences in their time system and temporal perspectives. This suggests that international marketers, when marketing their products and services in various regions of China, also need to adjust marketing efforts to salient temporal elements.

Section IV. China International Business

China is making the kind of market opening commitments to show that it is serious about liberalising trade and investment and that both European governments and their American counterparts are ready to speed up the pace of discussion toward World Trade Organization (WTO) membership. All sides appear to have become more pragmatic and flexible. However, there is still some way to go in opening up the China market, for example, in subsidising state-owned firms, in allowing free market access to financial services, distribution and other sensitive industries, and in the phasing out of non-tariff barriers. It is likely that restrictions on the trading activities of both Chinese and foreign companies will be removed in the next three years, allowing all firms established in China to import and export goods freely. The China market is, therefore, seen by many observers to have economic potential for foreign investors as we enter the 21st century. However, doing business in China has never been easy. Thus, this section mainly deals with changes and problems faced by these foreign investors in various areas such as accounting standards, technological transfers and market entries.

This section consists of five chapters. The first two chapters deal with accounting and tax issues in China, followed by two chapters in foreign technology transfer and one chapter in entry strategies of multinational companies.

Richard Maschmeyer and Michael DeCelles observe that the reform in financial accounting standards in China has reached a point of no return. In Chapter 15, they discuss the relationship between changes in accounting standards and trade reform, as well as the impact to foreign investors.

Given that foreign direct investment (FDI) is playing an increasingly important role in the development of the economy, the PRC Government has progressively introduced tax reforms as part of the policy of overall economic reform culminating in major reforms in 1994, which amended individual Income Tax, revamped Turnover (Sales) Tax and introduced various taxes including Value Added Tax. The developments taking place in the tax and trade reforms can be seen as part of the gradual alignment with international practices. Foreign enterprises face a bewildering array of regulations and license requirements to do business and are simultaneously coming under central provincial and local government jurisdictions. Reform of local taxes has emphasized codifying and unifying local taxes and to remove inappropriate tax items. Insights are given to taxes related to trade and economic reform and an attempt is made to assess implications for foreign investors. Key areas of economic reform since 1994 have been in taxation, foreign exchange, finance and foreign trade with three major objectives:

1. Accelerate the transition to a socialist market economy in order to attract further FDI.
2. Move toward closer compliance with international norms of trade in furtherance of China's application to join the WTO.
3. Standardize economic activities and regulatory frameworks to produce a more lenient business environment and efficient trading mechanisms to encourage a rapid development of the economy.

In Chapter 16, Daniel K. T. Li and his associates focus on how tax and trade reform in China affects foreign direct investment. The most recent round of tax modifications includes "Import Tariff Reduction" effective April 1996 reducing average tariffs from 35.9% to 23%. As part of its strategy to join WTO a target level of 15% has been set for the year 2000. The various measures and modifications introduced will have a significant impact on FDI and the performance of FIEs. Revenue from turnover tax has accounted for the vast majority of total tax revenue in the PRC. Three new turnover taxes have been introduced, comprising Value Added Tax (VAT), Business Tax, and Consumption Tax which replaced the Industrial and Commercial Consolidated Tax (ICCT). Effects will be felt by investing companies in areas such as decision making, capital structure planning and exchange risk management and will generally reduce returns on investment and adversely affect company cash flows.

Export processing has always been a high priority in the PRC's economic policy, especially in opening up to the outside world and attracting FDI. As a remedial measure to address deficiencies in the existing system, the Customs Duty Security System (CDSS) has been implemented, removing the requirement for a deposit of the tariff value of the imports, monitoring and control procedures have been improved which will reduce the opportunities for such fraudulent activities as tax evasion and smuggling and increase the penalties for malpractice. The reforms are moving towards establishing a domestic business environment and trading mechanisms which favour fair competition and place domestic and foreign invested enterprises on the same level playing field. They will also have a positive effect on channelling foreign investment to such priority industrial sectors as energy, infrastructure facilities, transport and the promotion of advanced technologies.

All economic reform measures implemented during the Eighth Five-Year Plan period demonstrate that China is making good progress in replacing direct economic control by economic means and with the development of regulatory frameworks. The Ninth Five-Year Plan promulgated in 1995 set long-term targets which aimed at achieving the transition from a planned economy to a socialist market economy for the year 2010, thereby affirming the open market policy and giving foreign investor confidence a boost. The taxation and foreign exchange system reforms will be the spearhead of the PRC's market opening policy as well as being the key components of the strategy for reform and development of industrial sectors given priority under national industrial policy.

In Chapter 17, a systematic look of the development of technology imports by China is taken and possible future directions of inward technology are suggested. A macro view is taken by D. X. Zeng, Oliver Yau and Raymond Chow from an extensive literature review and personal interviews with selected firms in China. Changes in the past few decades have been enormous from a starting point in 1949 when China began to take a rather systematic approach towards technology imports. Two major stages are identified. The first began in 1950 under highly centralized planning and control. The second stage, beginning with the open door policy from 1979 until the present day, is characterized by a more simplified and decentralized structure which has become progressively more flexible whereby opportunities have become more widespread for foreign technology transfer and FDI. At present, the value of China's technology and equipment imports exceed US$600 billions which include ten thousand projects, or approximately 70% in value which were financed by foreign exchange from the central government. Many of the projects have been related to major industrial development and the import of complete plant, often related to industries such as energy, transportation and raw materials. Other core projects are in the electrical, machinery and textile industries. Focusing on the fundamental industries in recent years, there has been a move towards acquisition of advanced technologies and economic benefits as well as exploring new ways for structural reform, together with a more decentralized structure where imported technology is obtained at the provincial and municipal levels and with the growth of small and medium size enterprises (SMEs) has come the recognition that enterprises should be able to import technology. Although most acquisition has been of production technologies, the trend has been away from complete plant and turnkey projects towards co-production licensing, consultancy and technical services provision. Technology imports have been obtained from more than 30 countries with the main suppliers being the United States, Japan and Germany.

Inevitably there have been problems in importing and transferring technology to China where there are limitations of infrastructure, trained and educated personnel and local supporting networks. In this chapter the authors emphasize that it is a very complicated strategy and more serious effects were felt on the former planned economy. It seems that not much emphasis was put on transferring the most advanced level of technologies and localizing the technologies. Undue emphasis has also been put on short-term economic benefits instead of achieving a balance in the level and structure of technology imports. These problems have limited the overall economic benefits which both China and its enterprises have achieved.

However, a number of important achievements have been observed from the import of foreign technology. Technological advancement has been speeded up and facilitated, bringing economic benefits. Product quality has been improved, resulting in a rapid growth in exports and their competitiveness. The economic base of China has been diversified, the self-developing capability has been enhanced and local technical expertise is now available. There are still many limitations on domestic enterprises that can reduce the positive impact of new technology, particularly the role of market development that has been led by foreign enterprises. With the growth in economic development and living standards, consumer's expectations have risen and the need to upgrade product quality is essential if domestic enterprises are to survive against joint ventures and wholly owned foreign enterprises (WOFEs). Improvements in technology that are manifest in product quality improvement are necessary if Chinese enterprises are to survive in the domestic market and if they are to succeed in the international market. The process of transformation of state-owned enterprises (SOEs) in particular is a cause for concern where the need to become operationally independent and responsible for their own profitability will take more than the mere transfer of appropriate technology. However, it is likely that such corporations together with the "three form of investments" (joint ventures, industrial cooperation enterprises and WOFEs) will be the most active participants in foreign technology transfers. The increased pace of technology transfer and the more decentralized and flexible framework under which it has been practised in recent years have made a significant contribution to the PRC's economic achievement when during the period 1991–1994 the highest average annual economic growth rate among major economies of the world of 11.7% was recorded.

An example of the Chinese management experience is given in "Buying International Technology for New Product Development" which is unusual in giving the buyer's prospective on technology transfer from a variety of overseas suppliers. Oliver H. M. Yau, Kwaku Atuahene-Gima and Raymond P. M. Chow identify a range of factors that influence the success of buying and using acquired technology. Each of these factors is discussed in relation to an in-depth survey of technology transfer to Chinese firms. Economic progress in China has been facilitated by the import of more advanced technologies. The government continues to play an essential role as facilitator of technology transfer in providing foreign exchange funding, in project approval, review of suppliers, approval of technology and in supporting contract negotiation as well as subsequent monitoring. Chinese enterprises generally see the role of government agencies as a positive one, and in compensating for lack of experience and expertise within the buying organization. Additionally, the government is able to coordinate and integrate a number of technology transfer projects enabling component and raw materials suppliers to upgrade their technologies making them appropriate for the firm's imported technology.

Before entering technology transfer arrangements, Chinese firms indicated that market studies have been undertaken to assess the specific requirements of customers and to forecast market potential. Such rigorous market evaluation exercises are necessary to justify and gain support of the government agencies in the acquisition of foreign technology. A free hand is given for firms to choose suppliers and products following justification of the need for the technology. In the search for suppliers government agencies are able to assist, but firms have gained knowledge of potential suppliers from foreign companies with representative offices in China, trade shows, foreign visits, technology exchange activities and from using overseas and Hong Kong Chinese as middlemen for facilitating exchanges.

The importance of acquiring the requisite level of technology is well recognized by Chinese managers with the government agencies having a preference for the latest technology. Few respondents had misgivings about the level of technology transferred, as overseas suppliers of technology were willing and able to give technical support and training and were willing to engage in a dynamic technology transfer process whereby upgrading occurs as local circumstances change to accommodate the improved technology. Few firms have in-house research and development facilities and are dependent on industry research institutes, which increases the importance of transfer of soft technology. To make effective use of the advanced technology transferred there is a need for the accompanying advanced management systems to introduce quality assurance and production control. Some evidence is given of the impact of the technology supplier to improvements in management capability through providing technical support and training.

Chapter 19 deals with entry strategies of multinational pharmaceutical companies (MPCs) in China. In this chapter, Gert Bruche covers a broad range of issues faced by these companies. Although there are unique aspects of the industry, many parallels can be drawn from other industries in various facets that are discussed. The issue of the timing of market entry is evaluated. Early entrants faced a risky, unfamiliar environment and found break even hard to achieve, but were able to build up a strong presence in the market prior to the intensely competitive period resulting from later entrants. These later entrants were able to avoid many of the mistakes made by early entrants to the market. Along with the timing of market entry, the MPCs had to face a rapidly changing administrative and structural environment progressing from an initial low level of institutional and legal infrastructure. Late entrants may find it more difficult to gain a foothold in the market as the regulatory framework becomes both more developed and at the same time more restrictive, and as China becomes more selective about the encouragement of foreign direct investment.

Professor Bruche charts the early strategies, progress and competition in the pharmaceutical market that is a major industry for overseas investment in China. The pharmaceutical industry is strongly research based and products are normally subject to patent protection. The factors and circumstances leading to MPCs achieving strategic market positions is analysed based on the richness of historical perspective and projections are made for the pharmaceutical industry in China into the 21st century.

A major influx of entrants to the China market occurred in the period 1992–1995. These companies were driven by the vision of the China market as one having economic potential in its 1.2 billion people and a rise in product imports, the low cost manufacturing base, the evidence of maturation of the pharmaceutical market with the sales success of pioneering joint ventures and the herd instinct — "if our competitors are there we must also be there." Market entry is identified in two stages, the first beginning from about 1981 and the second from 1991 and expected to continue to around 2000. Market entry modes are conventionally described as a sequence, but the business environment of China dictated a choice of approaches. Those MPCs not wishing to invest directly chose to use their Hong Kong operations as the base for exporting and selling to China. A small number of MPCs chose to invest directly in local production using equity joint ventures with shared management control. In the late 1980s, other MPCs chose this route following the success of exporting via Hong Kong after they had built up sales networks.

The prevailing government policy towards foreign enterprises in China was towards foreign investment partnership with joint managerial control. Emphasis was placed on establishing production capability and for this preoccupation MPCs paid a heavy entrance fee. During the 1980s changes began to occur in distribution and although remaining in state ownership, particularly levels two and three of the three-tier distribution system were no longer captive markets for the joint venture enterprises. In the market a dramatic change took place from a supply-driven market to a demand-driven one. Hospitals purchasing also changed and no longer were they captive markets. Thus came the switch from a production-driven to a market-driven industry.

The early 1990s saw changes to the administrative policy and the encouragement of foreign investment following the decline in the wake of the 1989 Tian'anmen crackdown. A spate of MPCs invested in production facilities using the contractual joint venture as the mode of entry. The China authorities were now willing to allow contractual joint ventures and MPCs could now choose joint venture partners with neither the interest nor the capability to manage a joint venture, but instead looking for portfolio investments. This gave the foreign companies management control. Existing equity joint ventures were also allowed to increase the foreign equity share and thereby improving management control. The opportunities for establishing wholly owned foreign enterprises (WOFEs) in the pharmaceutical industry are still very limited today. The authorities' requirements for high re-exports and a high technology transfer component prevent WOFEs from becoming a feasible option for MPCs entering the China market.

The early entrants to China's pharmaceutical market, circa 1989 had advantages in the marketing and distribution of their products. By gaining early recognition in product categories where competitor products were absent has given the early entrants leverage for extending their product range. They have built up relationships in the distribution channels and entered the market before the government imposed a more regulated regime. Later entrants have had advantages in that buyers have become educated, earlier strategic errors have been avoided and a pool of trained staff has been created. To some extent the late entrants are getting a "free ride", but they do face an increasingly competitive environment where it has become more difficult to win a piece of the customer's mind and established relationships to make market expansion less difficult. In most markets early entrants have achieved leading competitive positions measured by market share. It is estimated that the second period of the entry process will be completed around the year 2000 when all the ventures which are currently in the build-up phase impact the market and where the on-going health care reforms will largely be implemented.

Three key factors are identified in MPCs achieving success in the China pharmaceutical market, managerial persistence, financial commitment and continuous learning/adaptation to the rapid and often erratic nature of changes. It is likely that these factors hold true for most foreign investors to China. The operating environment may have got easier, but the lack of good managers is a re-occurring theme. Newcomers try to recruit experienced and able staff, and the shortage is made good by poaching good staff from existing ventures. In the face of competition from MPCs, as in other industries where there is a strong presence of world-renowned companies and brand names, the future of the local China pharmaceutical industry is under threat. A few companies not associated with joint ventures will survive and dominate the market for generic products.

Concluding Remarks

This book tries to provide the reader with tools for understanding, researching and managing China business. All contributions are grouped into one of the four sections, the environment, marketing, management, or international business in China. In each chapter, we also focus on a particular area of interest in China business. In addition to the contribution in providing insights into recent developments, problems that were encountered and challenges that are being faced by Chinese managers and foreign executives are discussed. We are confident that in understanding these problems and challenges it will help prepare strategies for enhanced performance in China in transition to the 21st century.

Section I
Business Environment in China

2

The Changing Economic Environment in the People's Republic of China

Kui-Wai Li

Introduction

A major international issue since the early 1980s is the liberalization in the two largest socialist economies of Russia and the People's Republic of China. Russia favoured political reform prior to economic liberalization, while China has chosen economic reform as the initial step and emphasized political stability. The results of liberalization and reform in the two socialist economies so far differ tremendously. While Russia is still experiencing political changes and economic decline at an average negative growth rates of 14.5% between 1991 and 1994 (Chang, 1995), China has achieved a remarkable degree of economic growth and its political rigidity is seen as a sign of stability for economic changes and market reforms.

Despite the various economic setbacks, China has experienced an economic growth path comparable to other Asian economies. As compared to six other major Asian economies (Indonesia, Malaysia, Philippines, Singapore, South Korea and Thailand) over the period of 1989 and 1997, China's average real Gross National Product (GNP) growth rate was the highest (Table 1). China is the only economy whose growth rate has kept at a two-digit level between 1992 and 1995.

Both Bell, Khor and Kochhar (1993, pp. 66–68) and Gao (1993) agree that China has undergone four stages of reform since 1978. The first stage

Table 1
Growth of GDP (1990 Price)

	1989	1990	1991	1992	1993	1994	1995	1996	1997	Average
China	4.3	4.0	8.2	13.0	13.5	12.5	10.5	9.5	8.8	9.4
Indonesia	7.5	7.2	7.0	6.5	6.5	7.3	8.2	8.0	4.6	7.0
Malaysia	9.2	9.7	8.7	7.8	8.3	8.7	9.4	8.6	7.7	8.7
Philippines	6.2	3.0	-0.6	0.3	2.1	4.3	4.7	5.8	5.2	3.5
Singapore	9.4	8.1	7.0	6.4	10.1	10.1	8.7	7.8	6.8	8.3
South Korea	6.4	9.5	9.1	5.1	5.8	8.4	8.9	7.1	5.5	7.3
Thailand	12.2	11.6	8.4	7.9	8.2	8.5	8.7	6.4	-1.3	7.8
Japan	4.8	4.8	4.3	1.4	0.1	0.6	1.5	3.9	0.9	2.3
USA	2.5	0.8	1.2	3.3	3.1	4.1	2.0	3.7	3.9	2.7

Source: *International Financial Statistics*, International Monetary Fund, various issues.

(1978–1984) was implemented in the rural areas under the "family responsibility system" through which rural households could sell their surplus of agricultural products in the free markets. The second stage (1985–1988) concentrated in the urban areas. A two-tier pricing system was introduced. Market mechanism was given a new dimension. Autonomy was granted to enterprises in setting their wages, and the division between party officials and enterprise managers were suggested by the then Premier Zhao Ziyang in 1987. The third stage (1989–1991) was highlighted by the government's effort to clarify the country's economic environment and rectify its economic orders so as to create a better condition for deepening reform. The fourth stage began in 1992 with Deng Xiaoping's important speeches made during his tour to the southern part of China. Since then, new confidence in China's economic reform was created and revived business activities produced a rapid growth pattern.

Acceleration in economic growth began in the second half of the 1980s (Table 2). Agricultural output grew at a higher rate between 1978 and 1980, due probably to the success of the "family responsibility system" introduced in the rural areas. The rise in income encouraged a higher average growth rate in consumption. Sales to consumers grew more than 20% in the period between 1978 and 1985. Inflation was mild then at less than 5%. The

Table 2
Nominal Growth Rates (%)

Year	GNP	Industrial Output	Agricultural Output	Sales to Consumers	Inflation
1952–57	—	20.3	3.3	13.6	1.7
1957–62	—	6.1	1.8	4.6	5.1
1962–65	—	17.5	14.2	2.8	−3.9
1965–70	—	10.2	4.5	4.7	−0.4
1970–75	—	10.3	4.7	8.7	0.1
1975–78	—	10.7	3.6	7.0	1.0
1978–80	12.3	10.8	18.8	20.9	4.1
1980–85	19.8	17.7	17.7	22.4	3.7
1985–90	21.2	28.2	22.3	18.1	12.4
1990–94	35.6	55.4	26.4	31.1	12.4
1995–97	27.8	23.8	20.9	10.6	9.5

Source: *China Statistical Yearbook*, Beijing, various years.

economy was obviously expanding within the existing framework, utilizing existing resources and capacities.

However, severe economic overheating appeared in 1984/1985. Rigidities in the economic structure surfaced while economic growth continued. Between 1985 and 1994, growth in GNP (exceeded 20%) were lower than growth in industrial output. Agricultural output declined since the 1990s, suggesting a growing dominance of the industrial sector. The high inflation since 1985 reduced the purchasing power of many households, and sales to consumers grew only at a rate similar to the GNP growth rate. Inflation, however, dropped drastically since 1995.

Unlike the 1980s, economic overheating in 1993/1994 resulted from the visit to southern China by Deng Xiaoping in 1992 led the authority to examine existing economic structure and identified new economic strategies. For example, the loose credit policy exercised by national banks has been questioned, and investments are considered not to be productive enough. Financial abuse, embezzlement of funds, and corruption in general are considered to be the most destructive elements in economic reform. Forty-eight senior cadres were punished by the Chinese Communist Party (CCP) for corruption in 1995, for example, and over 44% of all party discipline cases in the first half of 1995 were due to corruption. The party chief, Jiang Zemin has warned that corruption of officials will not be tolerated.[1] The pursuance of "marketization" in the 1980s is considered to be important in the revitalization of the economy, but quality improvement has often been overlooked. In the late 1970s and early 1980s, successful implementation of the market mechanism was the major concern. The division between party influence and the role of management in productive enterprises was the concern in the second half of the 1980s. However, the Austerity Plan initiated in 1993 imposed a quantitative restriction on the use of investment funds, and the Banking Law passed in 1995 urging for a sound financial performance is the latest concern in Beijing.

A sequence of economic events has taken place since the late 1980s. First of all, inflation has remained high since the late 1980s. In 1994, the retail and consumer price inflation hit 21.7 and 24.1% respectively, the highest since 1949.[2] A prolonged expansion in the money supply has been considered to be the cause of inflation. Cash expansion between 1992 and 1994 reached RMB 411.1 billion, equivalent to about 56% of the amount for the past 46 years since the founding of the People's Republic of China in 1949. The year-on-year growth of the money supply between January and September in 1995 reached 30.6%, which is higher than the rate of economic growth and price rise combined during the same period.[3] Two reasons accounted for the rapid money growth. One is the loose credit policy practised by banks. The other is the large fiscal deficit maintained by the Chinese authority since the early 1980s. The loose credit policy is the direct result of a low, or even negative, interest rate that persisted for a long time. A low rate of interest is thought to stimulate investment, but in fact it fails to screen out productive investment, and capital resources end up being channelled to unproductive projects. The desire to reduce regional disparity and political influence in the "central-local" debate has often resulted in bank loans given out for non-economic reasons. Similarly, many loss-making state-owned enterprises rely heavily on subsidies given out by the state. The so-called "triangular debt" problem created by these state-owed enterprises does produce a dilemma to the Chinese authority. On one hand, they lead to losses and financial resources have to be used to bail out these unproductive enterprises. On the other hand, the potential size of unemployment is equally threatening to the Chinese authority if these state-owned enterprises close down.

Reform in state-owned enterprises has become the focus of the Chinese authority since the early 1990s. The granting of "free" loans to state-owned enterprises has injected a large quantity of financial funds into the economy, but the productivity of these funds has been overlooked. Activities since the early 1990s, notably the Austerity Plan in 1993 and the Bank Law in 1995, aim to put a quantitative restriction on the use of financial capital, thereby forcing the users of funds, mainly the state-owned enterprises, to be more responsible and productive. A higher level of productivity is thought to be the solution to many of the macroeconomic constraints.

Macroeconomic Performances

Income and Consumption

The growth of nominal income since 1980 has experienced three peaks. The first peak appeared in 1984 and 1985 when the nominal growth rate of GNP reached 24% in both years (Table 3). The "family responsibility system" introduced in the rural areas permitted farmers to sell their produce in the free market at a higher price. A "ten thousand dollar household" (*wanyuanhu*) soon became a popular idiom in the rural areas. In this period, basic economic structure remained unchanged, but the impact of the free market introduced in the rural areas was large enough to bring about the rise in income.

The second peak appeared in 1988 with a growth rate of 24.8% (Table 3). Reform in the industrial sector began in 1984, mainly in the establishment of rural enterprises. These enterprises, commonly known as township and village enterprises, helped to absorb some surplus labour in the rural areas. This improved individual incentives and productivity. Various reasons have been given to explain the level of inflation and the overheated economy

Table 3

Changes in Income, Consumption and Inflation (RMB 100 million)
(% Change over Previous Year)

Year	GNP	Sales to Consumers	Inflation (%)
1978	3,624	1,265	0.7
1979	3,998 (10.3)	1,476 (16.7)	2.0
1980	4,518 (13.0)	1,794 (21.5)	6.0
1981	4,773 (5.6)	2,003 (11.6)	2.4
1982	5,193 (8.8)	2,182 (8.9)	1.9
1983	5,809 (11.9)	2,426 (11.2)	1.5
1984	7,205 (24.0)	2,899 (19.5)	2.8
1985	8,995 (24.8)	3,801 (31.1)	8.8
1986	10,221 (13.5)	4,374 (15.1)	6.0
1987	11,966 (17.1)	5,115 (16.9)	7.3
1988	14,922 (24.8)	6,535 (27.8)	18.5
1989	16,906 (13.3)	7,074 (8.3)	17.8
1990	18,545 (9.7)	7,250 (2.5)	2.1
1991	21,666 (16.8)	8,246 (13.7)	2.9
1992	26,651 (23.0)	9,705 (17.7)	5.4
1993	34,561 (29.7)	12,462 (28.4)	13.2
1994	46,670 (35.0)	16,265 (30.5)	24.1
1995	57,495 (23.2)	20,620 (26.8)	17.3
1996	66,851 (16.3)	24,774 (20.1)	8.3
1997	73,453 (6.7)	27,299 (10.2)	2.8

Sources: *China Statistical Yearbook*, Beijing, various years. *China Daily*, January 15, 1996.

in 1988. For example, the sequence of reform (Naughton, 1991), fiscal mis-management (Donnithorne, 1986; Huang Hsiao, 1987; Feltenstein and Farhadian, 1987), and rapid monetary expansion (Li, 1989; Peebles, 1991) have been suggested as the causes of inflation.

These two periods of high income growth also matched with high growth rates in consumption and inflation. Two peculiar situations appeared in the mid-1980s. The rise in income had led to a rise in demand for imported and non-traditional consumption goods. Price in these commodities rose rapidly. On the other hand, because of the emergence of new substitutes, the demand for many local and traditional commodities produced by state-owned enterprises dropped. A situation of excess demand in the modern sector coexisted with excess supply in the traditional sector. The price of goods in the modern sector rose faster than in the traditional sector.

Another situation was the hoarding activities exercised by both households and enterprises in anticipation of a rise in inflation and the rapid loss in the value of RMB. Households hoarded commodities and got ride of their surplus cash at a time of high inflation. Enterprises accumulated their raw materials in anticipation of a higher price in the near future. At the extreme, output could even fall if the hoarding of raw materials itself could produce a reasonable cash return. These hoarding activities added extra pressure on inflation. Political unrest in 1989 put a brake on the overheated economy.

The latest peak in economic growth began in 1992. The visit to Guangdong by Deng Xiaoping during the Chinese New Year in early 1992 produced new confidence in China's economic reform. Symbolically, Deng's visit reaffirmed investors that his strategy on economic reform remains unchanged. The growth in nominal GNP clearly experienced a jump between 1991 and 1992. In 1994, the growth rate exceeded 30% (Table 3). Growth in consumption first lagged behind but by 1994, its growth had caught up with income growth. Inflation also reached an unprecedented record of 21.7% in 1994.

One major concern in the rapid growth of income is the deterioration in income equality between the richer, mostly coastal, regions and the poorer, mostly interior regions. The richer regions, in general, grew faster than the poorer regions by around 50% between 1991 and 1994 (Table 4). The poorer regions, however, performed well with an average growth of 83.4% in GDP and 44.1% in the indices. Occasionally, there is evidence that a

Table 4

Regional Differences in Gross Domestic Product, 1994

(At Current Prices, RMB 100 million)

Region	GDP		% Growth in GDP		GDP Indice Growth	
	1994	1997	1991–1994	1994–1997	1991–1994	1994–1997
Below 500						
Tibet	45.8	77.0	5.0	67.9	32.5	58.2
Ningxia	134.0	210.9	86.7	57.4	31.7	42.9
Qinghai	138.2	202.1	84.0	46.2	29.9	33.8
Hainan	331.0	409.9	174.7	23.8	87.9	31.8
Gansu	451.7	781.3	66.4	73.0	38.5	39.4
Average			83.4	53.7	44.1	41.2
Between 501 and 999						
Guizhou	521.2	793.0	76.1	52.2	35.6	33.9
Xinjiang	673.7	1,050.1	100.6	55.9	48.2	37.3
Inner Mongolia	681.9	1,094.5	89.6	60.5	39.2	41.6
Tianjin	725.1	1,240.4	111.6	71.0	44.1	55.6
Shaanxi	846.7	1,326.0	74.9	62.4	38.2	37.3
Shanxi	853.8	1,480.1	82.7	73.4	21.3	42.0
Jilin	968.8	1,446.9	102.1	54.5	45.2	46.9
Yunnan	974.0	1,644.2	88.2	68.8	39.7	42.6
Jiangxi	948.2	1,715.2	97.8	80.9	54.7	56.4
Average			91.5	64.4	40.7	39.6
Between 1,000 and 1,999						
Beijing	1,084.0	1,810.1	81.0	67.0	46.7	44.7
Guangxi	1,241.8	2,015.2	139.5	62.3	68.2	50.6
Anhui	1,488.5	2,670.0	124.3	79.4	57.6	62.0
Heilongjiang	1,618.6	2,708.5	96.4	67.3	30.0	38.8
Fujian	1,685.3	3,000.4	170.9	78.0	81.7	66.8
Hunan	1,694.4	2,993.0	103.3	76.6	44.4	44.9
Hubei	1,878.7	3,450.2	105.7	83.7	50.6	56.0
Shanghai	1,971.9	3,362.2	120.6	70.4	51.2	54.1
Average			105.7	73.1	53.8	52.2
Above 2,000						
Hebei	2,187.5	3,953.8	139.5	80.7	59.2	54.8
Henan	2,224.4	4,079.3	112.7	83.4	50.2	52.9
Liaoning	2,461.8	3,490.1	105.1	41.8	44.3	35.8
Zhejiang	2,666.9	4,638.2	146.5	73.9	78.8	60.5
Sichuan	2,777.8	3,320.1	100.9	19.5	45.7	41.4
Shandong	3,872.2	6,650.0	113.9	71.7	66.2	53.9

Table 4 Cont'd

Region	GDP		% Growth in GDP		GDP Indice Growth	
	1994	1997	1991–1994	1994–1997	1991–1994	1994–1997
Jiangsu	4,057.4	6,680.3	153.4	64.6	75.7	56.1
Guangdong	4,240.6	7,315.5	138.2	72.5	80.6	55.2
Average			146.2	63.5	62.6	51.3

Source: *China Statistical Yearbook* 1995 and 1998, Beijing.

poorer region experiences a faster growth rate than a richer region. GDP growth in 1994–1997, however, has stabilized in all regions.

Output and Employment

Both industrial output and agricultural output have grown at a nominal rate by 4,980% and 1,683% respectively between 1978 and 1997 (Table 5). Industrial output growth exceeded growth in agricultural output in most years, reflecting the rising importance of the industrial sector. This is supported by a proportionate decline in the employment in primary industry. Total employment has increased by 73.3% between 1978 and 1997, but the proportionate increase in employment in the tertiary sector has almost doubled.

Although urban unemployment rate was kept low, there are two main sources of potential unemployment in China. One exists in the rural sector. No estimate has been given on the level of hidden unemployment in the rural areas. The other is the number of employed workers that have to be released if the loss-making state-owned enterprises are to close down. Industrial growth has overtaken agricultural growth in the second half of the 1980s. Rural workers are attracted to work in urban areas for higher wages and migration to seek employment in industrial areas has become popular.[4]

Under the previous centrally planned system, state-owned enterprises needed to fulfil production quotas. In return, workers' livelihood is being looked after and provided by state-owned enterprises. Typically, the survival of many state-owned enterprises relies heavily on state subsidies or

Table 5
Output and Employment

Year	Industrial Output (RMB 100 mil) (% change)	Agricultural Output (RMB 100 mil) (% change)	Employment (10,000)					Urban Unemployment Rate	Wage Index (Previous Year = 100)
			Total	Primary Industry (% share)	Secondary Industry (% share)	Tertiary Industry (% share)			
1978	2,239 (32.1)	1,397	40,152	70.5	17.4	12.1	5.3		
1980	5,154 (10.1)	1,923 (13.3)	42,361	68.7	18.3	13.0	4.9	118.2
1984	7,617 (17.9)	3,214 (16.9)	48,197	64.0	20.0	16.0	1.9	—
1985	9,716 (27.6)	3,619 (12.6)	49,873	62.4	20.9	16.7	1.8	121.6
1986	11,194 (15.2)	4,013 (10.9)	51,282	60.9	21.9	17.2	2.0	121.0
1987	13,813 (23.4)	4,676 (16.5)	52,783	59.9	22.3	17.8	2.0	113.3
1988	18,224 (31.9)	5,865 (25.4)	54,334	59.3	22.4	18.3	2.0	123.8
1989	22,017 (20.8)	6,535 (11.4)	55,329	60.0	21.7	18.3	2.6	113.5
1990	23,924 (8.7)	7,662 (17.3)	63,909	60.0	21.4	18.6	2.5	113.4
1991	26,625 (11.3)	8,157 (6.5)	64,799	59.7	21.4	18.9	2.3	111.7
1992	34,599 (29.9)	9,085 (11.4)	65,554	58.5	21.7	19.8	2.3	119.1
1993	48,402 (39.9)	10,996 (21.0)	66,373	56.4	22.4	21.2	2.6	123.4
1994	70,176 (46.1)	15,750 (43.2)	67,199	54.3	22.7	23.0	2.8	135.8
1995	91,894 (30.9)	20,341 (29.1)	67,947	52.2	23.0	24.8	NA	117.4
1996	99,595 (8.4)	23,429 (15.2)	68,850	50.5	23.5	26.0	NA	111.7
1997	113,733 (14.2)	24,588 (4.9)	69,600	49.9	23.7	26.4	NA	106.2

Source: *China Statistical Yearbook*, Beijing, various years.

"cheap" bank loans. Since economic reform, these enterprises have become a financial burden to the state.

Reform in state-owned enterprises, a new priority in 1997, aims to rejuvenate the state-owned enterprises.[5] Poorly managed state-owned enterprises are regarded as unproductive and a considerable amount of their capital is not geared for investment.[6] The "triangular debt," or inter-enterprises debt, is growing steadily. It is estimated that reform of the state-owned enterprises needs a bill of more than RMB 500 billion in the Ninth Five-Year Plan (1996–2000). The government requires RMB 280 billion to reduce debts of state-owned enterprises, including converting RMB 66 billion worth of debt into state equity and to cut the asset-liability ratio by 14%. A total of RMB 160 billion will be spent on re-employment of eight million redundant workers.[7]

The official policy in the reform of state-owned enterprises in 1997 is the so-called "grasping the big, enlivening the small" (*zhuada fangxiao*) policy. This policy aimed to accelerate the privatization of many small and some medium sized state-owned enterprises and focus reform efforts on around 1,000 of the largest enterprises.

One theoretical solution would be to select the more productive invest-ment projects, preferably regulated and monitored by a market interest rate (Li, 1994). Another aspect is to change the pattern of employment contract. The existing practice is that workers are given a fairly low wage, while a considerable amount of welfare provision is given by the state-owned enterprises. Such a practice cannot promote workers' incentive and adds a heavy financial burden on the state-owned enterprises. An alternative would be to raise the nominal wage of workers gradually but leave the provision of welfare to individual workers. The overall cost to the state-owned enterprises may not rise, but workers will have the incentive to organize their own welfare activities.

The government is revising the bankruptcy law to determine the fate of the loss-making state-owned enterprises. A new bankruptcy law was sub-mitted to the standing committee of the National People's Congress in December, 1995. The draft meets the needs of a market economy and protects creditors, and would apply to all enterprises including the collec-tive- and privately-owned enterprises.[8] In the meantime, China has tried to convert most state-owned businesses into limited holding firms as a step to shake up the state industry.[9] However, more loss-making firms will shut down as the bankruptcy reform is extended to 52 large cities. Firms with a

Table 6

Urban Employment (Year-End, in 10,000)

Year	Total	State-Owned Units	Collective-Owned Units	Foreign-Funded Economic Units	Overseas Chinese-Funded Economic Units	Private Enterprises	Individual	Jointly Owned Economic Units	Share-holding Economic Units
1978	9,514	7,451	2,048						
1980	10,525	8,019	2,425				15		
1984	12,229	8,637	3,216				81		
1985	12,808	8,990	3,324	6			339		
1986	13,293	9,333	3,421	12	1		450		
1987	13,783	9,654	3,488	20	1		483	38	
1988	14,267	9,984	3,527	29	2		569	50	
1989	14,390	10,108	3,502	43	4		659	63	
1990	16,616	10,346	3,549	62	4	57	648	82	
1991	16,977	10,664	3,628	96	69	68	614	96	
1992	17,241	10,889	3,621	138	83	98	692	49	
1993	17,589	10,920	3,393	133	155	186	740	56	
1994	18,413	11,214	3,285	195	211	332	930	66	164
1995	19,093	11,261	3,147	241	272	485	1,225	52	292
1996	19,815	11,244	3,016	275	265	620	1,560	53	317
1997	20,207	11,044	2,883	300	281	750	1,709	49	363
							1,919	44	468

Source: *China Statistical Yearbook*, Beijing, various years.

poor assets to liabilities ratio will be asked to shut down. In 18 pilot cities in 1995, 80% of the closed factories were under state-ownership. Another report suggests that bankruptcy has proceeded smoothly without causing social disorder.[10]

Recent experience shows that a rapidly rising number of workers are engaged in either private enterprises or foreign-funded enterprises in urban areas, and township and village enterprises in the rural areas (Tables 6 and 7). In the urban areas, state-owned and collective-owned units employ the largest number of workers, but their growth rate has been much lower than growth in the foreign and private sectors, especially since 1990. In the Ninth Five-Year Plan (1996–2000), the Chinese government has to create jobs to help 40 million urban labourers. According to the Ministry of Labour, about 54 million new urban job seekers will need employment, but the cities and town can provide only 38 million new jobs. In the 1991–1995 period, 34 million unemployed people found new jobs. The target of the Ninth Five-Year Plan (1996–2000) is that urban unemployment will be kept below 3%.[11]

Table 7
Rural Employment (Year-End, in 10,000)

Year	Total	Township and Village Enterprises	Private Enterprises	Individuals
1978	30,638	2,827		
1980	31,836	3,000		
1984	35,968	5,208		
1985	37,056	6,979		
1986	37,990	7,937		
1987	39,000	8,805		
1988	40,067	9,545		
1989	40,939	9,367		
1990	47,293	9,256	113	1,491
1991	47,822	9,609	116	1,616
1992	48,313	10,625	134	1,728
1993	48,784	12,345	187	2,010
1994	48,786	12,017	316	2,551
1995	48,854	12,862	471	3,054
1996	49,035	13,508	551	3,308
1997	49,393	9,158	600	3,522

Source: *China Statistical Yearbook*, Beijing, various years.

Money and Banking

Cash was considered to be the single most important measurement of monetary movements in the pre-reform period. However, the persistent large money growth rates have reduced the effectiveness of monetary policy. With the exception in 1985 and 1989, the growth rates of monetary aggregates reached two digits, exceeding 20% in many cases (Table 8). M0 grew faster than other monetary aggregates in the early 1990s, but the situation was reversed since 1995.

The most common monetary instruments are credit ceilings, reloans, reserve ratio, rediscount rate, open market operations and the interest rate.[12] Monetary policy in China since 1985 has been characterized by a "stop-go" nature. A loose monetary policy was adopted in 1986 and 1990, while a tight monetary policy was exercised in other years since 1985 (Tang and Li, forthcoming).

As far as the interest rate is concerned, China experiences a dual interest rate system: the official rates (the deposit and the loan rates of national banks) and the market interest rates (the interbank and loan rates of

Table 8
Money Growth Rates (%)

Year	M0	M1	M2
1985	24.7	5.8	17.0
1986	23.3	28.1	29.3
1987	19.4	16.2	24.2
1988	46.7	22.5	22.4
1989	9.8	6.3	18.3
1990	12.8	20.2	28.0
1991	20.0	23.2	26.5
1992	36.4	35.9	31.3
1993	35.3	21.0	24.0
1994	24.3	26.2	34.5
1995	8.2	16.8	29.5
1996	11.6	18.9	25.3
1997	15.6	16.5	17.3

Notes: M0 = cash. M1 = M0 + demand deposits of enterprises and rural collectives and other institutions. M2 = M1 + time deposits of enterprises + deposits of self-financed funds of capital construction + household savings deposits + other deposits.

Source: *China Financial Outlook*, Beijing: various years.

some financial institutions). There are also many types of deposit and loan rates. A negative interest rate has often been experienced during a high inflation period. For example, the highest interest rate in 1993 was 13.86%, but the retail price index was 13.2%. Li (1994) examines China's financial development in the first decade of reform (1978–1989) and argues that the interest rate has not been used as a "screening" device in ironing out unproductive investments. Credits are often given out due more to political reasons than to economic justifications.

National banks have faced with a dilemma regarding credit allocations. A rather conflicting "banks — state-owned enterprises — employment" relationship exists. National banks supply loans and credits to state-owned enterprises. In principle, state-owned enterprises borrow to invest. With a low interest rate, however, the opportunity cost of investment funds is kept to a low level. Problem arises, however, when these funds are either geared to unproductive investments or used for non-investment purposes or credits are given out due to non-economic reasons. Banks cannot choose their loan portfolio, and, for political reasons, have to financially bail out the economically weak state-owned enterprises. Bad and overdue debts form about 25% of the banks' portfolio in 1999, equivalent to about RMB 60 billion to RMB 70 billion. The "triangular debts" amounted to RMB 700 billion in September 1995.[13] Closure of a number of banks and trade and investment companies (TICs) in 1997 and 1998, such as the Guangdong International Trade and Investment Company (GITIC) has brought the debt level to a new height.

On the other hand, state-owned enterprises have to survive in order to provide employment for the majority of working labourers. Unless the rigid wage structure gives way to a more market-determined employment system, state-owned enterprises have to shoulder the employment burden. This burden requires a constant funding support from national banks. The debt accumulated by the state-owned enterprises is ultimately an employment problem.

The Banking Law passed in March 1995 formally restructured the banking sector. The 1995 Law is the result of negotiation and culmination of activities dating back to late 1979 when all national bank directors met (Byrd, 1983; Li, 1994; Tang and Li, 1997). Since 1984, the State Council decided that the People's Bank of China should function like a central bank. Between 1984 and 1993, many changes in China's banking sector have been introduced. For example, regional commercial banks appeared and trust and investment companies, financial companies, securities companies and urban credit cooperatives developed (Li, 1994). The 1995 Law formally declared the responsibility of various banks. The People's Bank of China becomes the central bank. There are three other groups of banks: policy banks, commercial banks, and state-owned commercial banks. Policy banks include the State Development Bank, the Agricultural Development Bank of China, and the Import and Export Bank of China. Commercial banks include national and regional banks, such as the Shenzhen Development Bank, and corporate company banks, such as CITIC Industrial Bank. The four older banks, Agricultural Bank of China, People's Construction Bank of China, Bank of China, and Industrial and Commercial Bank of China, become the state-owned commercial banks. Policy banks are restricted from commercial banking businesses, while the state-owned commercial banks, which are supposed to conduct their businesses strictly under commercial principles, can accumulate surplus, or profit, from their banking activities.

The main objectives of the 1995 Bank Law include: (a) the establishment of a central bank, which would oversee the activities of other banks; (b) the pursuance of a more effective monetary policy; (c) maintain a gradual reduction in the debt of state-owned enterprises; and (d) ensure a sound banking sector. Some argue that the 1995 Law may not be strong enough to reform the banking sector, but it definitely is heading towards a proper direction. Despite the tight monetary policy exercised at various times, the granting of loan credits ultimately is influenced by politics. The 1995 Law can be seen as a change in emphasis from the "quantitative" to "qualitative" use of bank loans and capital funds. The responsibility is given back to individual state-owned enterprise that "unlimited" granting of loans is no longer a viable channel. By imposing a quantitative restriction, enterprises are "forced" to either improve their productivity, or seek other channel of funds. It is only when the state-owned enterprises are financially independent, the "banks — state-owned enterprises — employment" relationship can be broken, and banks can become truly a financial institution.

Banking statistics show that loans are often larger than deposits (Table 9). As far as deposits are concerned, urban savings deposits are the largest source of deposit, and their growth rates have also been the largest (4,464%) between 1985 and 1997. Rural deposits have grown by less than 300% between 1985 and 1997. Treasury deposits are the smallest source of

Table 9

Deposits and Loans of National Banks (Year-end, RMB 100 million)

Item	1985	1990	1992	1994	1996	1997
Total Deposits	4,273.0	11,644.8	18,891.1	40,502.5	68,595.6	82,390.3
Enterprise Deposits	2,071.5	3,997.7	6,815.8	13,279.0	22,450.2	28,656.3
Treasury Deposits	368.4	380.4	230.8	862.3	1,274.2	1,572.4
Deposits of government agencies	325.8	614.8	687.5	857.8	968.9	858.6
Urban saving deposits	1,057.8	5,192.6	8,678.1	21,518.8	38,520.8	48,279.8
Rural deposits	449.6	850.3	1,409.4	1,063.2	1,364.1	1,533.0
Total loans	5,905.5	15,166.36	21,615.5	39,976.0	61,165.6	74,914.1
Industrial production enterprise loans	1,160.1	3,559.4	4,956.1	9,948.7	14,213.3	16,526.6
Industrial supply and marketing enterprise and materials supply department loans	380.8	653.0	818.8	1,016.4	—	—
Commercial enterprise loans	2,649.3	5,768.5	7,677.7	10,509.8	15,332.6	18,356.6
Construction enterprise loans	267.1	671.5	906.1	617.2	973.8	1,591.1
Urban collective enterprises and individual industrial and commercial household loans	321.3	831.26	1,166.5	2,158.3	3,101.7	5,035.8
Agricultural loans	416.6	1,038.1	1,448.7	1,143.9	1,919.1	3,314.6
Fixed asset loans	705.3	2,245.8	3,924.6	7,172.9	—	—
Loans to enterprises in 3 forms of ventures: Sino-foreign, cooperative enterprises, foreign-funded	—	—	—	—	—	1,891.0

Note: Loan items differ due to reclassification.
Source: China Statistical Yearbook, Beijing, various years.

deposit and their growth rate is lowest. Commercial enterprise loans form the largest proportion of loans, reflecting the growing importance of the commercial sector. Between 1985 and 1997, however, fixed asset loans experienced the highest growth rate (593%).

A tight monetary policy is expected throughout the Ninth Five-Year Plan (1996–2000). An economist from the State Council, Wu Jinglian, remarked that there is no shortage of credits, but the shortage of capital is mainly due to the problem of resource allocation and distribution rather than a credit squeeze.[14] Bank lendings are tightened by the introduction of a scheme under which a state enterprise will be issued a loan licence by the central bank. The licence will show the enterprise's debt burden, financial standing and ability to repay the loans. The scheme aims to help those debt-laden state banks to work out correct lending guidelines, and will put an end to the widespread habit of state enterprises "rushing to banks at the slightest hint of financial stress."[15]

Fiscal Policy and Reform

The reform of the fiscal framework has been slow. Typically, the state's revenue comes mainly from state-owned enterprises because they are the output generating institutions. Taxes from individuals form only a small portion of government revenue. Government expenditures usually exceed revenues because many social and welfare services are provided free by the state. Budget estimation has always been a problem. Political lobbying between the central and local governments, between agricultural development and industrial growth, and between heavy and light industries require special attention. The budget has become only a "paper" estimation in the fiscal year, while the reality is governed by the "extra-budgetary" revenue and expenditure accounts, which are the direct result of mainly regional and ministerial interests. Kornai (1986) suggests that a "soft" budget occurs in most socialist economies due to the state's weakness in budget control.

In the early 1980s, there was a considerable amount of goodwill in fiscal reform. The reformists believed that budgetary deficits distort resource allocation, weaken macro control and disturb various relationships. A "push effect" is distinguished from the "burden effect" of deficit budgeting. The former accelerates economic development in the short run, while the latter occurs when the enlarged purchasing power leads to inflation. The basic principle of budgetary balance is that "expenditure relies on the amount of income." Fiscal reform first began in 1980 with the substitution of profit tax (industrial and commercial tax, enterprise income tax, and fixed asset tax) for profit remittance. However, total fiscal revenue as a ratio of GNP declined from about 31% in 1978 to 17.8% in 1989 (Li, 1994, p. 46). There were subsequent changes introduced into the fiscal system. Wu (1989) discusses the two-phase development in the reform on profit substitution. The first phase began in 1983 when tax payments were substituted for profit delivery, while the second began in 1985 when profit delivery was replaced by tax payment to mitigate the contradictions caused by distorted prices. Donnithorne (1986), however, observes that the reform measures introduced in early 1980s were liable to abuse. Blejer and Szapary (1990) argue that there are "unintended consequences" in fiscal reform, including the result of a continuous decrease in the average tax rate and a tax elasticity less than unity for the enterprise profit tax.

China's budget has been in deficit for a large number of years, while the extra-budgetary accounts have been in surplus (Table 10). The overall "soft" budget has been in surplus until 1990 when the trend reversed and a severe deficit was experienced. The substitution of profit tax for profit remittance in 1985 had led to a rise in taxes, but at the same time a fall in revenue from enterprises. The two largest items of government expenditures are subsidies to loss-making enterprises and price subsidies, though both items have experienced a mild decline since 1990 (Table 11).

Experience from other developing countries show that there are limitations in perfecting the tax system. One major limitation is the low tax base, which refers to the number of taxable items. For example, economic activities in the informal sector usually do not fall into the government's tax net, and it is difficult for the government to regulate and monitor taxation in the informal sector. To formalize the informal sector requires the establishment of relevant institutions, and it takes time for an institution to function effectively. The second limitation is the extent of "taxability." Given any tax item, the concern is what will be the amount and how efficient tax is collected. Income tax exists, for example, but if income is low or below the subsistence level, the government may not be able to collect anything from the income tax. Furthermore, tax evasion and avoidance become widespread when the institutional structure is weak. The Chinese government suffered a total of RMB 21 billion of financial loss due to unpaid taxes in the first eight months of 1995. As of October 1995, the government had about RMB 23.6 billion uncollected tax and value

Table 10
Fiscal Performance (RMB 100 million)

Year	Budgetary			Extra-Budgetary			Overall
	Revenue	Expenditure	Balance	Revenue	Expenditure	Balance	Balance
1978	1,121.1	1,111.0	10.1	347.1			
1980	1,085.2	1,212.7	−127.5	557.4			
1983	1,249.0	1,292.5	−43.5	967.7	875.8	91.9	48.4
1984	1,501.9	1,546.4	−44.5	1,188.5	1,114.7	73.8	29.3
1985	1,866.4	1,844.8	21.6	1,530.0	1,375.0	155.0	176.6
1986	2,260.3	2,330.8	−70.5	1,737.3	1,578.4	158.9	88.4
1987	2,368.9	2,448.5	−79.6	2,028.8	1,840.8	188.0	108.4
1988	2,628.0	2,706.6	−78.6	2,270.0	2,145.3	124.7	46.1
1989	2,947.9	3,040.2	−92.3	2,658.8	2,503.1	155.7	63.4
1990	3,312.6	3,452.2	−139.6	2,708.6	2,707.1	1.5	−138.1
1991	3,610.9	3,813.6	−202.7	3,243.3	3,092.3	151.0	−51.7
1992	4,153.1	4,389.7	−236.6	3,854.9	3,649.9	205.0	−31.6
1993	5,088.2	5,287.4	−199.2	1,432.5	1,314.3	118.2	−81.0
1994	5,218.1	5,792.6	−574.5	1,862.5	1,710.4	152.1	−422.4
1995	6,242.2	6,823.7	−581.5	2,406.5	2,331.3	75.2	−499.3
1996	7,408.0	7,937.6	−529.6	3,893.3	3,838.3	55.0	−474.6
1997	8,651.1	9,233.6	−582.4				

Source: *China Statistical Yearbook*, Beijing, various years.

Table 11
Taxes and Subsidies (RMB 100 million)

Year	Taxes	Revenue from State-Owned Enterprises	Subsidies to Loss-Making Enterprises	Price Subsidies
1978	519.28	571.99		
1980	517.70	435.24		
1983	775.59	240.52		
1984	947.35	276.77		
1985	2,040.79	43.75		
1986	2,090.73	42.04	324.78	257.48
1987	2,140.36	42.86	376.43	294.60
1988	2,390.47	51.12	446.46	316.82
1989	2,727.40	63.60	598.88	373.55
1990	2,821.86	78.30	578.88	380.80
1991	2,990.17	74.69	510.24	373.77
1992	3,296.91	59.97	444.96	321.64
1993	4,255.30	49.49	411.29	299.30
1994	5,126.88	—	366.22	314.47
1995	6,038.04	—	727.77	364.89
1996	6,909.82	—	337.40	353.91
1997	8,234.04	—	368.49	551.96

Source: *China Statistical Yearbook*, Beijing, various years.

added tax (VAT), though RMB 10 billion is expected to be collected by the end of 1995. Tax delinquencies are said to be the major cause.[16]

The "central-local" issue in China has added complications to tax reform. Economic inequalities between regions and localities have made the economically weak regions reluctant to submit tax to the central government. The "richer" regions, on the other hand, want to keep their funds for further development. Furthermore, marketization has expanded the activities in the private sector, and a considerable number of individuals have secured a large earning. Tax evasion is common, and many individuals are very reluctant to pay tax.[17] A new attempt in tax reform was made in the Third Plenum of the 14th Party Committee in November 1993. The provision for the "Decision on Issues Concerning the Establishment of a Socialist Market Economy" aims to eliminate the distortionary elements in the tax structure, increase fiscal transparency, and reiterate the revenue sharing arrangements between the central government and localities.

The introduction of the VAT to replace the product tax and business tax is one of the major components in the 1993 programme. The VAT extends to replace the consolidated industrial and commercial tax previously applied to foreign enterprises. The tax structure has further been simplified. As far as the direct tax is concerned, the tax rate on profits for state-owned, collective and private enterprises is equalized, and the highest tax rate has been reduced to 33% from 55%. The personal income tax, the personal income adjustment tax and the individual enterprise income tax have been replaced by a new personal income tax schedule, which applies to both local households and foreigners.

A new "tax sharing system" is introduced to govern the often controversial "central-local" relationship. This system composes of three new revenue items: central fixed revenue, local fixed revenue and shared incomes.[18] To convince the provinces to accept the new system, the government guaranteed that each province's base revenue for 1994 would not be less than that of 1993, and 30% would be returned to the province if the VAT revenue collected by the central government from any province is higher than the 1993 level. The success of the new system depends largely on the incentive generated from local revenue collection, and on the degree of vigour through which the system is implemented in the central-local fiscal relationship.

Foreign Capital and Investments

There are three forms of foreign capital utilized in China. Foreign loans are made to China by foreign governments and international development agencies such as the World Bank and Asian Development Bank.[19] Direct foreign investment includes equity joint ventures which are a limited company jointly funded by the equity of two or more investors, contractual joint ventures which are enterprises where Chinese and foreign partners cooperate in operations and management, wholly foreign-owned enterprises, and joint development ventures which are limited to the exploration of offshore oil. The last form of foreign capital includes compensation, trade, export processing and international leasing (Nyaw, 1997).

The establishment of five Special Economic Zones (Shenzhen, Zhuhai, Shantou, Xiamen and Hainan), fourteen open-trade coastal cities, coastal economic development zones along the coastal region, and the New

Pudong Area in Shanghai have been regarded as an instrument in facilitating and attracting foreign investments. Foreign investments can substitute local capital and lead to a transfer of technology. Special treatments, such as tax exemption, and low labour costs are the main comparative advantages that attracted foreign investors. Despite the lack of infrastructural developments at the beginning, much capital from Hong Kong has been relocated to these regions.[20] One survey in 1995 shows that Shenzhen families are the wealthiest in China. The report finds that the number of families earning more than RMB 1,200 per month is 13 times higher than in Beijing. The average family income in Shenzhen is RMB 3,700 per month, 1.5 times more than families in Beijing.[21]

The "special" nature of these coastal Special Economic Zones has been challenged in 1995. If these coastal regions are "de-specialized," it is argued that foreign investment would begin to go inland because of their competitive edge in labour cost over the coastal areas, such as cities in the Pearl River Delta region. Another argument is that income in these regions is high and "special treatments" should no longer be given any more. However, the Chinese authority realizes that coastal economic areas have become the symbol of China's open door reform policy. De-specializing these areas would generate a new political debate. It was confirmed in late 1995 that the Special Economic Zones should be kept, but some of the special treatments would be changed. For example, from 1 January 1996, foreign-invested firms in Xiamen will no longer enjoy the duty-free privilege of capital equipment imports. This is a step the Chinese authority takes towards equal treatment of both foreign and local firms. At the same time, however, Xiamen would pioneer new measures to attract foreign investors, such as the expansion of the domestic market.[22] Companies will not enjoy tax holidays and special exemptions in China's Special Economic Zones, but these zones will be preserved so that experiments with other aspects of reforms can first be conducted in the Special Economic Zones.[23] The reassurance of the five Special Economic Zones is released in a Xinhua report, which revealed that the zones have been promised the following privileges:[24]

- A 15% income tax rate compared with the 30% charged elsewhere in the country.
- An above-average growth rate — about 15% — for the next five years.

- Authority to carry out new experiments such as offshore-financing, service and trade that are commonly used in foreign markets.
- Lesser incentives included import tariffs exemption for materials used in domestic construction.

Although the Special Economic Zones today have developed considerably as compared to other inland areas these zones, however, serve a very important function. They possess the richest experience in China's open door policy since 1978. Inland areas can draw lessons directly from their experience. Shenzhen, Guangzhou, or any coastal city can provide a lot of insights for the inland areas to pick up. In particular, the Special Economic Zones can also provide a "bridge" function between foreign investors and enterprises in the inner provinces. So far, Hong Kong has acted as a "bridge" for foreign investors to conduct their business in southern China. By now, the coastal cities can replace Hong Kong's "bridge" role. To maintain the Special Economic Zones is definitely a good strategic move for the open door policy.

Foreign direct investments are the largest form of foreign capital (Table 12). The value of foreign direct investment has increased tremendously over the years, especially in the 1990s. There is, however, a considerable difference between the contracted value and the utilized value. The largest foreign investors in China mainly come from the Asia-Pacific region. Hong Kong and Macau are by far the largest, and Taiwan has caught up with Japan and the United States as the second largest foreign investor (Table 13). A considerable amount of investments from Hong Kong, however, are overseas investments conducted from Hong Kong.

In regional terms, the largest recipients of foreign investments are cities in the coastal provinces. In 1994, the top 10 recipients of direct foreign investments are, in order of sequence, Guangdong, Jiangsu, Fujian, Shandong, Shanghai, Liaoning, Beijing, Tianjin, Sichuan, and Hainan. The industry sector receives the largest portion of foreign direct investment in value terms in 1993, followed by real estate, public residential and consultancy services; commerce, food services, material supply and marketing; and construction. In the early 1990s, however, there is a deliberate move by the Chinese authority to encourage foreign direct investment in the construction sector. For example, more foreign participation is called for in the ambitious transportation development plans in the next decade in highway construction. It aims to encourage the "build, operate and transfer" (BOT)

Table 12
Utilization of Foreign Capital (US$100 Million)

Year	Total			Foreign Loans			Direct Foreign Investments			Other Foreign Investments	
	No. of Contracts	Contracted Value	Utilized Value	No. of Contracts	Contracted Value	Utilized Value	No. of Contracts	Contracted Value	Utilized Value	Contracted Value	Utilized Value
1979–83	1,471	239.78	144.38	79	150.62	117.55	1,392	77.42	18.02	11.74	8.81
1984	1,894	47.91	27.05	38	19.16	12.86	1,865	26.51	12.58	2.24	1.61
1985	3,145	98.67	46.47	72	35.34	26.88	3,073	59.32	16.61	4.01	2.98
1986	1,551	117.37	72.58	53	84.07	50.14	1,498	28.34	18.74	4.96	3.70
1987	2,289	121.36	84.52	56	78.17	58.05	2,233	37.09	23.14	6.10	3.33
1988	6,063	160.04	102.26	118	98.13	64.87	5,945	52.97	31.94	8.94	5.45
1989	5,909	114.79	100.59	130	51.85	62.86	5,779	56.00	33.92	6.94	3.81
1990	7,371	120.86	102.89	98	50.99	65.34	7,273	65.96	34.87	3.91	2.68
1991	13,086	195.83	115.54	108	71.61	68.88	12,978	119.77	43.66	4.45	3.00
1992	48,858	694.39	192.02	94	107.03	79.11	48,764	581.24	110.07	6.12	2.84
1993	83,595	1,232.73	389.60	158	113.06	111.89	83,437	1,114.36	275.15	5.31	2.56
1994	47,646	937.56	432.13	97	106.68	92.67	47,549	826.80	337.67	4.08	1.79
1995	37,184	1,032.05	481.33	173	112.88	103.27	37,011	912.82	375.21	6.35	2.85
1996	24,673	816.09	548.04	117	79.62	126.62	24,556	732.76	417.26	3.71	4.09
1997	21,138	610.58	644.08	137	58.72	126.21	21,001	510.04	452.57	41.82	71.30

Source: *China Statistical Yearbook*, Beijing, various years.

Table 13
Six Largest Foreign Direct Investments in China (US$ Million)

	1990	1991	1992	1993	1994	1995	1996	1997
Hong Kong/Macau	1,913.4	2,486.9	7,709.1	17,861.3	20,174.8	20,624.9	21,457.9	21,954.4
Taiwan	—	—	1,050.5	3,138.6	3,391.0	3,165.2	3,482.0	3,342.3
U.S.A.	456.0	323.2	511.1	2,063.1	2,490.8	3,083.7	3,444.2	3,461.2
Japan	503.4	532.5	709.8	1,324.1	2,075.3	3,212.5	3,692.1	4,390.4
Singapore	50.4	58.2	122.3	490.0	1,179.6	1,860.6	2,247.2	2,607.0
South Korea	—	—	119.5	373.8	722.8	1,047.1	1,504.2	2,227.6

Source: *China Statistical Yearbook*, Beijing, various years.

Table 14
Percentage Share of Contracted Direct Foreign Investment in China by Sector

Sector	1987	1989	1991	1993	1996	1997
Farming and forestry	3.4	2.2	1.8	1.1	1.6	2.1
Manufacturing industry	47.9	83.3	80.3	45.9	68.9	53.1
Construction	1.5	1.2	1.1	3.6	2.7	6.1
Telecommunication	0.4	0.9	0.8	1.3	2.2	5.1
Commercial and catering	0.8	1.2	1.5	4.1	3.2	3.6
Real estate and public utilities and services	39.7	9.4	12.6	39.3	17.5	17.4
Others	6.3	1.8	1.9	4.7	3.9	13.6

Source: *Almanac of China's Foreign Economic Relations and Trade*, Beijing.

strategy.[25] The lack of investment in construction of infrastructure has been seen as a bottleneck in deepening economic reform in China. The percentage share of contracted direct foreign investment in the manufacturing industry has declined considerably since 1991, while the percentage shares in construction, real estate and public utilities and services, telecommunication, and commercial and catering have gone up (Table 14).

Economic Re-Orientations

The 1993 Austerity Plan and Reform of State-Owned Enterprises

By the end of 1980s, the Chinese authority, backed with a decade-long experience of economic reform, reexamined many economic issues. Although there was sanctions imposed by a number of Western countries following the 1989 Tian'anmen Incident, the economic situation stabilized and confidence was regained following the tour by Deng Xiaoping in spring 1992 when Deng spoke for a more rapid development of the "open door policy." Indeed, economic overheating came sooner than expected, and the Chinese authority was forced to react positively to the situation of rising inflation, while at the same time avoiding the mistakes made in the 1980s.[26] In July 1993, a 16-point Austerity Plan pioneered by Vice Premier Zhu Rongji was announced as an immediate instrument in curbing the credits given out by national banks, in stopping investments in sectors which are not thought to be in the national interest. The Austerity Plan consists of the following measures:[27]

1. Call-in loans which were diverted to speculative schemes;
2. Force workers to buy all government bonds that had failed to sell within two weeks;
3. Raise interest rates;
4. Force non-financial institutions to repay funds borrowed from financial institutions;
5. Impose a 20% cut in government spending and ban new car imports;
6. Suspend price reform measures;
7. Forbid the issue of new IOUs to peasants;
8. End dubious fund-raising schemes;
9. Control real estate speculations in the development zones;

10. Reduce the scale of infrastructure projects;
11. Control share-listing procedures on the stock market;
12. Reform the export financing system;
13. Force banks to tighten up their credit approval;
14. Strengthen the central bank;
15. Clear transport bottlenecks which cause goods to pile up; and
16. Send inspection teams to supervise compliance with the Plan.

Li (1995) argues that there are three major themes in the Austerity Plan: (a) the use of monetary controls and credit restrictions as the major instruments in cooling off the economy; (b) monetary order is thought to be more important than fiscal instruments; and (c) changing emphasis in investment priorities. The Austerity Plan was definitely a timely programme to restrict the widespread speculation in both the real estate and the stock markets. There is, however, a fundamental shift in the direction of reform. First of all, investments will no longer be based on popular demand. Rather, an investment strategy with infrastructural development is the top priority. The squeeze in credits conveys the message that the "quality" aspect in investment should be given an equal importance. The amount of funds invested should yield output and raise productivity. The 1993 Austerity Plan hopes that improvement in the quality of investment will lead to a rise in productivity and output, which in turn will ease the pressure on inflation.

The message of qualitative improvement in investments is not well understood. Many still regard the tight monetary policy as a mere instrument of quantity control and expect the restriction to be lifted after some time. Severe pressures, particularly from the regions and inner areas, have made the Chinese authority reluctant to introduce further policies. Indeed, the Austerity Plan and the tight monetary policy cannot be effective without corresponding policies to break the "bank — state-owned enterprises — employment" relationship. State-owned enterprises have to be made known that the state cannot bail them out endlessly. A successful policy requires the separation between the strong and the weak state-owned enterprises. Typically, state-owned enterprises along the coastal regions are economically stronger, and workers can have an easy access to the job markets. In the remote regions, on the contrary, state-owned enterprises need to be assisted financially. A policy package that can reform the state-owned enterprises should compose of three elements. Firstly, as far as bank credits are concerned, the interest rate should be used as a "screening device" in investment projects. A high interest rate discriminates against low return projects and more bank credits can be made available for high return projects. An effective interest rate policy must be applied by all national banks.

Secondly, state-owned enterprises along the coastal areas or in the economically "richer" regions should not be given subsidies any more. The huge debt accumulated by the state-owned enterprises is basically caused by two reasons: wastage in welfare and wage expenses, including the embezzlement of funds by officials, and unproductive investments. Increase in productivity includes a rise in output and the possession of modern management skills and techniques. In other words, for a productive investment project, the rise in output has to be coupled with the ability to sell the products. State-owned enterprises in the richer areas can adapt to market conditions easily, both in terms of output and employment. It makes sense for these state-owned enterprises to face up to market incentives than to rely on state assistance.

The third element in the reform of state-owned enterprises is time. The economically weaker state-owned enterprises in the remote regions should be asked to present a "timetable" such that their problems would be reduced, if not eliminated, gradually. Economically stronger state-owned enterprises obviously need less time in the transition period. Loss-making state-owned enterprises in the remote parts of the country require more time for improvements to be made. It would be appropriate that a longer time is given to those state-owned enterprises in the remote regions, while those state-owned enterprises situated along the coastal areas should be given a limited time in reducing their reliance on state funding, subsidies or bank credits. If each state-owned enterprises is given such a "timetable" in their pursuance of economic independence by raising productivity and restructuring the workers' wage agreements, in the meantime subsidies will still be provided by the Chinese authority. It is only when these state-owned enterprises fulfil their targets at the end of the period would the Chinese authority be released from the financial burden to bail out the loss-making state-owned enterprises.

A major obstacle in the reform of state-owned enterprises, however, is the extent of corruption among officials and the divergence of political interests between the localities and the central government. The policy, or strategy, so adopted has to be clear-cut, unbiased, fair and the objectives are made transparent so that the positive outcomes of the policy can be seen by all state-owned enterprises.[28]

Hong Kong 1997

The reversion of Hong Kong's sovereignty to China in July 1997 closes the final chapter of British imperialism in Hong Kong. The Sino-British Joint Declaration signed in 1984 between the United Kingdom and the People's Republic of China, and the agreement on the Basic Law provide the political and institutional structure for the post-1997 Hong Kong. In the period leading up to July 1997, various political tensions had emerged between the UK and the PRC, notably in 1987–1988 over the airport issue, the Tian'anmen Incident in 1989, and the Hong Kong Governor's introduction of democratic reforms in 1992–1993. Deng's "one country, two systems" policy has been received with mixed feelings in the territory.

Economically, Hong Kong is strong enough to undergo the historical change. China's open door policy since 1979 has provided a great number of economic opportunities for Hong Kong investors. First, the multiple expansion in the entrepôt trade has led to developments in Hong Kong's port and transport industry. Business activities in China have resulted in many foreign companies setting up their regional offices in Hong Kong. The cheap labour supply in the Pearl River Delta has attracted Hong Kong's industrialists to relocate their manufacturing plants to southern China. The People's Republic of China also invested massively in Hong Kong, making use of Hong Kong's international financial and communication positions. Hong Kong has served as the "bridge" and "gateway" between China and the international community (Kan, 1994). In the process, the economic structure of Hong Kong also changed. The manufacturing sector has declined drasti-cally, while the tertiary sector expanded remarkably, both in employment and in income. In fact, the Hong Kong economy has been overstretched, resulting in a two-digit inflation rate since the late 1980s until 1993–1994. Unemployment has been low, or even below 1%, until the early 1990s when industrial relocation generated a considerable number of unemployed factory workers. Unemployment exceeded 3% by 1995. Un-employment worsened after the Asian financial crisis in 1997–1998. By early 1999, unemployment rate exceeded 6%.

China has made it known that the Hong Kong economy should be in a good shape at the time of change over in 1997. Besides the avoidance of potential social discontent when unemployment is high, the Hong Kong economy does serve China in various aspects, even after 1997. Hong Kong will remain a financial centre, a window between China and the international community. China can learn from the lessons of economic achievements in Hong Kong. On the contrary, the survival of the Hong Kong economy depends also largely on the deepening of economic reform in China. The complementary nature of the two economies has become so tight that the fall of any one will cause economic disruption on the other. For the sake of Taiwan in the issue of national unification, China is likely to maintain an open and prosperous Hong Kong.

There are, however, uncertainties on the part of some citizens in Hong Kong. This is seen from the immigration figures and the channelling of financial capital away from Hong Kong. Cooperation between Britain and China, the identification of the Chief Executive for Hong Kong in the second half of 1996, and the way the democratic element in Hong Kong's political circle are the few non-economic, but sensible, issues that require extreme diplomacy in the last twelve to eighteen months before the transition. The Chinese authority has mobilized resources in order to ensure a smooth transition of sovereignty on 1 July 1997.

The unification between Hong Kong and China has positive implication on China's economic reform. While the Hong Kong economy is making progress at all fronts, the only choice for the Chinese economy is to catch up. This necessitates the continuation of the open door policy, market economy, and qualitative changes including modern management skills, advance telecommunication and so on. Unless drastic political changes occur, any economic "turn back" for China is out of the question. The reversion of Hong Kong's sovereignty to China in July 1997 has a great impact to China as well. The Chinese authority has to accept many economic and business values currently practising in Hong Kong.

The Ninth Five-Year Plan 1996–2000

Stability is considered to be the key to the continuation of economic reform in China. The Ninth Five-Year Plan calls for an annual economic growth rate between 8 and 9%, greater agricultural output, higher exports, increased infrastructural development and more development for outlying provinces. Job creation is another focus of the 1996–2000 economic plan. It aims to bring 70 million Chinese above the poverty line by raising grain production and exports at a rate higher than the growth in GDP. However, only 4% of GNP will be devoted to education.[29] Further liberalization in the financial sector is expected, especially after the Asian financial crisis and the closure of financial institutions. Firstly, full currency convertibility on the current account has been suggested, but after the Asian financial crisis, the Chinese authority will leave the idea aside for the time being.[30] The devaluation of the RMB in 1993 has led to a short time shock, but the currency stabilized considerably. This has stimulated further trade and foreign direct investment.[31] Secondly, regulations on the interest rate will further be eased, and a larger degree of market influence in the determination of the interest rate is expected. Commercial banks will be allowed to set their own rates within a range fixed by the authority, though the operation aspects have yet to be arranged. To make the RMB more acceptable in the international market, foreign-funded firms will be allowed to trade in foreign currencies more freely.[32] However, it would be unlikely that the Chinese authority would allow foreign banks to operate at the retail level in the near future. To ensure stability, the party leader, Jiang Zemin, outlined 12 major relationships in his address to the Fifth Plenum in October 1995. Reform, development and stability is the first relationship. The others are: construction, population, resources and environment; in-dustries; market mechanism and macro-control; speed versus efficiency; east versus west; the public sector; income distribution; open-up versus self-reliance; national defence; central versus regional; and material and cultural progress.[33] Although the political interpretation is that Jiang is using the address to make his manifesto for maintaining leadership, most of these 12 relationships are related to economics rather than to political activities. Provided there is political stability, economic reform will be China's dominant issue in future.

China's External Economy

Trade and official flows are the two important forms of external economic relations.[34] As far as the trade figures are concerned, China has experienced large trade deficits in the 1980s (Table 15). Large imports and the over-valued RMB were the major causes. In the 1980s, there was little enforce-ment on limiting imports of luxurious consumer items, although the authority only encouraged import of capital items. Furthermore, exports were mainly

Table 15

Total Value of Exports and Imports (US$100 Million)

Year	Exports	Imports	Balance
1978	97.5	108.9	−11.4
1980	181.2	200.2	−19.0
1984	261.4	274.1	−12.0
1985	273.5	422.5	−149.0
1986	309.4	429.0	−119.6
1987	394.4	432.2	−37.8
1988	475.2	552.8	−77.6
1989	525.4	591.4	−66.0
1990	620.9	533.5	87.5
1991	718.4	637.9	80.5
1992	849.4	805.9	43.5
1993	917.4	1,039.6	−122.2
1994	1,210.4	1,156.9	53.5
1995	1,487.7	1,320.8	166.9
1996	1,510.5	1,388.3	122.2
1997	1,827.0	1,423.6	403.4

Sources: *China Statistical Yearbook*, Beijing, various years.

manufactures of labour-intensive products, which were not too competitive in the world market. High inflation at home also discouraged exports.

Efforts to cut expensive consumer items after 1989 resulted in a trade surplus. China's major trading partners in Asia are Hong Kong, Japan, Taiwan, and South Korea. Major Western trading partners are the United States, Germany, Italy, France and Britain. Trade with Russia has exceeded most European countries. Trade arising from foreign investment enterprises has expanded considerably (Table 16), though the value of import is still larger than the value of export. Guangdong is by far the largest province favoured by foreign investment enterprises, while Shanghai is catching up gradually (Table 16).

Sino-U.S. relationship is by far the most important piece of inter-national economic relationship. When President Clinton came into office in 1993, political issues, typically the human right issue, are tied with economic issues. Bilateral trade and other economic activities with China could not be conducted smoothly because China was reluctant to give in to human right demands from USA, claiming that it is a domestic affair.

Table 16

Shares in Export and Import of Foreign Investment Enterprises Goods by Major Regions

Region	1992 Exports	1992 Imports	1993 Exports	1993 Imports	1994 Exports	1994 Imports	1995 Exports	1995 Imports	1996 Exports	1996 Imports	1997 Exports	1997 Imports
National (US$10,000)	1,735,619	2,637,070	2,523,717	4,183,320	3,471,297	5,293,417	4,687,587	6,294,271	6,150,636	7,560,380	7,489,986	7,772,135
Percentage Share												
Beijing	1.28	3.96	1.34	2.97	1.42	2.79	1.51	2.97	1.61	2.96	1.54	3.01
Tianjin	1.66	1.84	2.40	2.62	2.92	3.58	4.24	4.79	4.80	5.38	4.71	5.60
Liaoning	4.64	3.68	4.61	3.82	4.67	4.05	5.06	4.18	5.17	4.22	4.71	4.98
Shanghai	6.12	8.55	7.06	9.69	7.66	9.34	8.57	11.44	8.86	12.46	9.35	12.35
Jiangsu	1.74	6.39	5.96	7.36	5.92	6.61	6.26	7.74	8.24	9.35	8.95	9.63
Zhejiang	2.70	1.77	3.87	2.52	2.98	2.70	2.37	3.01	3.29	3.58	3.28	2.88
Fujian	11.11	9.49	9.86	8.54	8.27	8.21	7.56	7.44	7.32	6.64	7.07	6.75
Shandong	2.35	3.16	3.52	4.22	4.58	4.78	5.41	5.76	6.26	4.85	6.87	5.78
Guangdong	62.16	52.89	56.93	47.33	57.12	47.91	54.96	43.60	49.90	40.05	49.11	42.11

Source: *China Statistical Yearbook*, Beijing, various years.

Economically, the Sino-U.S. dispute hurt the U.S. relatively more than China. First, not all Western powers see China's human right issue as an urgent one. Secondly, economic recession in most Western economies has made China's unexplored market a potential for trade, export and investment.[35] China, in fact, managed to play one Western nation against another in terms of large trade deals and major foreign investment projects. China, therefore, is not short of potential economic partners. While American exports to China is low, the reverse is not so. Finally, in 1994, the Clinton Administration announced the delinking of trade and human right issues in the Sino-U.S. relationship. This opens a new era of Sino-U.S. relationship.

China is fully aware of the advantage it has in picking one Western nation against another in economic affairs. Most Western nations are looking to China as the next market they can conquer. China is also using her relationships with other Western nations as "trump cards" when dealing with USA. On the other hand, China's ambition to become a major world trade partner, to become a member of the World Trade Organization (WTO), and to have the RMB freely convertible in the world market are seen to be the "yardstick" the United States can use. In addition, the U.S. is prepared to use non-economic issues to influent the Sino-U.S. relation-ships. Non-economic issues include the human rights and piracy in tech-nological products. The USA's trade record with Japan in the 1980s had been one-sided, and it had proved to be difficult for the U.S. to lobby for more exports to Japan. Large trade deficit with Japan has become a major political issue in general elections. Armed with Japan's unfavourable ex-perience, it is not surprising for the U.S. to guard against massive import from China. While 40% of China's exports go to the U.S., only 2% of American exports make it to China. The U.S. trade deficit with China reached nearly U.S.$38 billion in 1995, and is growing at a rate of 25% each year. The magnitude of increase will soon surpass the American trade deficit with Japan.[36] The Chinese authority, however, argued that the trade deficit with USA has been exaggerated.[37] In 1995, China will export US$40 billion to USA and receive US$10 billion of foreign direct investment from USA. USA's exports to China were US$9.3 billion. Trade deficit is ex-pected to grow. The decrease in USA's trade deficit with Japan is matched with a rising trade deficit with China.[38] Fair trade, therefore, has become a condition for a normalization in the Sino-U.S. trade relationship. Various conditions have been imposed on China by the U.S. For example, China's has to clean up its piracy industry at home, especially copyright piracy at the retail level, has to expand imports from USA by lowering a great number of tariffs, and has to match with various standards if USA agrees to China's admission to WTO. In the application for entry to WTO, a major disagreement between the U.S. and China is the state of the economy. The U.S. wants China to be admitted as a "developed" country, while China wants to remain as a "developing" country. In the Asia Pacific Economic Cooperation (APEC) Forum in Japan in November 1995, the United States presented a "road map" on the entry into the new WTO to Wu Yi, the Chinese Foreign Trade and Economic Cooperation Minister. The "road map" outlines "steps China must take to reform its trade practices and meet WTO standards, including cutting tariffs and opening markets."[39] Charlene Barshefsky, deputy U.S. trade representative for Asian Affairs, remarked that the U.S. will continue to pressure China to follow the U.S. accord, and threatened to raise tariffs on millions of dollars' worth of imports from China (US$2.8 billion annually) if China fails to stop the piracy of American computer software and video cassettes.[40]

The Chinese leader, Jiang Zemin, responded by announcing a reduction of tariffs on 4,000 items, lowering them from the existing average of 36 to 25%. The U.S. welcomed the move and regarded that as a major step in China's trade liberalization, though the U.S. administration insisted that more measures to dismantle trade barriers are needed.[41] The self-interest of the U.S., especially in a time of general election, will make the U.S. administration reluctant to accept China into the WTO unless China liberalizes its trade and opens its domestic markets further. China's response has been consistent and firm, partly because of its favourable relationships with other European nations, and its strong reserve which has risen from US$52 billion to US$70 billion in 1995 as a result of the rise in trade surplus, though China's foreign debt stood at U.S.$10 billion.[42] President Bill Clinton has announced in May 1999 that China will most likely be admitted to the WTO by the end of 1999.

At the political front, the U.S.-Taiwan relationship has also been a major obstacle in the Sino-U.S. relationship. Taiwan President Lee's visit to USA in 1995 has sharpened the Sino-U.S. relationship. China began military exercises on the Taiwan Straits in late 1995 and early 1996, and Taiwan's election in March 1996 are sensitive issues which, hopefully, will not spill over to the economic front.

Conclusion

The Chinese economy has gone a long way since the beginning of reform in 1978. Despite the various ups and downs and the argument of wrong sequencing, China's economic reform has no parallel in history. Beginning with reform first in the agricultural sector and subsequently in the industrial sector, income has risen considerably. The establishment of Special Economic Zones has been a success in attracting foreign direct investment, especially from or through Hong Kong.

The current leadership in Beijing is pledged to pursue economic reform further. Since the 1990s, reform of state-owned enterprises has been given the top priority. State-owned enterprises are the largest state sector. There are two aspects in the reform of state-owned enterprises. The "hard" side concerns the financing of investment of capital, which involves activities in the banking sector. The "soft" side concerns the management of the enterprises, including the employment of workers. Successful reform in the state-owned enterprises will therefore solve the two problems of a sound banking practice and the employment of workers. A tight monetary policy has been used as an instrument in forcing the state-owned enterprises to use their funds efficiently and pursue qualitative changes in their investment activities.

The resumption of Hong Kong's sovereignty in 1997 requires China to adopt a more open strategy. This includes the use of Hong Kong as a base for modernization and reform, and the acceptance of various economic practices in Hong Kong. China has been able to pick one Western country against another in its foreign economic activities. The Sino-U.S. relationship, however, has remained the most challenging. Both parties have so far been able to separate economic gains and losses from political arguments.

Economic reform in China is changing from one with emphasis on quantity to one emphasized on quality. Reform in the financial sector and the state-owned sector is the top priority. Following the Asian financial Crisis, the Chinese Readers have become more cautious in the sequencing of economic reform, especially in the financial sector. There are still obstacles on the way, but the general attitude is that China's reform is progressing considerably.

Notes

1. *China News Digest*, 21 September, 24 and 30 November and 5 December 1995.
2. *China News Digest*, 19 December 1995.
3. *South China Morning Post*, 26 October 1995.
4. There is no formal record on the number of workers migrated, but millions of workers seeking for train and other transport services to return to their homeland before the Chinese New Year can be used as a rough estimate.
5. *China News Digest*, 17 December 1996.
6. *China News Digest*, 15 and 17 December 1995.
7. *China News Digest*, 5 December 1995.
8. *China News Digest*, 9 November 1995.
9. *China News Digest*, 4 October 1995.
10. *China Daily*, 14 December 1995, and *China News Digest*, 17 and 18 December 1995.
11. *China Daily*, 19 January 1996.
12. For a detailed discussion, see Tang and Li, 1997, pp. 13–42.
13. *South China Morning Post*, 2 November 1995.
14. *China Daily Business Weekly*, 21–27 January 1996, and *South China Morning Post*, 25 October 1995.
15. *South China Morning Post*, 2 November 1995.
16. *China News Digest*, 23 September, 7 and 13 December 1995.
17. Rules to curb tax evasion will be exercised on a massive scale (see *China Daily*, 17 January 1996). Tax collectors have been beaten to death. One report said that in 1994, over 100 tax collectors were beaten to death when they were performing their duties.
18. Central fixed incomes include mainly custom duties, tax on consumption, tax from central enterprises and financial institutions. Local fixed incomes include mainly income taxes and profit remittance of local enterprises, urban land tax, real estate taxes, vehicle utilization tax, and so on. Shared incomes are revenues collected from VAT at a share ratio of 75:25 between central and local governments (Wong, 1995).
19. For a discussion on official flows to China by the World Bank, see Jun and Katada, 1997, pp. 163–182.
20. Various reports conducted by the Federation of Hong Kong Industries show that southern China is the most popular destination of Hong Kong investors because of its low labour cost and geographical proximity. These annual surveys also reported the kinds of manufacturing industries most committed to investment in southern China.
21. *China Daily*, 15 January 1996.

22. *China News Digest*, 19 December 1995, and *Hong Kong Economic Journal*, 1 February 1996.
23. *China News Digest*, 27 October 1995.
24. *South China Morning Post*, 22 February 1996.
25. *China Daily*, 21 November 1995.
26. For example, according to a report by Reuters News Agency, total commitments of foreign investment to China during the first nine months of 1992 had far exceeded that of Indonesia, Malaysia and Thailand (see Nyaw, 1997, pp. 55–88).
27. *South China Morning Post*, 4 July 1993.
28. A considerable amount of discussion has been concentrated on the property right of the state-owned enterprises. The argument that private property right can naturally lead to improvement in state-owned enterprises is debatable. One should distinguish between the use right and the ownership right. State-owned enterprises exercise the use right, which is a strong incentive for the managers to run the state-owned enterprise effectively and efficiently.
29. *China News Digest*, 21 September 1995.
30. *South China Morning Post*, 14 November 1995.
31. For a detailed discussion on the foreign exchange market, see Wong and Lo, 1997, pp. 139–162.
32. *China News Digest*, 1 February 1996.
33. *South China Morning Post*, 9 October 1995.
34. For a discussion on official flows to China, see Jun and Katada, 1997, pp. 163–182.
35. Key leaders from Germany, France and Canada have visited China in 1994–1995, securing millions of trade and investment contracts.
36. *South China Morning Post*, 14 November 1995, and *China News Digest*, 13 November 1995.
37. *China News Digest*, 8 October 1995.
38. *South China Morning Post*, 7 October 1995.
39. *China News Digest*, 18 November 1995.
40. *China News Digest*, 16 and 31 December 1995.
41. *China News Digest*, 21 November 1995.
42. *China News Digest*, 9 January 1996, and *China Daily*, 8 January 1996.

3

The Legal Environment and Business Enterprises in the People's Republic of China

John D. Ho

Introduction

The first national Company Law applicable to both state-owned and private enterprises was enacted and promulgated at the end of 1993. The Law provides for the organization of modern Chinese enterprises with many features adapted from Western capitalist corporations. At least two factors account for the fact that it has taken the People's Republic of China four and a half decades to enact this Law. First, until 1978 preoccupation with political campaigns such as the Cultural Revolution made it impossible for the country to seriously focus its attention on rational economic reform. Second, the concept of a "socialist market economy" and the corresponding corporate structure provided for by the Company Law could not have been embraced until difficult ideological and legal issues about the role of state planning and socialist public ownership of the means of production are resolved. In this chapter, we examine the legal environment of the Chinese enterprise. In Section II, we trace the reconstruction of the legal environment after years of neglect. In Section III, we discuss the economy's shift from plan to market. In Section IV, we examine the legislation aimed at building a "socialist market economy." In Section V, we examine the formation, capitalization and operation of the modern Chinese enterprises under the Company Law. In Section VI, we examine the law related to bankruptcy of Chinese enterprises. Finally, in Section VII, we conclude by summarizing the challenges that still remain for the architects of the legal environment.

The Reconstruction of the Legal Environment

During the first decade of the People's Republic of China, the government nullified the Republic of China's Complete Code of Six Laws and promulgated a substantial number of laws and decrees, in an attempt to establish a "people's" legal system (Wang, 1993). Before Mao Zedong's Anti-Rightist Campaign began in 1957, China had for the first time implemented a substantial amount of systematic law, based mostly on the Soviet legal codes. This tentative start to lawmaking ended during the Cultural Revolution (1966–1976) amid an excess of ideological passion that brought forth what has been described as "legal nihilism" (Folsom and Finan, 1989). Law and legal institutions were dismantled in a frenzy of hysterical fanaticism. Law schools were closed; lawyers, judges, courtroom personnel and law teachers were taken off their jobs and sent to work in the countryside under primitive conditions. Politics, not law, became the yardstick and guide of behaviour.

The tide turned with the death of Mao in 1976 and the subsequent rise of Deng Xiaoping. The country began to refocus itself on economic issues. To facilitate economic reform, law was reinstituted and China underwent the most extensive period of lawmaking and legal training in its history (Folsom and Finan, 1989). Legal models of developed countries were borrowed to help the country embark upon a programme of economic reform to modernize the country by opening up itself to the outside world and revitalizing the domestic economy. The current legal system has been developed largely since the Third Plenum of the 11th Central Committee of the Chinese Communist Party held in late December 1978, which "swept away the chaos and led the country back unto a correct path" (Wang, 1993). After a brief pause as a result of the "June 4th Incident" of 1989, the policy of economic reform was reaffirmed after Deng's visit to southern China. The 14th National Congress of the Communist Party of China in October 1992 declared that in order to raise productivity and build the national economy, China had to adopt measures used in market economies and build a "socialist market economy" (Wang, 1993). As a market economy needs a different set of rules from a planned economy, this gave further impetus to accelerate the reconstruction of the legal environment.

From Plan to Market

Prior to 1978, the economy of the People's Republic of China was based on the model of the planned economy in which the government decided what to produce, how the products were allocated, as well as the prices at which transaction were made; profits of enterprises were remitted to the government and losses were subsidized by the government. However, the perspective must be kept that China's economy was never completely centrally planned. The number of commodities planned and distributed from the centre usually did not exceed several hundred, in contrast to the 60,000 such commodities in the former USSR. Instead, much of the planning occurred at the local level, uncoordinated by the central government. Much investment occurred outside of the economic plan; and a lot of planning took place only on paper (Johns, 1995).

The history of economic plans can be divided into three phases (World Bank, 1992). The period 1953–1962, covered by the first two Economic Plans, may be called the "Soviet period" in which relatively detailed "Soviet style" plans were used. This period included the period of the "Great Leap Forward" with its notorious consequences. The "pre-reform period," covering the years 1963–1977, which included the period of the Cultural Revolution, has been described as a period of "planning as propaganda," in which the plans were used to mobilize the population instead of being actual guides to specific policies and priorities. This period included the year 1968, when it was impossible to formulate an annual plan because of the political chaos. The "reform period" started in 1978 and is characterized by economic plans that attempt to make realistic assessments of the economic situation, and to provide for the country's overall development strategy by evolving towards a macroeconomic framework, using policy instruments such as interest rates, taxes and exchange rates instead of administrative directives. The scope of mandatory planning has been reduced, gradually to be overshadowed by "guidance planning" which gave enterprises greater autonomy. The direct determination of outcomes by the state continues to fall. Beginning in 1979, prices were gradually allowed to float. It has been estimated that the share of industrial production under the mandatory plan declined from 70% in 1979 to 16% in 1990. Similarly, the proportion of investment financed directly by the government budget dropped from 28% in 1981 to 8% in 1989, with the share financed by enterprises and especially banks correspondingly increasing to accommodate this change (World Bank, 1990).

The pre-reform planned economy operated almost entirely on the basis of socialist public ownership of productive resources. The socialist public ownership consisted of all-people's ownership (*quanmin suoyou zhi*) and collective ownership (*jiti suoyou zhi*). The all-people's ownership enterprises were of large and medium size, and were owned by the state; the collective ownership enterprises were of relatively smaller size and owned by the districts, street committees in urban cities, or townships in the rural areas (Qian, 1993). Unlike their counterparts in Western market economies, these enterprises lacked autonomy and therefore incentive. Being essentially administrative units of government, they were more concerned with bureaucratic relationships than market forces and efficiency. Amongst the numerous characteristics pinpointed as the source of their inefficiency were the "soft" budget constraint, micromanagement by the state, and the use of these enterprises to pursue aims unrelated to profit, such as provision of social welfare (Hay, Morris, Liu and Yao, 1994). Profit or growth maximization therefore was unlikely to be their principal aim. In fact, large profits could invite higher performance targets for the next period — a phenomenon sometimes referred to as "whipping the fast ox." Maximizing "organizational slack" so that the enterprise did not have to strain to meet its targets, and "satisfactory" profits, were what the manager sought (World Bank, 1990).

One of the principal objectives of the economic reform launched in 1978 was to stimulate economic growth by enhancing the incentive and efficiency of state enterprises, making them more responsive to market forces and competition. A private sector, albeit relatively small, was allowed to emerge. In order to institutionalize this change in the economy's orientation from a planned economy to a market economy, corresponding reform in the legal environment for the enterprise was inevitable.

Towards a Socialist Market Economy: The Legal Framework

It is well understood that for capitalist markets to function efficiently there should be a large number of market participants acting autonomously in competition against one another. Arms-length transactions and freedom of contract in the long run would weed out inefficient producers and lead to "optimal" allocation of resources (World Bank, 1990). Under the planned economy model, however, Chinese factory managers were administratively responsible to their superiors in the relevant ministries of the state bureaucracy and lacked the autonomy enjoyed by their western counterparts (Wang, 1992).

Freedom of contract was necessarily restricted by the demands of the system of economic plans placed upon the enterprises. Instead of seeking immediate profits, enterprises must conform their operations to requirements of the economic plans imposed on them by external authorities. Thus, for example, while Article 5 of the Law on Economic Contracts provided that economic contracts must be concluded on the basis of the principles of equality and mutual benefit, negotiated consensus, and freedom from "illegal interference" of outside parties, Article 11 imposed a duty on enterprises to conclude contracts in accordance with the requirements of mandatory plans where they were applicable. If agreement could not be reached, the disputed points must be referred back to the planning authorities, who could impose a "contract" of their own making on the contracting enterprises (Wang, 1993).

Indeed, when all state enterprises and the assets controlled by them belong to "the whole people," concepts that may seem ordinary for a capitalist market economy may not be applicable in the Chinese context. For example, when an enterprise making yarn supplies its products to a textile factory, there is no "sale" in the strict sense, as no change of ownership takes place, even though goods and money are exchanged. Only when products are transferred out and sold beyond the state sector (e.g., through retail outlets to private consumers) is there a change of ownership that gives rise to a true contract of sale. A whole body of "economic law" with a strong public law element therefore evolved to regulate the economic activities of the state economy (Wang, 1993).

Deng's reform to bring about a reduction of central planning and an increase in market orientation and competition made it necessary to provide a legal framework to give state enterprise managers increasing autonomy, as well as provide for the emergence of private enterprises.

Reform of State Enterprises

In order to give state enterprises greater autonomy, the People's Congress enacted the Law on Industrial Enterprises Owned by the Whole People (hereinafter "the State Enterprise Law") in 1988. The State Enterprise Law provides that state enterprises are legal persons under the Civil Law, with the same status and capacity to undertake obligations as all other legal persons. It also assigns responsibility for management to enterprise managers, giving them the power to decide production levels, make personnel decisions and generally oversee the enterprise. The role of the Communist Party is relegated to guaranteeing and supervising Party principles and policies in enterprises. While "ownership rights" are retained by the state, enterprise managers are given "operating rights." However, this separation of ownership rights from operating rights should not be confused with the separation of ownership and control in Western capitalist corporations. Under Article 71 of the General Principles of the Civil Law of 1986, ownership rights over property are defined as the rights of possession, use, benefit and disposition, while under Article 2 of the State Enterprise Law operating rights are made up of the rights of possession, use and disposition. Thus, with respect to state-owned property, state enterprises share the same rights as the state but not to the extent of the right of benefit. The exact nature of these rights has been the subject of much controversy. It has been argued that by granting state enterprises the rights of possession, use and disposition but not the right of benefit, the state has conveyed to the enterprises the right to endure and control costs on their own but not the right to enjoy the benefits (Wang, 1992). As a result, an enterprise would still have little incentive to maintain and improve fixed assets (Wang, 1992). At the same, since the central government still exercises extensive control over state enterprises through the rights of ownership, autonomy of enterprises is compromised. The problem is aggravated by the possible control exercised by regional state entities, which sometimes share property rights with the central government. As a result, policies of the central government are sometimes constrained or contradicted by ownership rights asserted by these entities that lie between the central government and state enterprises (Wang, 1992).

Another difficulty is although state enterprises are given the right to make personnel decisions, this right for the most part appears to exist only in name, and cannot be realized in practice. The State Enterprise Law and associated regulations only operate as instructions to the bureaucracy in charge of an enterprise. No mechanism has been created to ensure that the bureaucracy follow the law (Clarke, 1992).

The State Enterprise Law also provides for the "responsibility contract system," under which a contract is entered into between the supervising government agency and a state enterprise, stipulating major terms such as the appointment of managers and the distribution of profits. It has been observed that this system has failed to improve the efficiency of state enterprises and resulted in a short-term mentality in state enterprises (Wang, 1992).

Emergence of a Private Sector

From the point of view of socialist ideology, allowing private enterprises to exist presented even greater difficulties than modifying the organizational form of state enterprises as the concept of private business sharply conflicts with the socialist public ownership of resources.

The Constitution of 1975 and 1978 recognized only socialist public ownership. But the position of individual business was given limited recognition in Article 11 of the 1982 Constitution as the "individual economy" of urban and rural workers, and in the General Principles of Civil Law of 1986 (Conner, 1991).

The ideological difficulty was resolved at the Communist Party's National Congress in 1987 when Zhao Ziyang, then the General Secretary, advanced the theory that China was in the "primary stage of socialism" that began in the 1950s and was expected to last one hundred years thereafter. In this stage, the main goal was to develop production to meet the material needs of the people. While reaffirming the predominance of socialist public ownership, this theory asserts that a private sector may be allowed to exist to contribute production and employment that the state cannot provide. The 1988 Constitution adopted this pragmatic view and thereby legitimized profit-seeking private enterprise to develop within the limits prescribed by law (Art and Gu, 1995). The private economy is recognized as a supplement to the socialist public ownership economy. The state protects the lawful rights and interests of the private economy and exercises guidance and supervision over it.

In the Provisional Regulations of the PRC Concerning Private Enterprises promulgated on 25 June 1988, a private enterprise was officially declared to be a "profit-seeking economic organization with eight or more employees and whose property is privately owned." The rights granted to private enterprises and their investors were spelled out more clearly than those for individual firms. Private enterprises were specifically given the right to conduct their business autonomously, to determine the structure of the enterprise and hire and fire workers, and to determine the wage system and profit distribution of the enterprise. They were also empowered to enter into Sino-foreign equity or cooperative joint ventures with foreign or overseas Chinese enterprises or individuals (Conner, 1991).

In another ground-breaking move, the Chinese government has allowed individuals and private enterprises to buy small state-owned enterprises that the government deems itself unable to manage successfully and become full owners. Though significant, this programme of selling selected small state-owned enterprises does not evince a policy or goal to privatize the bulk of the Chinese economy, as China is committed to maintaining public socialist ownership as the dominant form for its economy (Art and Gu, 1995).

The Modern Enterprise System

The latest instalment in the reform of the legal environment of the enterprises came in the form of the Company Law enacted on 29 December 1993 at the Fifth Session of the Standing Committee of the Eighth National People's Congress and promulgated on the same day by the President of China. Under the new law, the corporation will become the most important form of Chinese enterprise.

The declared purpose of the Law is to promote the development of a socialist market economy (Company Law, Art. 1). It provides for the restructuring of the organization and management of state-owned enterprises, private enterprises, as well as branches of foreign companies by adapting international capitalist models.

Legal Person Status

Under the Company Law, a company is reaffirmed to be an "enterprise legal person" (Company Law, Art. 3); however, a branch of foreign company does not have Chinese legal person status (Company Law, Art. 203). As an enterprise legal person, a company shall "manage its affairs independently and shall be responsible for its profits and losses" (Company Law, Art. 5). In particular, it has the power to manage its business and organize its production independently for the purpose of increasing productivity and economic benefits, and for the maintenance and appreciation of its assets, subject to the "macro-management and control of the state" (Company Law, Art. 5).

Private Minority of State Enterprises

The Company Law permits sale of minority interests in state enterprise shares and this allows the government to draw private capital into state enterprises. It is important to emphasize that this reform must not be confused with privatization, which has been rejected as a path of development for the Chinese economy. The state will, however, maintain ultimate control and majority ownership of the largest enterprises (Art and Gu, 1995).

Private Enterprises

The Company Law also provides for the development of small private enterprises. Consistent with the view that public socialist ownership should remain the predominant sector in the economy, the Law envisions the private sector not as a substitute for state industry but rather as a necessary supplement that will be particularly useful in ameliorating current problems of unemployment and inefficiency in the national economy (Art and Gu, 1995).

Limited Liability

Two kinds of companies are recognized: a limited company or a joint stock company (Company Law, Art. 2). In either case, the company enjoys limited liability, and each shareholder assumes liability towards the company to the extent of the amount of shares held by him, and the company is liable for its debts to the extent of all its assets (Company Law, Art. 3). It has been observed that these forms of corporations correspond roughly to the British distinction between the limited company and the public limited company, or the American distinction between the closely held (or close) corporation and the larger (including the listed) corporation (Art and Gu, 1995).

The Limited Company

A limited company has 2 to 50 shareholders (Company Law, Art. 20). If a limited company is established solely by a state-authorized investment organ or department, it is a wholly state-owned company. Specifically, companies that manufacture "special products" or that are engaged in "special businesses" as determined by the State Council shall adopt the form of wholly state-owned companies (Company Law, Art. 64). What constitute special products or special businesses are yet to be clarified (Wang and Tomasic, 1994).

When a shareholder of a limited company intends to transfer his capital to persons who are not shareholders, the consent of over half of the shareholders must be secured. Those shareholders not consenting to the transfer must purchase the capital or will be deemed to have consented to the transfer (Company Law, Art. 35).

The Joint Stock Company

A joint stock limited company is established either through the method of promotion or the method of public issue (Company Law, Art. 74), and can be established only with the approval of the departments authorized by the State Council or the relevant provincial People's government (Company Law, Art. 77). There is no limit on the number of shareholders but the registered capital must be no less than RMB 10,000,000 yuan (Company Law, Art. 78). The company is obligated to set up a shareholders' general meeting and a board of directors.

With the approval of the State Council or the Securities Authority of the State Council, a joint stock company whose capital is at least RMB 50,000,000 yuan can become a listed company and have its shares traded on a stock exchange (Company Law, Art. 151). Unique to China's securities industry are the special provisions for state-owned enterprises of the Shanghai and Shenzhen stock exchanges that recognize three categories of shares: state shares, legal person shares, and individual shares. State shares bring state-owned assets into the company, and usually constitute over 50% of the total shares issued. Legal person shares are owned by legal persons, which can be government institutions, universities, companies, or collectives. Companies, as legal persons, may also purchase their own shares or those of another shareholding company. Individual shares are held by the employees of the company as well as members of the general public. Each individual cannot typically own more than 0.5% of these shares. The three kinds of shares are issued roughly in a 5:3:2 ratio. Only individual shares can be traded on the stock market, which account for a small fraction of the total shares (Qian, 1993; Johns, 1995). The division of shares into three categories enables the diversification of ownership and at the same time ensures socialist public ownership will remain the dominant form.

With approval, the shares of a joint stock company may also be traded on a stock exchange outside of China (Company Law, Arts. 85 and 155). Although the Company Law is silent on this, Chinese corporate stock is also defined by the nationality of the shareholders. "Class A" stock is available for purchase by Chinese citizens only; "Class B" is for foreigners; and "Class H" stock has been used for transactions on the Hong Kong Stock Exchange (Art and Gu, 1995). On 4 August 1994, the State Council promulgated the Provisions on the Listing of Chinese Joint Stock Companies Outside the Mainland of China, under which the Securities Commission of the State Council and its executive body, the China Securities Regulatory Commission, may enter into agreements with institutions in charge of securities outside the jurisdiction of China in regard to the listing of Chinese companies outside China (Wang and Tomasic, 1994).

The Shareholders' Meeting

In both the limited company and the joint stock company, the shareholders' meeting, composed of all the shareholders, is the "organ of authority" of the company (Company Law, Arts. 37 and 102), and its powers extend beyond those enjoyed by shareholders in Western corporations, including powers to: (1) decide upon the policies on the business operation and investment plans; (2) elect and remove members of the board of directors and decide upon their remuneration; (3) review and approve plans of profit distribution and for recovery of losses; (4) decide upon the issue of debentures by the company (Company Law, Arts. 38 and 103).

The Board of Directors

The board of directors is responsible to the shareholders' meeting (Company Law, Art. 46 and 112). One of its powers is to decide the business plans and investment programmes of the company. It is unclear how this power is to be shared with the shareholders' meeting, which holds a similar power.

The Legal Representative

The Company Law provides that the chair of the board of the directors is the legal representative of the company (Company Law, Art. 45 and 113). If the company does not have a board because of its small size, it will have an executive director who will be its legal representative (Company Law, Art. 51). The legal representative is subject to sanctions for the company's misconduct. He is personally at risk if the company engages in business beyond its authorized scope, conceals facts from registration and tax authorities, or hides property to evade repayment of debts. He may be fined or subjected to administrative sanctions, or if the offence constitutes a crime, he may be prosecuted (Art and Gu, 1995).

Registration and Scope of Activities

Consistent with the objective of developing a socialist market economy, the Company Law relaxes the requirements of registration of an enterprise to some extent. Previously, establishment of a new enterprise required approval to engage in the intended activity from the administrative agency in charge of the particular industry, which followed rigid, highly centralized planning processes (Art and Gu, 1995). However, despite the removal of this prerequisite in almost all cases, the law still tightly regulates incorporation, thereby maintaining state control over the scope of enterprise activities. Each company must apply for registration and obtain a business licence from the Company Registration Authority. The scope of a company's business activities is limited to those specified in its articles of association. A company may change its scope of business only by amending its articles of association "in accordance with the relevant legal procedures" and after registration of such amendments with the Company Registration Authority (Company Law. Art. 11). The scope of business of an enterprise has always been in practice carefully examined by the government and an enterprise will very often only have a limited scope of business. It is unlikely that government control in approving and amending the scope of business will be relaxed (Wang and Tomasic, 1994). The current Chinese approach has been compared to the "special" (as opposed to "general") incorporation processes followed in England and the United States until the early 1800s, when each instance of incorporation required special legislation (Art and Gu, 1995). Activities beyond the registered scope would not only be illegal but could also bring about contract disputes because they are *ultra vires.*

It is too early to assess the success of the Company Law in curing the problems of lack of autonomy and incentive. Although most business entities in China bear the word "company" in their names, only about 5% of them are currently governed by the Company Law. Most other companies are still government by the State Enterprise Law. Even some leaders in the government have trouble understanding the economic differences between these two enterprise forms, and some would propose that the government should enjoy veto power in all companies regardless whether they are governed by the Company Law and regardless of the government's proportional holdings in the company (Jiang, 1995).

Bankruptcy of Enterprises

The trend in the law towards greater autonomy for state enterprises is clear. However, ceding increased autonomy to state enterprises does not necessarily, by itself, enhance efficiency. With diminished accountability, the new autonomy has sometimes resulted in managerial abuses. Compared to the West, the stock markets are underdeveloped and are ineffective as watchdogs. In any case, only a small proportion of state enterprises is listed on the stock exchanges. Without the discipline of stock markets and with diminished oversight of government officials, some managers have abused their new autonomy and treated state assets like their own private property. Some are said to have purchased expensive foreign automobiles and other luxuries nominally for their enterprises (Art and Gu, 1995). Some enterprises have also used the new freedom to issue bonuses and increase other fringe benefits even when they are sustaining substantial losses (Wang, 1993).

For many years in the past, when a state enterprise sustained a loss, the prevailing practice had been either to write off the loss through state budget appropriations or take administrative measures against the enterprise, by closing, merging or changing its business operation. In either case, the employees in the enterprise would not be affected and would continue to receive wages, even bonuses. There were no bankruptcy cases in the first three decades of the People's Republic of China. The concept of bankruptcy was contrary to the philosophy of a planned economy, and the ideology that socialism was superior to capitalism practically precluded its use (Wang, 1993). As a unit of the state that operates according to economic plans beyond its control, the concept of bankruptcy of the state enterprise is fraught with theoretical difficulties. The ownership of assets of state-owned enterprises has also been the source of much confusion. When the Bankruptcy Law was proposed, opponents of the law argued that state-owned assets belonged to the state and not to the enterprise, and further, that state-owned enterprises were so closely tied to the state that bankrupting the enterprises meant bankrupting the state through its enterprises (David, 1994).

With the implementation of economic reform which resulted in a mixed economy comprising both planned and market elements, and with the policy of encouragement of competition among enterprises, it became inevitable that the government would gradually accept bankruptcy as a tool to enhance the financial discipline of enterprises (Wang, 1993).

Beginning in early 1985, the Chinese government began to experiment with a bankruptcy system to deal with enterprises that consistently sustained losses. The local bankruptcy regulations promulgated on 10 February 1985 by the Shenyang city government became the first bankruptcy law in the history of the People's Republic of China.

Subsequently, other local bankruptcies were instituted in Chongqing, Wuhan and to a more limited extent in Taiyuan. From mid-1984 to 1985, eight enterprises in the three major cities were issued bankruptcy warnings and were ordered to reorganize. Management was informed that unless substantial improvement occurred within one year, their enterprises would be declared bankrupt. In 1986, one of these, the Shenyang Explosion-Proof Equipment Factory, eventually became the first bankrupt enterprise (Wang 1993), and it was auctioned off to a local company (Folsom and Finan, 1989).

The National People's Congress adopted the Law of the People's Republic of China on Bankruptcy of Enterprises (hereafter "the Bankruptcy Law") on 2 December 1986, which became effective as of 1 November 1988. It applies only to state-owned enterprises. Article 3 provides: "Enterprises that sustain significant loss due to inappropriate management and are unable to pay off debts that mature will be declared bankrupt." Article 3 then exempts from bankruptcy proceedings enterprises that are engaged in public utilities or are of great significance to the national interest, and enterprises that have obtained a guarantee and pay their debts within six months. Bankruptcy petitions may be filed by both creditors and debtors. A voluntary debtor petition must be approved by the department in charge of the debtor state enterprise, thereby ensuring that the state maintains control. Even where petitions have been initiated by the creditor, the state may intervene. The state may block involuntary proceedings or use administrative means to close, terminate or change the product line of an enterprise. This enables the state to keep a check on the number of bankruptcies, and it would seem that without sanction of the state, a state enterprise will not be bankrupted (David, 1994).

The basic standard of bankruptcy of an enterprise is that it is unable to repay its debt. But unlike in a market economy, the test can be rather complicated. According to the judges, the standard is not a straightforward balance sheet criterion. Whether the loss is "significant" and whether is the loss is caused by "inappropriate management" are important issues. Sometimes losses by an enterprise may be a result of the government's policy on prices or subsidies, or inadequate energy supply and other public utilities. The inability of an enterprise to repay its debts in such circumstances may not necessarily lead to its bankruptcy. In determining whether an enterprise in question is or is not able to repay the debt, the overall condition of the enterprise such as its assets, credit situation, technology involved, and labour force employed would be taken into consideration. The policy is to protect state enterprises that sustain losses for reasons beyond their control from the reach of the punitive impact of bankruptcy proceedings (Wang, 1993). In particular, it is recognized that Article 3 implies that enterprises should not be put out of business when their losses are not due to poor management, although the Law fails to provide a standard for distinguishing good losses ("policy losses") from bad losses ("business losses"). As a result, bargaining and special pleading with the authorities may save an enterprise from bankruptcy, and the system continues to reward good bureaucratic connections. By February 1991, more than a year after the Bankruptcy Law became effective, only one instance of a state-owned enterprise being closed down through court action under the Bankruptcy Law had been reported (Clarke, 1992). Even after eight years of the promulgation of the Bankruptcy Law, very few enterprises have been declared bankrupt by the courts (Jiang, 1995).

The government is also worried about the possible social and economic ramifications of bankruptcies of state enterprises, as they play an important role in the delivery of social welfare, such as providing cafeterias, hospitals, and preschool childcare for their employees. There is no independent state-operated unemployment compensation or other social insurance system to ameliorate the effects of bankruptcy on workers. Another dilemma for the state is that unprofitable state enterprises may have taken out heavy bank loans to maintain production, and their bankruptcy could bring destabilizing losses to banks. Until inefficient state enterprises are in fact subjected to bankruptcies and similar painful adjustments, financial discipline for state enterprises will remain questionable (Art and Gu, 1995).

The bankruptcy of non-state-owned enterprises with legal person status is governed by the Civil Procedure Law adopted in 1991 (Wang, 1993), as well as local bankruptcy regulations. What has developed is a bifurcated, parallel system of law (David, 1994). The focus of the law is different. For example, unlike the Bankruptcy Law, under the Shenzhen Insolvency Regulations, which apply to Chinese-foreign equity joint venture companies, foreign cooperative companies in cooperative ventures, foreign-funded companies and Chinese-foreign (joint-stock) limited companies in the Shenzhen Economic Zone, and not to state-owned enterprises, debtor's petitions do not require the approval of the government department in charge. The state is not as concerned with protecting these enterprises from bankruptcy proceedings (David, 1994). Indeed, when a branch of a foreign company becomes bankrupt, the emphasis is on the protection of creditors. Under Article 205 of the Company Law, the assets of the branch of a foreign company is not permitted to be taken out of China until its debts are fully satisfied. Since a branch is not regarded as a legal person, where the assets of the branch are not sufficient to satisfy its debts, the foreign company in question will be held liable to repay such debts (Wang and Tomasic, 1994).

Conclusion

The legal environment is an important component in the development of a socialist market economy in China. It aims to give sufficient autonomy to the state enterprises so that they may operate with efficiency. At the same time, ultimate control of the means of production remains with the state, so that the socialist ideal of public ownership is not diluted. In order to enhance accountability and financial discipline, provisions for bankruptcy have been made. A supplementary private sector is also allowed to emerge to inject a degree of vitality into the economy by providing competition.

It is easy to criticize the law in China by pointing out its differences from Western capitalist counterparts. However, although China has been borrowing from the Western law, it must be remembered that China's aim is not to build a capitalist market economy.

If it can also be remembered that in the past, the Chinese government forbade any discussion concerning the establishment of shareholding companies, issuance of stocks to the public, or opening stock exchanges (Qian, 1993), not to mention private enterprises, it will be recognized that tremendous strides have been made in economic and legal reform.

The challenge is to perfect the legal environment. But this can only be done on an evolutionary and piecemeal basis because of the complexity of the problem. As early as in 1978, Deng recognized that there was a great amount of legislative work to be done, and in the beginning, laws could only be general and sketchy, and China should not wait for "the whole set of equipment" (Qian, 1993).

With the fast pace of legislative activities that has been taking place, there is an increasing tension between the old and new economic structures. At the same time, the tension between law and politics is always lurking in the background. An even greater challenge therefore is to ensure that legislation that has been enacted is given effect, and to minimize or eliminate the substantial gap between the legal norms and the enforcement of these norms (Jiang, 1995).

4

Stock Markets in China

David Yee-kai Chan

Abstract

Recently, the China stock market has become internationalized. A huge amount of capital came from foreign investors, most of them invested in B shares market.

There are five different types of ordinary shares (including A shares, B shares, C shares, H shares and N shares) which enterprises can use to raise capital and the China stock market has its own distinctive characteristics. These are studied under the aspects of (1) Turnover and Market Liquidity, (2) Concentration, (3) Sectoral Composition, (4) Clearance and Settlement, (5) Transaction Cost and (6) Taxation and Dividend Payment.

We found inefficiency in the new shares issue process and that the return of stocks examined had a high variability. Several problems exist in the China stock market and recommendations have been provided. They include cross-listing of shares at the Shanghai Securities Exchange and the Shenzhen Stock Exchange and the amendment of regulations.

Introduction

In the past, stocks in China carried a fixed income with maturity and were issued to raise funds for specific investment. They rather resembled bonds.

For example, certain shares had a guaranteed return and the issuing enterprises promised a buy-back after a specified period. Stocks were initially issued largely to employees, rather than to the public, sometimes in lieu of bonus payments. Trading in shares was legalized when the Shanghai Securities Exchange and the Shenzhen Stock Exchanges were formally recognized on 19 December 1990 and 3 July 1991 respectively.

History and Overview of the Shenzhen Stock Exchange

The Shenzhen Stock Exchange was formed in the Shenzhen Special Economic Zone adjacent to Hong Kong. In 1987, the Shenzhen Special Economic Zone was authorized to conduct experiments on establishing a securities market. The first flotation was arranged in May 1987 for the Shenzhen Development Bank via a new issue of shares, restricted to Chinese citizens. Between 1987 and 1990, six Shenzhen companies sold shares through the Shenzhen Stock Exchange. On 1 December 1990, the bourse was the first formally centralized stock exchange for stock trading. It officially opened on 3 July 1991.

The first B share, Shenzhen Southern Glass, was listed on 28 February 1992. In late April 1992, the State Council gave Shenzhen permission to accept listings from companies outside Shenzhen and the municipal government.

History and Overview of the Shanghai Securities Exchange

Since its official opening in late 1990, the Shanghai Securities Exchange — China's first and largest capital market — has achieved national coverage and has begun to link up with international stock markets with a turnover of RMB 500 million per year.

When it started to operate in 1990, the Shanghai Securities Exchange had only 46 seats in its spacious hall with only eight kinds of listed stocks and a membership of 25. In 1993, the exchange has six trading halls with 2,600 seats, 119 kinds of stocks, and a membership of 481. The amount of stocks listed has increased from RMB 290 million in 1990 to RMB 20.1 billion in 1993. Moreover, the total market value has grown from RMB 1.3 billion in 1990 to RMB 250 billion in 1993. All of these indicate the rapid growth of the Shanghai Securities Exchange.

The first B share, Shanghai Vacuum Electronic Devices was issued in

Shanghai Securities Exchange on 21 February 1992. Subsequently, there were 8 more companies listed in 1992, 12 in 1993 and 6 in early 1994, bringing the total of B shares to 27 by April of 1994. Most of the listed companies are Shanghai companies.

Types of Ordinary Shares in China's Equity Market

As enterprises sought new ways to raise capital, China's equity markets evolved faster than the government had foreseen. Now, there are altogether five different types of ordinary shares in China that enterprises can use to raise capital. They include:

A Shares

In terms of size and level of activity, the A shares market dominates China's equity markets. These shares are equivalent to ordinary equity as generally accepted in market economies. They are also known as individual or natural person shares. A shares are RMB denominated, and are the only domestic shares that can be legally traded on the Shanghai Securities Exchange and the Shenzhen Stock Exchange. However, A shares can only be bought and sold by individual or legal persons within the PRC. Overseas investors are not permitted to purchase A shares unless they purchase authorized joint venture mutual funds.

A shares are currently divided into three categories: Individual, Legal person and State. Individual shares are shares owned by any PRC citizen or corporation. This type of share can be further subdivided into "employee individual shares" and "public individual shares." Employee individual shares are those shares issued by the listed company and offered to employees prior to those offered to the public. The employee individual shares cannot be traded for at least six months after they are issued. Public individual shares are shares that the public can buy from the stock market and can be freely traded. At present, stocks that are listed on the Shanghai Securities Exchange and Shenzhen Stock Exchange are public individual shares.

Legal person shares can only be owned by government or quasi-governmental enterprises. These shares are highly illiquid and, in most cases, cannot be traded. State shares are also owned by the government and cannot be traded.

B Shares

B Shares are ordinary shares bearing the same voting or ownership rights and the same responsibility as A shares holders. The B shares market is denominated in RMB and traded in either US$ (in Shanghai) or HK$ (in Shenzhen) and listed only on the Shanghai Securities Exchange or the Shenzhen Stock Exchange. In addition, B shares can only be subscribed by foreigners, and residents of Hong Kong, Macau and Taiwan. However, PRC nationals are allowed to purchase B shares if they have foreign currency, overseas relatives or own Hong Kong entities. All after-tax dividends can be remitted to other countries.

H Shares

H shares are issued by PRC-controlled companies based in Hong Kong. To establish a legal avenue for overseas listing, H shares were officially created in July 1993. H shares are listed on Hong Kong Stock Exchange and traded in Hong Kong dollars. They can only be subscribed by foreigners and residents of Hong Kong, Macau and Taiwan.

N Shares

N Shares permit back-door listings of Chinese companies in New York through overseas registered holding companies. They are only traded in USA.

C Shares

C Shares are not found in ordinary market economies. They have been created in the PRC to designate holdings in state-owned enterprises by official bodies such as state institutions, other state-owned enterprises and government departments while individuals are not allowed to hold C shares. Chinese state institutions, enterprises and departments having legal person status are entitled to purchase such kind of shares.

Characteristics of China's Equity Markets

Compared with New York and Hong Kong, China equity markets are small and volatile and are not thoroughly understood by the public. In terms of total market capitalization, the two China stock markets are roughly 10% of Hong Kong. The Shanghai Securities Exchange and the Shenzhen Stock Exchange started to operate in 1991 with only 13 A share listings. The number of listed A and B stocks increased to 70 at the end of 1992, and to 203 in Shanghai and to 142 in Shenzhen by the end of 1994.

Market volatility of China's equity market is high. The 300% surge in the A-shares market in May 1992 was due to the lifting of price limits. The 70% downturn from mid-1993 to July 1994 was triggered by high inflationary expectations and the financial austerity programme introduced by the central government. The listing of 72 new A shares in 1993 and another 68 A shares in the first half of 1994 were due to the three-measure market rescue plan announced by the China Securities Regulatory Commission (CSRC) in late July 1994.

The characteristic of China's equity market are described in details as follows:

Turnover and Market Liquidity

Absolute Trading Value

As shown in Figure 1, to measure the market liquidity on the two stock exchanges, absolute trading value is used. Compared with the A shares market, B shares market is very thin, with very low turnover. For instance, on the Shanghai Securities Exchange, A shares turnover activity, in terms of the daily number of shares traded, exceeded 1,250 million shares and RMB 10,000 million of average daily trading on a number of occasions in 1994. The average daily trading volume in the third quarter of 1994 was 577 million shares with a corresponding daily value of RMB 4,772 million. In contrast, B shares turnover rarely exceeded 15 million shares and 50 million US dollars. The average daily trading volume in the third quarter of 1994 was 10 million shares with a daily value of RMB 44 million. It implies that in the third quarter of 1994, activity in the A shares market was greater than that in the B shares market by 55.7 times and 108 times, as measured, respectively, by the number of shares trading and by value.

Similar patterns are also found in Shenzhen. For A shares, the trading volume often exceeded 700 million shares and RMB 5,000 million in 1994. The average daily trading volume for A shares in the third quarter of 1994 was 300 million with a value of RMB 2,028 million. Whereas for B shares,

Figure 1
Average Daily Trading Values of A Shares and B Shares

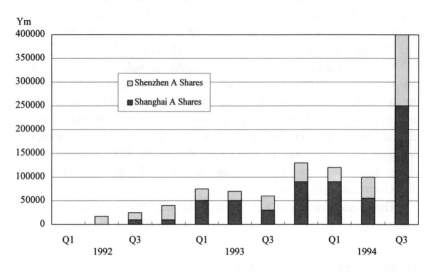

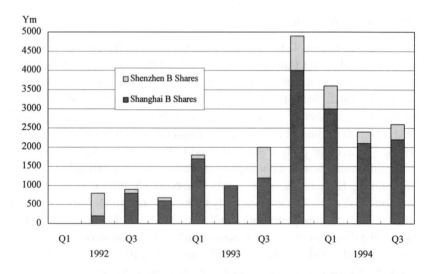

the volume of trading on the Shenzhen Stock Exchange fell from peak-levels reached in 1993. In 1994, daily volume of trading peaked at around 2 million shares and RMB 10 million. This compares to peaks exceeding 15 million shares and RMB 400 million on the Shanghai Securities Exchange.

Relative Turnover Rate

The relative turnover rate is also used to measure market liquidity on the two major exchanges. This ratio is defined as average daily turnover (value) divided by outstanding market capitalization. Since B shares market capitalization is much smaller than A shares market, the turnover rate is a more relevant measure of market liquidity than absolute trading values. According to Figure 1, for Shanghai A shares, the third quarter of 1994 daily turnover rate was 4.72 % versus 4.5% for Shenzhen. For B shares, the Shanghai turnover rate was 0.4 % versus 0.28 % for Shenzhen. Therefore, A shares markets have been much more liquid than B shares market on both the Shanghai Securities Exchange and the Shenzhen Stock Exchange.

Concentration

Members can have more than one seat on both exchanges. Despite the large number of members, trading is concentrated among a small number of members. Table 1 shows this phenomenon. The top ten members account for over 30% of all trades on the Shanghai Securities Exchange.

Table 1
Concentration Ratios of Member Firms Trading on the
Shanghai Stock Exchange (January 1995)

Rank	Market Share (%)		Funds	T-Bonds	T-Bonds Futures	B Shares	T-Bonds Repurchase
	Total	A Shares					
No. of Firms (Nos)*	314	302	272	98	307	37	37
Rank of Firms (Market Share)							
Top 1	10.6	4.5	19.2	14.4	10.6	12.0	16.3
Top 5	23.0	15.2	32.3	51.2	23.0	45.1	49.6
Top 10	32.5	23.6	43.1	65.5	32.5	74.9	66.3
Top 20	44.2	35.3	54.3	77.1	44.3	95.7	80.6
Top 50	64.6	51.2	67.1	88.1	64.6		

Source: *Monthly Market Statistics*, Shanghai Stock Exchange, January 1995.
Note: * Only the top 320 firms, in terms of total trading volume, were included in the sample.

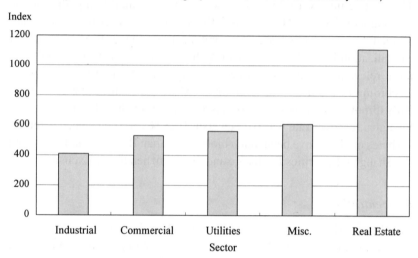

Figure 2
Shanghai Securities Exchange (Index value as of 27 January 1995)

Sectoral Composition

According to Figure 2, 59% of the shares listed on the Shanghai Securities Exchange are industrial companies. Commercial and miscellaneous companies account for another 29% while each of real estate and utilities enterprises accounts for around 6% of the number of firms listed.

Clearance and Settlement

As at 1 January 1995, A shares are settled at T+1 on both exchanges. Prior to January 1995, A shares are settled at T+0. In contrast, B shares are cleared at T+3 on both exchanges because of the need for payment to be made in foreign currencies and transactions to be recorded with global or regional custodian off-shore (e.g., in Hong Kong).

Transaction Costs

Buying and selling shares on the exchanges are subject to commissions, fees and stamp duties. Commissions and stamp duties are paid by both buyer and seller. Like other Asian exchanges such as Japan, trades are subject to fixed commission charges. Estimates suggest that total (two-sided) transaction costs (including a 0.3% stamp duty paid by both parties) exceed 1.5% on the Shanghai Securities Exchange and 2.0% on the Shenzhen Stock Exchange.

Taxation and Dividend Payment

Trades on the Shanghai Securities Exchange and the Shenzhen Stock Exchange are generally free of either capital gains or dividend taxation. In addition, there are no taxes on dividends. A remarkable feature of dividend payment in China is that cash dividends are rarely paid. When paid, dividends have taken the forms of new stock (normally stock options).

The New Share Issue Process

The Pre-Offer Process

There are quotas for issuing new shares. For example, the State Council Securities Committee (SCSC), the State Planning Commission (SPC) and the central bank (PBOC) jointly determine the new share issue quota for A shares. In 1993, the A-share quotas was RMB5.5 billion.

For each regional quota, the local securities authorities invite enterprises to request a listing, and make a selection based on some criteria. These criteria include the performance and sectoral development objectives of the enterprise. Local government selection criteria take into account the profitability and performance criteria of the exchanges. For example, in 1993, there were 100 firms which applied for A-share listing in the Shanghai Securities Exchange, from which only about 30 were approved from the Shanghai Securities Administration. Although these candidates are then required to seek the approval of the China Securities Regulatory Committee (CSRC) and the exchanges, approval at these successive levels is virtually automatic. While in principle any enterprise going public can list on either exchange, this is strongly influenced by local securities authorities.

In addition to approval by local authorities, companies desiring a B-share listing are also required the approval of the Ministry of Foreign Trade and Economic Cooperation (MOFTEC). However, overseas listing for H shares or N shares is not subject to quota but requires case by case approval, which has to be given by the SCSC, the SPC (in view of the annual overseas borrowing plan), the SRC (for approval of state ownership dilution) and the SETC (for conformity with industrial policy).

Actually, this process for listing differs considerably from a more mature market economy. In a mature market economy, the decision to list an enterprise would usually be determined largely by the exchange where it seeks listing. The criteria adopted by the exchange would typically include size, performance, and the extent to which compliance with the rules of the exchange would be expected. Therefore, the pre-offer process in China reflects the dilemmas of a transitional economy where the planning mechanisms for credit and investment coexist uneasily with new forms of markets. Enterprises selected for listing are unlikely to be the same as the ones that would have been selected by the market.

The Post-Offer Process

Once an issue is selected, a filing is made with the China Securities Regulatory Committee (CSRC). A filing fee of RMB 30,000 is paid by the enterprise and the CSRC undertakes a "due diligence" type analysis of the enterprise.

After the offer (IPO) is announced, there are a number of further steps before it starts the trading. Figure 3 shows the IPO underwriting process in China. After the announcement, and the publication of the prospectus, underwriters are chosen largely or by the local securities authority. Prospective investors obtain application forms from banks or brokers, at a small fee. Only retail investors are legally eligible to buy the application forms.

In China's equity markets, new issues have tended to be made in "lumps" or "tranches" in which lotteries typically determine (a) whether an investor is eligible to apply at all, and (b) which enterprise's shares he or she can buy.

Once the lottery is completed, winning shareholders pay for their shares, through cash or advance deposits at banks. Share ownership claims are then allocated, and trading can begin on the exchanges. The stylized IPO underwriting process has commonly taken as long as one and a half months; not dissimilar from the time taken for new issues in Hong Kong, Singapore, Taiwan and Thailand.

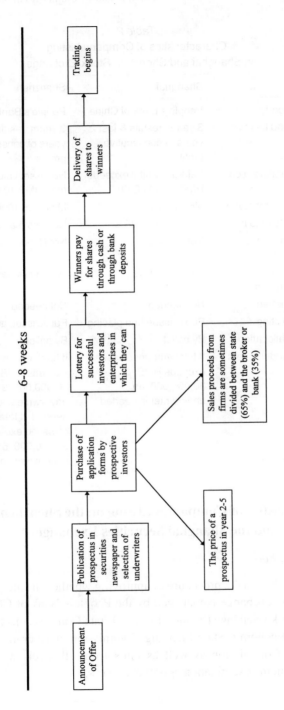

Figure 3

China: A Stylized IPO Process: Post-Offer to the Beginning of Trading

6-8 weeks

| Announcement of Offer | Publication of prospectus in securities newspaper and selection of underwriters | Purchase of application forms by prospective investors | Lottery for successful investors and enterprises in which they can | Winners pay for shares through cash or through bank deposits | Delivery of shares to winners | Trading begins |

The price of a prospectus in year 2-5

Sales proceeds from firms are sometimes divided between state (65%) and the broker or bank (35%)

Source: *World Bank 1995.*

Table 2
Characteristics of Company Listing
in Shanghai and Shenzhen Stock Exchanges

	Shanghai	Shenzhen
Regulatory body	People's Bank of China	People's Bank of China
Operation and financial record	3 years' results & last 2 years of consecutive profits	3 years' results & last 3 years of consecutive profits
Assets or capitalization	Paid-up capital exceeds RMB 50,000,000	Net asset value not less than RMB 10,000,000
Number of shareholders	Minimum 500	Minimum 1000
Shares held by the public	Not less than 25%	Not less than 25%
Profit and dividends forecast	Not needed	Not Needed
Time needed for examination and approval	Within 15 days	No specific requirement
Document signed	Not needed	Not needed
Methods of listing	Public issue and placing	Public issue and placing
Public offer allocation	By ballot	By ballot
Number of underwriters	If total amount of issued exceeds RMB 30,000,000, an underwriter is needed	If total amount of issued exceeds RMB 30,000,000, 3 underwriters are needed. If total amount of issued exceeds RMB 50,000,000, 5 underwriters are needed.

Characteristics of Companies Listing on the Shenzhen Stock Exchange and the Shanghai Securities Exchange

Regulatory body

In China, although the procedure of approving whether an enterprise can be listed on the exchange is managed by the People's Bank of China (issue) and the Stock Exchange (listing), local and state Commissions for Restructuring the Economy, State Planning Commission and Foreign Economic and Trade Commission as well as units from all levels would always participate in the examination approval process.

Trading Records

Enterprises that apply for a listing on the Shenzhen Stock Exchange or the Shanghai Securities Exchange are required to have a trading record of not less than three years under general circumstances. In addition, enterprises have to show two years' and three years' consecutive profits if they apply for listing on the Shanghai Securities Exchange and on the Shenzhen Stock Exchange respectively.

Assets or Capitalization

Regulatory bodies evaluate the enterprise by looking at its paid-up capital and its net asset value, (in fact not only its net asset value but its net tangible assets). For enterprises listing on the Shanghai Securities Exchange, the company should have not less than RMB50,000,000 paid-up capital, whereas for enterprises listing on the Shenzhen Stock Exchange, they should have at least RMB10,000,000 net tangible assets.

Number of Shareholders

The number of shareholders for an enterprise listed on the Shanghai Securities Exchange and the Shenzhen Stock Exchange should be at least 500 and 800 respectively.

Shares Held by the Public

Twenty-five percent of enterprises' shares listed on the Shenzhen Stock Exchange and the Shanghai Securities Exchange should be held by the public.

Documents Required

Both exchanges require companies to present essential documents to the authority in order to have an examination on the companies' situations (especially financial positions). The documents required by the Shanghai Securities Exchange are described in article 9 and 10 of "Procedures of the Administration for Trading of Securities in Shanghai," whereas the documents required by the Shenzhen Stock Exchange are described in article 17 of "Interim Procedures for Shares Issuance and Trading Management in Shenzhen."

Profit and Dividends Forecasting

Both the Shanghai Securities Exchange and the Shenzhen Stock Exchange require companies to state their profit forecasts in their prospectuses. However, as the joint-stock system is an entirely new element to a lot of companies in China, very often they do not have many opportunities to consider their dividend policies in detail. Therefore, there are no specific requirements on dividend policy in the Shanghai Securities Exchange and the Shenzhen Stock Exchange.

Time Needed for Examining and Approving Listing Application

It takes 15 days to analyse all listing documents received from the enterprises to see whether the enterprise can be listed in the Shanghai Securities Exchange. But there is no specific time needed for examining and approving listing applications in the Shenzhen Stock Exchange.

Agreement Signed

Since regulations set by the regulatory bodies change over time, no documents are needed to be signed between the Chinese authority and the enterprises.

Methods of Listing

Both the Shanghai Securities Exchange and the Shenzhen Stock Exchange are allocated by ballot.

Number of Underwriters Needed

If the enterprises apply for listing in China's equity market, the issue price, the number of shares issued and the issue expenses are affected by the regulatory bodies such as the People's Bank of China. On the Shanghai Securities Exchange, if the total amount of shares exceeds RMB30,000,000, an underwriter is required to carry out the underwriting process. Whereas on the Shenzhen Stock Exchange, if the total amount of shares exceeds RMB30,000,000, three underwriters are required. If the total amount of shares exceeds RMB50,000,000, five underwriters are needed.

The Efficiency of the New Share Issue Process

The efficiency of new equity issue pricing (i.e., pricing at levels close to what the market would be willing to pay) is crucial for an emerging market economy like China.

A Shares

Firstly, referring to Table 3, to those investors who are able to obtain application forms and win allocation at the lottery (RR1), the average returns or the average degree of underpricing of A shares is an extraordinary 733%. That is, the opening price has exceeded by seven times the offer price.

Secondly, the risk-adjusted returns for those investors who bought at the open and sold at the close on the first day (RR2) were on average quite small (1.9%). This points out that, at least on average over the entire period examined, brokers and dealers who legally abided by restrictions prohibiting them from acquiring IPO's in the lottery would have largely been precluded from enjoying the massive wealth transfers from the issuing enterprises (or the state) to investors.

Thirdly, the study suggests that if the price of a new issue at the opening of trading represents an overreaction or speculative bubble rather than the true economic or fundamental price, we should witness a significant decline in the stock's return in the aftermarket. An analysis of the data shows relatively small declines. The return to a buyer of the average IPO on offer who holds it for 60 days (RR6) was 667%, or not significantly lower than the gains to selling at the opening. Thus, the undervaluation of share prices at offer is real, and not a speculative phenomenon.

B Shares

An analysis of the underpricing results for B shares shows that the absolute degree of underpricing for B shares has been less than that for A shares, but is still extraordinarily large by international standards.

According to Table 3, on the first day's open, the average B shares exhibited a return of 281% over its offer price (RR1). Second, as with the A shares, returns to the "honest broker" on day one are at least relatively low (85%), and third, aftermarket seasoning made little difference to these

Table 3

China's Equity Markets: Underpricing of New Share Issues Risk-Adjusted Returns on Initial Public Offering
(A, B Shares: 1991 to 1994)

	Shanghai "A" shares					Shanghai "B" shares				
	Obs	Mean	Std Dev	Min	Max	Obs	Mean	Std Dev	Min	Max
RR1: Offer Price to Opening Price on T1	114	7.33	11.10	0.37	58.7	23	2.81	4.62	0.00	13.05
RR2: Opening to Closing Price on T1	114	0.02	0.13	-0.20	0.56	23	0.09	0.15	-0.12	0.44
RR3: Closing Price T1 to T20	114	-0.04	0.28	-1.45	1.17	23	-0.01	0.12	-0.30	0.25
RR4: Closing Price on T20 to T40	114	0.14	0.80	-0.38	5.65	23	0.06	0.08	-0.11	0.19
RR5: Closing Price on T40 to T60	114	-0.02	0.18	-1.20	0.48	23	0.00	0.22	-0.86	0.28
RR6: Offer to T60	114	6.67	13.94	0.11	76.4	23	1.92	3.09	-0.20	9.50

Source: Calculations based on data from the Shanghai and Shenzhen exchanges.

returns with (market) risk adjusted returns of 192% over the offer price after two months (RR6).

Causes of Inefficiency of the IPO Process

There are four reasons for the inefficiencies of the IPO process. First, underpricing in other countries has been associated with a relatively long elapsed time lag between the public offer and issue date (exceeding one month). This has created the problems of information leakage and herding behaviour, i.e., oversubscription and underpricing.

Second, due to weakness in disclosure and auditing standards, investors lack information about the true quality of the firm going public. A relatively high degree of investor uncertainty affects the efficiency of the IPO process.

Third, the allocation mechanism adopted for the new share issue affects the degree of underpricing. Non-discretionary allocation of shares, by mechanisms such as lottery, exacerbates the tendency to underprice. Investors do not even know which enterprise' shares they may require, making it impossible to undertake investment decisions based on fundamentals. The demand for equity is thus necessarily driven by speculation.

Fourth, the underwriting procedures and process significantly affect the efficiency of pricing of new offerings. Local underwriters enjoy the relative monopoly power. The selection of the underwriter is guided by the local authorities approving an enterprise for listing. Regional authorities tend to choose two or three local underwriters to syndicate an offering. Compared with some countries, such as USA, syndicates compete to become the new issue underwriters. Competition among underwriters has the potential of raising the offer price received by the issuer in a firm commitment underwriting, because the underwriters are willing to take more risk in order to win the underwriting contract. Local underwriters, however, may be relatively inexperienced.

Stock Price Volatility and Returns to Investors of the China's Equity Market

An empirical examination of the behaviour of prices and returns on the Shanghai and Shenzhen A and B shares markets shows that, due to the different investment clienteles in the A and B shares markets (small local retail investors for A shares and foreign institutional and wealthy investors for B shares), there are significant differences in the return and volatility characteristics of the two shares categories. The followings are the findings:

1. Returns (risk-adjusted) have, on average, been very low, on both shares categories and on both exchanges. However, returns are similar on the two exchanges, especially for A shares.
2. There is a significant difference between returns on B shares and returns on A shares. Returns on B shares at both exchanges have been relatively poor.

Looking at market behaviour in terms of volatility, the problem of extreme price volatility, which the Shanghai Securities Exchange and the Shenzhen Stock Exchange have exhibited since opening, is illustrated in Figure 4. For example, the Shanghai A share-index more than doubled in a single day, from 617 on 20 May 1992, to 1266, on 21 May 1992. On 17 November 1992 the Shanghai A share-index had fallen back to one-third of this level, to 393. Recently, this index was trading at the 400 level in July 1994 but by September 1994 it had risen above 900.

A more detailed analysis of the behaviour of the markets suggests:

1. A shares markets in both Shanghai and Shenzhen have exhibited far greater volatility than B shares markets.
2. The absolute sizes of volatility "jumps" in the Shenzhen A market have generally been less than those in the Shanghai A market. Figure 5 illustrates the standard deviations of share prices on both exchanges.
3. Volatility patterns in Shenzhen, in both the A and the B share markets, suggests that markets are thin and inefficient, and that information is dispersed slowly to investors.
4. Particularly large daily jumps in volatility have been noted on a few specific dates.

Actually, persistent and high levels of volatility would discourage a market's growth. More risk-averse investors are likely to seek alternative outlets for their savings. Excessive volatility has been common in other Asian equity markets at similar stage of development but the volatility observed in China exceeds Hong Kong, Korean and Taiwanese markets.

Figure 4

China: Shanghai and Shenzhen Share Indices and Volume of Trade

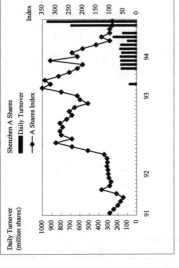

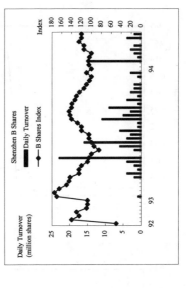

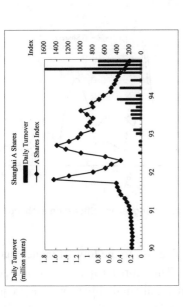

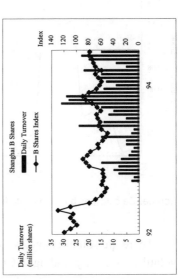

Figure 5

Shanghai and Shenzhen Share Price Variance (Ten-week standard deviation)

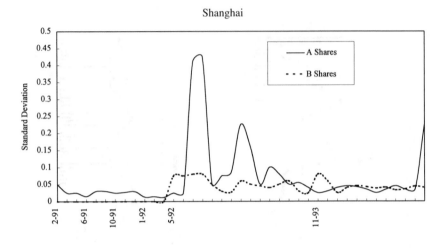

Shanghai

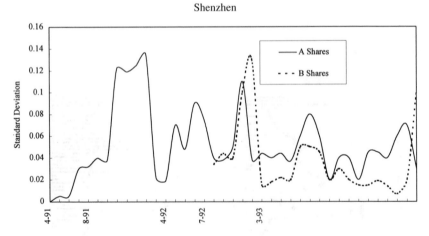

Shenzhen

Source: Calculations based on data from the Shanghai and Shenzhen exchanges.

There are some factors, which give rise to the low efficiency and high volatility of equity trading in China. The short-term horizons and specula-tive behaviour of poorly informed retail-small investors are frequently offered as explanations for volatility. However, the short-term behaviour itself is encouraged by a number of other factors:

1. The IPO process, including limited disclosure and the "lottery process" associated with the bunching together of IPOs.
2. The tendency of wealthy investors and brokers to engage in front-running behaviour that is nothing less than overt market manipulation.
3. The absence of an enforced capital gains tax, which would encourage shareholding for longer periods of time and short-term speculation.
4. The typical non-payment of cash dividends implies that the only way of realizing cash gains is by capital gains rather than by the dividend income flow.
5. The absence of large, stable institutional investors is certainly a factor.

Besides these factors, a major contributor to market volatility has been the succession of regulatory 'events' generated by the government. Specific instances of very big jumps in A share-price volatility, such as with the abolition of daily price limits in May 1992 and the announcement of the "support" package in July 1994, are clearly attributable to government policy decisions. While many of these announcements were ironically made with the intention of "improving" market functioning, and reducing volatility, such policy announcements, in practice, have enhanced volatility.

To reduce the volatility of equity trading in China, regulators can take the following actions:

1. The reintroduction of daily price limits — the advantages of price limits is that they suppress volatility and allow investors the time to revise their expectations about any given news item. It thus prevents excessive overreaction among relatively unsophisticated investors and limits the profit incentives of those who float such rumors.
2. The introduction of appropriately structured taxes on capital gains — in developed economies, government imposes a higher tax rate on short-term (under one year) capital gains versus long-term (over one year) capital gains. In view of the potential difficulties of tax collection in China, such a tax might require simplification. A transactions tax inversely linked to the time a stock was held would penalize those investors who take a short- rather than long-term

view. The information systems, to accurately track and historically record the buy and sell orders of individual investors, are not in place in China nor will they be for some time.

3. A more proactive stand on insider trading and front-running must be adopted by the CSRC, the PBC and the Exchanges.

However, the above policies are largely short term. Some long-term policies are encouraged. These may be achieved by at least three different routes:

1. Paying cash dividends by firms is encouraged. Enterprises must be given more discretion on dividend payments, and dividend announcements should be made at least annually.

2. Foreign securities firms such as Merrill Lynch and Morgan Stanley should be allowed to trade A shares. Such firms with their relatively sophisticated analytical tools and advice would likely add some degree of stability to the A shares market, at least in the long run.

3. The development of longer-term private pension and mutual funds should be encouraged. Such funds with their long-term horizon would counterbalance the largely retail-small investor oriented equity markets that currently exist.

Internationalization of China's Equity Markets

Like other emerging markets, China's equity markets are rapidly developing international links.

China has been very successful in attracting large private foreign resource inflows in recent years. Total private flows (on a net basis) jumped to $36 billion in 1993, up from $5 billion in 1990, and are estimated to have reached $40 billion in 1994. As shown in Figure 6, the total foreign direct investment in China increased drastically. Resource inflows to China have been increasingly skewed towards foreign direct investment (FDI), which accounted for more than two-thirds of the total net private investment flows to the country in 1993.

In contrast to other major emerging markets, the figure shows China's enormous share of developing country FDI, but its small relative share in terms of securitized flows, such as equities or bonds.

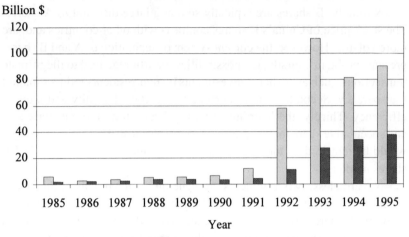

Figure 6
Total Foreign Direct Investment in China

	Number of Contracts	Amount Contracted (Million)	Amount Utilized (Million)
1985	3,073	5,931	1,956
1986	1,498	1,834	2,245
1987	2,233	3,709	1,647
1988	5,945	5,297	3,740
1989	5,779	5,600	3,774
1990	7,273	6,596	3,410
1991	12,978	11,980	4,366
1992	48,764	58,122	11,008
1993	83,437	111,436	27,515
1994	47,490	81,406	33,787
1995	37,126	90,300	37,700

Source: *Zhongguo Duiwai Jingji Maoyi Nianjian*, MOFTEC.

International Participation in China's Equity Market

Foreign Investment in B Shares Market

Overseas investor can invest in China through direct purchase of B shares listed on the Shanghai Securities Exchange and the Shenzhen Stock

Exchange. By the end of November 1994, the 28 B shares listed on Shanghai and 23 listed on Shenzhen had raised a total of US$1.3 billion.

Normally, B shares are typically sold at a large discount to A shares. The stock price of China's B shares contrasts with other countries and, are more volatile. However, the current system of separation of A and B shares presents problems. Firstly, the possibilities for arbitrage lead to illegitimate transactions, such as A shares investments by non-residents reduces market transparency. Secondly, share segmentation curtails liquidity and reduces efficiency. Thirdly, the learning benefits of permitting more experienced and speculative share market participants are also lost. These disadvantages would be removed by the synchronization through merger of the A and B shares markets.

Nevertheless, two arguments are generally offered against this. First, the limited convertibility of the RMB affects mergers. Second, the merger of A and B shares could encourage excessive inflows, which could crowd out domestic participation, thus, destabilizing the domestic market.

A range of alternative safeguards may be adopted. First, ceilings may be imposed on foreign investment, at the enterprise, sectoral, and individual levels. Second, participation may be restricted to known and approved large investors. Third, selective secondary equity market transactions with a destabilizing potential can be restricted. However, China must take care not to impose too many "safeguards," which could make entry unduly restrictive.

Tax Treatment of Foreign Equity Investment

It is recognized that the imposition of dividends or capital gains taxation may discourage liquidity and further reduce the attractiveness of portfolio flows relative to FDI. On balance, it is suggested that although a tax on dividends may be an unnecessary discouragement, a form of capital gains tax could be beneficial.

Overseas Listing of Chinese Equities: H shares

With the introduction of H shares, foreign investors can easily access to China equity market. Nine of the best internationally-known Chinese enterprises representing a total of $3 billion in value, were listed on the stock exchange of Hong Kong in the form of H shares in early 1994. By the end of 1995, another 22 companies were authorized for H share issues. Fifteen of the total of 31 approved companies had already established a listing on Hong Kong by the end of 1994.

As early as 1992, Chinese companies began to go further afield for raising capital, to the New York market. Due to the success of early H shares issues, the authorities permitted selected Chinese companies to officially approach the U.S. market.

International equity issuance can be beneficial to both issuing companies and foreign investors. From the issuer's viewpoint, it expands the investor base, which can lead to a higher stock price and a lower cost of capital; provides new markets for raising funds; enhances visibility of the issuing company and its products in international markets. From the investors' perspective, an international share listing (1) allows share trading and dividend payments in convertible currencies; (2) provides international diversification to institutional investors which are often prevented by their charters from investing in foreign currencies; (3) allows convenient and dependable settlement and custodian services; (4) and meets standard disclosure requirements.

A potential drawback of heavy dependence on offshore investment, however, is that a concentration of trading in domestic equities abroad could slow the development of local capital markets. Nevertheless, studies have shown that an international share-listing programme can produce an economy-wide benefit for the home country. This arises from the "spillover" effect on the pricing of domestically traded securities.

Problems Existing in the China's Equity Markets and Recommendations

There are several problems existing in the China's equity markets. They include:

Lack of an Appropriate Legal Framework

No perfect securities law and regulations were enacted to create a fine legal climate for foreign capital to come into China's equity market. It is recommended that the regulatory bodies has to establish a supervision and management system according to international practice to standardize the operation of the Shanghai Securities Exchange and the Shenzhen Stock Exchange.

Disqualification of Professional Practitioners

According to the Shenzhen Stock Exchange, only 30 people were employed by securities companies in the Special Economic Zone in the beginning of 1990. The number has risen to 300 by the end of 1990. Due to the short history of the trade, most of these personnel are far from experienced. The expansion of the China equity market in the future would demand increasing number of floor brokers, share registration personnel, qualified accountants, auditors and managers. These professional practitioners should be provided with appropriate training in order to standard the codes of conducts.

Availability of Supporting Infrastructure

There is insufficient infrastructure to support the operation of the China equity market. Supporting infrastructure includes (1) regulations pertaining to the trading of stocks and shares and to the operation of the stock exchange; (2) supporting banking services; (3) facilities available to investors outside the Shenzhen Stock Exchange; and (4) communication services should be increased.

Problems with Foreign Exchange

Difficulties on this score were not apparent when only A shares were traded. Since the Shenzhen Stock Exchange began to offer B shares to investors outside China, the situation has become more complicated. Since B shares are denominated in RMB, outside buyers must convert foreign currencies into RMB in order to trade in Shenzhen stocks. The exchange rate of RMB is set at the level quoted at Shenzhen Foreign Exchange Market on the day prior to the transaction.

However, since the RMB is not convertible in the international currency market, foreign investors have to face with the foreign exchange risks and liquidity associated with B shares. Moreover, as trading in B shares grows in volume, the amount of foreign exchange flowing in and out of the Shenzhen Stock Exchange will begin to affect the demand and supply for RMB, and hence the international competitiveness of Chinese exports. Conversely, the exchange rate of RMB will also have effects on Shenzhen's B share prices.

Non-Economic Problems

Experience has shown that government interventions in stock markets generally do more harm than good. In the past, the Shenzhen municipal government has on several occasions stepped into the market, with the declared intention of dampening black market activities and speculation. In mid-1990, when share prices skyrocketed, daily limit of + or −10% on fluctuations were imposed on 28 May. The permissible range was further reduced to + or −5% on 18 June, and again changed to an upper limit of to 1% and lower limit of 5% on 26 June. Other measures included an increase in stamp duty from 0.3% to 0.6%, and the imposition of a tax on dividends higher than the yield from a 12-month bank deposit. The daily limit was later lifted and the stamp duty was reduced. By doing so, investors' confidence towards the China's equity market is affected.

However, it must be admitted that politics exerts a heavier weight on the development of stock markets in China than in other Asian developing countries.

Recommendations

To improve the efficiency of the China's equity market, cross-listing of shares at two official exchanges of Shanghai and Shenzhen is recommended.

Cross-listing means the listing of enterprises at the other exchange style trading centres recognized under national law. Through the cross-listing of shares, liquidity of the stock will increase. In addition, investors can access more market information and illegal transaction like arbitrage across these two exchanges can be eliminated.

Apart from this, the reason why we recommend cross-listing is that, referring to Figure 7, the movements for the Shenzhen Stock Index and the Jingnan Stock Index are similar for the period September 1991–December 1995. It is believed that the factors affecting the movements of the two indices are more or less the same; for example, they are affected by political stability of China. Therefore, we suggest cross-listing of shares at these two exchanges.

Figure 7

Stock Indices of Shenzhen and Jingnan (Sept. 1991 to Dec. 1995)

Shenzhen Stock Index

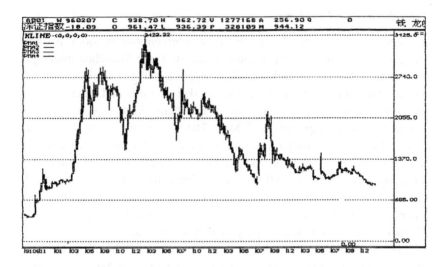

Jingnan Stock Index

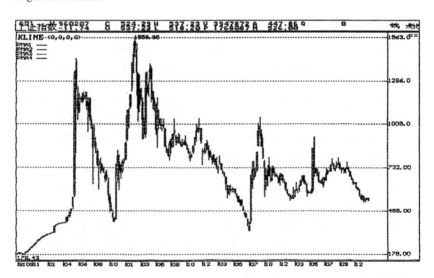

Conclusion

To attract more investors, China is taking measure to upgrade the performance of listed companies, standardize the publication of their information and the distribution of profits in a bid to raise the return on their investment.

Professionals believe that the prospect of the China's equity market is good. According to the *Securities Journal* in June 1996, Ching Ju Yeh, a senior investment of the HSBC Asset Management Limited, commented that "China's equity markets are still considered tiny compared with the size of its economy and the capital need of its industry. Whilst China's gross domestic product now accounts for around 24.5% of the Asia-Pacific region, its stock markets' market capitalization is just 0.3%."

The rapid increase in domestic savings and foreign direct investment in China contribute to the development of the China's equity market. Moreover, nowadays in China, most people are well educated. They no longer put their money in banks. They have some knowledge about the operation of the China's equity market. They believe they can get higher return from investing in stocks than from depositing in financial institutions.

It is believed that China can take advantage of such situation to be another important financial centre in Asia Pacific region. However, the regulatory bodies need to have strict supervision over business operation of the securities companies and the listed companies.

5

The Basic Framework of Forecasting RMB Exchange Rate: A Qualitative-Fundamental Approach*

Mun Kin-chok

Introduction

Since China's foreign exchange system was reformed in 1994, China's national currency, the Renminbi (RMB), has steadily strengthened against the US dollar. This is contrary to many projections that it should be devaluated because of high inflation. Whether the RMB would continue to appreciate in the future is questionable. A strong RMB would be unfavourable to China's exports, which still remains one of the important policy objectives of the nation. The prime reason for a strong RMB has been the government's tight money policy to curb inflation. The priority of government policy, however, will change when conditions change. If the government changes its priority, what would be its impact on the RMB exchange rate movement? To analyse the causes of RMB appreciation since 1994, this chapter provides business firms with a basic framework to forecast RMB exchange rate movement by using a qualitative-fundamental approach.

---

* This chapter was written in 1995, some views are still valid today.

Abolition of an Multiple Exchange Rate System

Before 1994 China practised two exchange rates: an official rate at 5.8 RMB per US dollar and a swap market rate with a lowest level of 10.5 RMB per US dollar. China decided to abolish this two-tier exchange rate system in order to meet the requirements of a market economy system to join the World Trade Organization (WTO). This two-tier exchange rate system was one of the barriers to China's entry into the WTO. It also has been unfavourable to foreign direct investment in China during the past years, as the official rate was applied to inflows of capital while swap market rates was used for capital and profit repatriation. As China moves from a planned economy to a socialist market economy, a number of socioeconomic reforms are required, and a single exchange rate system is one of them. Because of the above reasons, a devaluation of the official rate or a merge of the official rate with the swap market rate into one single exchange rate was deemed necessary. On 1 January 1994, a single and managed exchange rate replaced the previous two exchange rates by a single market rate at 8.7 RMB per US dollar — an official devaluation of 50%. Figure 1 shows the RMB exchange rate against the US dollar from 1989 to 1994.

Causes for RMB Appreciation During Inflation

With 20% inflation, many economic analysts considered whether China merged its two exchange rates would be successful. According to the purchasing power parity theorem, RMB should face a devaluation pressure against other currencies with a lower inflation rate. However, the RMB moved in the opposite direction against USD. Instead of a devaluation, the RMB/USD appreciated 4.5% in 17 months despite high inflation as shown in Figure 2.

The RMB case indicates that a currency with a very high inflation rate may not necessarily depreciate, if depreciation pressures can be offset by appreciation factors. The RMB appreciation case is explained by the following push factors: anti-inflation policy, austerity measures, capital inflow, trade surplus, expectation, and central bank's intervention.

Anti-Inflation Policy

Since 1992 China has faced a high inflation rate of more than 20%. This

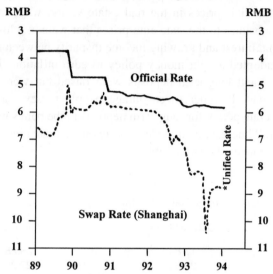

Figure 1
Exchange Rate of the RMB against the USD

Source: Adapted from *Hang Seng Economic Monthly*, January 1994.
Note: Month-end figures.

Figure 2
RMB/USD (Weekly) Exchange Rate

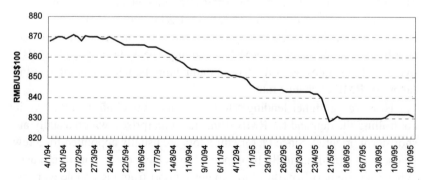

Source: Reuters.

inflation rate has occurred primarily because of an increase of foodstuff prices from China's price reform policy. Other causes for inflation were the rise of raw materials prices in the real estate sector, wage increase and government subsidies to the state enterprises that were in a loss situation. To avoid social unrest and growing income disparity between regions, the government adopted a tight money policy to curb inflation. The interest rates of short- and long-term deposits were raised but were still below the inflation rate. In order to encourage people to save, an inflation-compensation rate policy for long-term deposits in the banks was adopted. Thus the overall interest rate includes a basic interest rate plus an inflation-compensation rate as shown in Table 1.

Table 1
Overall Interest Rates of RMB Long-Term Deposits

	October 1994	July 1995
3-Year	17.86	25.25
5-Year	20.56	27.95
8-Year	23.26	30.65

Source: *Hong Kong Economic Journal*, 3 September 1995.

The increased overall interest rates for long-term deposits encouraged people to save and spend less. The total amount of time and saving deposits in the banks increased to US$290 billion at the end of 1994, an increase of US$70 billion within a year (*China Financial Outlook*, 1994 and 1995). The higher overall interest rates of RMB induced people to shift their deposits from foreign currencies, primarily US Dollar, to RMB deposits. As a result, the higher RMB interest rates increased the foreign exchange supply and the demand for RMB. Generally speaking, a rise of RMB's overall interest rates was effective in dampening people's spending and in favour of RMB exchange rate.

However, a higher lending rate from banks would not be effective in controlling the demand for RMB from state enterprises, which usually are short-term oriented. Since factory directors are usually appointed for a few years, they would naturally be expected to behave on a short-term basis. When they are in office, they have to get support from the people working in the factory. To achieve this they tend to spend more for welfare purposes. On the other hand, they also want to have some expansion projects to show their performance during their appointment. To meet these two objectives, they must borrow money from the banks as much as they can without paying much attention to how high the lending rate is. Under state ownership they tend to have less of a sense of responsibility for the repayment. Because of this state enterprise behaviour, a higher lending rate would not prevent them from borrowing. Before the responsibility problem of the state enterprises is resolved, any use of interest rate mechanism for controlling the demand for RMB from state enterprises is difficult.

To overcome this system-inherent problem, austerity measures seem to be more effective than an interest rate policy. Based on the above reason, direct control of bank loans to state enterprises was adopted in addition to a higher lending rate. Under the credit control policy, the RMB liquidity was effectively reduced and hence pushed up the RMB exchange rate. Another administrative measure for reducing the liquidity of RMB has been the selling of bonds to individuals and institutions. The higher overall interest rate policy together with the administrative measures effectively reduced the RMB supply on the market and hence a lower demand for foreign exchange.

Austerity Measures

Before the reform of foreign exchange system, domestic enterprises and institutions were allowed to retain up to 40% of their foreign exchange earnings in the form of retention quota. However, under the new exchange rate system, they are no longer allowed to retain their foreign exchange receipts but must sell them to designated banks. As a result, billions of US dollars that were previously on the accounts of domestic enterprises were gradually concentrated in the foreign exchange designated banks. The designated banks are not allowed to hold foreign exchange position in excess of the limits imposed by the central bank; any excess of their holdings must be sold to the China Foreign Exchange Trading System (CFETS) — the nationwide foreign exchange market (*China Financial Outlook*, 1995, p. 43). Under austerity measures, foreign exchange held previously by domestic enterprises was channeled to the foreign exchange market, thus increasing the supply of foreign exchange.

Austerity measures were used for the management of the demand for foreign exchange. For domestic enterprises, the purchases of foreign exchange, even in the new exchange rate system, are under control. To buy foreign exchange, domestic enterprises need relevant documents, foreign investment contracts or account settlement notes issued by the Ministry of Foreign Economic Relations and Trade.

Foreign firms can only sell foreign exchange to the CEFTS, but cannot buy from it, they still have to buy from swap centres. According to the original objective of the foreign exchange system reform, all swap centres will be abolished and replaced by an interbank market — the CEFTS. These swap centres are needed until the nationwide foreign exchange market is fully developed. Under austerity measures the foreign exchange supply and demand can be regulated to achieve the objective of China's monetary policy.

Capital Inflow

Under the new single exchange rate system, foreign capital inflow was stimulated by the 50% increase of purchasing power. Another factor for attracting foreign capital of foreign firms was the foreign firms' optimistic view on China's future economic development. China was the second most favoured place for foreign direct investment in 1994, second to the United States.

The third type of capital inflow was "hot money." "Hot money" aims at obtaining a higher interest rate from state enterprises that need money for expansion or other purposes but could not get credit loans from the local banks under the tight money policy of the government. For the purpose of arbitrage, "hot money" flowed in to meet the needs and demands of these enterprises by charging much higher interest rates than those of the local banks. The "hot money," however, was only a small portion of total capital inflow, about US$1–2 billion in 1994 (*Hang Seng Economic Monthly*, February 1995). The above three types of capital inflow to China increased the supply of the foreign exchange and strengthen the RMB's position.

Trade Surplus

The 50% devaluation of RMB improved the competitiveness of Chinese products on the international markets, hence the enterprises' incentives to export. In 1994 the trade surplus amounted to US$5.2 billion, compared with a deficit of US$19.4 billion in 1992. However, it is important to note that a 4.5% appreciation of RMB from March 1994 to mid-1995 could affect the export growth. Chinese enterprises were eager to promote their exports in order to generate foreign exchange even at high costs, thus they were able to compete in the international markets on lower prices. RMB devaluation plus penetration price policy stimulated exports and dampened imports, hence trade surpluses increased.

Expectation

Before the foreign exchange system reform, a number of foreign trading companies expected a merger of two exchange rates to be practised. "In order to benefit from such depreciation, they either postponed the 1993 foreign exchange receivable from exports to early 1994, or advanced the 1994 import payments before the end of 1993" (*China Financial Outlook*, 1995, p. 44). This expectation behaviour of foreign trading companies thus contributed to the increase of foreign exchange supply in 1994.

Central Bank's Intervention

Capital inflow for direct investment and "hot money" for receiving higher interest rates increased the supply of foreign exchange or demand for RMB, pushing up the RMB exchange rate. In order to reduce the appreciation pressure on RMB, the People's Bank of China (PBOC) constantly inter- vened in the foreign exchange market through purchases of foreign ex- change or sales of RMB. Without this central bank intervention, RMB would have been even stronger than the present rate at 8.3. However, a higher RMB appreciation could be unfavourable to China's exports. And central bank's intervention increased the supply of RMB, which had been contradictory to the government's tight money policy to curb inflation.

The Bases of Forecasting RMB Exchange Rate

Having analysed the causes for the appreciation of RMB during a high inflation environment in China, the bases of forecasting RMB exchange rate can be set up as shown in Figure 3.

1. Identify the priority of macropolicy

   As China is still in a transitional stage from a planned economy to a socialist market economy, the transformation process cannot be completed

Figure 3

A Basic Framework of Forecasting RMB Exchange Rate

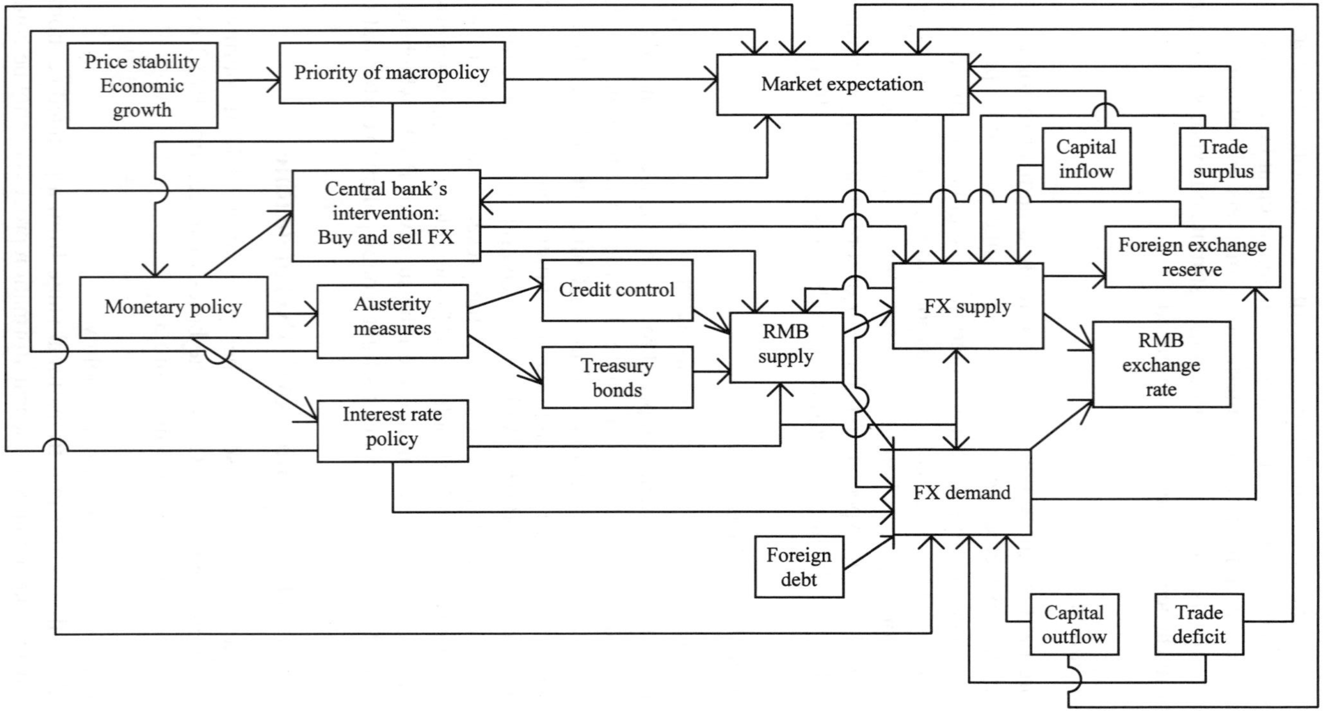

in the short-term. China's economic development will still be managed at the macro level for the foreseeable future, even though market mechanisms could be functioning in more economic sectors than before. For the purpose of exchange rate forecasting, an understanding of the priority of macro-policy is of vital importance to the business firms. A change of the priority of macropolicy objectives will possibly lead to a change of the direction of policies and related administrative measures.

If the objective of price stability is still a priority, a tight money policy will most likely continue. Under such circumstances, RMB exchange rate could maintain a stronger position against USD. If faster economic growth is emphasized, the RMB exchange rate could weaken by an easier money policy. But how can foreign business firms identify whether the government would change its policy priority or not? Some important signals or information need to be watched:

- The prime minister's annual policy speech at the Chinese People's Congress (CPC) held every March.
- The articles published in the People's Daily (the top official newspaper) about the future direction of macropolicy during the annual meeting of CPC and the Chinese People's Political Consultative Conference (CPPCC), both meetings held every March.
- The speeches of the president of the PBOC. The central bank and its other high-ranking officials could provide some clues about the future direction of monetary policy.
- The formal speeches or informal talks of the government leaders on the macropolicy directions.

The important speeches of government leaders in China will give information about the future direction of nationwide economic policy. Since the central government still plans and supervises the macro level economy, all provincial governments have to follow its decisions and policies. From this point of view, the impact of a change of policy priority on RMB exchange rate can be predicted. If the government leaders place more emphasis on economic growth or higher employment, this could be a signal for a change of policy priority or direction. This means an easier monetary policy would be adopted in a near future, indicating a possibility of weakening RMB.

Since the RMB exchange rate is still regulated by the central bank, any prediction of RMB exchange rate movement must first understand the government's policy priority. A central bank's policy cannot, however, deviate from the national policy. So an early understanding of a possible change of the government policy priority would provide business firms the most important base of forecasting RMB exchange rate. Based on the nature of a managed exchange rate system in China, a qualitative-fundamental forecasting approach like this appears to be useful.

2. Signals of a turning point of RMB exchange rate movement

After identifying the direction of policy priority, firms operating in China should pay attention to the signals that may influence the RMB exchange rate movement as reflected by the indicators stated below:

*   The inflation rate drops to 15% — the target of China's macropolicy in 1995, providing more room for an interest rate cut.
*   The inflation-compensation rate for long-term bank deposits is falling.
*   The banks relax their credit control on domestic enterprises.
*   The forced purchase of government bonds in all institutions stops.
*   Capital inflow slows down or begins to decrease.
*   Trade balance surpluses are declining.

The above indicators could be the signals for a depreciation of RMB in the future. Since the RMB exchange rate is managed by the central bank, a drastic downturn movement of RMB is unlikely. A depreciation of RMB would most likely be smooth and the volatility of RMB is rather low because of the central bank's intervention. Another reason for RMB's low volatility is the nature of its nonconvertibility, under which the central bank is in a good position to manage effectively. The exchange rate is backed up by China's high foreign exchange reserve of 70 billion US dollars in 1995, the fifth largest position in the world.

3. Other factors

The RMB exchange rate movement could also be influenced by other factors:

*   Entry to World Trade Organization.
*   Foreign debt redemption.
*   Move to a free convertible currency.

When China enters the WTO, a large part of the domestic market has to open up to foreign countries. If the increase of imports is larger than that of exports, this will lead to trade deficit and the foreign exchange reserves would decrease. Another unfavourable factor to RMB exchange rate is China's foreign debt redemption. In 1995 China must repay its foreign debts of US$20 billion (*China Financial Outlook*, 1995, p. 46). This foreign debt redemption will increase the demand for USD, but it can be offset by increased foreign reserves. The third pressure on RMB exchange rate may arise when China starts to move to a free convertible currency, which needs a high foreign exchange reserve to support.

Example: Forecasting the RMB Exchange Rate Movement for 1996

As this chapter is prepared (autumn 1995), the RMB exchange rate movement in 1996 is forecast by using the above basic framework.

1. Identify the priority of macropolicy

The first step is to identify the government's priority of macropolicy in 1996. In 1995, anti-inflation has been the first priority of the government. The target of the macropolicy is to reduce the inflation rate to 15%. The inflation rate of the first eight months in 1995 was on the average 17.2%. It is expected that the inflation rate will decrease to 15% at the end of this year.

Following the declining inflation rate, the inflation-compensation rates for long-term deposits have been slightly reduced. The overall interest rates of RMB long-term deposits from July to October are shown in Table 2.

Table 2
Overall Interest Rates of RMB Long-Term Deposits

	July	August	September	October
3-Year Deposit	25.25	25.23	24.88	24.31
5-Year Deposit	27.95	27.93	27.58	27.01
8-Year Deposit	30.65	30.63	30.28	29.71

Source: *Hong Kong Economic Journal*, 3 September 1995.

In four months, the overall interest rates of 3-year, 5-year and 8-year deposits have been reduced 3.72%, 3.7% and 3% respectively. Would lower inflation rates and lower overall interest rates for long-term deposits be signals for a change of the present tight money policy? To answer this question, it is important to examine the government leaders' speeches as published in the official newspapers to see whether any clues to a change of the macropolicy's priority can be found.

Having analysed the speeches of the government leaders in recent months, clues to a change of the priority of macropolicy have not been found. This would suggest that anti-inflation policy is still the priority of macropolicy. Chen Yuan, vice-president of the PBOC, indicated that China will adopt a "steady-to-tight" money policy for several years, however, a too-tight control of the RMB supply would lead to economic recession and therefore it should also be avoided. On the other hand, the inflation problem cannot fundamentally be solved within a short period of time. China needs more time to strengthen its monetary tools for stabilizing the economy.

Recently, Director of the State Planning Commission and President of the PBOC also indicated that a "steady-to-tight" money policy should be adopted despite a fall of retail price index (*Wen Wei Po*, 16 September 1995). As the increase in food prices in the past years were primarily due to price controls and heavy government subsidies, the prices, though they fell in the past months, are still considered to be at a high level and unstable. Furthermore, the provincial governments and enterprises still have a strong drive to invest. A relaxation of credit control would push up the prices again.

Based on the speeches made by the government leaders, senior officials, president and vice-president of the PBOC, China's monetary policy in 1996 will still be on the restrictive side, but not so "tight" as in the previous two years.

2. Other important objectives of government's economic policy

Beside anti-inflation as the first priority of the government's economic policy, there are also other important policy objectives which cannot be ignored, such as development of mid-west China, development of the agricultural sector, large infrastructure projects and improvement of state enterprises' economic efficiency. All these are important to the government's economic policy in the coming years. To achieve these objectives, the government has to allow banks to increase loans to support the above-mentioned plans and projects. Based on this, a "steady-to-tight" money policy is likely to be adopted.

3. Macropolicy more important than trade policy

The RMB appreciation in the past 20 months has been unfavourable to exports. The minister of the Ministry of Foreign Economic Relations and Trade (MOFERT) indicated that China's exports had severely been hurt by the RMB appreciation as the growth rate of exports began to decrease consecutively for several months in 1995. But the minister warned trading companies that they should not expect a devaluation policy to be undertaken by the government, rather they should use other measures to boost their exports (*Hong Kong Economic Journal*, 13 September 1995). The speech of the minister of the MOFERT gave an important message that the policy a ministry at anytime must give way to the macropolicy. Even though a devaluation policy would favour the nation's exports, it will not be adopted if it has a lower priority in the agenda of government policy.

4. High foreign exchange reserves

Foreign exchange reserves in China increased at a fast rate during 1992–1995, from US$20 billion in 1992 to US$70 billion in 1995. In four years China has the fifth highest foreign reserves in the world. This puts the PBOC in a good position to intervene the foreign exchange market together with its administrative measures. This also means that a large RMB devaluation is unlikely to happen in the future.

5. Forecast

Based on the above analysis, the RMB exchange rate movement can be forecast as follows:

- Since a "steady-to-tight" money policy will be adopted, credit relaxation would be applied to only selective sectors. An overall credit expansion is unlikely, hence the pressure on RMB devaluation is low.
- If there is a devaluation pressure on RMB, the PBOC will be in a strong position to stabilize the exchange rate by using monetary tools plus its austerity measures, which are not available to most central banks in free market economies. This would be one of the special characteristics of a socialist market economy in which a direct control of credit in the banking sector is allowed. By using a mixed approach — monetary tools plus direct control, the PBOC is

therefore more influential on stabilizing exchange rate than its counterparts in western countries.

Should the RMB depreciate, 4.5% would probably be the upper limit as this is the maximum percentage of appreciation in the past 16 months. It is possible that the PBOC would not allow a RMB depreciation to exceed this psychological point. On the whole, the devaluation of RMB would be slow and limited.

Conclusions

The most important base of forecasting the RMB exchange rate movement in China is to understand the major difference in central government's economic role between a socialist market economy and a market economy in Western countries. In a socialist market economy like China, the central government has much more influence on the economy than its counterparts in Western countries with respect to the direction of nationwide economic development and price stability. All provincial governments, state enterprises and banks must follow the central government's policy in order to maintain uniformity between their policies and actions. Once the policy priority is identified, it would be easier to predict which direction of the monetary policy of the PBOC would move to, and hence the RMB exchange rate movement.

In a socialist market economy, a quantitative-fundamental analysis based on a number of economic indicators or a technical analysis should be less useful than a qualitative-fundamental approach to a forecast of the direction of the RMB exchange rate movement as proposed in this chapter. However, the use of this method is based on the premise that the RMB is not a convertible currency. The forecasting methods, which are used in a market economy with a fully convertible currency and highly developed foreign exchange markets, are less useful in a socialist market economy, where these two conditions are not existent.

China is planning to make RMB a free convertible currency by the year of 2000. If the inflation rate in China by that time is still be higher than that of the US dollar or other major international currencies, the RMB would face devaluation pressures. To avert such foreign exchange risk under a fully convertible currency, China would probably adopt a step-by-step approach to RMB convertibility, that is, the principle of convertibility would be applied first to its current account, and then its capital account. In the early stage of convertibility, local residents would probably not be allowed to freely buy foreign exchange, but this restriction should be relaxed when the confidence on RMB and market mechanism in the foreign exchange market is well built up.

When RMB reaches the stage of fully free convertibility, its exchange rate will probably not be as stable as at present, its floating range would become wider than that of the present managing rate system. When RMB becomes an international currency, a higher volatility of its exchange rate is unavoidable.

6

Chinese Cultural Values: Their Dimensions and Marketing Implications*

Oliver H. M. Yau

Introduction

With one-fifth of the world's population, China has the greatest number of consumers in the world. Businessmen in international trade will often find themselves dealing with Chinese consumers. Waldie (1980) has warned international managers in Hong Kong to examine the cultural differences between Chinese and Western people in general when making management decisions. An English term can have a different meaning in a Chinese situation. For example, in Western culture, maturity means "to be able to express one's genuine self, to be free from the constraints of what other people think, to confront others because of the consequence of being individualized or different" (Waldie, 1980). But, for the Chinese, maturity means a movement towards a harmonious integration into the social fabric of the family, as well as the institute at which one is working. Thus, it is crucial and beneficial for international marketing managers to understand the Chinese way of life and value systems. This is the objective of this chapter.

* An earlier version of this chapter appeared in *European Journal of Marketing*, 22 May 1988.

Chinese Cultural Values

Researchers in the study of Chinese cultural values may find it amazing that Chinese values have formed a clear and consistent system for generations (Kindle, 1983; Hsu, 1970). Of course, it does not imply that the values and the system have not been changed. In fact, the Chinese cultural value systems have recently undergone rapid change. For example, during the Cultural Revolution in the People's Republic of China, the orthodox doctrine of Confucianism, which is the foundation of the Chinese value system, was severely criticized and deeds according to the doctrine strictly forbidden. Thus, the classical Chinese value system was disrupted and efforts are now being made to rebuild it. Other Chinese-dominated societies, such as Taiwan, Hong Kong and Singapore, have also shown inevitable changes in the value systems during the process of rapid social and economic change (Shivery and Shively, 1972).

Some studies have revealed that Chinese cultural values have indeed changed. In a cross-cultural comparison of human values, Morris (1956) found that there was no noticeable difference in the value systems of sub-samples of university students from four large cities in China. Yang (1977) replicated Morris's study and found that there was a change in hierarchy of the value systems of college students. However, his findings also imply that some of the traditional Chinese values are still held by young Chinese nowadays.

Adopting the methodology from Kluckhohn and Strodbeck (1961), Lin (1966) tried to uncover the value orientations of Hong Kong school students and their parents. He found, within variational limits, that the younger generation had changed considerably, as compared with their parents, with regard to time, man-nature and relational orientations. It would be a mistake, however, to conclude that these findings indicate the traditional Chinese value orientations in Hong Kong have been completely eradicated in the transition to modernization. Firstly, mastery of traditional Chinese learning is regarded as an important prerequisite for achieving status among the intellectuals in Chinese society (Lin, 1966). Second, strong vestiges of the Chinese heritage are rooted in the family and kinship relations and not in the educational institutes (Hsu, 1947, 1963, 1972). As for individual Chinese, family is a source that constantly diffuses cultural influences on them throughout their lives. Even though they may deviate from the traditional value orientations at some point in their lives, they tend to be assimilated again by their Chinese culture and enjoy their authority and social status as they grow old. Some researchers have argued that education would introduce new values, which would gradually replace the old ones to shape an industrialized society in which family and kinship relationships could not survive (Shivery and Shively, 1972). However, this may not be so.

Traditional values will not necessarily be a stumbling block to industrialization or economic development. The success of the Japanese, which has a similar culture to the Chinese, is a typical example. Hong Kong and Taiwan are two good examples of how cultural values have served to make their respective economies unique. It has been proven during the past 30 years that the prosperity of Hong Kong and Taiwan is not only due to the acumen of the Chinese businessmen, but also to the considerateness and perseverance of the labour force who always try to be in harmony with their employers.

Classification of Chinese Cultural Values

The Chinese cultural values are largely formed and created from interpersonal relationships and social orientations. This is shown in the work of Confucius, whose doctrine is still a basic pillar of Chinese life today. To describe the Chinese culture, it is therefore more suitable to adopt the value-orientation model of Kluckhohn and Strodbeck (1961) which has the same emphasis. The following is a description of each of the Chinese cultural values according to Kluckhohn and Strodbeck's classification, with possible marketing implications discussed for each orientation (see Figure 1):

1. Man-to-nature orientation;
2. Man-to-himself orientation;
3. Relational orientation;
4. Time orientation, and
5. Personal activity orientation.

Chinese Cultural Values and their Marketing Implications

Man-to-Nature Orientation

The Chinese regard man as a part of nature, and believe that man should not try to overcome or master nature but has to learn how to adapt to it so as to

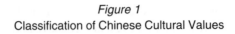

Figure 1
Classification of Chinese Cultural Values

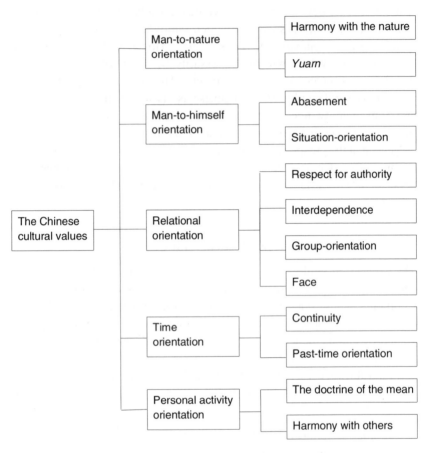

reach harmony. This is because the Chinese believe that nature has the Way (Tao) by which all things become what they are (Chan, 1963). It was said that the Way cannot be told:

> There are existence and destruction, life and death, and flourish and decline .... What is eternal has neither change nor any definite principle itself. Since it (the Way) has no definite principle itself, it is not bound in any particular locality.

Therefore, it is not wise to hold too tight on to what one has got or lost. There is no such thing as fate or misfortune in life, as they are entangled with each other, as well as causes of each other (Wei, 1980).

Apart from the doctrine of the Way, *Yuarn* (Karma) is another important belief that has been rooted in the heart of most Chinese. This belief prevailed well before the time of Confucius (BC 557–479), as he once said: "Life and death are fated; wealth and honours hinge on the will of providence" (Legge, 1960). It resembles the important doctrine, Karma in Buddhism, which was spread to China from India in the Han or Tang Dynasty about 2,000 years ago. Hence to a certain extent, it still has the Buddhist meaning of Karma. However, after 2,000 years of assimilation, its meaning has deviated from its origin. *Yuarn* can be referred to as predetermined relations with other things or individuals, which are far beyond one's control.

The existence or absence of interrelations with the universe is predetermined or governed by a powerful external force. This force could be supernatural, or a social law that is too sophisticated to be understood by human beings. The Chinese believe that friendships or even marriages are predetermined. When *Yuarn* exists, it leads to the chance that two men, living thousands of miles apart, could meet each other and become friends. It also leads employers to find employees with which they may be very satisfied. Furthermore, *Yuarn* will come to an end. When it does, couples have to divorce and friends separate.

Despite its tragic sense, *Yuarn* also has its positive side. The concept of *Yuarn* leads to self-reliance. People cease to complain about their circumstances and try to save themselves from the natural consequences of their own acts before they accept their fate. For example, an individual could beg for *Yuarn* by giving alms and doing charitable deeds in secret so that the interrelations of himself or his family with the universe may be established. A businessman may believe that doing business ethically will bring him *Yuarn* of prosperity. Furthermore, though things are predetermined, he has to try positively to seek for interrelations with others (or things) in order to find out whether he has got *Yuarn* or not. According to the concept, the interrelations among people are always passive. But it is only those who take an active part in searching for, and trying to establish it, who can successfully have *Yuarn*.

Potential Marketing Implications for Man-to-Nature Orientation

The man-to-nature orientation has some implications in marketing. According to these two doctrines, it is possible to expect that a Chinese consumer who believes in them would generally have low expectations towards the product he is going to purchase or consume, or that when the performance of the product does not meet with his expectations, he would feel less dissatisfied because he thinks he has to conform to *Yuarn*.

The Chinese have a great tendency to attribute failure of products/ services to fate rather than to the company from whom the product was purchased, or even the manufacturer. Hence, they are reluctant to complain about products that do not meet with their expectations. Thorelli (1982) includes this evidence in his recent study on Chinese consumers. Therefore, objective measurement of dissatisfaction, such as frequency of complaints, does not adequately reflect the affective attitude of consumers towards products, and, thus, is not a good measure of marketing effectiveness (McNeal, 1969; Cavusgil and Kaynak, 1982). Other means of measurement of consumer satisfaction or dissatisfaction are needed.

Man-to-Himself Orientation

Abasement

By studying the child-rearing practices of Chinese families, one can observe dramatic differences from Western cultures. From an early stage, a child in a Chinese family is brought up to understand the legitimate role of him/herself in front of others. Chinese are used to believing in modesty and self-effacement, two important virtues that a child, as well as a subordinate, uses to cultivate him/her mind. In the past, individual Chinese would call themselves "the worthless" before their teachers, and "the unfilial" child before their parents. This sort of behaviour is still very common in today's Chinese society. For example, Western people will tend to say "thank you" when praised by others, but Chinese people will be prone to say "No, I am not worthy" in the same situation. Furthermore, Chinese try to avoid saying "No" when asked to express opinions. They believe that saying "No" will embarrass or offend others. Thus, to reply in an indirect or sarcastic way is the best way to express disagreement.

Situation Orientation

Chinese today are frequently regarded as situation-oriented and pragmatic (Hsu, 1963). Again, this is due to child-rearing practices during which children are taught by parents, uncles and aunts, and other adults in the (extended or joint) family. They are therefore liable to exposure of many points of view. Consequently, Chinese children learn that circumstances have an important bearing upon what is right or wrong, and compromise in most cases is inevitable. Western children, on the other hand, are usually brought up under the guidance of one set of parents, are rarely exposed to various points of view, are kept in a more closed relationship with life's events, and grow up with concepts of one right way to do things (Kindle, 1982). Thus, comparatively, the Chinese are less dogmatic and tend to be more flexible in following a learned principle. The root of this Chinese cultural value is in Lao Tse's doctrine of the Way.

Potential Marketing Implications for Man-to-Himself Orientation

In marketing, the value of abasement may have possible implications for sales force management. It can be used as a supplement to other sales force selection techniques, such as objective testing, personal interviews and background investigation. If an effective salesman has to be aggressive and positive-minded by American standards, Chinese tend to be bad salesmen. However, in Chinese society, aggressive salesmen might frighten customers, who may be humiliated. For example, Chinese buyers like to have their shopping in a free environment without interference. If a salesman in a retail store is too eager to help and approaches a customer who has not decided what to buy, the customer will feel uneasy and go away. The proper thing to do is to deep a distance from the customer, but, at the same time, let him/her know that he is always ready to help.

The value of situation orientation has particular implications for service marketing. Because of this orientation, Chinese tend to enjoy available things. In the United Kingdom or other Western countries, it is commonplace for consumers to queue up to buy tickets for a movie or to cash a cheque. Customers are requested or assigned to a counter to be served. The Chinese prefer a short queue, even though the waiting time is the same. Moreover, Chinese are anxious to choose the person whom they are familiar with to serve them. Therefore, unless there is no other alternative,

Chinese tend to feel more dissatisfied with the serving system and are more likely not to re-purchase than their counterparts in the U.S. In Hong Kong and even in Taiwan, the multiline waiting system is usually adopted, except for some English and American banks.

Relational Orientation

Respect for Authority

The Chinese have a strong respect for authority. They are prone to trust totally without questioning. In a classroom, Chinese students expect their teachers to "teach" them, as well as guide them. Students will feel they are learning nothing if asked to express their opinions or to solve a problem by themselves. It is the same in psychological therapy. Chinese patients usually request the psychologist to teach them what to do, and do not believe that trying to find out the solution themselves in consultation with the psychologist is a better way to cure their illness.

The early root of the Chinese respect for authority is in Confucius's five cardinal relations, between sovereign and minister, father and son, husband and wife, old and young, and between friends (Hchu and Yang, 1972). These relations have served effectively to control social behaviour in society. Chinese have to observe and act according to the norms prescribed for each instance of interpersonal relations Thus, the king must be kingly, the minister ministerly, the husband husbandly, the wife wifely, brothers brotherly, and friends friendly. It is not surprising to see that Chinese today still prefer to address someone in more structural or hierarchical type terms than Westerners. For example, people in the People's Republic of China used to address Mao as Chairman Mao in order to show respect for his authority. A child is not allowed to call his father's friends by their names. And a venerable man with seniority in an organization is addressed by adding the term "old brother" before his surname.

This value has particular implications for advertising. Since the Chinese have such respect for authority, directing them to what is right or wrong, advertisement will tend to be more effective when opinion leaders stand up in commercials recommending products/services to their target consumers. Opinion leaders for Chinese consumers include older people, political leaders, family elders and authoritarian types. Kindle (1985) pointed out that Chinese are much more likely to be influenced in their purchasing by opinion leaders than are consumers in the U.S.

Interdependence

The flexibility of the Chinese in dealing with interpersonal relations comes from the principle of "doing favours," which literally signifies one's honour to another. Favours done for others are often considered what may be termed "social investments," for which handsome returns are expected. The following Chinese proverbs clearly reveal this:

> If you honour me a linear foot, I should in return honour you ten feet.
> A horse received must be returned by an ox; a case of presents received is
> to be acknowledged by a case of presents in return.

Almost every Chinese is brought up to be highly conscious of "doing favours" and to practise it heartily but not in an immediate and hasty manner. They believe that the reciprocity of doing favours between man and man should be as certain as a cause-and-effect relationship. It should be continuous so that affinity for each other is well established.

The application of the principle of "doing favours" has a tremendous influence on social, as well as business, behaviour. It maintains relations among Chinese people by the presentation of gifts, which they regard as a form of *Li* — propriety. Small businessmen often believe that following the principle of "doing favours" is of utmost importance in making the business go smoothly so as to earn more money. They exchange their favours (help) when supplying goods or credits without signing any legal documents, and believe that the signing of any legal document will terminate the reciprocity of doing favours.

Face

Face is a concept of central importance because of its pervasive influence in interpersonal relations among Chinese. Hu (1944) examined 200 Chinese proverbs and classified face into two types, *lien* and *mien-tsu*:

Lien "represents the confidence of society in the integrity of ego's moral character, the loss of which makes it impossible for him to function properly within the community" (Hu, 1944). *Mien-tsu*, on the other hand, "stands for the kind of prestige that is emphasized ... a reputation achieved through getting on in life, through success and ostentation" (Hu, 1944).

Mien-tsu can be characterized in both quantitative and qualitative terms (Ho, 1972). The amount of *mien-tsu* a person has is a function of his social status. It varies according to the group with which he is interacting. A manager may have more *mien-tsu* before his subordinates, but not in a group of intellectuals. *Mien-tsu* may be claimed on a variety of grounds. It may be obtained either through personal qualities, or derived from non-personal characteristics, such as wealth, social connections and authority through personal efforts (Ho, 1972).

Mien-tsu can be lost or gained when there are changes that constitute a departure from the quality or quantity of one's claim. *Mien-tsu* can normally be gained by obtaining favourable comments from the interacting group or community, through exemplary behaviour, superior performance or knowledge, or enhancement of status, by formal promotion to higher office, etc. *Mien-tsu* may be lost when conduct or performance falls below the minimum acceptable standard, or when some essential requirements corresponding to one's social position are not satisfactorily met with. Since the standard and requirements are social expectations held by the group with whom he is interacting, the possibility of losing *mien-tsu* may not only come from his own actions or behaviour, but from how he is expected to behave or be treated by other members in the group. Chinese are always under strong constraint to meet the expectations of others so as to maintain their *mien-tsu*, as well as to reciprocate a due regard for the *mien-tsu* of others. The concern for *mien-tsu* exerts a mutual restrictive, even coercive, power on each member of the social network. Thus, the Chinese always try to avoid causing others to lose face, which is regarded as an aggressive act by those whose face has been discredited, but to protect others from losing it, which is an act of consideration.

Lien differs from *mien-tsu* in that *lien* is something that everyone is entitled to by virtue of his membership in society; it can only be lost through misconduct. Thus, it is meaningful to speak only of losing *lien*, but not of gaining it.

The loss of *lien* is more serious than that of *mien-tsu*. This is because when *mien-tsu* is lost, it can more easily be regained. But when *lien* is lost, an individual's integrity of character is cast in doubt, or even destroyed. For example, prostitutes and thieves are all people who renounce their concern for *lien*. The disregard for *lien* can therefore lead to a total transformation of one's social identity.

The significance of *lien* cannot be fully appreciated without realizing its close relationship with the concept of *ch'ih*, which, in the Chinese context has literally the same meaning as the word "shame" in English. King and Myers (1977) suggested that in Chinese culture, *lien* (face) is an incomplete concept. They demonstrated a dichotomy between the Chinese face-shame complex, in contrast with the Western sin-guilt complex. *Lien* implies the presence of *ch'ih*, which is one of the fundamental requirements of being human. Thus, Mencius declared that "a man without a sense of *ch'ih* (shame) is not a man" (see *Mencius*, one of the *Four Books*). Losing *lien* is experienced as *wu ch'ih* (without a sense of *ch'ih*). In cases of complete loss of *lien*, committing suicide may be a final resort to show the presence of *ch'ih*. Even in today's Chinese society, women often commit suicide to demonstrate their innocence following the misfortune of being raped.

Group Orientation

The concept of face is in conflict with individualism, which assumes the individual's well-being or interest. Hofstede (1980), a European scholar, used the term "collective" instead of "group oriented." He indicated that the Chinese, as well as Asians, are collectivistic, although his list of values was incomplete. The collectivistic nature of the Chinese is reflected in the Chinese family and kinship system (Hsu, 1968). Hsu argued that "the primary concern of a majority of Chinese was to protect and enhance their private kinship interests." He indicated that the Chinese regard the kinship system as a basis for relating to others. It means continuous and long-lasting human ties, which do not have clearly defined boundaries. For example, in many European countries, the parent-child relationship legally comes to an end when children reach the age of 18 or 21, after which parents lose their say over their children's marriages. The Western husband and wife also maintain individual privacy, which cannot be intruded on except by invitation. Efforts at discipline by grandparents and other adults in the family system are regarded as interference. Thus, there exist in the family system dividing lines which make the boundaries clearly defined, and human ties supersede each other rather than being additive (Hsu, 1968).

The Chinese tend to behave in the opposite way. When getting married, children still regard seeking approval from parents as mandatory and necessary (Salaff, 1981). Sometimes, decisions of parents are final. Sons and daughters after marriage are still liable to support the family (in terms of their parents or parents-in-law), even though they may live apart. Furthermore, they spend their leisure time preserving a viable relationship with parents and parents-in-law by a variety of activities, such as having tea in Chinese restaurants, or feasting at home on Saturday or Sunday evenings. Normally, parents live with one of their children (usually the eldest son) even after his/her marriage. Therefore, in contrast with Europeans or Americans, marriage for a Chinese means an increase of psycho-social involvement with his/her parents or parents-in-law. Marriage is not only an affair between the bride and the bridegroom, but an occasion for the family to reciprocate affection to friends and other members in the kinship system (Salaff, 1981).

Chinese may well be able to sacrifice themselves for benefits that largely accrue to a particular social unit, or even to society as a whole. In a poor Chinese family daughters and the eldest son may have to forgo their educational opportunities by going out to work so as to secure economically the whole family (Salaff, 1981). When making decisions, an individual Chinese should always take into account other members of the family, in contrast with the husband-wife joint decisions in the West. He/She is more motivated towards achieving the goal of the (extended) family or the group that he/she is affiliated with than with individualized self-fulfilment. Wilson and Pusey (1982) have confirmed this in the investigation of achievement motivation and small-business relationship patterns in Chinese society. They found that group orientation correlates more significantly with achievement motivation in the Chinese sample than in the American sample.

However, there is one thing worth mentioning. Chinese are only group oriented towards those social units with whom interactions have been established. They follow the appropriate social norms regardless of their own private views. But they appear to be quite suspicious and cold towards strangers with whom relationships have not been established.

According to the above discussion, it is to be expected that satisfaction with a product may not be derived solely from one's expectations towards, or disconfirmation with, the product, but from other members of the family. This is especially true in an extended family.

Potential Marketing Implications for Relational Orientation

The values of interdependence and face are particularly meaningful to the study of gift-giving behaviour. To the Chinese, gift giving is one of the ways to build up relationships with friends. There are festivals in the Chinese Lunar calendar, such as the Chinese New Year, the mid-autumn Festival and the Dragon Boat Festival, when gifts are presented to friends or superiors. Differing from Western societies, there are certain norms that Chinese obey when giving gifts. For example, gifts presented should be expensive enough to match the income of the givers, so that they are giving face to those who receive their gifts, and that they gain face at the same time because they are thought of as being sincere. For friends, gifts of comparable or even higher value should be returned as soon as possible. In marketing products that can be regarded as gifts, the packaging of these products is extremely important. They should be packed prestigiously and beautifully in red, which means happiness and good luck, and priced at a level to match their packaging. When such products are launched by well-known firms or manufacturers, the prices can be set higher than competitors' as the Chinese believe in established brands and companies.

From a different angle, the concept of interdependence is important for Western executives working in Chinese society. They should be reminded that off-duty personal behaviour, through which the relationship with the community is built, is highly important to the firm's image and its effectiveness.

Several aspects of the value of group orientation are noteworthy in marketing, too. First, because the Chinese are strongly collective may imply that informal channels of communications are important in Chinese society, compared with those in the U.K. Chinese consumers tend to rely more on word-of-mouth communication. Because of the high contact rate among group members, communications among Chinese consumers for a given product idea may be diffused very quickly. Furthermore, given that informal channels of communication carry both facts and rumours, Chinese consumers are much more likely to rely on, and make use of, the rumour moiety of the informal channel, rather than what is actually claimed for the product officially (Kindle, 1985).

Second, Chinese consumers tend to be more brand loyal than their counterparts in the West. Chinese consumers often endeavour to conform to group norms and therefore tend to purchase the same brand or product other members of the group recommend. In other words, if a reference group has established a product as the normative standard, Chinese consumers are not likely to deviate from the accepted product on their own by switching to a competitive product.

Third, since Chinese are only group oriented towards social units with which close interactions have been established, consumers tend to confine their activities to a small social circle. Hence, they are members of a small number of reference groups. This may be one of the reasons that mass advertising through formal channels (e.g., television) is of limited potential for attracting attention when using reference groups, which are often small in size. In Hong Kong, Winston, an American cigarette brand, has been suffering from a continuous decline in sales because of improper use of reference groups in its advertisements.

Fourth, the concept of the extended family is important to advertisements of family products. Unlike consumers in Western societies, the Chinese concept of family is one of the extended family, which includes even distant relatives. Therefore, if an advertisement, which attempts to persuade consumers to buy a family product, includes only husband, wife and children, it does not really show a picture of a family at all. Other members of the extended family, such as grandfather and grandmother, should be included to make the advertisement more persuasive.

Time Dimension

Past-Time Orientation

Klukhohn and Strodbeck (1961) noted that the Chinese have a strong preference for past-time orientation:

> Historical China was a society which gave first-order preference to the past-time orientation. Ancestor worship and a strong family tradition were both expressions of this preference. So also was the Chinese attitude that nothing new ever happened in the present or would happen in the future; it had all happened before in the far distant Past.

Van Oort (1970) believed that Chinese people were very history-minded:

> A second culture value is the principle of respect for the past, or almost veneration of history. If there is one people in the world that is history-minded, it is certainly the Chinese people.

He did not attempt to explain why it was, but Burkhardt (1953) clearly stated:

China has always been a conservative country ... which held to the belief that what was good for their forefathers, and had been tested by countless generations, was sacrilege to tamper with.

No doubt, the Chinese have a strong admiration of their culture, which has a history of thousands of years. The following proverb clearly depicts the feeling of most Chinese: "Among the three unfilial duties, to have no heir is the greatest." There are three reasons why having no heir is unfilial. Firstly, it is necessary to have an heir to extend the biological life of parents and ancestors. To carry this duty is not difficult, but the most fundamental. Secondly, it is necessary to pass down the Chinese culture to the next generation. To do so, parents have to provide the best education they can for their children. The most important thing is that parents should have a deep knowledge of the Chinese culture. Thirdly, it is necessary to fulfil the hopes that parents or ancestors have failed as yet to accomplish (Yang, 1979).

The salient ethnological fact about Chinese culture is that it is, and always has been, based fundamentally and predominantly on agriculture, which provided the economic margin of security for the people. In contrast with pastoral peoples, the Chinese were prone to be more risk averse and less innovative because, in order to secure a stable or increased food supply, it seemed safer for them to follow the traditional methods which had been proven workable for thousands of years.

Continuity

The Chinese believe that interrelations with things and others are continuous. Once a relation is established, it can hardly be broken. Hence, the Chinese proverb: "If you have been my teacher for a day, I will treat you like my father for ever."

Potential Marketing Implications for Time Orientation

The values of past-time orientation and continuity also imply that the Chinese tend to have great brand loyalty. Unless the product or brand being used proves very unsatisfactory, they are not likely to switch to purchasing other brands or products. This point of view is also shared by Crow (1937), who pointed out that the Chinese are "the world's most loyal customers," with a high degree of brand consciousness. Furthermore, Chinese consumers, especially married ones, are likely to consider opinions, values and influences of deceased relatives and respected figures in their current consumption choice. Attention should be paid from time to time to these opinions and values when producing advertising copy.

Activity Orientation

As for the activity orientation of the Chinese, the evidence is conflicting. As mentioned earlier, the Chinese have been greatly influenced by the doctrine of the Way, which emphasized the "being" orientation. However, the Chinese have found themselves conforming to behaviour according to *Li* (propriety), which denotes a system of semi-formal norms of behaviour. Jarvie and Agassi (1969) gave a description for the predominance of this value orientation:

> The highest value in China is to live properly, which particularly concerns being polite and obeying the rules; and this makes even the social aspect of personal transaction of supreme importance. In other words, in traditional China, being considerate to others is equated with ... strict observance of the accepted code. To observe the code is to be human; to forget it is to become barbarian.

However, Jarvie and Agassi did not mention the doctrine of the Mean which has been the most important Chinese cultural value (Chu, 1979). The Mean, according to Confucius, was referred to as "being without inclination to either side" (Legge, 1960). Confucius did not believe in suppression of passions and impulses, but in regulation of them so as to achieve internal harmony. The Chinese, therefore, are taught not to let primitive passions and impulses be completely repressed or unrestrictedly satisfied. To explain what is meant by the Mean, Confucius declared:

> The gentleman does what is proper to the station in which he is; he does not desire to go beyond this. In a position of wealth and honour, he does what is proper to a position of wealth and honour. In a poor and low position, he does what is proper to a poor and low position ... In a low situation, he does not court the favour of his superiors. He rectifies himself, and seeks for nothing from others so that he has no

dissatisfactions. He does not murmur against Heaven, nor grumble against men. ("The Doctrine of the Mean, XV," Legge, 1960).

Thus, a concern for the Mean leads to a high degree of moral self-control or self-regulation, at least publicly, for the individual Chinese. His family members or intimate friends are the only channel to whom to express his inner feelings. Hchu and Yang (1972) also supported this point of view in their study on the individual modernity and psychogenic needs of Chinese college students. It was found that more socially-oriented Chinese students tended to blame or punish themselves when reacting to frustration. In a similar vein, Yang (1981) also found that traditional Chinese were more cautious and more conforming in verbalizing their responses. In retrospect, China has never been an aggressive country in world history. Traditional Chinese were depicted as non-military and self-contented people (La Barre, 1948; Russell, 1922). This can be useful in explaining why, today, only on rare occasions would one see a Chinese lose control and become angry, insulting or threatening in public (Kindle, 1982).

Potential Marketing Implications for Activity Orientation

One of the potential marketing implications for the value of activity orientation concerns complaining behaviour. As previously mentioned, Chinese tend not to take public stands, such as complaining to manufacturers, companies or to consumer councils when they encounter unsatisfactory products or services. One of the explanations is that they regard taking public action as something very serious. Careful consideration is given before deciding whether a public action is the proper way to solve the problem concerned. Legal action, which is regarded as extreme behaviour, is normally not considered at all. Marketing managers who wish to obtain data on the satisfaction/dissatisfaction of Chinese consumers should play a more active role, rather than waiting for the consumer to feed back.

The doctrine of the Mean may influence Chinese consumers' attitude to adopting new products. Chinese consumers are slow to accept new fashions or technology, and resist marketing innovations involving complicated features. Of course, it may be because Chinese are more risk averse, as previously mentioned, or because they regard adopting or using a new product as an extreme behaviour which is not proper in their position.

Summary

This chapter has attempted to investigate the underlying dimensions of Chinese cultural values, in terms of Kluckhohn and Strodbeck's classification, and their potential marketing implications. In recent years, Western thought and ideology have played an important part in the cultural changes of many Chinese societies, especially in Taiwan, Hong Kong and Singapore. It seems that it is time to investigate the expected relationships between Chinese cultural values and other determinants of consumer behaviour. Furthermore, Chinese cultural values can also be used as an effective basis for market segmentation (Yau, 1986), and help in understanding whether theories of consumer behaviour, which were built on Western premises, can be transplanted to Eastern cultures.

7

Changing Consumer Value
in a New Business Environment*

Stephen Shek-lam Lau

Introduction

China has gone through different stages in its historical development. After overthrowing the Manchus in 1911, the Republic of China led by the Nationalists was set up until it was taken over by the Communists in 1949. Due to constant internal and external conflicts, the economy of China was in a state of total collapse. The livelihood of the Chinese people in general was poor. Such a hardship of life continued and further degenerated during the Cultural Revolution up until the 1970s. Any economic breakthrough at that time was not possible owing to the political isolation by the West. The breakthrough came about when diplomatic relationship was reestablished with the United States in 1972 and the open-door policy was implemented in 1979. There have been drastic changes in China since its economic reform began. Since 1979, China has shown enormous social and economic developments. The Special Economic Zones (SEZs) are examples of economic success, industrialization and modernization.

Since the beginning of economic reform, the economy of the People's Republic of China has improved significantly. In less than a decade, the per

---

* An earlier version of this chapter appeared in Antonio and Steele, 1996.

capita Gross Domestic Product (GDP), reached US$2,660 and Gross National Product (GNP) US$540. The steady GDP growth in China is 9.8%, the highest in the world. There has been substantial GNP gains since 1991, from 2% in 1990 to 10% in 1991 and 15% in 1992. Growth of economy has increased at an annual rate of 11.5%. In the first six months of 1992, foreign investment figures show a 130% increase (US$3.358 billion) compared with the same period of 1991. Also in the first half of 1992, the economy is estimated to have notched up 12% growth, industrial production 18% increase and retail sales up 14%. With these encouraging results, government policies were revised to attract more investments. In June 1992, China granted the Yangtze River basin the rights to use preferential policies to attract more foreign investments. These rights were previously limited to Special Economic Zones (SEZs).

If the economy continues to grow at this speed, soon the People's Republic of China will be able to compare favourably with its Asian partners in terms of both national economy and the standard of living. Some economists even predicted China to become the fifth dragon. At present, the economy of the Newly Industrialized Countries (NICs) is impressive, the 1995 per capita GDP in Hong Kong is US$23,080, Singapore $21,493, Taiwan $13,235 and South Korea $10,534. The GDP growth is 4.2%, 9.1%, 6.0% and 6.8% for Hong Kong, Singapore, Taiwan and South Korea respectively. The per capita GNP of Singapore is US$26,400, Hong Kong US$23,200, Taiwan US$12,265 and South Korea US$10,076. With reference to the yardstick of nominal per capita GNP, Hong Kong and Singapore are among the richest countries. They are comparable to the United States, France, Germany and Great Britain. Although China is still far behind the NICs in terms of per capita GNP, in one or two decades, the economic situation of China will be at par with the NICs. The economic development of Taiwan is a very good example. In 1962, Taiwan's per capita GNP was only US$162. After 30 years, it reached the significant amount of US$12,265, surpassing many countries in the West. Under this favourable environment, China will definitely change into a different world. It is the purpose of this chapter to indicate the new elements emerging from the Old World.

Traditional Value System

Before the Communists took over China in 1949, traditional family values, especially those of a Confucian persuasion, were the sole determinant of family lives and individual behaviours. Thus, we have the prevalent Chinese character of a collective identity by emphasizing blood ties and family relationships, i.e., a lineage system by referring to blood or affinity. Loyalty to one's family group and ancestors is deemed important. Since the traditional family structure is based solely on patrilineal and patrilocal factors, the male is de facto the more authoritative and powerful between the two sexes. Subsequently, the female has to adopt a subordinate role, in terms of authority, rights of inheritance, rights to be educated or even rights to work. This characteristic of male dominance creates the inequality of sexes, and finally becomes the norm in all spheres. In the practice of child-bearing, for example, the family would normally opt for a son rather than a daughter. The result will not only give them all the advantages of being a male in this patriarchal society but also satisfy the value of filial piety towards the ancestors, which is fulfilled by producing a male descendent to continue the lineage line.[1]

For a long time, the Chinese is based on an agrarian economy relying on farming products for daily needs. The uncertainty of production creates an attitude of thrift. The traditional Chinese becomes cautious in spending, both in terms of food consumption and other expenses. The unending insecurity in the possession of material goods and wealth forces the Chinese to be diligent in their daily activities. Diligence and thrift is the general mentality of the traditional Chinese, and such an attitude is important for safeguarding the life and daily necessities of each individual member. A well-structured family economy provides a base for the proper continuation of "Chinese familism." Familism gives rise to many of the Chinese national characteristics, e.g., filial piety and being conservative, authoritative, dependent, obedient, courteous, modest, prudent, diligent, thrifty, patient, law-abiding, etc. (*Far Eastern Economic Review*, 1993)

Communist Social Values

After the Communist Party took over China in 1949, a socialist value system and Chairman Mao's ethical teachings were introduced to replace the traditional ones. The propaganda of "new man and new earth" is used frequently in the building up of Chinese socialism. Since the whole socialist principle is basically antagonistic towards familism, the practice of inequality is challenged and totally abolished. It emphasizes the horizontal social structure rather than the hierarchical Confucian model. Equality among the sexes is widely enforced in all spheres; it is exemplified by the equality in work and pay and the status of women in society is guaranteed. The traditional value of patriarchy is further weakened by the introduction of the one-child policy. This policy aims not only at controlling population growth but also at abolishing the prevalent mentality of filial piety. The Communist Party reiterates again and again the necessity of individual sacrifice towards the party and the nation rather than the family. The ideal of family obligation and family ties are undermined. The extreme of such a belief is demonstrated by the Cultural Revolution from 1966 to 1976. Destruction was made in both social and the cultural dimensions. Orientation of life is totally lost. During our recent interviews with the Chinese, we always try to find out remnants of the communist ideal as well as the traditional ones so that the new value systems will be contrasted and compared with the older ones.

In this chapter, we shall use three research surveys done in China between 1993 to 1995. The 1993 project was on the changing family values in Shanghai; in 1994, we made a comparative study of three cities (Beijing, Shanghai and Guangzhou), concentrating on the family relationships between parents and children. The status of women in Beijing was our third project in 1995. The data of these three projects will be used to present a picture of China today. It is hoped that the behaviour and mentality of the present-day Chinese can be clearly depicted.

Background of the Present-Day Mainland Chinese

Profession and Education

If we use our survey data to describe the distribution of professions in China, we can see that quite a high percentage, 40.6%, of Shanghaiese belong to the category of labourer such as manufacturing, construction and transportation sectors, compared to 28.7% in Beijing and 27.4% in Guangzhou. The commercial category comes second; there are 18.1%, 17.6% and 16.0% in Guangzhou, Shanghai and Beijing respectively. In Guangzhou, we can find more males working in the commercial and labour industries than in the service industry and the education field, with the latter two having a higher percentage of females. There are more males than females in the work force both in Beijing and in Shanghai except for the service industry in Shanghai. Nevertheless, the working opportunity for females in China is not lacking. Nearly half of the people belong to the state enterprises, 52.9% in Shanghai, 49.2% in Beijing and 45.8% in Guangzhou. 30.5% in Shanghai and 23.5% in Beijing are workers whereas there is only 15.2% in Guangzhou. The highest percentage, 21.3%, of people in Guangzhou are in administrative jobs followed by 19.8% as clerks and sales personnel. The education standard in Guangzhou is relatively higher than that in Shanghai and Beijing, 32.5% finished tertiary education and 30.9% finished high school. In Beijing and Shanghai, only 17.2% and 17.8% respectively are graduates and 27.4% in Beijing and 27.5% in Shanghai are high school leavers. As the new economic structure begins to take shape, employment is shifting from the concentration in factory work to commerce and office administration. The demand for educated professionals has encouraged people to attain higher education standards. This can be seen clearly in Guangzhou.

Income

People in China earn much more now than they did before the implementation of the open-door policy, when the majority of household earnings were less than RMB200 per month. In 1993, our survey in Shanghai recorded RMB952. The result of our 1993 Shanghai survey reveals that 49.8% of families admitted having a substantial gain in their earnings compared with five years ago (1988). 82.6% of the families believed that the improvement is mainly due to better opportunities today than before (Lau and Kwok, 1994). The income increase in 1995 is even more significant.

When we look at the 1995 individual income, we can observe that people in Beijing earn relatively less than people in Shanghai and Guangzhou. In Beijing, 24.7% earn between RMB301 and RMB450 and 20.6% between RMB451 and RMB600. Only 6.6% have an income of over RMB1,001. In Shanghai, 21.9% earn between RMB751 and RMB1,000, 19.2% RMB451 and RMB600, and 13%, which doubles that in Beijing, over RMB1,001. The best income is found in Guangzhou, 29.2% earn RMB751 to RMB1,000 and 20% earn RMB1,001 and above. The average individual income for Beijing, Shanghai and Guangzhou is RMB521, RMB676, and RMB805, respectively. The average individual income in these three cities is RMB669. Although individual income has increased significantly, one recent national survey launched by the People's University shows that 65% of the workers wish to increase their income (*Economic Daily*, 1 July 1996).

As far as family income is concerned, 26.5% in Beijing earn RMB801 to RMB1,200, 20.1% RMB401 to RMB800 and 18.1% RMB1,201 to RMB1,600; only 9.4% earn RMB2,401 and above. In Shanghai, 22.2% earn RMB2,401 and above, 20% RMB801 to RMB1,200 and 19.3% RMB1,201 to RMB1,600. The family income is much higher in Shanghai than in Beijing. The highest income is in fact in Guangzhou, 30% earn above RMB2,401, 20% RMB1,201 to RMB1,600 and 18.4% have an income of RMB1,601 to RMB2,000. The family income in Guangzhou is three times as much as in Beijing. The average family income for Beijing, Shanghai and Guangzhou is RMB1,397, RMB1,851 and RMB2,074 respectively. The average household income in these three cities is RMB1,789. The difference in earning corresponds to the degree of development in Beijing, Shanghai and Guangzhou. Compared with her Asian partners, the present earnings of the Chinese are insignificant. But if we take into account the fact that the expenses of the Chinese families on rental, transportation, water and electricity are still subsidized by the government, the cash availability is abundant. Therefore, the buying power of Chinese citizens is higher than that of those in the other Asian countries.

Present Socioeconomic Situation

After the "opening up" of China, the influx of foreign capital has given rise to a vast number of private and joint-venture enterprises on the mainland. In 1992, there are altogether 130,000 firms with foreign investment, producing about 25% of China's export and 9% of the gross value of industrial output (Wong and Mok, 1995). In 1994, foreign investment in China amounted to US$33.7 billion (Tsang and Ma, 1995). In addition to multinational and joint-venture companies, some 15,470,000 households were registered as private businesses in 1992 (Li, 1994). If we include the unregistered small family enterprises, the number can hardly be estimated. Modern marketing techniques lead to the rebirth of the advertising industry. The number of advertising agencies increased from 10 state-run agencies to 7,000 mostly non-state-run agencies in 1988. Advertisements influenced directly the consumption habits of the Chinese (Sklair, 1995; Lull and Sun, 1988; Rice and Lu, 1988; Schell, 1987, 1988; Huang et al., 1992).

Table 1

Social Environment of the NICs

	Pop. (m.)	Infant Mortality per 1,000	Life expec- tancy	Literacy Rate %	People per TV	People per Tel.	Pop. Growth %
Singapore	3.1	4	76	91.6	2.6	2.0	2.0
Hong Kong	6.3	5	78	91.2	3.0	1.5	2.1
Taiwan	21.5	4	75	93.2	3.1	2.4	1.0
South Korea	45.2	8	72	97.4	3.4	2.3	0.9
China	1,215.5	31	71	80.0	6.7	36.4	1.2

From the figures shown in Table 1, we can observe that the social environment is very similar among the Newly Industrialized Countries. The situation in China is not too dramatic even with the immense population size and relatively lateness in the economic development. One important reason is that prior to the open-door policy, products supplied on the market were limited or even non-existent. This is due to the fact that economic activities were labelled as capitalistic, therefore they were totally absent in China during and after the Cultural Revolution. Consequently, an enormous amount of savings has been accumulated. According to estimation, "savings in banks amounted to some RMB1.05 trillion (US$194.5 billion) as of July 1992" (*Asian Business*, November 1992). The figure from the State Statistical Bureau is RMB1.2 trillion (*Far Eastern Economic Review*, 23 April 1992). In October 1995, The *China Daily* reported that Chinese individuals saved RMB2.68 trillion. Individual bank deposits continue to grow, the first quarter of 1996 reported RMB3.33 trillion. (*Wall Street Journal*, 13 July 1996). Since there is no shortage of money supply, it is not difficult to ameliorate the living standard of the people. After the economic reform, whenever there are products available on the market, people will not hesitate to acquire them. In recent years, demand is always higher than supply in the market. Thus, inflation went up as high as 27% in 1994. Parsons (1993) believed that China is in its third wave of consumer buying, from the buying of bicycles, watches and sewing machines to refrigerators, TV sets and washing machines, followed with air-conditioners, telephones, video-cameras and modern toilets. If economic stability continues, the third wave may cumulate in the mass buying of private cars by the end of the millennium (Parsons, 1993). In 1995, 0.45 million cars were sold, and it is estimated that the number will go up to 1.2 million in the year 2000 (*Time*, 16 October 1995). Driving schools have emerged to be important enterprises, and at present, there are more than 3,000 such schools all over China. There are around 30 million Chinese possessing a driving licence. The driving licence enables them to drive their own cars or become professional drivers. As a matter of fact, transportation personnel have increased significantly in recent years.

The increase in working opportunities and earnings improved the economic situation of the younger generation, thus the income gap between the two generations disappeared. The market economy has broken down the privilege of occupational prestige and income of the older generation as in previous years. According to our survey, the majority of married couples with children do not receive any financial support from their parents, 66.4% in Beijing, 74.5% in Shanghai and 81.8% in Guangzhou. Only 24.5%, 17.3% and 15.2% in Beijing, Shanghai and Guangzhou respectively receive money occasionally from their parents. There is a dramatic decrease when compared with the 39% claimed by the 1985 five-city survey (Tsui, 1989; Gao, 1986). The family becomes more self-supportive with improvement in the economic situation. As we have observed, Guangzhou is one of the richest cities in China; it is not astonishing to find that merely 3% rely on parents for financial support. We therefore believe that intergenerational inequalities as claimed by Davis-Friedmann (1983) have diminished by the introduction of the market economy. The younger generation becomes more self-supportive financially, and thus they are more independent minded in terms of both attitudes to life and spending on daily necessities.

If this new economic system continues, many unwanted consequences will follow: inflation, high cost of living, bankruptcy of state enterprises, unemployment as well as consumerism. All these will create more problems to the older generation than the younger ones as savings or pension benefits of the elderly people could no longer cope with the rising inflation and cost of living. It is possible that in future more and more elderly people will rely upon their children for support. Will filial piety be totally abandoned if the people can no longer cope with the ever-increasing cost of living or rising attitude of consumerism? This unfortunate situation could be tempered if the pension scheme in China was well structured, but this does not seem to be the case, and so children might have to take up the responsibility of old age support. However, the one-child policy in China makes the practice of filial piety more difficult, if not impossible. In future, one married couple would have to take care of four old people. As there are more consumer goods and entertainments on the market, it becomes more difficult to fulfil the duty of filial piety if one has to choose between personal satisfaction and family obligations. Guangzhou is a good example, only 36% said that they always support their parents versus 52.4% in Shanghai and 60.6% in Beijing. It is probable that traditional family values of intergenerational dependency would be disrupted more easily during economic progress. Consumerism is the most serious cause. Let us see the changing consumer habits.

Consumption Habits

The increasing incomes in China have created a new group of consumers who have different attitudes and life styles than those on low incomes. In China, "Retail sales of consumer goods for October 1992 were US$14.7 billion, up 18.1% for the same period a year ago. And a growing number of these purchases were of foreign brands" (*Public Relations Journal*, July 1993). Admiration for foreign brands is so strong that even local Chinese products have to be labelled by Philips, Sanyo, Mitsubishi, etc. (*Economic Daily*, 24 July 1996). According to our 1993 survey in Shanghai, people tend to spend more money on personal items like food, clothing, entertainment, savings and, especially, investment, which was unbelievable a decade ago. This is not astonishing if the supply and range of products is so abundant and people will definitely spend more money to upgrade the quality of life (Lau, 1996). This relatively new mentality of consumerism has a significant impact on traditional value systems. Guangzhou is a good example with comfort of life taking priority at the expense of filial responsibility.

From our surveys, an analysis of the variation in spending habits between 1988 and 1993 showed that food was the major expense in 1988 and this remained the case in 1993. The only significant decrease was in the categories of executive/professional and entrepreneur, 6.3% and 6.7% respectively (Table 2). In particular for executive/professional, spending on clothing, entertainment, investment and savings shows a significant increase. Spending in order of priority is: clothing, investment, saving and entertainment. On clothing, the executive/professional increase in proportion of income spent was 2.4% from 1988 to 1993, which represents an increase from 11.8% to 14.2% of total expenditure. This could be explained

Table 2
Spending Habits According to Professions

	Professional Executive		Clerks/Party Officials/ Technicians/ Teachers		Entrepreneur		Sales/ Servicing		Unemployed Pensioner Housewife Student/Other	
	1988 %	1993 %	1988 %	1993 %	1988 %	1993 %	1988 %	1993 %	1988 %	1993 %
Housing	3.7	4.0	4.7	4.1	2.7	3.8	3.5	3.8	2.5	3.4
Food	40.8	34.6	34.9	33.3	32.9	26.2	34.7	32.3	45.0	41.1
Clothing	11.8	14.2	14.2	12.7	14.1	14.0	17.7	17.4	12.0	13.3
Entertainment	3.8	5.4	4.0	4.5	6.3	4.1	6.1	6.1	3.8	4.8
Child-caring	18.7	15.7	17.5	14.8	16.2	12.0	14.4	14.3	11.8	11.9
Cosmetics	1.1	1.5	1.9	2.3	1.3	0.9	3.1	12.9	1.4	1.8
Personal development	3.7	2.9	4.5	3.2	0.8	0.6	5.2	3.9	3.8	1.8
Saving	14.8	17.0	16.5	20.8	19.3	12.3	13.8	15.2	18.5	3.4
Investment	1.6	5.8	1.8	4.1	7.4	26.1	1.7	4.1	1.0	18.5

by the professional needs of this category including frequent contact with the outside world since the economic reform, which tempts the professional to dress like their foreign partners.

As for the share of earning devoted to investment, the most outstanding is in the entrepreneur category which shows a triple increase, i.e., from 7.4% to 26.1%, compared with savings, food, child care and entertainment which decreased by 7.0%, 6.7%, 4.2% and 2.2%, respectively. This is due to investment opportunities, e.g., stocks, private business, which were absent for a long time. People use this new economic environment to increase wealth by investing in opportunities showing higher returns. Therefore, it is not surprising to find a net increase of 18.8%. No other category can be compared with the entrepreneur in this aspect. However, we still found a 4.2% increase in the professional/executive and 2.3% in technician/clerk categories. As for the share of earnings devoted to saving, entrepreneur is the only category to decrease, while others either remain stable or registered between 1.5% increase for sales/servicing industry and 4.4% for clerks/technicians/teachers/party officials.

It is worth noting that spending on child care registered a drastic decrease across the board, except for the sales/servicing category, which remains stable. One reasonable explanation is that people have become richer and family expenses more diversified, therefore income and expenditure have to be better planned and regulated. Child-caring expenses have to be trimmed down in order to meet other expenses.

Spending Habits According to Education

Responses showed the importance of savings, which registered an increase across all three categories of education level. It was the second major area of income alteration in 1993 after food. As for investment, similar progress was registered in 1993, but with the highest increase directly linked to the level of education, i.e., university/post-secondary + 3.5%, secondary/ junior high + 2.1%, and lastly for primary + 0.2% (Table 3). It is possible that education lessens the traditional fear of investment risks and makes people realize that investment can, on the one hand, protect the value of money against inflation and, on the other, be viewed as proper economic activity. Such an accepted view of investment by the highly educated shows clearly that a new mentality towards money and economic exchange is budding in China.

Table 3
Education Levels and Spending Habits

	University/ Post-Secondary		Secondary/ Junior High		Primary/ No Education	
	1988 %	1993 %	1988 %	1993 %	1988 %	1993 %
Housing	3.7	4.0	3.1	3.5	3.8	4.8
Food	39.2	35.7	40.6	36.9	49.1	45.6
Clothing	14.7	13.9	12.6	13.6	11.8	13.3
Entertainment	5.7	6.6	3.8	4.6	1.3	1.6
Child-caring	14.9	12.5	15.2	14.4	8.2	6.2
Cosmetics	2.0	2.3	1.5	1.9	1.1	1.0
Personal development	6.6	5.1	3,4	2.7	0.3	0.7
Saving	12.1	15.4	18.1	18.7	23.8	25.9
Investment	1.2	4.7	1.7	3.8	0.6	0.8

However, this same mentality does not exist in the least educated category since these people spend only 0.8% on investment versus savings. This might be due to job security, opportunity of earning and a conservative view on investment. Generally, they believe that saving is more secure than investment. Such thinking is understandable because of parents' responsibility towards their children in providing money for wedding expenses for sons, which involves an amount of twenty to thirty thousand yuan, or paying the child care expenses of grandchildren. Thus, they hesitate to take risks on investment.[2] Although the medium term category of spending, e.g., saving and investment, remains the dominant category among lower levels of education or one fourth of their total earning (26.7%), the highest level of education category is the one which registered the highest increase in medium term spending, i.e., one fifth of their total earning (20.1%), an increase of 6.73%.

Changing Attitudes

The new life styles and consumerism have accelerated young people's tendency to develop individualistic attitudes, replacing both the traditional and the new social values, which were destroyed by the Cultural

Revolution. Such individualistic attitudes are shown by "increased apathy in regard to political and public affairs and a growing interest in material comfort and individual conjugal units." A recent survey showed that 68.3% of workers and employers thought the most important change during the economic reform starting in 1979 was a desire to "earn as much money as possible by working hard so as to modernize family life," which means to "buy modern household appliances and raise living standards." (Tsui, 1989) In another survey of 247 young people, it was reported "that 44.8% had no interest and little confidence in current social and economic reform.... In general, the attitude concerning the purpose of living ... was to create a better material life for oneself and one's conjugal family, and try to do something good for others and society as well.... This value orientation was different not only from the unselfish, collectivist orientation emphasized by the Communist Party, but also from the traditional familism, which called for self-sacrifice for parents and ancestors." The ideal of total devotion to the family and the state is being replaced by individualism. A survey in Beijing also found that "80 per cent of those aged 15 to 25 wanted to set up financially independent families and maintain some physical distance from the parents." (Tsui, 1989) It is evident that present-day Chinese have become more individualistic, independent, free from elders' supervision and devotion to traditional familism. Individualism will definitely disrupt the harmonious relationship between generations. In the following sections, we shall describe family relationships.

Pension Scheme

Entering the 21st century, the population of senior citizens will increase drastically, which is mainly due to the decreasing trend of birth and death rates. According to one study, in the year 2040, the age group of 65 and above will reach 12.5% to 15.6% of the whole population. Some scholars even estimated that the figure would reach up to 20%. Recently, the Bureau of National Statistics estimated that 9.8% of the whole population would be over 60 years of age at the end of 1994. Facing such a large number of old people, special attention should be given to social problems brought about by this alarming increase of old-age population, among which life after retirement is definitely an important issue.

The social welfare towards the aged mainly includes the guarantee of their income as well as medical care. The present Chinese pension scheme includes free medical care and a monthly pension of 70–80% of the basic salary. As a matter of fact, the basic salary does not include various allowances, consequently many of their incomes could remain to be two-thirds of what they previously earned. Such an amount is ample for having a basic living, especially when continuing to occupy housing from their work units. High inflation rate is the only factor that could drastically decrease the living standard of retired people. For example, in September 1994, the annual inflation rate reached 27%, and the serious impact on the retire can be easily imagined. Moreover, the pension scheme in China is restricted mainly to those living in the city working for government bureaux, party units, education, cultural and scientific institutions, and those in the light industry and handicraft industries making up to 26% of the total labour force. The pension of all private enterprises will be taken care of by the employers. However, most of the pension schemes of the non-government sectors do not include medical care. According to information in 1981, only 45% or 8 million out of 18 million retirees are eligible for pensions. In the 1984 *Beijing Review* it was pointed out that the number of citizens enjoying a pension scheme reached 13 million in 1983. At present, the Chinese government is revising the social security system.

Those who have neither income nor pension are eligible to seek help from the community which provides such benefits as food, clothing, medical care, housing and funeral expenses. Four per cent of old people received such community service in 1984. Old people who have only a meagre pension or even none at all will have no choice but to rely upon the family as the most important source of support. According to Liu and Hong, 75% to 84% of the old people live with younger generations. Again, if we take the 1985 five-city survey, the three-generation family from 1950 to 1982 remains at 20%. The possible answers to this phenomenon are the tradition of filial piety in the Chinese culture as well as the help that the old people can contribute at home, e.g., child-caring and doing household chores. There seems to be no drastic change of the three-generation family in today's China. According to our 1995 survey of three Chinese cities, the highest percentage is 39.2 in Beijing, with 29.1% in Shanghai and 25.4% in Guangzhou. The increased percentage is a sign of aged parents relying on their children for financial support. This living arrangement can temporarily solve the problem of the old people. With the ever increasing standard of living, accompanied by high inflation, the present amount of pension received is insufficient to make ends meet, thus the burden will definitely fall upon the younger generations. Tensions and later conflicts will naturally result.

Living Arrangements

Family Type

At present, the majority family type in the cosmopolitan areas is the two-generation family. According to our recent survey data of three Chinese cities (Lau and Kwok, 1995), the nuclear family remains the highest in percentage, 63.7% in Guangzhou, 60.3% in Shanghai and only 49.6% in Beijing. The majority of households have 3 people, more than 20% of these families have 4 people. These correspond closely with the 4th National Census Data of the Chinese Statistical Bureau: 65.7% in 1990 are two-generation families. Thus, it is not uncommon in recent years to see Chinese sociologists use the term "nuclear family" to designate the contemporary Chinese family structure. They believe that both industrialization of the cities and the improved economic situation of peasants will necessarily lead to an upsurge of nuclear families as in the West. (Liu, 1991; Pun, 1991). Traditional family values are replaced by an utilitarian exchange value between members.

Following the common practice in China, most of the unmarried children are living with their parents, 90%, 91.8% and 90.7% in Beijing, Shanghai and Guangzhou respectively. In normal circumstances, they move away from their parents after they get married, but this is not always the case. We have 43.5%, 43.4% and 27.1% for married without children versus 41.5%, 38.7% and 23.6% for married with children in Beijing, Shanghai and Guangzhou respectively still living with their parents (Table 4). One of the main reasons is the long waiting time for allocation of housing from their work units. It depends on availability and seniority. As an interim measure, they will stay with their parents until their own quarters are allocated.

Even if it is not due to the problem of allocation of quarters, very often young couples need their parents' assistance in taking care of the new baby, and so larger family unit is formed. Our survey figures show that 34.3% in Beijing, 23.6% in Shanghai and 16.5% in Guangzhou responded that parents are the ones actually responsible for child care even though many of the young parents expressed the intention of taking care of their own

Table 4
Relationship between Parents and Children

| | | Single | | | | | |
| | | Beijing | | Shanghai | | Guangzhou | |
		f	%	f	%	f	%
Living with parents	Yes	443	90.0	459	91.8	451	90.7
	No	49	10.0	41	8.2	46	9.3
Contact with parents	Frequently	434	90.8	455	91.5	434	88.6
	Sometimes	40	8.4	42	8.5	53	10.8
	Never	4	0.8	—	—	3	0.6
Parents give me money	Frequently	217	46.2	209	41.9	110	22.3
	Sometimes	152	32.3	106	21.2	191	38.7
	Never	101	21.5	184	36.9	193	39.1
Parents taking care of me	Yes	316	66.8	378	76.2	317	64.7
	No	157	33.2	118	23.8	173	35.3

| | | Married without Children | | | | | |
| | | Beijing | | Shanghai | | Guangzhou | |
		f	%	f	%	f	%
Living with parents	Yes	174	43.5	186	43.4	105	27.1
	No	226	56.5	243	56.6	283	72.9
Contact with parents	Frequently	265	69.7	301	70.7	203	52.7
	Sometimes	105	27.6	116	27.2	166	43.1
	Never	10	2.6	9	2.1	16	4.2
Parents give me money	Frequently	30	8.0	34	8.0	11	2.8
	Sometimes	110	29.3	90	21.1	70	18.0
	Never	235	62.7	302	70.9	307	79.1
Parents taking care of me	Yes	70	18.8	135	31.8	42	10.9
	No	303	81.2	289	68.2	342	89.1

Table 4 (Cont'd)

		Married with Children					
		Beijing		Shanghai		Guangzhou	
		f	%	f	%	f	%
Living with parents	Yes	153	41.5	161	38.7	87	23.6
	No	216	58.5	255	61.3	282	76.4
Contact with parents	Frequently	237	66.6	279	67.1	164	44.7
	Sometimes	110	30.9	124	29.8	179	48.8
	Never	9	2.5	13	3.1	24	6.5
Parents give me	Frequently	32	9.1	34	8.2	11	3.0
money	Sometimes	86	24.5	72	17.3	56	15.2
	Never	233	66.4	310	74.5	302	81.8
Parents taking care	Yes	62	17.5	113	27.6	33	9.0
of me	No	292	82.5	297	72.4	333	91.0

children; the figures were 40.4% in Beijing, 65.9% in Shanghai and 54.5% in Guangzhou. For young couples both parties work naturally, making it most cost effective to rely on their parents rather than taking up no-paid maternity leave. Even though the young couples themselves are actually the one taking care of the child, the majority of them will again turn to their parents for help in case of need; there are 72.4%, 81% and 79.3% in Beijing, Shanghai and Guangzhou respectively.

Family Relationships

The relationship between parents and children is still close even if they live apart; 32.6% of Shanghaiese admitted that they will meet several times a week with their parents whilst only 14.8% in Beijing and 12.9% in Guangzhou had such frequent meetings. Nevertheless, 17.1% in Beijing, 22.6% in Guangzhou will meet every fortnight. The married couples agreed that their contacts with parents are frequent, those without children have the most frequent contacts (Table 4). Only 6.5% in Guangzhou admitted that they have no contact with their parents. Such an intimate relationship between family members provided them with a base for entertainment and mutual help. 44.1% of the respondents in Beijing, 48.2% in Shanghai and 54.5% in Guangzhou will always gather together whenever they are free.

Such close family relationships lead us to ask how far they will sacrifice for their family members. When asked if they would sacrifice the child-care money for the urgent need of their siblings, 46.8% in Beijing, 44.5% in Shanghai and 52.3% in Guangzhou answered affirmatively. The figure is even more encouraging in giving an definite answer, there are 32.6% in Beijing, 37.6% in Shanghai and 15.9% in Guangzhou. Such a sacrifice would be impossible if their relationships were poor. From the above, we can see that the traditional extended family support is not lacking in present-day China even though the family structure has become nuclear. Sociologists used the term "Intimacy at a Distance" to explain this Asian/Chinese family setting. Since the traditional extended family is no longer possible in present-day society, living close by can serve the same purpose as the traditional extended family. (Kuo and Wong, 1979; Chen, 1991; Jernigan and Jernigan, 1992).

Family Conflicts

If the family members in China relate so closely with one another, it is unavoidable that there are conflicts among themselves. 49% in Beijing, 50.1% in Shanghai and 69% in Guangzhou admitted having occasional conflicts. The most common cause of conflict is the attitude towards life, 20% in both Beijing and Shanghai and 25.3% in Guangzhou gave this as the major cause of family conflict. Such a contrast on the attitude to life between generations might be an important issue as the economic and social development is so drastic that individuals have not struck a right balance in life. It is also because the present education system has not provided enough guidance for young adults. Traditional ideals become the second major cause of family conflict in these cities, Guangzhou 21.1%, Shanghai 14.1% and Beijing 10.9%. From these figures, we can observe that the contrast in opinion between generations is directly related to the influence from the recent socioeconomic development. This is again confirmed by conflicts in family consumption, the highest is in Guangzhou 18.8%, followed by Shanghai 9.3% and Beijing 8.5%. The traditional value of thrift is gradually disappearing. Consumerism started to take root especially among the younger generations. It is also interesting to find that Beijing people are more concerned with their future prospects, 9.6% versus 5.2% in Shanghai and 6.3% in Guangzhou. One important remark to be noted is that issues on morals, politics, or state policies are neither controversial nor interesting topics for discussion. This is dangerous especially when China's economic and social structures are both developing rapidly. Social responsibilities will definitely be undermined if apathetic attitudes are found for these values.

Old Age Support

In our survey, we undertook an in-depth investigation of old age support under the present retirement scheme. People were asked about the necessity of old age support, 52% of Shanghaiese affirmed it as extremely necessary, and 46.4% as necessary. In Beijing 45.5% replied that it is extremely necessary and 49.5% that it is necessary. Guangzhou seems to be the poorest in supporting the elderly, only 31.9% responded extremely necessary and 65.3% necessary. In all these cities, only a very small number of people responded negatively, 5% in Beijing, 1.6% in Shanghai and 2.8% in Guangzhou. The proportion between males and females are relatively similar in Guangzhou, but, in Shanghai, 6.2% more females than males believed old age support to be extremely necessary. 5.8% more females in Beijing expressed the necessity of old age support. The overall opinion of the people is quite encouraging owing to the fact that filial piety is not yet absent. 43.1% of people in Shanghai believed that the main reason for old age support is the traditional idea of piety whilst 41.5% in Guangzhou and 36.5% in Beijing chose obligation or duty as the main reason. Only 11.1%, 6.3% and 9.9% in Beijing, Shanghai and Guangzhou respectively answered by referring to the financial difficulty of the parents (Table 5). This idea is again confirmed by the reason for not practising old age support, 46.7% in Guangzhou, 44.5% in Shanghai and 39.5% in Beijing expressed that parents are financially self-sufficient. Moreover, only 15.4%, 7.7% and 7.6% of retired persons in Shanghai, Guangzhou and Beijing respectively receive pension benefits. It is evident that retirement benefits are not widely provided to the retirees. However, the present financial situation of the aged is not yet too critical since many of them have enough savings to pay for their living. The Chinese tradition of filial piety is still prevalent even though the elderly have enough money to pay for their daily necessities.

Nevertheless, there is always a discrepancy between the ideal and the real. When asked about the actual practice of old age support, 60.6% in Beijing, 52.4% in Shanghai and 36% in Guangzhou said that they always support their parents. 10.4%, 20.3% and 31.3% in Beijing, Shanghai and

Table 5

Main Reason for Old Age Support

	Beijing		Shanghai		Guangzhou	
	f	%	f	%	f	%
Traditional ideal of piety	131	31.6	198	43.1	154	35.5
Obligation	151	36.5	124	27.0	180	41.5
Parents' demand	2	0.5	2	0.4	11	2.5
Parental satisfaction	36	8.1	34	7.4	26	6.0
Financial difficulty of parents	46	11.1	29	6.3	43	9.9
Personal satisfaction	35	8.5	56	12.2	16	3.7
Avoid condemnation by others	2	0.5	1	0.2	—	—
Others	11	2.7	15	3.3	4	0.9
Total	414	31.7	459	35.1	434	33.2

Guangzhou respectively answered sometimes. Only 15.1% in Beijing, 16.7% in Shanghai and 17.4% in Guangzhou said that they had never supported their aged parents. This group, however, was mainly the unmarried and the age band of the majority ranged between 19 and 29 years. The married couples take up the duty more responsibly than single persons, 63.6% in Beijing, 53.4% in Shanghai and 36.7% in Guangzhou have always supported their parents. In Beijing, most of the married couples are industrial labourers working in construction and transportation whilst in Shanghai and Guangzhou, the servicing industry takes the lead. It appears that the lower class tends to be more attentive to the needs of their parents.

Most of our respondents use their own money as a means of supporting their elderly family member. Guangzhou people use this means more often, there are 56.4% for the single, 55.5% and 55.7% for married without children and married with children respectively whilst in Beijing it is 47% for those married without children, 46.8% for married with children and 33.3% for the single. In Shanghai, a similar percentage was found for both single and married with children, 39.8% and 39.7% respectively whilst there are 41.5% for those married without children. Thus we can conclude that in Guangzhou more single people use money as a form of old age support whilst in Beijing and Shanghai it is found more common among those married without children.

In these three cities, we observed that "helping their parents by means of manual work" is another important way of old age support after giving money. For the unmarried people, there are 28.1% in Shanghai, 22.4% in Beijing and 17.5% in Guangzhou. We can assume that if the young people are not financially ready to help their parents, then some kind of manual work can be an alternative. However, such kind of effort is absent for those who are married; instead, many married couples use "visits to the parents" as an important sign of respect. It varies from 11.8% to 19.4%. The other more popular means is giving gifts to parents. The highest percentage is found in those married without children in Guangzhou; there are 21.2% followed by the single in Beijing 20.2%, and 18.9% for those married without children in Shanghai.

More than half of the respondents across the board said that they are giving money monthly to their parents. This is shown more by single persons of which, 60.4% in Guangzhou, 58.9% in Shanghai and 46.6% in Beijing gave their parents money regularly. However, 21.5% and 22.1% of the single people in Beijing and Shanghai respectively have never given any money to their parents compared with only 4.4% in Guangzhou. This can also be explained since the youths of Guangzhou are richer compared with those of Beijing and Shanghai, thus making it more possible to give money to their parents. For the married group, there is a significant number of them giving money on feast days or New Year's Day ranging from 16% in Beijing to over 20% in Shanghai and Guangzhou.

In comparing the percentage of giving money to the parents, the highest is married with children, followed by married without children and lastly single persons. Most of them will give 10% of their salary to parents, the highest one is 49.3% in Guangzhou, 44.9% in Beijing and 42.8% in Shanghai. However, many respondents give 20% of their salary, 24.9%, 21% and 21.2% in the above three cities. It is interesting to observe the phenomenon that families with direct expenses, i.e., those married with children registered a higher percentage than the other two groups. One probable explanation is that they have experienced financial hardship in raising children and respond more positively. The age groups that have always supported their parents are between 30 to 39, 67% in Beijing, 59.1% in Shanghai and 43.8% in Guangzhou, and between 40 to 49, 69.6% in Beijing, 56.6% in Shanghai and 35% in Guangzhou. It is also shown clearly that when individuals become more mature, they will show more respect for traditional values of supporting the elderly. It is, however, interesting to find that 17.6%, 12.6% and 5.9% of single people in Beijing, Shanghai and Guangzhou respectively surrender all their salary to the parents. Although Guangzhou has the lowest percentage, yet it is compensated by 19.8% who give one third of their salary to their parents.

Parental Expectation

Personal achievement is the most important parental expectation for their children, which was expressed by 36.6% in Beijing, 52.2% in Shanghai and 39.8% in Guangzhou. Possessing a higher education qualification comes second, chosen by 19.6%, 24.3% and 19.8% in Beijing, Shanghai and Guangzhou respectively. Lastly, in Beijing and Shanghai, 19.6% and 6.2% respectively choose contribution to the country and 11.8% in Guangzhou opt for earning more money. Personal achievement can best be obtained by having a good education; a majority of parents expected their children to have at least university education. Present-day Chinese are conscious that educational qualifications help one to adjust better to society and it is also beneficial to the country as a whole.

Working for the business sector is the first preference of parents for their son's career (46.1%). The second preference (25.9%) is seeking employment in academic/professional research. In fact, a high percentage of people (29.3%) are employed as civil servants, while the number employed in the business sector is considerably lower, a mere 18.1%. For daughters, many parents (37.8%) preferred them to be employed in academic/professional research, 22.3% for the civil service sector and 21.9% for the business sector. In reality, 18.1% of females work in the business sector, 17.4% as civil servants and 15.1% in academic/professional research. However, 43% of our female respondents are housewives, unemployed and students (Table 6). It seems that the business sector is one of the most popular careers for both sons and daughters even though the percentages are still low at present. As the economy continues to grow, opportunities and demand from the field of business increase. It is certain that business professions will become the most attractive to work in especially with the superior monetary returns.

Table 6
Parent-Preferred and Actual Jobs of Sons and Daughters

	Son				Daughter			
	Preferred Job		Actual Job		Preferred Job		Actual Job	
	f	%	f	%	f	%	f	%
Academic/ professional research	126	25.9	15	12.9	181	37.8	13	15.1
Business	224	46.1	21	18.1	105	21.9	16	18.1
Entrepreneur	12	2.5	3	2.6	10	2.1	4	4.7
Civil servant	75	15.4	34	29.3	107	22.3	15	17.4
Military personnel	6	1.2	4	3.4	2	0.4	1	1.2
Others	43	8.8	39	33.6	74	15.4	37	43.0
Total	486	100	116	100	479	100	86	100

Education

With the new economic environment, parents tend to invest heavily in children's education. In our 1993 survey, only 16.4% of respondents wanted their children to begin working earlier while 69.6% preferred higher education for their children. Only 14% wanted their children to work and study at the same time. They are more willing to support their children in obtaining an education than to have them working to earn money at an early stage. It is quite common these days for young children to depend on private tutors to assist them in their homework. Fees range from RMB50 to RMB100 per session. The main purpose of private tuition is gaining entry to a good school. In some schools, donations are acceptable for gaining entrance, and parents even donate money in order to secure a place for their children. The amount of such donation ranges from RMB10,000 to RMB50,000, depending on the status of the school. As from 1997, China will implement the "new higher education policy of the user pays." University students will have to spend more than RMB5,000 per year in tuition fees. Such a burden will necessarily fall upon the shoulders of parents. Nevertheless, Chinese parents will never hesitate to make such an investment owing to the Chinese cultural ideal of educating the young. This is especially true with the promising rewards for educated professionals. According to our survey, 91.4% in Beijing, 91.5% in Shanghai and 78.0% in Guangzhou prefer their sons to obtain university or postgraduate education. The figures for daughters are also comparatively high, 83.9%, 84.9% and 67.8% in Beijing, Shanghai and Guangzhou respectively. Thanks to the one-child policy, at last, females in China have a better chance of obtaining equal treatment with males.

The present-day females also have a higher expectation of themselves than in the past. In our recent 1996 Beijing survey, 43.8% of females wished to obtain a university education, 17.6% opted for postgraduate level and 13.4% aimed even higher towards obtaining a master degree. It is evident that a higher education qualification is the ideal for the majority of females. As far as parents are concerned, 55.2% of Beijingese no longer make any distinction between boys and girls, and only 21.5% still prefer the traditional mentality of educating sons rather than daughters. Such a traditional mentality is seen to be losing ground.

Consequently, the status of women changed significantly compared with the past. In a five-city family survey. "81 per cent of all married women were working and their wages made up 42 per cent of an average family income. This economic independence and indispensable contribution to the family have given women increased bargaining power and changed their subordinate position in the family" (Tsui, 1989). In fact, even the sexual mentality of the female has indicated a sharp departure from the traditional, as well as socialist morality in China. One survey reported that "30 per cent of young females considered it all right to have sex before marriage, and a survey in 1987 reported that more than half of the abortions in a large city were among unmarried women" (Dai, 1987; Tsui, 1989). Here, it is shown clearly that the puritanical attitude of women toward sex has totally changed.

Conclusion

Owing to the chauvinistic and xenophobic attitudes of officials of the Manchu Dynasty, China isolated itself from the rest of the world. After the establishment of the Republic in 1911, owing to constant civil wars within China and the invasion of Japan right before the Second World War, the whole social environment as well as the environment for economic development was completely destroyed. The living conditions of the

Chinese were poor. After the Communists took over China in 1949, the economy was still underdeveloped because of the "planned economy" endorsed by the State. This fragile economic growth was further hindered by the Great Cultural Revolution. The people's economic situation was similar to that existing during the 1940s. After the "open door" policy was implemented, economic performance has taken a big stride forward in terms of national growth, GNP, foreign investments, job opportunities, individual income and savings. The infrastructure of various cities has changed completely into an entirely new setting: new airports, transportation and highway networks connecting important cities and harbours. The new infrastructures provide better supporting services for business activities. Together with preferential government policies for foreign investments, new commercial centres, hotels and condominiums are mushrooming in many places rather than only in the SEZs.

Even though a great majority of the Chinese are employed as workers and labourers in state enterprises, 20% of the professionals are in the field of commerce because of the monetary return and benefits provided, and more and more people are attracted to jobs related to business. It appears also in our findings that parents have preference for their children to take up a position in the business field. In order to achieve such a goal, investment on educating the younger ones was never a serious concern even though it involves employing private tutors or making large donations to schools to gain entry. The parents in China still seem to be traditional and single-minded in their expectations of their children; goals like personal achievement, possessing higher education qualifications and contributing to the country are objectives for most of them. Owing to the recent socio-economic development, mentalities of the younger persons have shifted toward individualism and consumerism. Conflicts between parents and children centre around attitudes to life and traditional ideals. The desire to earn as much money as possible so as to modernize family life is the common objective for 68.3% of young adults. At the same time, there is increasing apathy in regard to political, public and moral issues. These attitudes can be dangerous to social reform. Although the traditional ideal of filial piety is still a key concern for most of the young people, there are clear indications from Guangzhou that such a practice has begun to decrease. It is possible that traditional values might be traded off for comfort in life and consumerism.

We have seen that China has undergone a tremendous change in terms of physical, social, economic development, as well as people's attitudes and behaviour. All these new elements give China a new face much different from the past. Modernized China seems to identify more closely with the global community in many aspects. In any case, it is definitely not the one that we used to know.

Notes

1. The following references are helpful for a better understanding of China's family values: Fei, 1962; Levy, 1965; Yang, 1974.
2. The amount of 2,000 and 4,000 yuan estimated by Chen Xiangming (1985), seems to be too little. According to our interview in Shanghai, most of the people admitted that such an expenses involve not less than a five figure amount.

Section II
Business Management in China

8

Confucianism and Management

H. L. Chan, Anthony Ko and Eddie Yu

The recent revival of interest in "Confucianism" represents the effort of searching a new paradigm in management theories. Modern management used to be synonymous with Western management, characterized mainly by Scientific Management, which has been modified by the emphasis on human relations (Elton Mayo), quantitative methods (Management Science), system theory, and contingency approach.

Japanese Management came to the scene in the early 1980s as a result of the economic miracle and rapid economic growth of Japan. Westerners were also fascinated by the "Eastern" way, which was believed to offer an alternative to the Western models. Chinese management has also come into the scene, as Confucian value is believed to be largely responsible for the economic success of Japan and the four Asian Dragons (see Kahn, 1979; Hofstede and Bond, 1988; Tai, 1989), and China, the homeland for Confucianism, is forecasted to become the super economic power of the 21st century. From the Western perspective, although there is still a long way for Asia to catch up and become economically preeminent, the West still has a lot to learn from Confucian values (Prowse, 1996, p. 6).

A mounting interest has been accumulated as both scholars and management practitioners seek firstly, to understand more about China, and thereby prepare themselves for doing business with China. It is agreed that one has to start with Confucianism, which had controlled Chinese education, society and government for some 2,000 years and played an essential role in making China what it is (Chan, 1986, p. 11). And secondly, to look for a clue to improve one's own country's economic/enterprise performance, particularly the need for a model more suitable for Eastern culture.

Many reports written by academics and practitioners have been published on this subject. What is most needed is to find a theory linking Confucianism and its influences on management thinking and behaviours of Chinese business people, and how these can affect the practices of organizations and economy in general.

The meanings of "Confucianism" discussed in various literature often differ. Broadly speaking, they can be categorized into three groups (Wang, 1993):

1. A school of thoughts represented by Confucius, as distinguished from Daoism, Legalism, etc.
2. The Chinese philosophy, referring to Confucianism as the core, incorporating other schools of thought.
3. A system of common cultural traits observable among the communities in China and its neighbouring countries. These traits have been incorporated with other influences to form indigenous cultures in different communities.

These definitions are in fact related, as shown in Figure 1.

This chapter holds the position that it will not be very meaningful to

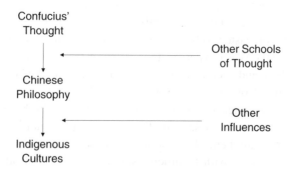

Figure 1
Meanings of "Confucianism"

attempt to clarify what is the pure and original Confucianism. The Confucian thought as it is nowadays is the result of continuous reinterpretations in history and has incorporated influences of various schools of thought. It is, however, important to understand some of the essential philosophical elements that have been inherited and last till today. The chapter begins with the background characteristics conducive to the development of Confucianism. It then identifies some key characteristics of Confucian thought, and discusses their influences on Chinese management styles and systems.

The Origin

Confucius (551–479 B.C.) is considered as the founder of the Confucian school. He was the first private teacher in Chinese history. His ideas were recorded as scattered sayings in *Analects*, or *Lun yu*, compiled by his students.[1] Mencius (371?–289? B.C.) and Xun Zi (third century B.C.) developed Confucianism further by providing essential interpretations. Confucian values were regarded as the natural choices of human nature, and were accepted among many schools of thought, such as Daoism, Moism and Legalism before the Han Dynasty. It was Dong Zhongshu (179–104 B.C.) who convinced Emperor Wu of the Han Dynasty to make Confucianism the state teaching. The status of Confucianism was raised at the expense of other schools of thought. To qualify as a member of the ruling elite, one had to pass the examinations based on the Confucian classics. Novels, drama, poems and folk songs were written, which embellished all Chinese people in Confucian tradition (Bond and Hwang, 1986, p. 215). Apart from the periods of political and social disorder during Wei, Jin, Southern and Northern Dynasties (220–589 A.D.), when intellectuals turned to Daoism or Buddhism, Confucianism remained its dominant position in the Chinese history. In Sung (960–1279 A.D.) and Ming Dynasties (1368–1644 A.D.) in particular, a large number of prominent Confucian scholars such as Cheng Yi, Cheng Hao, Zhu Xi, Lu Jiuyuan, Wang Yangming reinterpreted Confucian philosophy by incorporating Daoism and Buddhism.

According to Fung (1948, p. 16), philosophers are conditioned by the environment in which they live. It is necessary to trace and understand the geographical and economic background leading to the development of the early Confucian thoughts. Figure 2 shows a comparison made by Fung (1948) between the early Greeks and Chinese in the factors influencing their philosophies.

Figure 2
Background Characteristics for Ancient Greek and Chinese Philosophies

	Greek	Chinese
Geographical Factors	Maritime	Continental
Economic Factors	Commerce	Agricultural Subsistence
Social Systems	City	Family

Unlike the Greeks, who lived in a maritime country and engaged in commerce, China is a continental country with its massive population engaged in agriculture at a subsistence level. Confucianism was a suitable ideology by encouraging self-restraints and distribution of limited resources according to a prescribed hierarchical political and social order. To provide sufficient food for survival, agrarian production was emphasized as "the root," and commerce was slighted as merely "the branch." Those engaged in exchange were ranked as the lowest in the traditional social hierarchical classes of scholars, farmers, artisans and merchants.

The merchants of a maritime country tended to be accustomed to change because they had more opportunities to meet different people and see new things. They had to encourage novelty in order to meet the demand of customers and increase sales of their goods. On the other hand, the way of life of the farmers in China was to follow Nature, and they desired no change and could not conceive of any change. Inventions or discoveries were therefore often discouraged.

Since the farmers are in frequent contact with Nature, they are inspired by the movement of moon and sun and the succession of the four seasons. They are led to believe in the theory of cyclical nature of life, which is the major ground for the doctrine of golden mean. They avoid the extremes and "remain cautious even in time of prosperity, and hopeful even in time of extreme danger" (Fung, 1948, p. 20), because they believe the dawn will come soon after the darkest period, and misfortune will arrive immediately after great pleasure.

Farmers in China have to live and work on their land, they are tied to their family and community in a particular place. Every individual is born to be a part of a prescribed network of relationships. Intensive agriculture also requires them to cooperate with each other in maintaining irrigation systems, transplanting the seedlings and harvesting the crops (Cheng, 1980,

p. 55). The mutual dependence among themselves has made harmony a necessary virtue.

Confucianism is developed as a theoretical expression of this social system, where social organization is an extension from the family system. The Chinese social system may thus be called the family state, in contrast to that of the Greek merchants who lived in towns and organized their society around the city state. A family state is more autocratic and hierarchical, because in a city state "there is no moral reason why one should be more important than, or superior to, another," but "in a family the authority of the father is naturally superior to that of the son" (Fung, 1948, p. 26).

Humanism

The fundamental belief of Western philosophy is man's rational faculty, which can deduce abstract and universal principles discrete from facts or experience. In China, philosophy takes the place of a religion. Men are not made by God. God was originally human, and "the supernatural world is basically an objectification of the humanistic spirit" (Wu, 1972, p. 9). Chinese philosophy is derived from man's concrete experiences, and man is emphasized as the centre of the things (Chan, 1986, pp. 18–19). For example, according to Mencius, man's experience of immediate feelings like the response to a scene of a child about to fall into a well is the beginning of virtues (Cheng, 1972, p. 160).

Humanism in the West emphasizes the intrinsic value of a human being as a free and independent individual. In Chinese humanism, a human being's potentialities are realized only through the relationship with other human beings (Wu, 1986, p. 6). Confucian humanism is practised as a way of life. It is concerned "with the practical question of advancing the well-being of the individual and the order and harmony of society and State" (Cheng, 1972, p. 163). Five conceptions may be analysed:

> First, Man is the centre of the universe and therefore human dignity must be upheld; secondly, Man is by nature good, not conceived of sin, and therefore, requires no redeemer from Heaven; thirdly, Man has common sense and he should be able to judge for himself; fourthly, any decision made by man ought to be to his own advantage; and finally, culture, of which religion and philosophy are but a part, is a tool of life and Man is in a position to use it for his own benefit. (Cheng, 1980, p. 118)

Confucius believed that good government depends on good men ("sage"). "When good men are in office, government is efficient, just as when the earth is fertile, plants flourish." (*Chung Yung*, p. 20).[2] Man is a social being and the original human nature is goodness of human nature. For the Western philosophers like Plato, a man chooses to be good after knowing what is good or evil. Education is required to transform man from ignorance to enlightenment. But for Mencius, it is not a matter of knowledge but is entirely a matter of nature. Education is only required to help one to return to his nature. Therefore, Confucians have greater trust in human nature and Western thinkers have more trust in knowledge (Allinson, 1989, p. 17). They believed that goodness of human nature is "nothing but a fulfilment of the inherent nature-virtue in man." (Cheng, 1972, p. 147)

All men are born with "seed of humanity," which makes man different from animals, and potentially every man can cultivate and become a sage. Even Xun Zi, who argued that human nature was bad, had "faith in man's ability and potential and his initial willingness to better himself" through education and training (Cheng, 1972, p. 148).

Harmony in human relations is maintained through the practice and perfection of the five constant virtues: *ren* (love and benevolence), *yi* (righteousness), *li* (propriety or rites), *zhi* (wisdom) and *xin* (sincerity or trustworthiness) (Zhang, 1992, p. 126). According to Confucius, *ren* is to love people (*Analects*, XII: 22). A human being extends in a graded love towards other people through *li*, a patriarchal and hierarchical system.

Confucius said: "To return to the observance of the rites through overcoming the self constitutes benevolence" (*Analects*, XII: 1). *Li* is a manifestation of *ren*, which prescribes the appropriate relationships with others. *Zhi* is the cognitive ability in distinguishing good from bad, which, together with *li*, forms the basis of righteous and sincere attitude (*yi* and *xin*). As a result, the ideal behaviour is characterized by *zhong* (loyalty) and *shu* (reciprocity). *Zhong* means fulfilling one's duty with all strength in accordance with one's conscience. *Shu* is a principle of "Do not impose on others what you yourself do not desire" (*Analects*, XV: 24). Figure 3 shows how the various Confucian virtues are related and enhanced.

Self-Cultivation

In the *Great Learning*, Confucius said: "Great wisdom consists in fully perfecting intelligence, in restoring morale to the people, and in attaining

Figure 3
Implications of Confucian Virtues on Attitudes and Behaviours

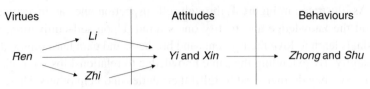

the highest good" (*Ta Hsueh*, p. 2).[2] One should cultivate oneself, regulate the family, govern the state and achieve peace in the world.

> By gaining insight into the nature of things, they came to know the highest good. By apprehending the highest good, they became honest with themselves. By becoming honest with themselves, they acquired the right attitude. By acquiring the right attitude, they developed themselves. By developing themselves, they guided their families. By guiding their families, they established moral order in their states. By establishing moral order in their states, they brought peace and prosperity to the whole country. From the highest official to the ordinary people, all need to recognize that self-development is fundamental. (*Ta Hsueh*, p. 4)

One may become a sage through cultivation of a moral life by achieving perfection of *ren*, unlike Plato's philosopher kings "who were fully developed in intellect or the rational part of the soul" (Wu, 1972, p. 11).

The process of cultivation requires the fulfilment of one's duties. One of the duties is "self-inspection" to gain a clear insight into what one has done in accordance with *ren*. Constant effort is needed to eliminate selfishness, which blocks the way to harmony (Neville, 1989, p. 71). As Zeng Zi said:

> Every day I examine myself on three counts. In what I have undertaken on another's behalf, have I failed to do my best? In my dealings with my friends, have I failed to be trustworthy in what I say? Have I failed to practise repeatedly what has been passed on to me? (*Analects*, I: 4)

Filial piety is stressed as the most fundamental virtue. One can learn to cultivate *ren* by first loving and respecting his own parents and brothers in the family, then extending the love and affection to society at large. Individuals are therefore envisaged to relate to society "in terms of a continuing permeation of the quality of the character of the individual throughout the ever-broadening circles of society" (Mei, 1986, p. 326).

As illustrated in Figure 4, through self-inspection one can investigate, extend the knowledge and rectify one's mind. Upon self-cultivation, individuals learn to love their parents and brothers, and gain harmony within the family. By extending the same knowledge to relationships with others in society, they do their best to fulfil their duties and help others whatever they wish others to do for themselves, and thereby achieve peace in the world.

Figure 4
Self-Cultivation and Society

Society:	Zhong, Shu
Family:	Filial Piety Brotherliness
Individual:	Self-Inspection

Wu Lun

Unlike the contractual type of relationships in the West, morality in Confucianism is personalistic and particularistic, and is defined in terms of duties in certain specific relationships, or in an individual's specific role in the social hierarchy. (Alston, 1989; Wokutch, 1990).

One's status in social hierarchy in China determines his/her duties to others. (Richman, 1969, p. 243) The social status or rank of everybody, according to Confucius, has to be appropriately named. Therefore, when Confucius was asked what he would do to rule a state, he replied: "The one thing needed first is the rectification of names." (*Analects*, XIII: 3.) He held that, in order to maintain a well-ordered society, it would be essential to have the rectification of names, which means appropriate names with appropriate duties: "Let the ruler be a ruler, the subject a subject, the father a father, the son a son." (*Analects*, XII: 11). As explained by Fung (1948, p. 42):

> Every name in the social relationships implies certain responsibilities and duties. Ruler, minister, father, and son are all the names of such social relationships, and the individuals bearing these names must fulfil their responsibilities and duties accordingly. (Fung, 1948, p. 42)

Age largely determines the hierarchical relations. Every member in a family has a special "name" given according to his/her age in relation to other members. An older brother is named *"gege"* and a younger sister is called *"meimei"* (Laaksonen, 1988, p. 66).

Three out of the five cardinal human relationships (or *wu lun*) belong to family. *Wu lun* are the relationships between sovereign and subject, father and son, husband and wife, elder brother and younger brother, friend and friend, which "exemplify the nature of all social relationships" (*Chung Yung*, p. 20). Confucian classics, especially *Xiao Jing*, described extensively the duties of sons in filial piety. The relationship is predetermined and permanent. Being good as a son can be seen as the root of *ren*. It was deduced that,

> It is rare for a man whose character is such that he is good as a son and obedient as a young man to have the inclination to transgress against his superiors; it is unheard of for one who has no such inclination to be inclined to start a rebellion. (*Analects*, I: 2)

The father can never be wrong and commands the unconditional respect and loyalty from his son, and in return, the father will take care of his son. For example, referring a case of a father who stole a sheep, Confucius said the son should cover up for his father and the father should cover up for his son (*Analects*, XIII: 18).

The basic hierarchical relationship between father and son is a model for extension to other social relationships. Family is not simply the primary social unit, but all social organizations tend to be patterned after the family. For example, emperor is "Son-of-Heaven," the local magistrate is called "parent-official," good friends are "sworn brothers" (Mei, 1986, p. 331).

The advantage is to provide commonly accepted rules of give and take in efforts and resources distribution. Everyone knows his/her place (social rank), abides by it, and behaves in accordance with the roles and duties prescribed to the specific social rank, as shown in Figure 5. The result is a long time harmonious and stable society.

Figure 5
"Names" and Behaviours

| Social ranks specified by "names" | → | Rules and duties prescribed for particular names | → | Appropriate behaviours |

Management Implications

Figure 6 illustrates how the key elements in Confucianism have been translated into management orientations, which in turn affect the Chinese management styles. Humanism results in a morality orientation in management, which emphasizes motives rather than results, virtues and good intentions rather than clear and comprehensive systems in organizations. The spirit of self-cultivation leads to the achievement orientation, which managers generally characterized by hard-working, thrift and perseverance. The concept of *wu lun* prescribes an orderly human relationship, which, causes the importance of family interests, *guanxi*, and paternalistic leadership. Figure 7 summarizes these relationships in a diagram.

Morality Orientation

Correct behaviour is seen as more important than results (Punnett and Zhao, 1992, p. 80). Western managers in decision-making tend to estimate

Figure 6
Confucianism and Chinese Management

Key Elements in Confucianism		Management Orientations		Characteristics of Chinese Management
Humanism	→	Morality	→	Simple structure Benevolent leadership Emphasis on motives
Self-Cultivation	→	Achievement	→	Hardworking Thrift Perseverance
Wu Lun	→	Relationship	→	Familism Paternalism Importance of *guanxi*

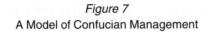

Figure 7
A Model of Confucian Management

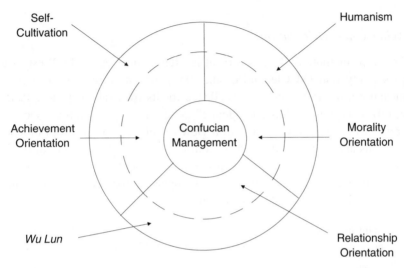

possible consequences of various actions and select the one likely to have the most favourable and the least unfavourable consequences. Chinese managers, however, tend to judge an action in terms of the appropriateness of motivation and the intent of the manager, as determined by moral principles. A "good" manager must be right and reliable, whose mind "is the source of any successful action: where there is a sincere and earnest desire, nothing is impossible" (Li et al., 1992, p. 98).

The leadership style is characterized as "benevolent consultative paternalism." All followers are expected to be loyal and submissive to hierarchical positions. Loyalty and personal virtues are emphasized in recruiting and promoting employees.

In return, the followers expect those in higher positions to be virtuous and benevolent, like father looking after the welfare for his sons. Chinese are said to prefer strong leaders with their mandate depending on merit (Clark, 1982, p. 65).

The emphasis is on virtue in leaders to set moral examples. Systems and regulations are seen as relatively unimportant. The control relies on the effectiveness of self-discipline and self-restraint. Both leaders and followers are sensitive to face-keeping. Anyone who fails to fulfil the duties prescribed to his/her specific social role will lose face (Chao, 1990, pp. 585–586).

Achievement Orientation

The need or motive of achievement is often conceived in the West as a personality trait (McClelland et al., 1953), which is intrinsic in nature, meaning a desire to achieve excellence for its own sake (Spence, 1985, p. 69). It is criticized as an "agentic" perspective which defines success "by a personal achievement with a view of self as separate from others" (Parsons and Goff, 1980, p. 351). Confucianism is not limited to intrinsic motivation. Instead, the highest form of achievement is defined as "sageliness within and kingliness without." It emphasizes on self-cultivation and the extension of personal virtue to benefit the world:

> in his inner sageliness, he accomplishes spiritual cultivation; in his kingliness without, he functions in society. (Fung, 1948, p. 8)

Chinese are believed to be in general high in achievement motivation (McClelland, 1963; Hofstede and Bond, 1988). The emphasis of the Chinese on education, working hard, patience, thrift, and perseverance are believed to be the key principles of Confucian teaching (Hofstede, 1991, p. 165).

In a reinterpretation of Weber's thesis, Hwang (1990) concludes that Confucianism puts a high value on achievement. Even though traditional Chinese society is not conditioned by the formal rationality required for developing industrial capitalism, there is a strong achievement drive implied in the *rendao* (way of humanity). It is evident that given an appropriate business environment, Chinese are generally high in achievement-oriented behaviours. In Hong Kong, for example, the phenomenon that the Chinese people reject the fatalistic view of future and continue to strive hard for success is attributed to Confucian ideology and a favourable situation of equal opportunities in Hong Kong (Lau, 1982; Lau and Kuan, 1988).

Interviews with Chinese entrepreneurs have discovered an universal drive for achievement.

> It was the urge to control, to take charge of events, to be master of the situation, and to achieve this by carving out an area of life in which such control could be exercised. (Redding, 1990, p. 88)

Another study on Chinese entrepreneurs in Hong Kong also found that they possess a high sense of achievement, unwilling to be employed even if the salary level is high, and attributing their success to their own hard work (Tuan et al., 1986, p. 78).

Relationship Orientation

Chinese organizations typically operate like an extension of the family system. The relationships between superior and subordinates are viewed as father-son or master-servant. Family-type obligations and personal relationships are valued in holding the organization together (Richman, 1969, p. 244) Family interests take the priority. Most important positions are generally taken by family members.

There is no clear division between ownership and management. Authority is usually centralized in the owner. Production, sales and management are highly centralized in the hands of the owner and his/her kins. Managers in the higher-level tend to believe that their authority is "based on some type of natural law, rather than on a clearly defined contractual type of role in the organization, or on specific skills and knowledge." (Richman, 1969, pp. 244–245).

Human relationships in Chinese organizations tend to be more important than to "things." The relationship between employers and employees is supposed to be long lasting. (Tai, 1989, p. 25) The concern of Chinese managers is more on achieving harmony in relationships. Decision making is based less on individual utility maximization, but on achieving harmony in the group. Competition is discouraged for reducing conflicts (Li et al., 1992, p. 103). Personal relationships are often used to get the things done. Proper application of guanxi is important for doing business in Chinese societies (Punnett and Zhao, 1992, p. 80).

Conclusions

Since the late 19th century, China has experienced a series of political turmoil. In their search for a new philosophy to adapt to and catch up with the modern world dominated by the West, the Chinese intellectuals have little time for understanding, evaluating and synthesizing the past with the influx of Western ideologies. The past tends to be simply rejected in favour of anything modern and popular in the West. (Cheng, 1972, pp. 156–157)

The purges in the 1950s and 1960s were especially destabilizing for the Chinese concept of family (Whyte and Parish, 1984; Yang, 1966). The Cultural Revolution encouraged children to report on their parents and to examine and criticize themselves. The result was a disruption in the harmony with self and family that is the heart of the integration dimension. (Ralston, 1992, p. 670)

The "Four Modernizations" programme since the late 1970s has in effect been translated as "Westernization," which encourages a larger degree of freedom for individuals, but at the same time weakens the family as a cohesive force (Mei, 1986, p. 332). Besides, as a result of industrialization, the rural underemployed migrated to cities looking for jobs, sons were no longer dependants, women were freed from their traditional roles. An "individualism by default" has thus occurred in China (Levy, 1962, pp. 225–240). Chan (1986, pp. 25–26) argued that China's individualism has been excessive in recent decades, with individuals believing that they are above society and are unable to cooperate and work together.

Tradition is not static, "it has to be both surpassed and created afresh" (Shao and Wang, 1989, p. 18). To search for wisdom from the tradition, reinterpretation of Confucianism is necessarily a continuous process (Kam, 1980). For example, a "cognitive selection" has occurred among the Hong Kong Chinese, who selectively retain Confucian doctrines according to practical needs of accomplishing economic objectives in the new circumstance. Successful industrialists and merchants, instead of scholars, enjoy the highest admiration in social status. Nepotism is now based not on affective but instrumental considerations (King, 1987). Performance becomes an essential criterion, alongside with relationship and loyalty, for recruitment and promotion considerations. (Cheng, 1993). It is hoped that, through such transformation of the traditional Chinese thoughts, the paradigm of Chinese management can be established and improved to meet the needs of the organization in the future.

Notes

1. *Analects*, Translated by D. C. Lau, Hong Kong: The Chinese University Press, 1992.
2. *Ta Hsueh, Chung Yung*, Translated by A. J. Bahm, Taiwan: Confucius Publishing Co., 1994.

9

Managing Political Risks in the People's Republic of China

H. L. Chan

Political risk is the "negative perceptions emanating from internal stability, intergovernment relationships, anticipated or unanticipated government actions, or government discontinuities all brought about by social, economic, or political imperatives existing in a country's internal or relevant external environment" (Fatehi-Sedeh and Safizadeh, 1989, p. 4). Political risks, like other environmental factors, are implicit in any investment decision and are often viewed as the probability of the occurrence of some political events which may result in a loss of assets and/or profit (Kobrin, 1982). Questions like: "Will there be a power struggle after the ageing strongman die? Will there be fights with neighbouring countries? Will the new leaders solve the nation's economic problems and further promote prosperity?" (Linn, 1995, p. 28) are often asked by China watchers and managers with great interests.

   The outlook for the PRC is very uncertain. As Nathan (1990) pointed to the fact that virtually no important political events since the founding of the PRC in 1949 had been foreseen by the China specialists. Another writer said: "Put any 12 economists in a room, and you may end up with 13 opinions. But if the subject is the Mainland China then the number of views is almost unlimited" (Heath, 1993). Opinions on the PRC's future differ significantly. According to a survey of senior executives in 1,000 international companies, the PRC was rated the most attractive investment target. The results were said to imply no significant concerns of political stability, legal framework, bureaucracy and exchange controls (Hughes, 1994, p. 1). In another survey, however, the business confidence on the PRC was ranked the lowest among the countries in this region (Linn, 1995). However, these researchers were probably addressing two things separately: the attractiveness of financial opportunity and the political risks in the PRC. In practice, an investment decision will be reached by making tradeoffs between risks and opportunities. The more attractive the financial opportunity, the more willing a firm will be to undertake a higher political risk (Daniels and Radebaugh, 1989; de la Torre and Neckar, 1982; Fatehi-Sedeh and Safizadeh, 1989).

This chapter attempts to systematically examine the risks associated with the PRC's modernization programme, which has encountered obstacles and generated unintended consequences. It will trace the problems of economic reforms, to provide an understanding of the likely sources of the political risks for businesses in the PRC. Finally, ways of managing political risks will be discussed.

Problems in Reforms

In 1978, an economic reform aiming at the modernization of industry, agriculture, science and technology, and defence, was initiated in the PRC. A partial "marketization" is advocated, in the hope that private enterprises can supplement the central planning system and provide employment opportunities. Another reason for the reform is suggested (Gold, 1989; King, 1986) to be the need to alleviate fears in Hong Kong and Taiwan that the PRC will not touch private business after its reunification with the two areas. After the June 4th Tian'anmen Square Incident and the collapse of Communist rule in Eastern Europe and the former USSR, the pace of economic reform increased rapidly, as shown in the widely publicized Deng Xiaoping's tour of South China. It was believed to be an awareness of the urgent need to revive the confidence of people in the Chinese Communist Party (CCP). The leaders in the PRC understand that the survival of CCP rests on rapid economic reform (Conable and Lampton, 1992). Since the late 1980s, however, the PRC economy appears to encounter increasing problems. The economic reforms appeared to have reached a dead end (Nathan, 1990, p. 119).

The essence of rural reform was the abandoning of collective ownership, breaking up the fields into small pieces and offering a contract responsibility system to each family household. Privatization and higher prices for agricultural products have increased work incentives and peasants are allowed more flexibility to engage in sidelines and commercial crops with more favourable returns. Since 1985, except for 1990, however, growth in the primary sector has been lagging behind other sectors of the economy. A major problem is the fragmentation of land with little prospect of improving productivity. Each family is allocated small and scattered strips, described by Hinton (1991, p. 16) as "noodle land," which are so narrow that "not even the right wheel of a cart could travel down one man's land without the left wheel pressing down on the land of another." The reliance on the contract system has also led to short-term behaviour. Roads, irrigation systems and other public facilities have not been properly maintained. Ruthless exploitation of land and natural resources has resulted in wastage, environmental pollution and ecological destruction.

In the industrial sector, half of the state enterprises were suffering a loss. Drastic reorganization, restructuring or bankruptcy of state enterprises can hardly be implemented before the creation of unemployment insurance system and a more active labour market. The efforts to reform enterprises are concentrated on "revitalization" by granting greater autonomy to the managers of state enterprises, who are made accountable for the performance of their firms. Individual managers may sign a contract with an enterprise to operate a production unit or a project at a price or a guaranteed output, and in return, these managers will receive rewards upon fulfilment of the contracted obligations. After fulfilling the state plan, enterprises are permitted to engage in production and sell directly in the market.

The contract responsibility system can only stimulate productions at the initial stages and was criticized as being "based on the oversimplified thinking that the separation of operation from ownership and the introduction of the market mechanism alone would improve the efficiency of enterprises and lead the whole economy to success (Zhai, 1992, p. 9). Many of the large state enterprises are still equipped with the equipment and technology of the 1950s, which will require very substantial amount of new capital investment to replace and renovate. It was estimated that only 10% of the existing industrial equipment is at the technology level of the 1970s or 1980s, 20–25% of equipment requires replacement and renovation, 35% of them was seriously obsolete and should be written-off immediately (*China Times Weekly*, 7–13 November 1993, pp. 56–57).

Township and village enterprises are frequently propagated as providing what seems to be the only hope for the unemployment problems in the PRC. They are developed spontaneously with almost no laws or regulations as guidance, "doing whatever they can get away with" (Linn, 1993, p. 2). Nevertheless, it is doubtful if these township enterprises will have places for the surplus rural labour, which is estimated to be 240–260 million by the year 2000 (O'Leary, 1990).

Figure 1 summarizes the dilemma constantly confronted by the PRC leaders. Economic reform, which aimed at alleviating social discontent, has encountered increasing difficulties in advancing productivity in the agricultural and industrial sectors. The decentralization of economic decisions has encouraged regionalism and weakened macro-control of the system. It has also resulted in unintended consequences, which have aggravated social discontent. First, the abandonment of Marxism has challenged the legitimacy of the CCP and left an ideological vacuum. The "open-door" policy has brought in foreign influences and increased people's expectations. Second, income disparity has increased between those who have benefited and those who have not benefited from the reform. A "money-first" mentality and an emphasis on short-term gains have prevailed and, due to loopholes in the legal system, crime and corruption have grown rapidly. Third, due to the complexities of the problem and the weakening control, the PRC leaders appear to lose direction and determination, which result in frequent policy shifts.

Figure 1
Sources of Political Risk in the PRC

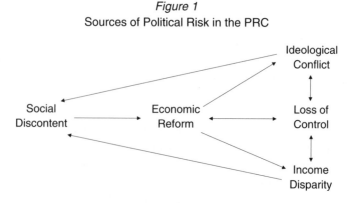

Ideological Conflicts

Economic reform for the present Chinese leadership is a means to maintain its unity and stability rather than part of an ambitious long-term process to achieve an ideal society in the PRC. Official documents still indicate that the PRC should go for a "socialist market economy," the definition of which is so flexible that it can fit in anything the government wishes to do. Such pragmatism is not unfamiliar to the audience of Chinese politics. The famous saying of Deng Xiaoping: "Any cat which catches mice is good cat" has profound influence on Chinese value, which casts aside any ideology and moral issues to give way to economic growth. Although the leaders in the PRC insist that they reject any fundamental political reform, economic reform has already weakened the party's control on the economy by stressing technical competence and profit-making ability instead of the role of political ideology and loyalty to the communist party (Meaney, 1989, p. 203). As Tseng (1993, p. 50) observed: The reform, though not sufficient in themselves to democratize the PRC, could "speed up the process of dismantling dependency on authority."

One can readily observe the changes taking place with declining influence of the communist party and the government as a whole on economic affairs. The exodus of officials to private business and the loosening control of the government, however slow and gradual, are in effect transforming the political system. Orthodox Marxism and Maoism are officially acknowledged as not appropriate for today's China (*People's Daily*, 7 December 1984). But there has been no replacement thus there is a "value vacuum." The whole populace appears to be mobilized and directed to the aim of getting rich for oneself, which is praised as "glorious" and as the road towards "modernization." Money thus becomes the only yardstick for measuring success, and is a powerful incentive to people after a long period of material deprivation. With the official line advocating "to get rich is glorious," individuals respond actively towards monetary incentives at work and any opportunities of earning money.

The reformers in the CCP thought that the PRC could remain essentially socialist in nature while bringing in foreign capitalism. However, the opening has brought about more potential ideological conflicts (Woodard, 1986, p. 78). The improving communications and knowledge have exposed a growing number of people to capitalist values which are likely to stimulate their demand for freedom as a higher priority than the emphasis on stability and growth. The legitimacy of the CCP is threatened as the people have increasingly realized that after 40 years of sacrifice for socialist constructions, the country still remains one of the poorest in the world. Any attempts to tighten political control with increased ideological campaigns and crack downs are becoming less effective. The Chinese are described by Pye (1968, p. 115) as "among the world's greatest masters of the art of coping." People in the PRC have learned quickly the tactics of apparent compliance to get around official political campaigns.

A conspiracy theory is being circulated: The West is uneasy about the PRC's fast economic development and is actively pursuing a strategy to Westernize Chinese and promote separatism among Hong Kong, Taiwan, Tibet by promoting democracy, human rights and other bourgeoisie culture (Chanda and Kaye, 1993, pp. 12–13). Therefore, despite the need to continue the open-door policy, the PRC government is constantly on guard to reduce the dependence on foreign trade and investment which are "sources of dangerous ideas and instruments of subversion" (Sullivan, 1992, p. 52). Raddock (1986, p. 32) predicted that in the event of serious economic setbacks, the PRC might blame the West for its domestic problems, "all to avoid internal rebellion deriving from the unfulfilled expectations which the post-Mao era had created."

Income Disparity

By allowing market forces to rule, unequal distribution of income has resulted, which is contradictory to the ideological commitment to egalitarianism. Farm income remained unchanged despite good harvests in 1989 and 1990, as bumper crops saturated market and reduced prices for agricultural products (Kobayashi, 1992, p. 13).

The official newspaper admitted a widening income gap as the ratio of average income between rural and urban residents had reached 1 to 2.7 in 1992 (Gao, 1993, p. 1). Between the most impoverished and the most developed provinces, the gap was even larger at 1:3.55 in 1992, as compared to 1:1.73 in 1980 and 1:2.2 in 1978 (Zhang, 1993, p. 30). The gaps have been attributed to the massive exodus of job seekers into the coastal cities. A reservoir of discontent and the emerging jealousies between the haves and the have-nots may easily lead to disturbances and revolt (Shambaugh, 1988, pp. 6–7).

At the same time, the PRC government has failed to set up a regulatory framework and orderly marketplace. Laws and regulations appear to be applicable and effective only to those citizens with no power and means to get around the rules. Enforcement of law has been limited to a small range of officials, because there is neither democratic process nor a free press to monitor the power of government officials. Crackdowns on crime and corruption remain empty slogans. According to Bakken (1993, p. 31), the trend of crime rates in the PRC has surged since the beginning of economic reform in 1978. The government's crackdown on crime, like the "severe blows" (*yanda*) campaign of 1983 managed to halt the trend only temporarily. It is suggested that the public security system in the PRC had meant to be a tool of "proletarian dictatorship" in the 1950s, and was unable to cope with "normal" crimes. From 1985 onwards, the number of serious criminal cases has increased 40% each year. Many of the so-called "economic gangs" are "protected by elaborate webs of bribery and official connivance" (Hood, 1992, p. 2) Economic reforms in the PRC seem, in reality, to be a process of transforming and expanding political power into economic power. The process has effectively transferred the state's assets into the hands of party officials or their families who, in order to acquire the maximum benefits, will need to retain their grip on power. It is, therefore, perhaps natural for them to free the economy (for their own profit) while tightening control over politics (to suppress any countervailing power which may challenge their interests). Lee (1990, p. 30) suggests that the prevalence of corruption is due to the centralization of power and the losing control over the behaviour of cadres and officials. With a lot of ambiguities and loopholes in laws and regulations, and many departments each empowered with one single aspect of authority, private businesses are operating in a vague and confused legal environment and are, in addition to paying income tax and regulatory tax, forced to share their profit in the form of various fees, charges and contributions to the local authorities. As Perkins (1986, p. 67) remarked, "individuals and enterprises must make their way through a minefield of complex and often contradictory rules and regulations. Success is achieved, not by rigid adherence to the rules, but by careful selection of which rules to follow and which to ignore."

As Ch'i (1991, p. 27) pointed out, few things are likely to be more enraging to the ordinary Chinese than the worsening discipline of party cadres, which causes them to lose confidence and hope for the future under the present system. Deprived of any channels to address their discontent, people have become alienated from their work and lost respect for the law.

The impact of corruption will continue to erode the fundamental legitimacy of the government among the masses. When the level of corruption surpasses the threshold of tolerance, the stability of the political system will be at risk.

Loss of Control

Solinger (1984, p. 298) attempted to explain the frequent fluctuations in economic policy by changes in the priority among three often contradictory values: egalitarianism, bureaucratic control, and productivity. Economic reform since 1978 could thus be understood as the pursuit of productivity which "requires incentives that give short shift to egalitarianism, and [it also] demands a flexibility for the play of market forces, which runs in the face of tight planning." She may be right in explaining the situation before the late eighties, when those who were in power had a clear vision of the values they wished to pursue and what kind of country they wanted to build. The direction of policy appears to be less clear since then, especially after the June 4th Incident. The leadership is probably preoccupied with the increasing problems that have emerged. As Hamrin (1990, p. 211) observed, the Chinese leaders were "riding the tiger," "seemingly in the driver's seat but actually hanging on for the ride."

Instead of quick and wholesale reform, which would require the government to make many far-reaching decisions, gradualism, the method of "crossing the river by feeling the stones" has been the key characteristic of the PRC's economic reform. Policies are often poorly conceived, and the reform does not follow a predetermined pattern. Half-formed ideas are experimented. There is no sign of any large-scale programme of privatization, but a gradual increase in the influence of the market through changes in prices, incentives, subsidies, subcontracting or takeovers of small state enterprises by non-state and foreign firms, and a number of showcases of converting medium and large state enterprises into stock companies.

The secret of success, therefore, does not lie in any comprehensive planning in the central government, but rather in their doing less planning work, by decentralization, by letting the leaders in grassroots areas take initiatives, going their own way and taking the responsibility themselves. The gradualist approach to reform has avoided the confusion and chaos of "shock treatments" like Eastern Europe. However, the PRC's reform policies tend to be inconsistent, with little long-term vision and no coordination; it has primarily relied on trial and error. The implications of this is the lack of a clear direction, coherent policies and relatively low long-term investments in infrastructure, agriculture and environmental control, which require large capital and in many cases coordination from the central authorities.

The decentralized economic decision from Beijing to local authorities and enterprises also tends to encourage the expansion of local bureaucracies and becomes a threat to national unity. Provincial and local authorities have a great incentive to expand investment by obtaining bank loans at low interest rates. They write their own policies and present Beijing with *faits accomplis* instead of first securing approval (Kohut, 1993, p. 21). They attempt to retain more of the tax revenues instead of transferring them to Beijing. Many state or collective enterprises take advantage of preferential tax treatments by changes of identity to foreign-funded enterprises, or submit fraudulent claims for export rebates (Sender, 1993, p. 52). As a result, the government deficit has grown from 0.8% of GDP in 1985, to 2.9% in 1990 and over 3% from 1991 onwards. Government revenue as a percentage of GNP has dropped consistently from 16.6% in 1990 to 13.9% in 1993 and an estimated of 11.8% in 1995 (*Ming Pao*, 1995). The central government lacks the personnel and resources necessary to monitor and control the compliance with regulations. It has adopted a system of "venal control" (Liu, 1992, p. 710). A "weak centre, strong localities" set-up begins to emerge. A recurring theme in Chinese history is that whenever the centre was weak, local leaders would attempt to establish their own kingdoms and resulted in warlordism or civil war (*Asiaweek*, 1993, pp. 18–19).

Consequences of Political Risks

Since economic performance is recognized as the sole criterion of ensuring political power, the CCP has, in effect, trapped itself in a position where it is forced to continue its open-door policy and keep the economy booming in order to justify its own existence. There is an emphasis on economic growth, but little has been done to provide the needed investment with low yields and heavy capital commitment. At the same time, economic reform tends to stimulate upsurge in demand, which easily results in bottlenecks in the supply of raw materials and needed infrastructure, and leads to sharp inflationary pressures. The features of the PRC economic policies, therefore, reveal a zigzag path. Drastic policy shifts have occurred in cycles: promotion of economic reform leads to overheating of the economy, which necessitates retrenchment and recentralization. The rigid control results in economic slowdown, causing higher unemployment and labour unrest. It is followed by a relaxation of central control, and so on. The frequent policy shifts are not only wasteful, it also erodes the credibility of the government in general. Any new policy is expected to have a short life span.

According to Wu (1993, p. 18), there were large oscillations in GNP growth in the eighties, featuring differences as high as 11%: 14.6% in 1983–1984 and 3.6% in 1988–1989, which were much larger than other developing countries. Thailand's GNP growth, for example, was highest in 1988 at 11% and lowest in 1982 at 3.2%; South Korea was highest at 12.4% in 1986 and lowest at 5.4% in 1985.

The problems seem to be interlocking and mutually reinforced. Attempting to tackle any one single problem is likely to be an impossible task as it is invariably connected to many other visible or invisible problems. For example, the austerity programme to cool down the overheating economy has met strong resistance from regions and interest groups within the CCP. The credit squeeze will force state-owned enterprises to close down with massive layoffs, the victims of which, lacking social security protection, are likely to create unrest.

These problems have become entangled with power struggles leading to leadership changes and shifts in the path of future economic reform. As Gu (1991, pp. 150–152) argued: "The lack of a strong man firmly guiding a central government has traditionally been associated with chaos and civil war." The ageing leaders at all levels of the government and the lack of any effective and stable system for leadership succession mean that policy continuity may not survive its creators (Woodard, 1986, p. 78). It is often thought that, since a majority of the leadership's offspring is involved in business, they would not be interested in strenuous ideological debates about political direction. On the other hand, the power struggles upon Deng Xiaoping's death may be more severe than those in the past, due to the competition for a share of the economic benefits.

The consequences of the political risks on businesses in the PRC can be summarized in Figure 2. Ideological conflicts imply an unstable political climate where the CCP is constantly threatened for its legitimacy to rule and as a result may reverse the open-door policy. Income disparity aggravates

Figure 2
Consequences of Political Risk in the PRC

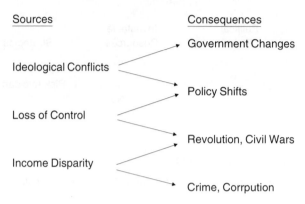

crime and corruption, and may accumulate the social discontent to a point of riots and revolution. A further loss of control in the central government may be reflected in ambiguous and frequent changes in policies, and the possibility of chaos and civil wars.

Political Risk Management

A number of possible strategies in managing political risk are described below. It should be noted that the classification is only for the convenience of analysis. In practice, at a given time, a combination of strategies is often used. For example, a firm forming a joint venture with the host government may in effect transfer some of the risk to an influential organization, which has enough incentive and capability to ensure the firm's continued well-being, and thereby implement both strategies of risk avoidance and transfer. Presumably, firms with greater resources are likely to adopt a more aggressive and an extended combination of risk management strategies. Small firms constrained by resources will have to limit their choices to more defensive and a fewer combination of strategies. A possible decision model is suggested in Figure 3.

Risk Avoidance

One of the natural responses to political risk is to avoid "by not owning,

Figure 3
A Decision Model of Political Risk Management

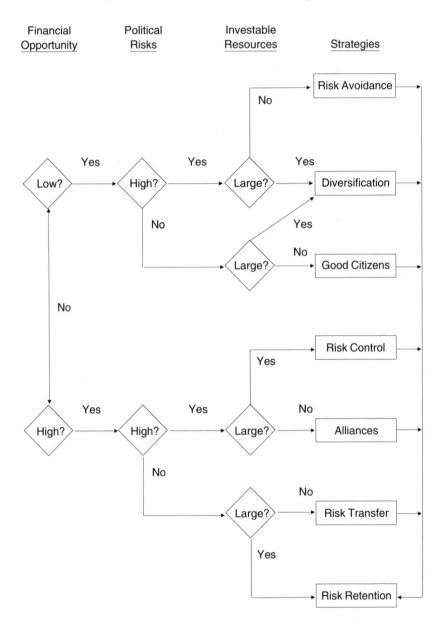

operating or entering into a certain field of business or activity" (Ting, 1988, p. 193). The shortcoming of avoidance is the possible suboptimization of benefits by missing a potentially favourable investment opportunity, in the event that the future political environment may be better than expected.

Instead of totally avoiding or solely bearing the risks, payback periods for investment projects can be shortened to enable frequent evaluation of performance (Locke and Latham, 1990, p. 332). In the PRC, Hong Kong and Taiwan investors are known to limit their risk exposure by investing in export processing and assembly ventures with small capital and short payback periods. They have been able to tap the PRC's massive supply of cheap labour, while avoiding the risks of heavy investment commitment in an uncertain political environment (Forestier, 1988, p. 21).

Risk Transfer

It is possible to reduce the risk exposure by sharing the ownership of a project with others, for instance through joint ventures or selling shares to the public. Alternatively, the investment in a project can be structured with a minimum of equity capital and a maximum of loans, preferably from the host country, so as to transfer some of the risk exposure to the creditors (Banker, 1983, p. 159).

A major strategy for international business to cope with the political risks of its investment in a foreign country is to procure formal political insurance. Such insurance is usually government-backed. For example, U.S. companies investing in less developed countries may insure with the U.S. Government's Overseas Private Investment Corporation (OPIC). However, due to the extreme complexity of making actuarial estimates, the scope of political insurance is usually limited to the loss of physical property. The insurance coverage offered by OPIC, for example, is applicable only to extreme cases like expropriation of assets after the Vietnam War, which is too narrow with respect to the risks resulting from increasing government intervention in less developed countries (Banker, 1983, p. 158). It is reported that in the PRC the state-run People's Insurance Company has accepted political insurance since 1982–1983, but so far has very little business even after June 4th Incident (*China–Hong Kong Economic Monthly*, 1993, p. 36).

Risk Control

Another important political risk management strategy is to prevent loss due to government intervention by increasing the indispensability to an economy, and thereby enhancing the bargaining power vis-à-vis the government. A company with control over technology and export markets may not only thwart the potential competitors, but also deter unfavourable political actions (Poynter, 1985). U.S. joint ventures in the PRC, for example, were reported to manage political risks by retaining control over some key inputs, such as research and development, and access to international markets (Daniels et al., 1985, p. 55).

Investment projects widely regarded as symbolically or materially important may enjoy protection from home and host governments. A classic case is the Beijing Jeep, a joint venture between Beijing and General Motors, which ran into serious troubles due to the lack of foreign exchange. In June 1986, the then U.S. Secretary of the Treasury James Baker visited Beijing and stressed the importance of the project as a symbol of Sino-American cooperation. The PRC government responded by granting immediate relief to some joint ventures, including Beijing Jeep, which had suffered from foreign exchange shortage.

Diversification

With operations located in different countries, the companies can reduce dependency on one country and thereby neutralize the political risks of operating in a single country (Kogut, 1983; Mascarenhas, 1982; Poynter, 1985). For example, overseas Chinese business community in Southeast Asia is well-known to diversify broadly so that it can take high risks and still maintain overall profitability (Overholt, 1982, p. 26).

Good Citizens

Overseas diversification may be difficult for smaller firms, which have to focus their limited resources in one location. Besides, investment incentives offered by other countries tend to be available mainly to large scale and high technology projects, and the costs of diversifying could be prohibitive, and their operations less accessible and convenient. They have little bargaining power vis-à-vis the political authorities, and it can be easier and less costly for the host government to expropriate or intervene in them (Overholt, 1982, pp. 37–38). It may be more sensible for them to adapt to the demands of the PRC government, and to maintain the profile of good corporate citizens.

Private companies in the PRC were reported to express openly their loyalty and support to the government policy (*Ming Pao*, 1992). Some Hong Kong companies' investments in the PRC were not profitable but offered a means of showing goodwill. Prominent businessmen have also been keen to donate generously to charitable and economic projects (Rafferty, 1989).

Alliances

It is common for businesses in less developed countries to be involved in local politics and coopt political support by maintaining good relationships with politicians and civil servants. Joint ventures with host governments, the most dominant form of business organizations for multinationals investing in developing countries, are found to be the main instigator of intervention (Poynter, 1985). In the PRC, *guanxi*, or personal relationships, are often cited as the important key for doing business, which provides information for risk reduction, and chance to exploit business opportunities (Manion, 1991; Frankenstein, 1987; Stewart and Keown, 1989).

Conclusion

Woodard (1986, p. 72) noted the complexity of risks in the PRC, involving a wide range of political and economic risk factors. The PRC's economic reforms, promoting decentralization and marketization, appear to have been a partial success as the economy has grown impressively, with a general increase in the standard of living especially along the coastal regions. On the other hand, the same reforms have perhaps stimulated regionalism, income disparity, crime and corruption, and economic overheating, which have resulted in social discontent, worsened the ideological conflicts and threatened the legitimacy of the political leadership. Instead of avoidance of risks and missing the opportunities of a potential favourable market in the PRC, a decision model for political risk management strategies has been suggested. It is necessary to be alert to the changes of government policies, remain flexible and adaptive, and establish good relationships with the PRC government and its officials.

The 15th Party Congress and Beyond

The year 1997 has been a successful year for China. It began in spring when Deng Xiaoping died. It was a sad occasion to have lost the great leader, but Deng's death did not result in any political or social unrest. Rather than creating additional uncertainty, analysts saw that positively and regarded Deng's death actually cleared uncertainty. The reversion of Hong Kong's sovereignty to China on 1 July 1997, was hailed as a success. There was no disturbance, and the hand-over took place peacefully and magnificently. The Chinese leaders appeared in Hong Kong and the Special Administrative Regional Government of Hong Kong sworn in the early hours of 1 July 1997. The World Bank meeting in Hong Kong in September provided an opportunity for the world to see that "business is as usual" in Hong Kong.

Other than the Fifteenth Party Congress meeting in October, the Chinese leaders appeared in other regional and international occasions. President Jiang Zemin's summit meeting with President Bill Clinton in November was seen more of a success for China. President Clinton has agreed to resume the export of hi-tech products to China prior to President Jiang's visit. Huge exports of hi-tech products from the United States to China is expected in 1997 and 1998, thereby easing the Sino-U.S. trade deficit pressure for President Clinton. The two presidents met again in the APEC meeting in Vancouver only ten days after the November summit. President Jiang Zemin, similar to the previous two APEC meetings, announced that there would be further reductions in import tariffs. It has been regarded as a gesture that China is eager to enter the World Trade Organization. President Jiang also met the Soviet President earlier in the year in order to bring further understanding in the border issue. Prime Minister Li Peng visited Japan in early November 1997, and succeeded in seeking Japanese assistance in the further opening of the services sector, notably banking and finance, which has been regarded to be the obstacle in service trade liberalization conditioned in the World Trade Organization accession.

President Clinton is making a return visit to China in the early half of 1998. Judging by the friendly atmosphere in the Sino-U.S. trade since 1996 (for example, in contrast to the early 1990s during the first term of President Clinton's Administration, U.S. trade ministers and officials since 1996 have not openly and regularly complained about the various aspects of China trade), one is optimistic that President Clinton will announce that China's accession to the World Trade Organization will be agreed by the United States.

On the economic front, China has done extremely well in 1997. China's State Statistics Bureau has announced that economic growth in 1997 is 8.8%, while GDP has reached US$900.9 billion. Trade surplus is expected to reach US$ 40 billion (three times larger than the 1996 surplus), while the trade volume is US$320 billion (grew more than 10% as compared to 1996). Foreign currency reserves topped US$140 billion, about US$35 billion more than 1996. The forecasted consumer price index for 1997 is 2.8%. Such a buoyant state of the Chinese economy is hailed as the success of the Austerity Plan initiated by Zhu Rongji in 1993, which put a brake on a considerable number of unhealthy economic and investment projects, and redirected China's overall investment strategy from one emphasizing on "quantity" to one focusing on "quality", or from an "extensive" to "intensive" investment policy.

Politically, the Fifteenth Party Congress reaffirmed the leadership of President Jiang, while the position of Zhu Rongji has risen to number three, right after President Jiang and Prime Minister Li Peng. Reform of the state-owned enterprises (SOEs) is the core in the economic agenda. As explained earlier, SOEs reform has crucial implications on employment, banking reform and ultimately economic growth and stability. For example, the *China Daily* reported on 31 December 1997, that over 25% of rural workers numbering 450 million feared that they could be out of work, and the rural labour pool is projected to increased by 13 million before the turn of the century. The *People's Daily* reported in mid-December 1997, that laid-off workers are poorly qualified for re-employment. The Xinhua News Agency reported on 18 December 1997, that the Chinese government will increase the amount of financial assistance to eliminate bad debts owed by reforming state enterprises. The bad debt amounted to RMB30 billion.

The SOEs reform has been in the mind of the Chinese leadership for a number of years. Before the Fifteenth Party Congress, the official policy on SOEs is to "keep the large, release the small SOEs", meaning that the state would financially look after only the designated larger SOEs, while the smaller SOEs, particularly those in the coastal provinces, are encouraged to solve their own problems. This effectively means that small SOEs can choose whatever ways to "privatize" their assets, operation and production.

In recent years, various "privatization" strategies have been practised by the SOEs, including joint partnership with either a Hong Kong or overseas company, putting up for sale or floating shares in Hong Kong after financial restructuring.

The share-holding system has been announced and adopted officially in the Fifteenth Party Congress. Analysts regard it as the great leap towards "privatization" of enterprises. The basic mechanism in the share-holding system is that each SOE will restructure its production and management, while the assets can be sold and distributed to private individuals or organizations. The ultimate objective is that the system will help to solve the financial debt accumulated by the SOEs. Achievements in financial efficiency would bring further improvements in production and eventually in management. It intends to have a "virtuous circle" impact on the economy.

There are a couple of issues that the share-holding system did not address, at least directly. Many consider that the major problem in most SOEs lies in the management. In 1986, the share-holding system was practised for a short while. The management of many SOEs forced their workers to buy shares by retaining part of their wage. It effectively become a "wage pooling" rather than a shareholding system. Workers become shareholders, but the management remained unchanged.

A more critical issue is the "mini-society" nature of the SOEs, particularly the larger ones. Chinese SOEs contain a production division, as well as divisions, typically, in housing, primary school, clinic, transportation, entire workers and social welfare. Nominal wages are low because all other living costs are provided by these divisions. The production division is the largest, if not the only, revenue-generating division, while other divisions are expenditure-making divisions. In a central planning economic system, the state is the ultimate boss, subsidies and low cost bank loans could be made easily. In a market economy, it would be more appropriate to break the "mini-society" nature of the SOEs by separating the various divisions and letting each division to become an independent enterprise with revenue and expenditure accounts. The same division from various SOEs can combine to become a larger enterprise. It is only through such a specialization of production that each enterprise will become financially and managerially sound.

It is hoped that the newly introduced share-holding system would indirectly solve these two problems. Nonetheless, optimism has been expressed on the share-holding system. First, the SOE reform is seen as the last obstacle in the completion of China's economic reform, making room to rapid growth in income, consumption and investment. Both national banks and enterprises in general look forward to the success of the system. The lending rate was lowered by 1.5% in late October, 1997. The cut was aimed to relieve interest burdens of the SOEs. It was announced at the end of 1997 that the freeze on the upper lending limits by the state-owned commercial banks will be removed from January 1998 onwards. Instead, the People's Bank of China will issue quarterly directives to state-owned commercial banks.

One other worry is whether the success of the shareholding system would lead to another period of economic overheating. Certainly, the Chinese authority is more prepared to use monetary policy instruments than fiscal policy instruments in regulating the shareholding system and the path of economic reform ultimately. Chinese leaders have also become very alert to economic changes. For example, the Asian currency crisis in November 1997, did not spill over to the Chinese economy, but the Chinese authority has certainly gained lessons from the crisis.

Conclusion

Despite the success in 1997, the following three years would be the true testing period for the economic policy adopted by President Jiang and Prime Minister Zhu Rongji. The Chinese economy is expected to grow by 8% in 1998. Inflation would remain low, unless drastic increases in money supply through fiscal expenditures and bank loans lead to another period of economic overheating. Many feared that the Asian currency crisis in November 1997 would bring an economic downturn in the Asian region, and China would suffer in the form of a lowered level of exports and foreign direct investment. President Clinton's visit to China in early 1998, and whether China's accession to the World Trade Organization would be finalized, is critical to China's exports in 1998 and beyond. Nonetheless, it is fair to argue that most Western countries are keener to expand trade with China than with other lower-tiered Asian economies. Some economists, indeed, argue that the depreciation of the Chinese currency in 1994 was the economic root of the Asian currency crisis in November 1997, because China's expanded exports had replaced similar exports from other Asian countries, such as Thailand and Malaysia. This assumes that in the short run, world demand for exports would remain constant.

10

Motivation and Strategy of Multinational Service Firms: Japanese Multinational Banks in the People's Republic of China

Abby Sin and Thamis W. C. Lo

Introduction

Since 1978, China's "open door" policies and economic reforms have resulted in a dramatic increase in foreign trade and investment. As China has striven to quadruple its industrial and agricultural output by the end of this century, foreign entrepreneurs have recognized the potential and have entered the market. In response to these opportunities, foreign (multinational) banks began to build up their own presence in China.

In Chinese history foreign banks were equated with "foreign imperialism" (Reynolds, 1982). The Communist Party had blamed the role that foreign banks played in China for many of the ills of pre-revolutionary Chinese society. After China's opening up to the outside world in 1979, the role of foreign banks was recognized by the Chinese officials. They believed that foreign banks could help equip China to become a full-fledged international trader, by assisting in the modernization of its domestic financial system as well as supplying capital, financial expertise, and banking technology.

Several studies focused on the banking system in China and foreign banks' activities in China since 1978 have been conducted within the past ten years. After studying three service industries in China, namely, hotels, supermarkets, and banking, Ho and Lo concluded that international service firms could have a significant role to play in the transferring of service technology into China and the "revolutionizing" of its service sector which was vital to its attainment of the Four Modernization goals (Ho and Lo, 1987). Wolken discussed the restructuring of China's banking system under the economic reforms and the role of the nation's finances and foreign banks (Wolken, 1990). He believed that if economic reform was to be successful, China's financial institutions would have to undergo further changes to improve their ability to perform the important functions of financial intermediation; if foreign banks were allowed to go beyond merely having representative offices, they could become a positive force in transforming the Chinese banking system. Dipchand et al., after analysing the trends which emerged in the financial system in China, found that the economic and social reforms since 1978 had prompted changes in the financial system, including banking reforms (Dipchand, Dodds, McGraw and Chen, 1991). It was concluded that China placed great emphasis in developing international linkages and Chinese banks expanded overseas while foreign banks established branches and offices in key commercial centres in China, even though the Tian'anmen Incident might have added a great deal of uncertainty to China's future. These studies provided some inroads concerning the development, importance, and roles of foreign banks in China.

Despite the importance of multinational banks in the China market, there is no organized study concerning the behaviour and strategies of these banks in China. Since Japanese banks are the largest banking group (in terms of the total number of representative offices and branches established in China), and the largest lender in China, it is important to study their behaviour and strategies in the China market. By using Japanese banks in China as a case example, this chapter attempts to explore the motivations and strategies of multinational banks in entering the China market. Since no previous organized research studies have been conducted on this topic, this research will serve as an exploratory study and it is hoped that it will facilitate better understanding of the problems and potentials of the banking industry in China, as well as the motivations and perspectives of Japanese banks and other multinational banks in the China market. It is further hoped that this study will serve as a benchmark to stimulate subsequent research related to multinational banks and other multinational service firms in China in the future.

Japanese Banking Activities in the PRC

Growth of Japanese Banks

Within this century, the Japanese banks will be the largest investment bankers in the world. They will dominate the foreign exchange markets. They will dominate the Eurobond markets. They are already the biggest, richest, best connected banks in the world. Almost one third of the world's 100 largest banks are Japanese (Waterhouse, 1990); the world's six largest, whether measure by Tier One capital or by assets, are all Japanese (*The Banker*, 1993).

In recent years, they have come to dominate banking in the area of highest economic growth — Southeast Asia. There has been a sharp increase in lending and trade-related financing by Japanese banks in Asia and other Pacific Rim countries. Almost 40% of the Japanese banks' international networks are now located in Southeast Asia. Two of the most dense overseas networks of Japanese are in Hong Kong and China (Baume and Gupta, 1991). It is apparent that at the heart of the Japanese banks' strategies for overseas growth, China is one of the important places to develop (*Foreign Bankers in China*, 1987).

Historical Development of Japanese Banks in the PRC

The development of relations between China and Japanese banks since the founding of the People's Republic of China (PRC) can be roughly divided into the following four stages (Yang, 1987).

The first stage covers the years between 1950 and 1961. Bilateral trade between the two countries at that stage was mainly done on a non-governmental barter basis. The annual volume was less than US$100 million, with China registering a habitual trade surplus. There were no direct agent relations between banks of the two countries at that time. Trade accounts were all settled by the Bank of China and the Japanese banks (mainly the Bank of Tokyo) through their branches in London, and all letters of credit were issued or forwarded through London.

The second stage covers the years from 1962 to 1972. Direct ties between banks in China and Japan were finally established under the guidance of the three political principles and the three trade principles of Sino-Japanese relations. The Bank of China successively established agent bank relations with 19 Japanese banks such as the Bank of Tokyo, the Fuji Bank, the Sumitomo Bank, the Mitsubishi Bank, the Sanwa Bank, the Tokai Bank, the Mitsui Bank, the Daiwa bank, and the Industrial Bank of Japan.

The third stage covers the years from 1973 to 1978. Due to the rapid development of Sino-Japanese economic, trade and technological cooperation, and the drastic relaxation of control on the part of the Japanese government over direct monetary transactions conducted by Japanese financial organizations, the number of Japanese banks with which the Bank of China had established agent bank relations increased from 19 in 1972 to 31 in 1978.

The fourth stage is from 1979 up to the present moment. With the new situation coming from the open-door policy and the friendly cooperation between Chinese and Japanese banks since 1979, financial relations between the two countries entered into a new era. According to the Bank of China's publication, the Export-Import Bank of Japan, a Japanese government agency, was the first to open a representative office in Beijing in 1979 after China adopted the open-door policy. After the first establishment, Japanese banks came one after another to China and became the most active foreign banking group in China. They showed a "presence" strategy by opening representative offices and branches. They have the largest number of banking offices (including representative offices and branches) in China among all foreign countries. In Shanghai (which began its resurgence especially in the financial sector reform since September 1990), Japan has the most banks represented, with about one-third of all the branches and another one-third of all the representative offices established over there (*The Banker*, 1994). Moreover, Japanese banks have become the most aggressive institutions in China. Of all private lending to China, some 60% come from Japan. Of China's US$40 billion total debt, about $10 billion is held by Japanese government agencies and another $10 billion by Japanese banks (Lake, 1990).

Operations of Japanese Banks in the PRC

Some of the Japanese banks are following the movements of their principal manufacturing clients to establish low-cost bases, and also the Overseas Development Aid Programme (ODA) of the Japanese government to enter the China market. China alone received 13.2% of all ODA assistance. Now consider a remarkable coincidence: wherever there is Japanese aid, there will be Japanese banks.

The linkage between the ODA programme and Japanese banks is simple. Much Japanese aid is for projects involving Japanese contractors and trading houses, which are backed by Japanese banks. The banks, through setting up their presence in China, have been key beneficiaries of such activities. Following the government lead, a consortium of Japanese private banks headed by the Bank of Tokyo extended US$10 billion from 1979–1985 (Kim, 1986).

In China, the Japanese banks can maintain their home customers because of the loyalty and cohesiveness of a typical bank-centred group — which include a city bank, a trust bank, an insurance company, a general trading company and a variety of manufacturing and service industry firms. Unlike the arm's-length relationship between US companies and their financial institutions, it is standard practice for Japanese banks to hold shares in companies they lend to. Likewise, a deal struck by a trader or manufacturer within a bank's commercial grouping will often lead to new businesses in project/trade financing, settlements, guarantees, and/or leasing. This time-honoured, unwritten corporate practice results in extensive cross-shareholding within the industrial/trading/banking groups, and creates a powerful "full-court press" that non-Japanese competitors would find tough to beat in the China market.

In China, Japanese banks are more eager to make loans to local customers. Western banks generally insist on full disclosure by loan applicants, a requirement that Chinese organizations, which normally prefer to disclose as little financial information as possible, would be reluctant to comply with. Even if they did agree to release their books, the balance sheet might not prove very useful in determining the creditworthiness, given that loans made by domestic Chinese banks are routinely approved or written off by pulling political strings. In contrast, the Japanese are more willing to trace down the ownership of a particular enterprise. Lending limits are tiered, based on whether the enterprise is affiliated with national, provincial, municipal, country, or town government (Thurwachter, 1990). Therefore, the local Chinese customers are more willing to approach the Japanese bankers when they need money.

Not only are the Japanese banks aggressive, but they are also willing to offer competitive pricing and low interest rates in order to penetrate the China market. The most critical factor is undoubtedly their low cost of funds due to the tax-sparing clause in the Japan-China double taxation treaty, which was signed in the early 1980s. The treaty enables Japanese banks to lend to Chinese enterprises at less than their own cost of funds. It assumes that the Chinese side would withhold 10% of the interest payments due to Japanese banks in order to cover their own tax liabilities. Under this tax treaty, Japanese banks are given a tax credit for the same 10% back home, so as to avoid double taxation. Therefore, Japanese banks are able to offer loans to Chinese enterprises below their own cost of funds — and still make a profit. The clause secures a very satisfactory overall margin, ensuring that banks from countries without a comparable agreement are in no position to compete (Thurwachter, 1990). Some Western countries, such as Germany and Belgium, have similar tax agreements, but the amounts of money available from their banks under this formula have been relatively limited.

Apart from the tax relief on loans made in China, the willingness of Japanese banks to work on paper-thin margins also accounts for the aggressiveness of Japanese banks in the China market. Japanese financial institutions, which seek intensely for opportunities to lend to China, have proven to be willing and able to offer interest rates lower than their European and US competitors (Kim, 1986). Japanese banks have been willing to make the so-called Kamikaze loans, loans on which there is little or no profit, in order to gain entrance into new markets. This can be explained by their ultimate objective — "survival," which means long-term profitability. They consider income on a long-term basis when calculating business opportunities fifteen to twenty years in advance (Loong, 1987). They stress asset growth, believing that profits will naturally increase in the long run together with asset growth.

After the Tian'anmen Incident, almost all major foreign creditors decided to defer new loans to China. However, Japanese banks never truly stopped lending to China, and nine of the ten largest have made at least one China loan since June 1989. They either claim that negotiations were underway before the ban; or that the money went to a Japanese company; or that the loan was made to the Hong Kong office of a Chinese company. Because of the perceived risks, the loans have also been made at higher than usual premiums, making them very profitable. One example was a 1989 US$30 million loan by Industrial Bank of Japan, Sumitomo, Sanwa and Dai Ichi Kangyo to China International Iron and Investment Corporation, priced at between 75 and 100 basis points above LIBOR (London Inter-Bank

Offered Rate — the interest rate paid to each other by top-rated London banks for Eurodollars) (Lake, 1990).

Apart from the fact that perceived risk is higher than before, the internal problems of Japanese banks have made them less eager and more wary than when the door was first opened a decade ago. The Japanese banks said that this was due to the Agreement amongst the Basle Committee on Banking Regulations on minimal capital adequacy ratios (8%) and the decreased asset value due to the crash of the stock market in Japan. Therefore, they would like to maintain a better asset quality and provide the loan with a spread that is not as thin as before (personal interview with key personnel from Japanese banks in Hong Kong).

Methodology

To ensure the continual growth and enrichment of their services in China, it is common for Japanese banks to be strategically positioned not just on the mainland but also in Hong Kong (*Foreign Bankers in China*, 1987). Therefore, the Japanese banks have built up an exceptionally strong network in Hong Kong. Among the banks operating in Hong Kong, Japanese banks constitute the largest group by number and assets. In 1990, the Japanese were the largest banking group with 31 licensed banks; followed by American (20 licensed banks); and then Chinese and Hong Kong (15 licensed banks each).

Given its advantageous position, excellent infrastructure and supporting facilities/services, as well as the good business and cultural linkages with China, Hong Kong has often been mentioned as a gateway to China (Ho, 1984; Campbell, 1986). Hong Kong is extremely well-informed about current developments in China. Coupled with its other advantages, Hong Kong's role in China trade and investment is indisputable. Thus, these Hong Kong-based firms are on the frontier in the field and their experience and insights should be of paramount importance to those parties concerned (Wang, 1984; Lo and Yung, 1988; Lee and Lo, 1988). Therefore, this research will focus on the Japanese banks based in Hong Kong and it is envisaged that the study will provide insight to the understanding of this subject.

After discussing with experts in the field, in view of the foreseeable difficulties in arranging interviews with the potential respondents, it was decided that a mail survey would be conducted. A questionnaire was designed for the mail survey. The questionnaire attempts to probe the motives behind the Japanese banks' decisions in entering the China market. The respondents were also asked to express their opinions on the importance of the China market to their banks, major problems they encountered, their attitudes toward risks as well as their opinions on the competitive advantage of the Japanese banks.

The questionnaire was mailed to the personally identified Managing Directors or Chief Representatives of the Japanese banks that are listed on the Directory of the Hong Kong Japanese Club. It was assumed that the Managing Directors or Chief Representatives, being the top decision-makers of the banks, would be in the best position to comment on the their banks' initial entry motives and strategies in the PRC. From the directory, 53 Japanese banks were identified. One of the limitations of this survey was that it could not cover those Japanese banks that did not have representative offices or branches in Hong Kong. Nevertheless, it was worth noting that this list of 53 Japanese banks in Hong Kong included 8 out of the top 10 Japanese banks and 14 out of the top 20 Japanese banks respectively (*The Banker*, 1994).

Before the actual mail survey was conducted, a pre-test of the questionnaire was conducted with two of the banks in the sample. The first and second mailings were sent out respectively on February and March 1992. A telephone follow-up was conducted after the second mailing. A total of 23 usable questionnaires (43.4% response rate) were obtained after the two mailings and the telephone follow-up. Follow-up letters and telephone calls were used to stimulate as large a response as possible from the Japanese banks.

Some of the banks refused to complete the questionnaire because it was their policy to keep information confidential, or it was their headquarters in Japan that was responsible for the China business. Although the issues included in the questionnaire are perceived as sensitive, the response rate was higher than other similar surveys. This reflects that the respondents (including non-participating banks) were taking the issues very seriously. Nevertheless, the authors caution that in view of the small size of the sample, and the possible non-response biases, the findings presented in this chapter should be interpreted with these limitations in mind.

Apart from the mail questionnaire survey, in-depth interviews were conducted with key personnel from three Japanese banks actively involved in the PRC market in order to explore more deeply the issues involved so as to develop further insights.

Findings of the Survey

Company Profile

A total of 23 Japanese banks responded to the survey. The response rate was 43.4%. Thirteen of them conducted some financial activities in China and were classified as "participating banks," while ten of the Japanese banks did not have any financial activities in China and were classified as "non-participating banks." These ten banks answered a special section of the questionnaire specially designed for them.

Among the participating Japanese banks, seven of the 13 banks have representative offices or branches in China. The number of representative offices and branches are shown in Table 1.

Table 1
Respondents Profile

Number of Representative Offices in China	Frequency
0	6
1	2
2	1
3	2
4	1
5	1
Number of Branches in China	Frequency
0	11
1	1
2	1

The profile indicates that seven Japanese banks preferred to show a "presence" strategy by establishing representative offices and branches in China. Only four Japanese banks have established three or more representative offices in China. As expected, an intensive network of Japanese banks is not common in China because approval must be obtained from the People's Bank of China and the cost of maintaining an office is high in China.

Moreover, six of the participating Japanese banks do not have any representative offices and branches in China but they can participate in the China market by using their Hong Kong licensed banks. They can serve

China adequately by flying the bank representatives from Hong Kong to China on a regular basis. In this way, their business will not suffer and the cost can be kept low. Before establishing representative offices or branches in China, Hong Kong can act as a base in which to gain experience and build up a network before becoming highly involved in the China market.

Table 2
Motives in Entering the PRC Market

Motive	Frequency
Huge potential market	10
Sustained and rapid economic growth	6
Sino-Japanese economic interdependence	5
Profitability	4
Service the customers	2
Its significance presence in Asian region	2
Expand its international network	1
Geographical proximity	1
Not risky	1
Total	32*

* Some banks gave less than 3 reasons.

Motives for Entry

The participating banks were asked to state the three most critical reasons for engaging in financial activities in China (Table 2). "Huge market potential" was expressed by ten of the 13 respondents as the most important motive. This huge market potential can provide ample market opportunities for expansion of business for Japanese banks; therefore, they are attracted to enter China.

Moreover, "sustained and rapid economic growth in China" was mentioned six times as a motive for entry in China. The favourable economic conditions in China can increase the demand of the multinational bank services. In general, the open-door policy and modernization programme of the economic development are the main motivators for the Japanese investors and bankers. It provides a lot of opportunities for multinational banks. Therefore, it stimulates the Japanese banks to prospect this potential gold mine.

Table 3
Reasons for Not Entering the PRC Market

Reason	Frequency
High political risk/risky	6
No customers' need	4
Small operation of the bank	3
Lack of international regulations and rules	2
Wait and see	2
Scarcity of relevant information	1
Sufficient to have a office in Hong Kong	1
Unfavourable atmosphere for financial activity	1
Low potential market	1
Total	21*

* Some banks gave less than 3 reasons.

"Sino-Japanese economic interdependence" was perceived as the third important reason to enter the China market. Both China and Japan have a long-term common interest in each other's welfare. With its rich capital and advanced technology, Japan is bound to be the most important supplier of capital goods and management know-how to China. On the other hand, China, with its vast manpower and natural resources, looks to Japan as its major market for minerals, agricultural products, and light and labour-intensive manufactured goods. Both countries have benefited significantly from bilateral economic cooperation. Therefore, close cooperation between the two countries has provided opportunities to the Japanese banks.

"Profitability" was mentioned four times by the participating banks as a reason to engaged in financial activities in China because they envisaged that quite a reasonable return could be made from business activities in China.

It is interesting to note that "service the customers" was mentioned by only two participating banks as the most important motive. This result seems to contrast previous service industry-related studies (Terpstra and Yu, 1988; Dunning, 1993); international banking studies (Goldbery and Saunders, 1980; Nigh, Cho and Krishnan, 1986; Terpstra and Yu, 1988) as well as Lo and Yung's study on foreign advertising agencies in China (Lo and Yung, 1988). This preliminary finding is especially interesting in the light of the usually strong bank-client relationship in the Japanese context (Thurwachter, 1990). It seems that the market-seeking behaviour of Japanese banks in the China market, which might be due to "historical desire," is so prominent that even the "crucial" "service the home clients" motive has to subside.

For the ten non-participating Japanese banks, their main reason for not participating in financial activities in the PRC was "high political risk/risky" (mentioned six times) (Table 3). They viewed that the environment was not favourable for engaging in financial activities. Moreover, "no customers' need" was mentioned four times. These banks did not enter the China market because very few of their customers were engaged in business activities in China. Besides, "small operation of the bank" was mentioned by the banks for not entering the China market. The small operational size of the non-participating banks also limited their expansion into China.

Perceived Importance of the PRC Business

The participating banks were asked to assign the degree of importance of the China banking business during the various periods. The results in Table 4 were obtained. Nine out of 13 banks said that the China business was only "moderately important" to their banks right now. The Japanese banks were rather "realistic" in rating the importance of the China business to their banks because their scope of business was relatively limited at the moment.

According to the research findings, the importance of the PRC banking business to the bank is increasing as time passes by. Three out of the 13 respondents said that it will become extremely important ten years from now. This reflected the fact that the respondents understood that penetration of the China market required patience and a long-term perspective. This long-term view implies that the respondents maintain an optimistic attitude towards the future of China. The willingness of Japanese banks to take a long-term view of the market can be explained by their concept of calculating business opportunities 15 or 20 years in advance (Coleen, 1985). Their optimistic attitudes could be explained by some of the Japanese bankers' views that banking regulations for foreign banks would be more favourable, that economic development would be sustained, and that Sino-Japanese economic interdependence would continue to boom in the

Table 4

Importance of the PRC Banking Business to the Participating Banks

	Frequency			
	Not Important	Moderately Important	Very Important	Extremely Important
Right now	1	9	2	0
5 years from now	1	7	3	1
10 years from now	2	4	3	3

future (personal interview with the Japanese bankers in Hong Kong). A special study conducted by Japan's Nippon Credit Bank showed that financial market developments assume special significance in China because the country needs more capital from both domestic and external sources for economic development. China also needs to improve its financial institutions and markets to meet the new demands placed on them because of the changes brought about by the adoption of reform and open-door policies. Therefore, it has concluded that the prospects for further development in China in the long-term are "exceedingly bright" (*Survey Asia*, 1991).

Business Objectives

Long-term objectives of participating Japanese banks were identified and highlighted to show their focus and direction in the future. They were requested to rate the importance of three long-term objectives — market share, growth, and profitability.

As shown in Table 5, growth was expressed as "very important" and "extremely important" by five banks and one bank, respectively. Market share was expressed as "very important" by two Japanese banks only. Profitability was rated by seven and two Japanese banks as "very important" and "extremely important" for the long-term objectives. The finding showed that among the three objectives, profitability was perceived as the most important one in the long term. Thus, growth and market share are just the "means" to the "ends" even for the Japanese in this context in the long-term horizon.

Table 5
Long-Term Objectives of the Participating Banks in the PRC

	Not Important	Moderately Important	Very Important	Extremely Important
	Frequency			
Growth	1	5	5	1
Market share	6	4	2	0
Profitability	1	2	7	2

Perceived Importance of the Banking Services

In China, foreign banks are limited in its business scope. Plans to allow foreign banks to undertake local currency business are reportedly under serious consideration, although initially this is likely to be on a very restricted basis (*The Banker*, 1993). According to the regulations, foreign banks are not allowed to operate retail banking. Therefore, they usually service three categories of customers — foreign investors from home country, local customers (central government or provincial authorities, state-owned corporations and financial institutions) and foreign-invested enterprises. The common business services are project financing, trading financing, advisory services and consultation as well as commercial loans.

As shown in Table 6, in evaluating the importance of the various banking services provided to the PRC, more than half of the participating banks rated commercial loans and project financing as "very important."

The perceived relatively higher importance of commercial loans by the Japanese banks can explain their dominant position and aggressive attitudes towards lending in the PRC. The Japanese banks believed that China would rely increasingly on commercial bank loans to satisfy its demand for foreign capital.

China's ambitious modernization plans will need a lot of foreign money. There are so many projects that have been approved which would require financing from the banks. The Japanese banks have already identified projects they considered "bankable." Therefore, project financing was perceived to be relatively more important in China.

Although Sino-Japanese trading volume is increasing, the respondents

Table 6

The Perceived Importance of Banking Activities for the Participating
Japanese Banks in the PRC

	Frequency			
	Not Important	Moderately Important	Very Important	Extremely Important
Project financing	2	4	7	0
Trade financing	6	4	2	1
Advisory services and consultation	3	6	3	1
Commercial loans	0	6	7	0

reflected that trading financing was relatively less important and favourable than commercial loans and project financing.

Major Problems Encountered

When asked to name the three major problems encountered in engaging in financial activities in China, the participating banks overwhelmingly named "inadequate and incomplete regulations and law" and "political instability" as the major problems (Table 7). "Scarcity of relevant information" and "lack of international business practices and knowledge of the Chinese parties" were also mentioned three times.

The Japanese banks believed that the unstable political situation would hinder economic development and discourage foreign investment. This means uncertain opportunities for the Japanese banks under political instability.

The regulations and law for foreign bankers were perceived as incomplete and inadequate. The legal environment in China is still very much under development, from an almost "standing still" position 15 years ago. Not only are the banking regulations for foreign banks vague, but also no standard legal recourse on defaults has been formulated in China. For example, the guarantee and security for making loans are not well defined. Such problems will make the Japanese banks become more cautious about drawing up ambitious expansion plans in China.

Previous studies showed that the lack of organized data was a common problem encountered by multinational advertising agencies (Lo and Yung,

Table 7

Problems Encountered by the Participating Banks in the PRC

Problem	Frequency
Political instability	4
Incomplete and inadequate regulations and law	4
Lack of international business practices and knowledge of the Chinese parties	3
Scarcity of relevant information	3
High lending risk	2
Lack of borrowers	1
Tension with USA	1
Tax	1
Big culture gap	1
Communication problems	1
PRC's bids of loans are very severe	1
Difficult to gain approval from foreign exchange authority	1
Keen competition from domestic banks	1
Total	24*

* Some banks gave less than 3 problems.

1988) and foreign investors in general (Wang, 1984; Lo, 1986) in China. For foreign banks in China, information is important for banks to lend to local customers. Scarcity of reliable information and data — on both individual borrowers and the country — was also one of the pitfalls Japanese banks encountered in China, even though these Japanese banks, like the sogo shosha, are very "strong" in commercial intelligence gathering ability. Many major Chinese government-owned corporations, for example, refuse to discuss their business in detail or release financial figures. Even if the companies have the annual reports, they contain few facts and figures. Therefore, it is difficult to get reliable information for the foreign banks to identify the borrowers' background.

Since China remained a closed economy for many years and has only been opened up relatively recently, the Chinese parties usually demonstrated a lack of exposure to relevant international business practices and financing knowledge. This leads to serious problems of understanding and communication during the negotiation process, as the Chinese parties have different practices and thus consensus is difficult to arrive at. In addition, the inadequate business knowledge of the local Chinese customers often result in a misinterpretation of the contractual terms which would eventually lead to the breaking of the contract in the future, causing losses to the bank. Therefore, the foreign banks often are required to teach their local clients to use the relevant documents, when dealing with export and import businesses. Besides, sufficient discussion and consultation must be made with the Chinese counterparts in before the contracts are signed.

Although the non-participating banks did not engage in any activities in China, it is justified to ask them to state the problems they might expect to encounter in engaging in financial activities in China. "Problem loans" was stated as the major problem (Table 8). They expected that the problem loan cases might require rescheduling.

Attitude towards Risks

One of the crucial elements in international bank decision making is risk evaluation. This reflects bankers' expectations on the current business environment and influences their future move. The participating banks were asked to assign the degree of perceived risks before and after the

Table 8

Problems Expected by the Non-participating Banks in the PRC

Problem expected	Frequency
Problem loans	7
Political instability	2
Frustrating negotiation	2
Unfavourable economic condition	2
Lack of regulations and laws	2
Lack of Chinese customers	1
Lack of information	1
Less experience by Japanese banks	1
Total	19*

* Some banks gave less than 3 problems.

Tian'anmen Incident (1 = Not risky, 2 = Moderately risky, 3 = Very risky, 4 = Extremely risky).

Table 9 shows that the perceived risks of the participating banks in political, credit and legal aspects were more or less the same before the Tian'anmen Incident. However, after the Tian'anmen Incident, these risks were perceived to be higher. The increase in perceived risk related to the political aspect was higher than those related to the credit and legal aspects. Moreover, the paired t-test shows that the differential reaction to political risk was significant after the Tian'anmen Incident. It thus appears that even the Japanese banks, well-equipped with the "long-term" and "realistic" view related to the necessity to take substantial risks to profit from the China market in the long-term (Campbell, 1987), was somewhat "shocked" by the Tian'anmen Incident as far as political risk was concerned.

For the non-participating banks, all the risks were perceived slightly higher, though not a single risk showed a significant difference.

Table 9

Differences in Perceived Risk before and after the Tian'anmen Incident by the Participating Banks (Paired t-test)

	Before	After	t-value
Political aspects	2.231	2.846	−2.89*
Credit aspects	2.308	2.386	−0.56
Legal aspects	2.385	2.692	−1.74

* Significant at 0.05.

Competitive Advantages of Japanese Banks

As indicated in Table 10, five out of the 13 participating banks stated that their main competitive advantage was "building up *guanxi* with the government officials and business corporations." "Intensive network in China" and "good supportive/motivated staff" were mentioned three times as the competitive advantages of Japanese banks.

The Japanese are well versed in the Chinese art of *guanxi*, the personal connections that are necessary for any business deal. Hence, they are in almost unanimous agreement that good personal relationships between senior Chinese officials and business corporations is an essential element contributing to the success of foreign banks. A good "*guanxi*" can be built up by initiation of the top managers, such as the chief executive, with the key decision makers in China. A good relationship can increase customer base and get more information to interpret the Chinese government's policy and business practices.

Table 10
Competitive Advantages of Japanese Banks

	Frequency
Long and well established relationship with the PRC officials, counterparts	5
Various network in China	3
Good supportive/motivated staff	3
Experience in banking know-how	2
Long history in China	2
Joint venture financial institutions	2
Large mother country customer base	1
Geographical proximity	1
Low operation cost	1
Simple corporate structure	1
Total	21*

* Some banks gave less than 3 advantages.

The Japanese banks use the "presence" strategy in China. They believed that various banks network can increase their advantages in China. The representative offices and branches not only can serve their customers, but also act as a channel to build up close relationship with the government and provincial officials.

The Japanese know that to understand the Chinese culture is important. Therefore, one logical solution is to hire "overseas" Chinese executives to work in China, and they are usually drawn from Hong Kong. This is because they are Chinese by origin and can speak various Chinese dialects, able to understand the Chinese way of thinking and the Chinese style of interpersonal interaction. It would thus be easier for them to approach the local customers. Besides, the Japanese think that learning Chinese is not a "luxury." The Japanese staff learns Chinese before working in the China market so as to gain confidence from the local customers. In this way, the

Japanese banks can build up a strong motivated staff that help them to penetrate the China market. In contrast to the study by Lo and Yung surveying foreign advertising agencies in China (Lo and Yung, 1988) and other reports related specifically on banking industry in China (*Economic Digest*, 1994), which identified the lack of qualified skilled staff as a problem, the Japanese banks seemed to deal with this issue so nicely with their competitive advantage such that not a single bank, in the previous discussion on major problems encountered, mentioned lack of qualified skilled staff as a major problem (see Table 7). It seems that the European and American banks have to face the Japanese challenge in this aspect and start to narrow the gap (Enderwick, 1990).

Business Results to Date Measured up to Expectation

In the survey, nine out of 13 participating Japanese banks showed that their overall business results in the PRC to date satisfactorily measured up to their expectations (Table 11). This may be accounted for by various reasons: maintaining good relationship with government officials, having no bad debts or being able to provide information and services to customers. Thus there would be strong grounds for suggesting that a majority of the Japanese banks have tried to set realistic expectations of the Chinese environment, and have provided the right services, competence and strategies to survive in the China market, despite the difficult business environment.

Table 11
Overall Business Results in the PRC to Date Measured up to Expectations

	Frequency
More than satisfactory	0
Satisfactory	9
Less than satisfactory	4

Four out of 13 participating Japanese banks showed that they were dissatisfied with the China results due to the thin spread and relative profitability when compared with other countries.

Conclusion

To conclude, China will continue to improve its banking industry to meet the new demands placed on them because of the changes brought about through the adoption of economic reforms and open door policies. Multinational banks will continue to enter the China market and play an important role in the future.

Among the multinational banks, it is apparent that Japanese banks are motivated into entering the PRC market by long-term expansion plans as well as attracted by its huge market potential. Although the Japanese banks view China as less favourable after the Tian'anmen Incident, they are still committed to the China market as before.

In view of the future development of multinational banks and multinational service firms in the China market, they should continue to focus on more long-term penetration strategies that would enable them to gain further inroad into the China market.

Section III
Marketing in China

11

Reform of the Distribution System in China

Oliver H. M. Yau and Li Yi-jing

Introduction

The distribution system is one of the most complicated elements of marketing in China. Reforms and the open-door policy have been carried out for 18 years, during which a gradual transformation from a traditional economy into a socialist economy has given rise to a vigorously developed commodity market. This has led to, inter alia, a shift of emphasis from unified acquisition, unified distribution, national-uniform price, single channel and monopoly in the domain of circulation into a circulation system that contains multiple economic components (in terms of the forms of ownership), multiple means of management, multiple channels, reduction in segments and levels of circulation, high efficiency, smooth circulation and an orderly *san duo yi shao* ("three mores and one less") market economy. The reforms have faced many difficulties, but changes are renowned and have attracted worldwide attention.

As early as 1986, in the article "Marketing and Marketing Research in China: Some Observations on the Distribution System and the Problems of Marketing Research" (Yau, Li and Lo, 1986), we made an initial analysis of the condition of China's distribution system at that time as well as commenting on China's reform prospects. The essay is concise and comprehensive. Since reforms were in an initial stage at that time, the concept of the market economy was not well known. China was still in the economic stage of adhering to the fundamental principle of relying mainly on the planned economy and supplementing this with market regulation. As a result, our analysis was not profound enough. Because of the intensification of reforms, today, we will, once again, review this topic. We believe that this review will benefit studies on the reformation of the Chinese distribution system.

Review of the Development of Reforms to China's Distribution System

Reforms have been carried out for more than ten years. The fundamental process of the development of China's commodity market can be roughly divided into three stages.

The Initial Reform Stage (1979–1984)

Since the Third Plenary Session of the 11th Central Committee of the Communist Party of China held in December 1978, the reform of China's economic system, which first took place in villages, was gradually extended to cities. The commodity market was restored and began to develop. According to the basic direction of the economic reforms, adhering to the fundamental principle of "planned economy supplemented by market force adjustment," which was confirmed by the central government, commodities were not the first goods to break through the means of production, and thus, they could not be circulated in the market. The key points of the early attempt at "promoting commodity circulation" in the reform of management of the economic plan were as follows:

1. To foster the dominant role of commodity market; to optimize its structure; to enlarge the autonomy of enterprises; to adopt a management contract responsibility system in all large or medium sized state-owned enterprises in the areas of retailing, catering and service; and to adopt a policy of "modification, transformation and lease" in small enterprises. The Ministry of Food was transformed from an administrative model to a management one. Collective ownership was restored in the Federation of Supply and Marketing Co-operatives, in villages to be controlled by the people instead of

the government. While developing the state-owned enterprises, collective and individual businesses, catering services and food businesses were also simultaneously restored.

2. To enlarge the objective parts of the commodity market and to reform purchase and sale policies, mainly aiming at reducing the types of commodities. Originally, in 1978, there were 274 types of planned commodity, which were controlled by the Ministry of Commerce. But in 1984, the number of commodities was reduced to 60 types. Means of production also relaxed control of some planned management. During the period from 1979 to 1984, the ratio of unified distribution of steel products dropped from 77% to 62%, while coal dropped from 58.9% to 51.6%. As far as purchase and sale policies were concerned, the state monopoly on the purchase and marketing of daily necessities was abolished, while four forms of purchase and sale — namely planned purchase and marketing by the state, planned state purchase subscription and selective purchase — have been carried out.

3. To reform the circulation system of commodities in the market. The previous division of labour in towns and countries was changed to a division of labour in respect of commodities, thus violating the "three fixed" models (i.e., fixed administrative supply districts, fixed supply targets and fixed plow back price rates) of the wholesale of daily necessities; while methods of inter-regional management, small-scaled linked management, consultative plow back price rate and mark-up price rate have been carried out. Apart from mandatory plans, first, second and third level wholesale enterprises and state-owned retailing enterprises are also allowed to make agreements directly with industrial production enterprises on making orders, replenishing stock and selling goods on a commission basis. Wholesale enterprises are also allowed to take part in the retailing industry, and vice versa. Some industries are allowed to sell commodities on their own. Unreasonable price ratios and price differences have been adjusted, and price controls in small shops have been relaxed.

4. To strengthen the macroeconomic control measures and to foster the commodity market system; to abolish the Ministries of Commerce and Food, and the All-China Federation of Supply and Marketing Cooperatives; to establish a new Ministry of Commerce,

which will be mainly responsible for organizing the circulation of all commodities in the country, unifying leaders and making arrangements for markets in both cities and counties, and reconciling business activities with different economic components; to strengthen the networks of retailing businesses and the service industry; to restore pedlars' market in cities and counties; to set up wholesale markets for small shops; and to build trading centres. The Means of Production Service Company, which is subordinated to the Ministry of Materials and Equipment, also established a comprehensive exchange market.

Comprehensive Reform and Development Stage (1985–1991)

China's economy stepped into a new era of city-based comprehensive reform from the time of the Third Plenary Session of the 12th Central Committee of the Communist Party of China held in October 1984. Reports from the 13th National Congress in 1987 also clearly suggested the "enhanced establishment and nurturing of socialist market economy," gradual intensification of market reforms and the "planned commodity economy," forcing the commodity market to develop in full swing. Major reforms are as follows:

1. To cultivate the commodity market:
   - separate the functions of political organs and enterprises;
   - transfer the power of 17 first level supply and purchasing stations of industrial products previously under the Ministry of Commerce to the city in the locality;
   - transfer the power of most second level wholesaling stations previously under provincial government to the city in the locality;
   - encourage horizontal integration of the economy (e.g., integration between industrial and commercial enterprises; agricultural and commercial enterprises; agricultural, industrial and commercial enterprises; and within the commercial circle itself);
   - form commercial corporations;
   - try out the "one supply and purchasing station in one county system";
   - introduce auctions and conglomeration for trial implementation in order to transform state-owned small enterprises;

- urge large to medium-sized enterprises to implement contract systems and experiment in the share system;
- activate state-owned enterprises to realize "Four Reformations" (namely operation, pricing, allocation and labour deployment), together with system reformations in personnel, work force and allocation.

2. To widen the objective scope through:
   - blending command and directing planned management skills with the latter being the mainstay. Ten commodities are to be controlled under command management, including four agricultural (foodstuffs, edible oil, cotton and tea) and six industrial products (sugar, iron wire, nail, chemical fertilizers, pesticides and scrap iron). Thirteen commodities are to be controlled under directing management, including five agricultural (hogs, small cotton velvets, jute and bluish dogbane, wool and cattle-hide) and eight industrial products (cotton cloth, polyester/cotton fabric, medium-long fibre cloth, wool fabrics, famous wine, washing powder, galoshes and iron pots.)
   - monopolizing agricultural data for the production of chemical fertilizers, pesticides and agricultural moulds;
   - monopolizing the colour TV set business;
   - adopting diversified sales and purchasing means for general daily industrial products, like the agency system.

3. To establish a circulation system:
   - establish different types of economy and multi-channel circulation, different forms of operation, reduced layers of distribution meeting the direction of material flows, and a network facilitating the development of the commodity economy;
   - break through the top-down allocation mode of the vertical circulation system and the state-operated centrally controlled structure.

4. To release market price controls:
   - allow the market to control prices of some daily necessities industrial goods and main non-staple foodstuffs in the city;
   - narrow the price scissors of industrial and agricultural products, sharply increase the purchasing price of food, which has not been changed for 25 years, adopting a unified price for buying and selling;

- smooth out the grain and edible oil price system.
5. To enhance macroeconomic regulation and develop the market system:
   - functional changes to the Ministry of Commerce; increase departmental administration of all industry; divert their focus from micro perspectives to macro control;
   - restructure the market, encouraging mainly wholesalers;
   - set up a market adjustment fund and reserve system for important products, so as to build up a specialized food reserve system;
   - clear up troublesome defaults, strengthen laws and set up industry associations.
6. To fix an official price for production materials:
   - to integrate guiding prices and market prices to form a price management system;
   - to adjust the scope of distribution for materials earmarked for unified distribution by the state.

China suffered from a sluggish market and was going through rectification processes between 1989 and 1991. Many wholesale channels and wholesale companies were reorganized. The contradictions of the old system were exposed, forcing state-owned wholesale enterprises to transform from administrative to managerial systems. However, most enterprises still suffer from a slump in the market due to strict policy controls and exposure to the external environment. Reform is more difficult as most people still think of the market economy under interference from both "the Left" and "the Right."

In-Depth Reform Stage (1992–Present)

Since Deng Xiaoping's visit and speech to the southern Special Economic Zone in 1992 in which he indicated the will of the 14th National Congress, there has been a breakthrough in the national understanding of the market economy. The 14th National Congress of the Communist Party of China clearly suggested that "the chief objective of the economic reform of China is to establish a socialist market economy." Since then China's economic reform, open-door policy and development have stepped into a new era. At the same Congress, the Central Committee passed a resolution which urged the reform of the existing commodity circulation system to develop the commodity market further, to establish a wholesale market of large scale agricultural products, industrial consumer products and production materials in the origin of selling, production or collecting and distributing centres of the important commercial goods, strictly allocating the limited pilot point of futures market. Circulation enterprises need to change their operating systems in order to become involved in market competition so as to enrich their economic benefits and to play a leading role in developed and developing wholesale markets. To promote distribution modernization, a fully functional commodity market network will need to be constructed according to the needs of commodity distribution, which will integrate operations of different sizes, economic forms and modes of operations. The core content of the economic reforms is to develop the market and hence to cultivate an integrated market system. The gradually deepening reforms exhibit the following main features:

1. To establish a market main body; speed up change in enterprise operation systems; set up a modern circulation enterprise system; improve contract systems and share-holding systems; to explore the reform of the "local-people-run-state-owned-businesses" policy in small scale enterprises; to try out share-holding cooperation systems in supply and marketing; to intensify the level of systemization in enterprises; to establish and develop business groups; and to explore formation and development of chain operations. Wholesale enterprises are to perform both wholesale and retail operations, develop sole distributors and agents, and build wholesale markets utilizing warehouse and storage spaces. A further aim was to break through the trade barrier by allowing foreign investment in retail business. A few Sino-foreign joint venture retail enterprises were first authorized to establish operations in Beijing, Shanghai, Tianjin, Dalian, Qingdao, Guangzhou and the five Special Economic Zones, which served as testing points. Twelve such projects were reviewed and approved during the early part of 1994.

2. To widen the scope of market: up to 1992, the number of commodities under the planning of the former Ministry of Commerce had been reduced to only 12. Four new forms of materials control and distribution for production supplies were implemented. These are: directive planning, government purchase contracts, negotiated

purchase orders between suppliers and users, and open market purchases.

3. To enhance macroeconomic regulation and reform the commodity market. Also to abolish the former Ministries of Commerce and of Materials and Equipment and establish the Ministry of Internal Trade. The new authorities will be the functional departments of commodity circulation for the whole of the country. To relate market data and production data in order to accelerate the unification of domestic and foreign trade. To speed up the transactions of county markets, local markets and international markets within the country so as to develop a large scale market, and circulation and trade. According to the philosophy of "emphasizing services and minimizing government interference," there will be reforms in commercial administration organizations; formation of group co-operation; continuation of the completion of the food reserve system and market risk system; establishment and completion of market regulation; and enhancement of the commercial information network. Also to implement the open policy for the price of grain and oil to operate (staple products market under free market); abolish the use of food coupons to end 40 years' of controlled procurement and distribution in China; and to open the price of food and catering services to market forces.

4. To cultivate the commodity market system, most cities have used city planning to accelerate the network establishment of commercial and food and catering services industries. To build modernized large-scale shopping arcades, hotels and shopping centres to a high standard. Specialized markets have been developing relatively fast, especially trade centres, wholesale markets and futures markets. Since the establishment of the Northern China Timber Wholesale Market in May 1992, there are a total of 20 production materials exchanges all over the country and 15 national markets for wholesale of production materials. Until 1992, there were more than 1,000 markets for wholesale of production materials, over 550 material trade centres, 1,000 industrial consumer product wholesale markets, 1,858 agricultural products wholesale markets and 79,188 pedlar's markets.

A Comparison of the Distribution System Model of the Traditional Planned Economy and the Recent Distribution System Model

Traditional Distribution Model

Commerce and industry are separated in the traditional distribution system (see Figure 1). The producer and distributor belonged to different departments. This led to a disconnection between production and distribution. For example, according to government production planning, production is monitored by the Ministries of Light and of Heavy Industry. The final products will be distributed to the different departments. As shown in Figure 1, the distribution system can be divided into two main streams: the production system and the commerce system. It is obvious that the production system controls the distribution of industrial products (production materials) and the commerce system controls consumer products (consumption materials). These two systems are under the control of the State Council.

Production System

The State Economic Commission is the highest authority in the industry hierarchy. Beneath it are the Ministries of Heavy Industry and of Light Industry. The lowest level consists of production factories like mobile and machine manufacturing. After meeting production targets made by the Commission, production units can sell excess products to other factories or end consumers. Other than that, they can also subscript materials from other supply units. The government will distribute specialized products to enterprises or end users according to their situation.

Commerce System

The Finance and Economics Committee was the highest authority in the Commerce System before 1981. Its function was then absorbed by the State Economic Commission. It monitors three main bodies: the Ministry of Foreign Economic Relations and Trade, the Ministry of Commerce, and the Materials and Equipment Bureau. Under these three main bodies are three levels of wholesale stations. They are: the 1st level wholesale station

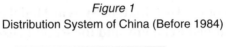

Figure 1
Distribution System of China (Before 1984)

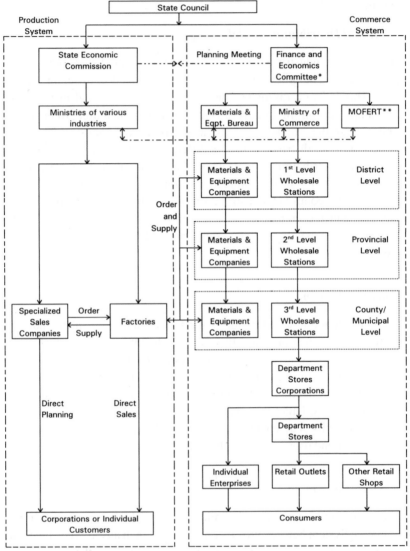

*   Abolished in March 1981, function absorbed by State Economic Commission.
** Ministry of Foreign Economic Relations and Trade.

(District level); 2nd level wholesale station (Provincial level); and 3rd level wholesale station (County/Municipal level). The 3rd level wholesale stations are responsible for the distribution of products to department store corporations or materials and equipment companies, in which products will be distributed to different branches. The cooperatives and branches will work out the optimal way to distribute products to end consumers.

Communication and Cooperation between Systems

Light industry has been paying more attention to Chinese economic reforms. In 1983, Ma Hong pointed out that the growing rate of light industry should be sped up and should become faster than that of heavy industry. He suggested that various heavy industry departments should also produce consumer products, especially durable consumer products. This would avoid a lack of coordination between production and distribution systems and hence build up different levels of communication channels. Moreover, the State Planning Commission would work out long- and short-term economic planning so as to bridge the work of the State Economic Commission and the Finance and Economics Committee. At the level of Ministries of various industries, there were informal contacts between the Ministry of Foreign Economic Relations and Trade, the Ministry of Commerce, and the Materials and Equipment Bureau to help solve the following problems:

- to appropriate a proportion of finished products for export;
- the Materials and Equipment Bureau to distribute industrial and consumer goods as planned by central government;
- to understand the demand and distribution of light industrial products.

After meeting country-wide targets, the Ministry of Light Industry can distribute finished products to different retail outlets. In fact, the Materials and Equipment Bureau has purchased products from the Ministry of Light Industry and then resold them to other enterprises. This helps solve some of the shortcomings of a planned economy.

The Chinese distribution system has experienced a tremendous evolution since the economic reforms began in 1979. The implementation of responsibility systems encourages workers and peasants to work harder to earn increased profits. More finished products have been poured into distribution channels. In 1981, the State Council suggested changes to the market distribution system. This helped open up more channels for products to reach the market by decreasing the consignor's buying time and shortening the distribution time. However, the traditional distribution system still has many disadvantages, although these are gradually diminishing due to the system transformation. Disadvantages include the following:

1. Too much emphasis on the direct and exclusive control of enterprises and top-down administration. A single channel disconnects the multiple level of production and distribution;

2. Enterprises do not comprise the main body of the market. They have no price-setting rights. Prices are fixed by the country. However, since there is a discrepancy between the central government and the market, overpricing or underpricing usually takes place as central government ignores the demand and economic differences of different regions;

3. Distribution is still based on the principle of equality, history and key regions. The principle of equality means that every unit will be given the same quantity of products regardless of the price, location and types of product. Distribution is based on historical principles. No amendments are made. Merits can still be found under this guideline. If evaluation and feedback of past distribution have been recorded, amendments can be made to reduce the difference between supply and demand. In the case of key regions, the quantity of products distributed depends on whether a region is designated a key region or not. Key regions will be allocated more. This method of distribution is based on the assumption that the demand of key regions is greater than that of non-key regions, and thus larger quantities should be distributed to key regions. This assumption has narrowed the gap between supply and demand of different regions, but still ignores the role of marketing in the distribution system;

4. The system shows that there were imbalances between supply and demand, or prices set at an inappropriate level. Before products deteriorate, traditional distribution systems will not try to sell all the products in order to minimize loss and waste;

5. Outdated infrastructure and bad conditions, lack of management systems and appropriate transportation are the main causes of

sluggish circulation. For instance, products mildew because of inappropriate storage;

6. Bad service attitude. This is mainly due to low income and long working hours. The "iron bowl system" lacks both positive and negative stimulation. Workers are lukewarm to their work and their attitude is bad. It has been said that "[we] get $36 whether [we] work or not."

New Tangible Product Distribution System

Figure 2 indicates the latest product distribution system originating from deepening reforming stage in 1997. Superficially speaking, there is no big difference in terms of structure between Figure 1 and Figure 2, especially the left side of the two figures. During the 13 years from 1984–1997, reformation of the product distribution system experienced great difficulties, but the transformation, which can be seen by making a comparison between the two figures, attracted great public attention. Figure 2 outlines the main parts of the distribution system and brings out the direction of the transformation supplemented by some practical examples and figures.

Both the production and distribution areas are managed by the State Planning Commission. The production area is under the control of the State Economic and Trade Commission. A sub-system was produced to replace the main distribution system in 1984. The State Economic and Trade Commission consists of two associations: the Chinese General Association of Light Industry, and the Chinese General Association of Textile Industry; also one bureau, the Civil Aviation General Administration of China and 14 divisions (see Figure 2). Different departments have their own production enterprises and supply and marketing companies. Production enterprises have different forms of ownership, which are not the same as traditional ones.

Following state planning policy, specialized sales companies can supply products directly to the business enterprises and individual consumers for reproduction or reselling. They can also sell some products not provided by the state directly to those organizations, i.e., once the production enterprise fulfils the State targets, they can fill orders from other resources trading centres or different kinds of wholesale companies by using their extra production capacity or manufacturing products subject to market demand and selling them directly to the wholesalers.

Figure 2

Distribution System of Tangible Products in China (1997)

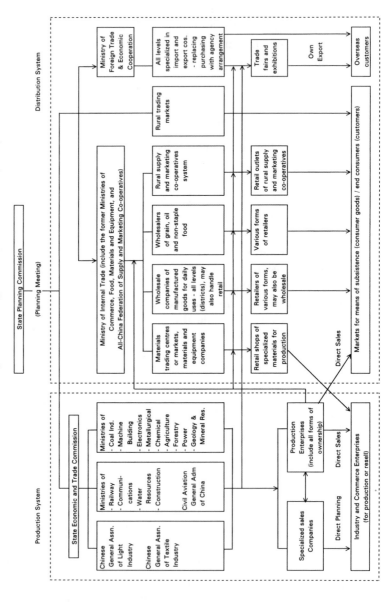

The coordination of production and distribution areas is based on results of the planning conference held between the State Economic Commission, Ministry of Internal Trade and Ministry of Foreign Economic Relations and Trade. Circulation policy planning is traditionally drawn up by the State Economic Commission and Finance and Economics Committee. The Materials and Equipment Bureau and Ministry of Commerce used to have different functions, but recently they have been merged into the Ministry of Internal Trade, which further strengthens the circulation efficiency of industrial, commercial and agricultural products. Import and export circulations are managed by the Ministry of Foreign Trade and Economic Cooperation, which used to be the Ministry of Foreign Economic Relations and Trade. As a result of the reforms, this Ministry has been assigned to manage specialized export companies by using the agency system instead of the purchasing system. This demonstrates that the Ministry of Foreign Trade and Economic Cooperation is not responsible for any losses created by unsaleable or unpopular foreigner-oriented products. They can also reject agents for those unsuitable products. These arrangements are much more flexible than before. The Ministry of Internal Trade includes the functions of the former Ministries of Commerce, Food, Materials and Equipment and All-China Federation of Supply and Marketing Cooperation. Four channels are identified.

The first channel is to distribute products purchased from production enterprises through the Materials and Trading Centre or materials and equipment companies to retail shops specializing in different production materials. These products will then be resold to industrial and commercial enterprises or be used in production. This is an industrial channel. Products are not usually sold to end consumers directly. The Material and Trading Company and Exchange Centre was formed by the change of the former Materials System from an administrative unit to an enterprise unit. The Chinese Statistical Annual Report in 1992 showed than there are more than 550 centres of this kind.

The second channel is to distribute industrial daily use products directly to buyers or end users through a regional wholesale company. Products can also be distributed to different types of agent or retail shops where they will then be sold to the buyer or consumers. This channel is more complicated than the original three levels of wholesale station. The wholesale stations in various levels have in fact been gradually transforming into trade centres, open markets and different types of wholesale market. Wholesale companies also carry out retailing, and retailers can purchase products directly from manufacturers. The circulation system also allows different types of retail ownership, including privately owned, individual enterprises, joint ventures, inland associated enterprises and collective enterprises. The Sino-foreign venture is only currently on trial and is restricted to retailing. In 1992, six cities and five Special Economic Zones were appointed to be pilot areas. The six cities are Shanghai, Beijing, Guangzhou, Tianjin, Qingdao and Dalian. The five Special Economic Zones are located in Shenzhen, Zhuhai, Shantou, Xiamen and Hainan. The State Council approved a total of 18 Sino-foreign ventures for department stores by early 1998 (see Table 1 of Chapter 13 in this book).

Various types of ownership have activated the development of department store retailing. Large-scale shopping centres, supermarkets and department stores have grown like mushrooms after the rain. The increase in fast food chain stores and chain supermarkets facilitate the knowledge of department store retailing and improve the retail environment. Shopping becomes a leisure activity in daily life.

The third channel is the distribution of grain, oil and non-staple food to various retail shops, where products will then be resold to consumers. This channel diversifies the supply of grain, oil and non-staple foods. As there is a great increase in products packaged for supermarkets and meat retail shops, products are well presented which strengthens sales potential despite the increase in production costs.

The fourth channel is mainly for the circulation of agricultural products. The Rural Supply and Marketing Cooperative purchases agricultural products from farmers and resells them to retail outlets.

The fifth channel is similar to the market town for farm products. Farmers sell their products directly or run small scale wholesaling in the market. The selling may take the form of barter trade or monetary exchange. Wholesale products will be purchased by the rural supply and marketing cooperatives in the fourth channel and then resold to other cooperatives and retail outlets.

The Ministry of Foreign Trade and Economic Cooperation is another important stream in the circulation domain. It manages specialized import-export companies of various levels. Enterprises in the production system in Figure 2 can also act as agents to export products to other countries through import-export companies.

Identification of Main Problems in the Reform of the Distribution System

A comparison of distribution systems between Chinese traditional planned economy and market economy was made to show the general trend in developments in the Chinese distribution system. Although these reforms promote the Chinese economy to a great extent, many problems are still left unsolved.

Mixed-Up Function of Political Organs and Enterprises

An enterprise's right to make decisions on product circulation has not yet been confirmed. The transformation of managerial mechanisms is also incomplete. Enterprises cannot stand on their own to make business. They are not mature enough to become market leaders. The deep-rooted reason for this is that the process of Chinese reforms is "from the top down." A confused relationship exists between political organs and enterprises. Property rights are not clearly identified and there is a mixture between functions, resulting in a confused line of responsibility for government organs and enterprises. Wholesale enterprises have to perform functions on main supply lines and reserves. They cannot decide themselves whether to become wholesalers or retailers. Nor are they capable of taking full responsibility for their own profits and losses. The reformation of State revenues and expenditure, tax revenues, human resources, the labour force, allocation and social security are incompatible and out of synchronization, resulting in difficulties in the transformation of the business system, especially for government-owned enterprises with heavy staff burdens, and large retail expenditure. As a result, these enterprises are unable to compete fairly in the marketplace.

Unsuccessful Price Reforms

Relaxation and adjustment of the price system is incomplete, so enterprises have problems in setting proper prices for their products. State-fixed prices are not strong enough to regulate the pricing system and so result in confusion between the state-set price and market-adjusted price. Due to a lack of proper management and control, the market-adjusted price can easily be marked up. The price regulating mechanism is imperfect, resulting in high inflation.

Incomplete Market System

The internal market suffers from the problems of serious decollation, regional blockades, town and county separation, industry strongholds, department monopolies and intensified competition in buying and selling. Regions and departments emphasize self-interest and evoke the *da er quan, xiao er quan* ("large and comprehensive" and "small and comprehensive") self-sufficient economic system. This leads to the integration and assimilation of regional economies. Barriers between different regions and departments and the mix of politics and enterprises has been exposed in the market. The domestic and overseas markets are still separated. Reforms of the external trade system are still not in place, and so external trade and internal trade are divided. The commodity market demonstrates a lack of unified planning. People are encouraged by the market and set up enterprises blindly. This wastes resources, and results in a large market with few transactions.

Lack of Regulation and Market Disorder

When the market is active, people tend to store up their goods to make better bargains or produce fake goods to attract more consumers. If the market is in a sluggish condition, default payments, "triangular debts," breach of contract and corruption are not uncommon. These result in a vicious cycle. Two reasons contribute to these phenomena. First, the new market and trading regulating system is not well-developed and is imperfectly set-up. Second, the macro economy is not strong enough to support the changes, and there are few system regulating measures. A unified authoritative market administration structure has not been developed, resulting in multiple departmental, legislative and administrative controls.

Conclusion

The Chinese socialist economy is a public ownership oriented market economy. To establish a truly socialist economic system and develop the market as a way to allocate resources, the establishment of a comprehensive distribution system is crucial. From a different angle, it can be said that "the market economy is the distribution economy." The distribution system is important in organizing social economic activities, facilitating in-depth market development, accelerating social reproduction, relieving different regulating factors in economic development, and integrating various production elements and resources effectively. Speeding up the reform of the product distribution structure and developing a market economy system requires reform of the distribution system. In a nutshell, establishing a modernized and market-oriented economy is an arduous task; it is inevitable that this cannot be achieved in the short term.

12

Chain Stores in China: Development, Problems and Prospects

Sha Zhen-quan, Oliver H. M. Yau and
Raymond P. M. Chow

Introduction

Following on the heels of department stores and supermarkets, chain stores are the new "Third Revolution" in retail organization. Alvin Toffler, an American futurologist, in *The Third Wave* (1980) predicted that by the year 2000, turnover in chain stores will occupy half of the total retail sales in the USA. Around the world, this industry is already well established in developed countries, and its adoption is gaining momentum in developing countries elsewhere.

In recent years, the operation of chain stores has attracted much attention from the Chinese government, the commercial sector, and mass media circles. Several relatively better developed operations are being presented as "model chain stores," highly praised and vigorously promoted by the government, and actively publicized by the press. In response to this publicity and pressure, and in view of economic benefits, those companies that can adopt the chain store organization do well, while those less prosperous small and medium-sized retail enterprises assume the label of "chain store" in an attempt to boost sales, basking in borrowed light. Meanwhile, foreign-funded chain stores, armed with abundant capital resources and rich experience, fortify their "beachhead" outlets in one form or another in many cities in China. Some even caused a sensation in the retail trade.

What caused such "chain store" upsurge in the Chinese market? What problems arise in the course of its development? What lessons can be learned? This chapter explores different aspects of these questions in seeking useful insight in guiding further development in China.

Exploration of the Factors Leading to the Growth of Chain Stores in China

Chain Stores Defined

In this chapter, "chain stores" are defined as "retail organizations consisting of two or more units under a single owner. All units generally carry the same (or similar) lines of merchandise, designed and decorated similarly, and rely on centralized buyers to select merchandise" (*Collin's Encyclopedia*, 1995, Vol. 15, p. 422).

Chain Operations in the History of China

While chain stores are popular and highly developed in overseas markets, and are now being introduced into China as a form of advanced retail operation, the origin of chain store-type organizations can be found in China's past. Using the product life cycle concept to model the development of chain stores in China, the following three developmental stages can be observed.

Embryonic Stage (?–1949)

Although it is not possible to determine exactly when the form of chain store operations started, it has been proved that the ancient courier posts (*yizhan*), armed-courier services (*biaoju*) and herbal medicine shops (*yaopu*) in China were operated as chain stores. However, in the past several thousand years, Chinese society followed a tradition that emphasized agriculture (physiocracy) and gave less attention to or even played down the role of commercial activities. Yet, the chain store form of business continued, being passed down through generations and exists still today. Famous examples are the Qiao Jia Shan Pastry Shop and the Zheng

Zhang Laundry and Dyeing Shop in Shanghai. Although these chain stores run relatively few outlets and their mode of operations may not be standardized, they are strong evidence supporting the claim that the origin of chain stores lies in China rather than in the United States (Li, 1994).

Chain Stores in the Period of Centrally Planned Economy (1950–1978)

After the liberation of China, the centrally operated commercial system (*shangye tixi*) was owned and controlled by the State, under a unified policy with guiding principles of state monopolistic purchase and supply. For instance, staple food shops in all cities were under the administration of the Staple Food Bureau. They supplied almost the same sorts of items at the same prices, and the citizens were obliged to buy from these stores using the food coupons issued by the respective local offices of the State Food Bureau. Such a commercial system, somewhat similar to chain stores in that they were all owned by the state and sold similar merchandise, differs radically from the concept of modern chain store operation today.

Firstly, there are differences in the macro-environmental conditions. The unified commercial system was the result of the planned economy. Under this system, all supplies were distributed according to the central plan, and the outlets were under the control of the same administrative unit. Participation of other enterprises and individuals was forbidden or restricted because the system was monopolistic and did not have the fierce competitive pressures of market economies. Adoption of the chain store mode of operations by retailers in China fortified the strength of the corporation, benefiting from lower cost through mass production and economy of scale with reduced risk.

Secondly, under the planned economy system, the state-owned enterprises were all governed by related departments and thus had no autonomous power. Fundamentally, they were just administrative units. While on the one hand this facilitated the central government in their planning and control of the distribution network (*fenxiao xitong*), on the other hand it led to high costs and low operating efficiency. In contrast, modern chain store operations are a business. The corporation and all its retail outlets constitute a unified and integrated economic entity in pursuit of economic benefits under the mechanism of the market value system in an attempt to maximize profits at the lowest cost.

Thirdly, with the state-owned commercial structure of the planned economy system operating under the monopolistic purchase and supply mechanism, price was determined and controlled by the government without taking into consideration the needs and wants of the consumers. Modern chain store enterprises operate according to the unified purchase but diversified distribution concept that offers the freedom of choice of suppliers. Retail prices and sales tactics are determined based on the market demand and supply conditions.

Lastly, competitive marketing strategies were not needed in the state-owned commercial structure operating within the planned economy system. There was no unified shop name, layout and appearance, and the operations were not standardized. The government maintained the outlets even if they were operating at a loss. On the contrary, modern chain stores operate with a unified corporate image and standardized business practices. They strive for continued enhancement of market share by employing competitive marketing strategies and capitalizing on modern scientific and management techniques.

Chain Stores under Planned Economy System Facing Severe Challenges

Since the implementation of the revised staple food purchase and supply policy by the State in May 1991, there have been marked changes in the cereals and edible oil market in Guangzhou. The gap between the negotiated and equilibrium prices has almost been closed. As a result, sales at equilibrium price dropped drastically, while newly formed private individual business and collectively-owned enterprises selling cereals and edible oil at negotiated price increased substantially. Some unlicensed hawkers even openly offer to sell their products in front of the staple food shops. The monopolistic position of the state-owned outlets in the planned staple food distribution network has been demolished. A new multi-ownership, multi-channel, multi-trading-mode form of business is gradually taking shape, with intensified competition. The retail system under the administration of the Municipal Department of Cereals Management is incurring losses. The "chained" staple food shops under the planned economy system is now facing severe challenges (*Guangzhou Daily*, 15 October 1991).

There are marked differences between the planned economy and market economy systems. Common characteristics, however, can also be identified. We can therefore name chain store operations in this period as the stage of "chain operations under the planned economy system."

According to the definition of the modern chain stores, it would be more appropriate to consider these two earlier developmental stages as the states of "associated company" (*lianhao*) or "amalgamation" (*lianhe*). Such operations should perhaps be treated as the early form of chain store operations in China.

Upsurge of the Modern Chain Stores — The "Entry Stage" (1979–Present)

Up to the end of 1994, the number of outlets ran by several large chain store groups in China was insufficient to break even financially. According to the General Manager of the Shanghai Hualian Supermarket Group that ran 11 outlets in 1994, the group could break even with over 20 outlets, and could ensure profitable returns with 40 (*Guangdong–Hong Kong Information Daily*, 8 June 1994). That is to say, economies of scale could not be achieved due to the small number of outlets. Despite the above, fundamental changes in the operating concepts, the level of technology employed, the number, size and scale of the retail outlets did take place during this developmental stage. This third stage can be treated as the period of transition from entry to growth phase using the product life cycle concept.

In 1986, the Tianjin-based Lida Group built the Lida International Plaza in Tianjin and began to establish chain stores both in and outside of the country. This was the first chain operation in China since the economic reforms. It heralded the beginning of the development of the chain store system and made valuable contributions to the exploration of the formation of modern Chinese-style chain store operations. In 1991, the Chinese government began to put forward the strategic concept of "Rapid Circulation, Megamarket, Big Business" (*da liutong, da shichang, da shangye*) to foster momentum in the reform of the distribution system, and at the same time to set a specific path to explore the ways and means to establish and develop chain store operations. Since then, chain store operations have begun to develop on a relatively larger scale in China, as can be seen in the following reports:

Rapid Development of the Modern Chain Stores in China

On 20 September 1991, the Shanghai Lianhua Supermarket Corporation, the first supermarket chain company in China, was founded in Shanghai. Its first outlet in the Quyang district was opened on the same day. Marching forward with their slogan of "Lianhua is right next to you," they choose, as their target market, the newly developed residential districts that are highly populated yet have few commercial establishments. The Lianhua supermarket outlets are not large in size, mostly between 500 to 800 sq. metres; they operate 12 hours daily, and deal primarily with daily necessity items, 60% of which are non-staple food and the rest daily consumable (Li and Ma, 1995).

Also developing rapidly is the Hualian Supermarket Company, another supermarket group in Shanghai. In addition to their own direct chain outlets, Hualian expanded through the development of franchised stores. On 20 August 1995, six supermarkets in the Pudong district of Shanghai and Wuxi formally joined the Hualian franchising chain. This represented expansion both in operations — from chain stores to franchised outlets, and in geography — beyond the city boundary. Since this move, the Hualian Group has developed plans to increase the number of their franchised outlets to about 30 in the coming three years (*Xin Min Wan Bao*, 20 August 1995).

The development of chain operations in Guangzhou can also be traced back to the mid-1980's. According to incomplete statistics of the Commerce Committee of the Guangzhou Municipal Government, as of June 1995, there were 25 state-owned or collectively-owned chain store corporations in Guangzhou, with altogether over 190 retail outlets. Operating as convenient stores, supermarkets, speciality shops, etc., these chain stores included department stores, restaurants, and shops selling clothing, food and non-staple necessities, vigorously promoting distribution in the Guangzhou area (*Guangzhou Daily*, 15 September 1995).

Although formally classified statistics of the chain store business are not available, a general observation can be drawn from the above cases and from the data released by the various cities. In 1995, in Guangdong province, total sales of the chain stores that focus on retailing amounted to over RMB 5 billion. This accounted for approximately 2.5% of the province's total retail sales of the year, double that of 1994. Chain operations in Shenzhen, Guangdong developed even faster and recorded total turnover of RMB 2.25 billion in 1995, representing 10.5% of their total retail business. In 1997, the total number of chain store outlets in China reached 14,000 (Chain Stores Association of Guangdong; *Market Daily*, 8 July 1998), an increase of 43% over the prior year. Total sales through these outlets amounted to RMB 42 billion, representing 1.5% of total national retail sales, and 40% increase over 1996. These statistics demonstrate powerful momentum in the development of the chain store business in some of the cities in China. They are further depicted in Figure 1.

Figure 1
Number of Chain Outlets — Selected Cities in China, 1995 & 1997

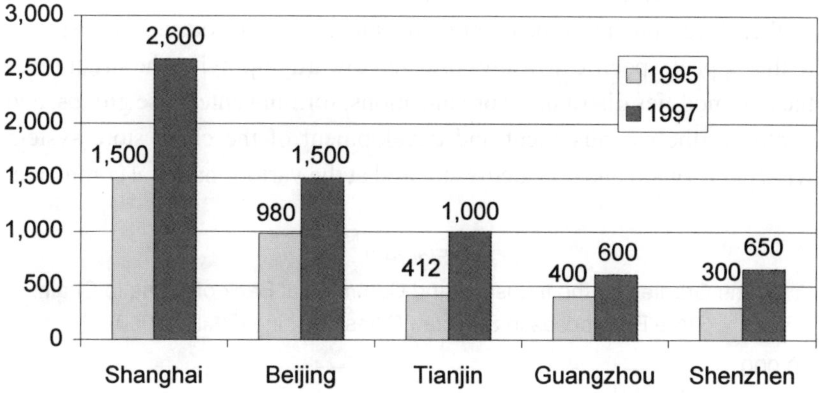

Source: The Chain Stores Association of Guangdong.

Causes for the Revival of the Chain Store Business in China

Attention and Encouragement of the Chinese Government, Publicity in Mass Media

Attention, support and active promotion by the government have been significant and indispensable contributing factors to the development of the chain store business in China. In the course of modernizing their product distribution mechanism, many developed countries have taken measures to enhance the structure of their distribution systems through stimulating the development of chain store operations. The Japanese government has been most persistent, and the effect is remarkably noticeable. Since the launch of their policy on promoting retail chain operations in the 1960s in almost all of their major political platforms, the Japanese government has advocated and promoted financial subsidies to support the development of chain operations in the retail business. Among these, particular emphasis has been given to chain stores in the form of voluntary integration and franchising. From this standpoint, the Japanese government has been instrumental in the growth and advancement of the retail business (Li, 1994).

After the speech made by Deng Xiaoping during his inspection tour to South China in early 1992, a breakthrough in the conceptual understanding of the market economy was achieved. The Chinese government stated explicitly, "Reformation of the current product distribution system, and further development of the commodities markets must occur." In response to this appeal, specific measures directed toward improving the structure of the commodities distribution organizations, forming enterprise groups, and exploring the establishment and development of the chain store system were put forward and repeatedly stressed at the various national commerce,

Figure 2

Loans Granted by the Industrial and Commercial Bank of China to Chain Store Enterprises in Selected Cities of China (RMB10,000)

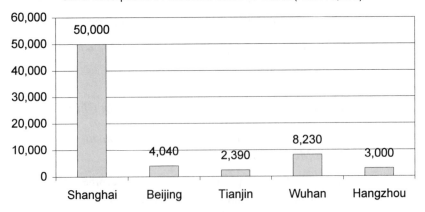

Source: The Chain Stores Association of Guangdong.

economic and trade conferences. Seizing the opportunity, the mass media also actively publicized the campaign that led to a "chain stores explosion" in China. In the meantime, local governments at different levels added their active support:

Active Supports from the Government

In terms of financial support, the Beijing Municipal Government determined that a loan of RMB200,000 will be granted to each new convenience chain store establishment, and RMB2 million to each supermarket. The Finance Authority of the respective municipal, county or district governments will subsidize 25 per cent of the interest payment for three years. A further loan of RMB50,000 will be granted by the municipal, county or district governments to each convenience store added according to plan (RMB 500,000 for supermarket), repayable after three years. Capital repayments will be put into a chain store developmental fund for recurring use (*The Investment Times*, 29 September 1995) (see Figure 2).

Regarding taxes, the Commerce Committee of the Guangzhou Municipal Government brought forth that for the newly established chain operations, a one-year exemption on income tax would be granted counting from the date of the commencement of the business, subject to audit and approval. The chain operations as a stand-alone accounting unit will be treated as an independent taxpayer and will be required to pay the unified tax to the tax authority. Similar policies have also been promulgated by the Beijing, Nanjing and Chengdu municipal governments (*The Investment Times*, 29 September 1995).

On shop space, the Tianjin Municipal Government stipulated that for property sold to the chain stores enterprises, price will be fixed at the construction cost of the building; if rented, three years rental will be waived (*The Investment Times*, 29 September 1995).

On simplification of the procedures on business registration, the Chengdu Municipal Government announced that the chain stores group and its branch outlets can apply to the local commerce and industry administration authorities for unincorporated trading license on a unified arrangement (*The Investment Times*, 29 September 1995).

While different strategies are employed by the local governments, they all demonstrate determination to respond to the call of the central government to support the development of chain stores. Through the adoption of this modern chain stores form of commercial structure, the Chinese government seeks to accelerate the pace of the reform of the distribution system, reduce the cost of the distribution operations, curb inflation of prices, prevent fake products and products of poor quality from entering the distribution network, and hence improve the efficiency of the entire economy.

Increase in Productivity

To cope with the development of chain store operations, a higher level of industrial production is necessary. Unified multi-store operations and the self-selection mode of the supermarkets require manufacturers to supply products of standardized specifications, of stable quality, in multiple varieties, with high process contents, and with excellent packaging and labelling, to enhance the engagement of the unified business strategies, uniform pricing, and the application of high standard technical skills in promotional tactics, as well as to facilitate self-servicing of consumers.

Since the economic reforms, rapid growth in the productivity of China has been evidenced. The following are some examples:

Improved Product Availability

Beer had been a product in short supply in China, and was only available in limited quantity in a few big cities. However, the sellers' market was turned into a buyers' market in just over ten years. For imported brands alone, mostly manufactured by joint venture factories, there are already over twenty types in the market, such as Heineken, Carlsberg, San Miguel, and Pabst, available in various sizes in bottles and cans (*Market Analysis Report* — China Pabst Brewery Group Company).

In the old days, some food products such as confectionery items were only sold in bulk, and shop assistants had to weigh each sale before the transaction could be completed. Most items available for sale are already packaged or in deluxe packaging now (Sha, 1992).

While quality, variety and specification of the products made in China still cannot fully satisfy the needs of the chain store operations, considerable improvement has been observed in the past ten years. Chinese-made products are gradually replacing imported ones, and are taking up more shelf space in the chain stores.

Sizeable Increase in the Total Income of Individuals in China

With regard to the distribution of food and daily necessities, the advantages of chain stores are their centralized, sizeable and professional operations. To capitalize on these strengths requires that the household income must reach a level to produce stronger purchasing power. Only when a certain income level is attained will the consumption power then be increased and will the consumers be able to afford the added value for the refined processing such as cleaning, cutting and repackaging, etc. that would be reflected in the selling price of the products.

Shanghai is a good example of such evolution. In the 1990s the per capita income of the residents in Shanghai was already very close to that of the level of Hong Kong in the 1970s, at which time the supermarket chain operations began to boom there. In the case of Hong Kong, the launch of the health ordinance on the control of rice was the leading cause that pushed up the sales of rice in the supermarkets, which also increased demand for other items and drove the rapid development of the supermarket business in Hong Kong. For Shanghai and the other cities, the announcement made by the Chinese government in 1992 to allow cereal commodities to be traded in the marketplace, hence ending the historical central purchasing and supply mechanism, brought about the reform of the cereal retail chains and facilitated the evolution of the supermarkets.

The Exemplary Role of Foreign-Funded Operations

The year 1992 saw a breakthrough in the restrictions on the participation of foreign enterprises in the retail industry of China. A few testing points for Sino-foreign joint venture or cooperative venture retail enterprises were allowed to be established in Beijing, Tianjin, Shanghai, Dalian, Qingdao, Guangzhou and the five Special Economic Zones (SEZs). The vast consumer market of China has been a major attraction to foreign companies, which want to be among the first to enter the market. However, even though the Chinese government announced the opening up of the retail business, it still was not easy for a foreign firm to enter through the normal channels. As a result, those that were too impatient to wait, took various "circuitous," "flanking" and "flexible" routes to set up their beachhead outlets in major cities. These created considerable disturbances in the domestic retail industry, and many eye-opening experiences for the state-owned enterprises.

Exemplary Role of Foreign-Funded Operations

Through a local cooperative arrangement, the Giordano Group of Hong Kong established direct outlets in Beijing Road, Changti Road and Renmin South Road of Guangzhou in September, 1992. Utilizing modern scientific management techniques to regulate their business processes, Giordano launched products with their unique character to satisfy the needs of the consumers, their outstanding customer service to induce purchases, and their attractive remuneration to stimulate enthusiasm of the employees. "All these provided valuable exposure to the state-owned enterprises, and also spur us on" (*Guangzhou Daily*, 21 March 1993).

Problems Encountered by Chain Stores in China

While the development of chain stores in China continues to pick up tremendous momentum, there have been problems that should not be forgotten. From the retailers' point of view, some of these are problems resulting from subjective factors while others have external causes.

Some of the State-Owned Chain Stores Are Just Chained in Form; Structural Reform Has Yet to Be Realized

Regardless of the form of the chain, be it formally established, voluntarily amalgamated or created through franchising, the fundamental economic theory of economy of scale is the underlying concept of chain operations. However, for some of the state-owned chain stores, this concept is simply the adoption of a common shop name, unified shop front design and standardized advertising. The outlets are not willing to let go of their control in procurement and in financial and human resources management. They agree only to join the chain in form, but not in substance, especially with regard to the reassignment of powers. On one extreme, some base-level leaders take the view that under chain operations, they would have to surrender their authority. In so doing, they would violate the spirit of "strengthening the autonomous power of the enterprises," an injunction continuously promoted under the reform.

In the West, some of the chain operations were originated by the self-initiated, cooperative efforts of small retailers that integrated themselves to form chain stores to counteract the threats exerted on them due to the expanded power of the large corporations. Small state-owned retail shops in China also have such an "amalgamation" status.

Structural and Policy Issues

Outlets of the Beijing Lucky Chain Stores are formerly the branch stores of the Beijing West-Town District Non-Staple Food Company. Formation of the chain was a decision of the company and not that of the desire of the outlets. They are operating 20 outlets now. According to their General Manager, the combined total volume of the incoming merchandise of these 20 stores is still not as big as that of a large shopping arcade. Their distribution centre still could not satisfy the needs of such multi-stores operations. They are short of operating capital, and even experience difficulties in settling the medical bills for their staff. There are still many unfavourable structural and policy issues in the organization (Li and Ma, 1995).

The Need for the Government to Review the Policy Issues to Facilitate the Practical Operations of the Chain Stores

Although all local governments take chain stores and supermarkets as their focal point for major developments, there are still difficulties hindering the advancement of chain store enterprises, due mainly to the lack of solid supportive policies. Some domestic chain store enterprises consider that the biggest problems they face in running their business come from various administrations and the involvement of many government organizations. Under the existing review and approval process, to open up a chain store, a firm must apply for various permits for the sales of different products (e.g., cigarettes, spirits, medicine, and imported fruit) from respective government offices, in addition to the business license. Apart from these bureaucratic problems, the various kinds of inspections demanded by the offices are also administered under different government bodies. For example, food products are subject to quality inspections not only by the district and the municipal consumer councils, but also by epidemic prevention stations of both the district and municipal authorities. For imported items, port and frontier inspections are also required (*The Investment Times*, 29 September 1995).

High Operating Costs of Chain Stores Make It Difficult to Survive

The current operating costs of chain stores are maintained at a high level, mainly due to the following three reasons. Firstly, there are high rental expenses, especially those for properly organized stores. Even when they take over small shops that were running in the red, the supplemental expenses are still huge. For example, Shanghai Hualian spent about RMB 4.8 million on rental expenses for their 11 outlets in 1993. Adding on the depreciation expenses of over RMB 2 million caused the corporation to run at a loss.

Secondly, the small number of outlets find it extremely difficult to distribute the allocated expenses. Economies of scale have not been achieved.

Thirdly, some supermarket chains are very concerned about their shop security and hence are reluctant to reduce the number of cashiers, merchandisers and inspectors. Incremental labour costs for the processing and packaging of the acquired items such as meat, vegetables and fruit are also substantial. As a result, some chain stores find themselves in a vicious cycle: higher costs force them to increase their selling prices; increased selling prices turn customers away; a smaller customer base in turn raises relative costs; and the stores end up with even greater losses.

Development of the Chain Stores Has to Rely on the Concerted Support of Society

Even though productivity improved drastically after the economic reforms in China, there are still limited products suitable for selling in chain stores. A recent survey conducted in January 1996 in the supermarkets in the five major shopping arcades in Guangzhou revealed that the proportion of locally-made products on the shelves (although increased compared to the prior years) was only about 40%. The primary reason behind this mismatch comes from the still unmet challenge of satisfying the needs of consumers in terms of product quality, packaging, labelling and specifications. Taking bar-code labelling as an example, computer systems are being installed in some of the privately-owned and joint venture chain stores to improve their process and management efficiencies; however if bar-codes are not incorporated into the products supplied by the manufacturers, it is still difficult if not impossible for the chains to realize some gain in their operating efficiency. Some manufacturers still have not applied to the China Commodities Coding Centre for the assignment of unified commodity code numbers for their products. The Centre has branches all over China and administers the assignment of commodity code numbers following international standard practices. Some chain stores are thus creating their own coding systems. As one recent report noted:

Unmet Challenge of Satisfying Needs of Consumers

In his speech made at a press conference on the occasion of the opening of the Hutai Branch of the Shanghai No. 1 Department Stores Company Limited, the biggest retail store in China, Mr. Wang Guanqun, Vice General Manager said, "There is an extremely limited number of items available in the China market that are suitable for distribution in the large supermarkets. Manufacturers in China must exert tremendous efforts to develop and produce various kinds of products suitable for supply in the supermarkets." The Hutai branch had planned to put 8,000 items on sale in their supermarket; however after their three to four months of elaborate planning and searching efforts, they still could not come up to the desired level, as only slightly over 6,000 items were made available. The Majority of these 6,000 plus items do not carry bar-code labels on them (*Huanan Jingji Journal*, 16 December 1993)

Some Thoughts on the Development of Chain Stores in China

To Intensify Research Efforts and Training and Development of Human Resources in Modern Enterprises

For a long period of time, under the influence of the State's emphasis on production and low attention to distribution, tertiary institutions and schools for professional training shifted their research effort to other areas of interest, or areas related to the commercial field. Some research projects conducted by academics and their students were redirected to address issues in the industrial management area. The situation might have been different if primary efforts on training, education and research had been directed to focus on retailing after the launch of the economic reforms. A Chinese proverb says, "It takes ten years to grow trees, but a hundred to rear people." If this had been done, there would have been a batch of talented, first-line personnel with good modern business education. Such a situation has been identified in Shenzhen:

Lack of Talented Business Persons and Theoretical Research

One of the factors hindering the development of the large-scale commercial establishments in Shenzhen is their lack of talented business persons. Figures in the retail industry of Shenzhen commented, "In Shenzhen, there is generally not enough attention devoted to talent of the people. We are short of not only better educated people with experience of working in large shopping centres and with understanding of new business concepts, but also of talent to work on theoretical research in the commercial area." (*The Investment Times*, 20 October 1995)

It is therefore imperative that China must eliminate such a deficiency in training and development and in basic research. It must recognize the important role that retailing is playing in the national economy, and must strengthen the efforts in business research and the development of human resources with modern business education. Only then would there be sustaining power to support the development of the business activities in China heading toward a positive route for further advancement.

A Correct Perception of the Distinct Meaning of "Chain"

Chain stores are a new form of organization, not just a fine-tuning of the mode of retailing, nor simply restructuring of the constructs of merchandising. To boost sales, some retail shops in China simply changed their names and have themselves administered like chain stores. This would probably not bring them any substantive improvement in business volume and profit, and neither the shops nor consumers would benefit from such superficial refinements.

Reliance on the In-Depth Reform of the Economic System

The success of chain stores, especially those state-owned ones, has to rely on further advancement in the reform of the economic system. Only when enterprises truly become an integral part of the market economy and a mechanism for the profit-seeking motive can be developed such that compensation to the management of enterprises is linked to the economic performance of the business, will a balance between the benefits to the operators and that of the shops be maintained.

Integration of the Technological and Social Factors

Various forms of retail operations can be engaged in under the chain stores mode of organization, such as department stores, supermarkets, convenience stores, etc., which are determined by different technological and social factors. Technological factors refer to those basic elements relating to the strategies and tactics employed by the retailers (e.g., pricing strategy, auxiliary facilities, shop location, etc.), and social factors encompass those characteristics relevant to the target customers (e.g., living conditions, car ownership, etc.). In order to adopt and diffuse a successfully acquired foreign retail system, careful consideration must be taken to match the technological factors of the system with the specific social characteristics of the system. Modifications or renovations might sometimes be necessary to cope with the unique environment in China. One example is the warehouse-type operation:

Chain Operations or Transfer of Retail Technology?

Warehouse stores, having great vitality, are very popular in the Western society, and have become one of the main streams in the retail industry in the world today. However, the warehouse stores acquired and established in Shenzhen encountered tremendous problems: citizens of China do not always purchase in bulk; unavailability of parking space in front of the shops also do not induce institutional buyers; high rental for outlets operating in the downtown districts, and etc. (*Nanfang Weekend*, 1 September 1995).

Taking just the few most essential technological and social factors for comparison, it may become obvious that the difficulties experienced by the

Shenzhen warehouse stores, some of which are organized as chains, are fundamental problems resulting from not understanding the technological characteristics of warehouse store operations and the matching social conditions. These characteristics are not typical of chain stores elsewhere in the world. Table 1 below shows a comparison of different social and technological factors applicable to warehouse stores in USA and China.

Table 1
Social Factors and Technological Factors

Warehouse Stores in USA		Warehouse Stores in China	
Social Factors	Technological Factors	Social Factors	Technological Factors
Larger living space, larger refrigerators	Low price strategy, facilitate bulk purchases	Smaller living space, smaller refrigerators	Low price strategy, but small price differentials
High household ownership of cars	Plenty of parking space	High bicycle ownership, low household ownership of cars	No parking space, some even do not have parking space for bicycles
Higher populations in suburban areas	In suburban districts where rental is lower, self-service, lower labour content	Higher populations in urban or residential districts	In urban districts — high rentals, self service but labour savings not so significant

A Need to Master Research on Business Strategies

We have observed that some of the better performing retail shops, especially those large shopping arcades, would tend to employ an expansion tactic capitalizing on the strategic location of shops. This investment strategy appears to be a risk avoidance approach as compared with the setting up of branch operations in other areas, since the business volume in the initial period could not be guaranteed and the payback period would also be difficult to forecast. However, in the longer term, the return on investment might not be appropriate, and the risk might not be totally eliminated. Some of the shops that took this approach in expanding the operations on the same shop site began to see negative growth in their marginal profits. It is therefore advisable to note that a good location today might turn out to be a less than satisfactory site tomorrow. On the other hand, a less preferred location could work out to be a profitable outlet due to improvement in traffic conditions and relocation of inhabitation, etc. In their investment decision process on selecting new outlets, the retail enterprises in China usually use rental expenses as a base to determine the break-even sales volume, which will then be adjusted to project the future turnovers based on the experience of their managers. Some might appoint a marketing consultant firm to perform a feasibility study. If the projected revenue exceeds the break-even sales volume, they will then proceed with analysis of other factors, and make their final selection and decision. Such an analytical approach, in general, would seem to be crude and incomplete. We therefore recommend that the retail operators in China intensify their efforts in their business investment evaluation process, focus on analysis and research into the relevant strategies of the chain operations, so as to develop a more comprehensive and rational framework for their investment and business processes and at the same time provide substantive benefits to consumers.

Conclusion

Structured on a substantial collection of secondary data, this chapter presents a general overview of the development of chain stores in China, and at the same time highlights some directional questions for further discussion and research. The year of 1996 was the first year of the implementation of the "9th Five-Year Plan" in China. Looking ahead into the beginning of the twenty-first century, it can be anticipated that there would be significant development in the chain operations in China, in which the state-owned chain stores, being the main stream of the distribution network, would continue to play a leading role. The following newspaper extract from the *Guangzhou Daily* (15 September 1995) indicates the direction of this development:

Setting the Path for Future Development

In August 1995, the Guangzhou Municipal Government called a commercial chain business operations working conference, signifying that speeding up of the reform of the chain stores business as one of the major

---

reconstruction projects of Guangzhou. During the "9th Five-Year Plan," the municipal government plans to support the restructuring or establishment of ten supermarkets or convenience stores chains, with a total of 80 to 100 outlets. It is anticipated that by the year 2000, the total number of commercial chain operations will exceed 40 per cent of the state-owned and collectively-owned establishments in Guangzhou, its total sales would represent over 50 per cent of the total turnover of these establishments. At the same time, it has plans to foster and develop 20 large size chain business groups, with ten modern multi-municipal, multi-provincial and multi-national chain organizations, to cope with the building of a commercial centre in Guangzhou (*Guangzhou Daily*, 15 September 1995).

Like Guangzhou, other cities of China have also announced plans to support the development of chain stores during the "9th Five-Year Plan." During the Asian Pacific Economic Cooperation Conference held in Japan in the later part of 1995, General Secretary Jiang Zemin announced that China would further open the retail market and would allow more establishments of Sino-foreign joint venture retail operations. This would undoubtedly create moderating effects on the development of chain stores in China.

Since the economic reforms, the retail industry in China has undergone a major evoluation. After the Third Round Meetings of the 11th National Congress of CPC, the State began to enhance the growth of the economy through promoting the development of various economic constructs, and allowed the rapid development of private business in the distribution system. On the one hand, the evolution of private businesses created competitive pressures on the state-owned enterprises; on the other hand, this motivated the reform of the state-owned and collectively-owned retail industry, and enhanced the growth and prosperity of the market. The retail industry is now facing another evolution: the gradual loosening of restrictions on the entry of foreign capital in the retail business and foreign participation and technology-stimulated competition at a higher level. To attain the desired objectives through such evolution in the distribution system, China should employ various advanced retail technologies and management skills with a high degree of flexibility, and it should improve the marketing management capability. In so doing, modernization of the

China retail industry could soon be achieved (*Nihon Keizai Shinbun,* February 1993).

Even taking competition into consideration, opening the retail market will bring more good than harm to the local economy. It will stimulate joint efforts of the state-owned retail enterprises in the following ways:

- to develop their businesses;
- to bring domestic capital together to create sizeable operations (chain stores can benefit from economies of scale);
- adopting modern skills and technologies in business management;
- better utilization of logistics and other related supports in a more cost-effective manner;
- capitalizing on the publicity and influence gained from the power of size to attract interested parties; and
- to step up the franchising operations.

Once economies of scale can be achieved, most problems encountered by the chain stores today can easily be resolved. Chain stores in China can advance further in development and will eventually benefit the growth of the entire economy.

13

Foreign Investment in Tertiary Industries in China: A Retail Sector Perspective

C. S. Tseng

Deng Xiaoping's surprise visit to southern China in the spring of 1992 reaffirmed the government's intention to continue with the economic reforms and become more open to the outside world. The message from the visit was backed up by subsequent Central Committee and State Council documents, but of particular interest was Document No. 5 issued in June 1992, which urged the provincial and local authorities to faster development of tertiary industries. According to the official definition used in China, primary industries refer to agriculture; secondary industries refer to construction and manufacturing; and tertiary industries refer to retail, foreign trade, warehousing, finance and insurance, accountancy, real estate, restaurant, culture, education, health, etc.

Since then, market access restrictions have also been relaxed in services industries such as retailing, banking, accounting, advertising, and insurance. Among all the service sectors, the most prominent is the retail sector. Many new commercial districts are being set up in major cities throughout China. Old commercial districts are being redeveloped and shops renovated: examples are Nanjing Lu, Huaihai Zhonglu, and Sichuan Beilu in Shanghai. Many foreign-owned department stores/speciality shops such as Sincere, Lane Crawford, Isetan, and Crocodile garment shops have also been set up. In the past, many shops were closed at night and now many of them are open until late at night even on Sunday.

This chapter attempts to focus on the historical development of as well as foreign participation in reforms of the retail sector in China. Theoretical implications will also be discussed.

Reforms of Distribution and Retailing

In China, before the economic reform, retail distribution of consumer goods was under state monopoly. The so-called three-tier structure consisted of specialized corporations under the Ministry of Commerce or local Commercial Bureau divided along product lines to handle specific categories or groups of goods. For instance, the distribution of household electrical appliances was under the control of the metals, transport, electrical and chemical companies, a corporation under the first Commercial Bureau. The three-tier structure comprised the First Level Purchasing and Supply Enterprises (FLPSEs), the Second Level Purchasing and Supply Enterprises (SLPSEs) and the Third Level Wholesalers (TLWs). The FLPSEs were located in three cities only, namely Tianjin, Shanghai and Guangzhou. Reporting to the Ministry of Commerce in Beijing and the local Commercial Bureau, the FLPSEs purchased goods from all over China, accepted imported goods, and then distributed these goods to the second tier of the system, the SLPSEs. The SLPSEs operated at the provincial level; each reported to the Commercial Bureau of the province and also to the local government department taking charge of commercial matters. They were normally located at capital cities of the provinces, and were responsible for purchase of goods from FLPSEs and then distribution to the TLWs in the various cities and counties, which in turn redistributed to local retailers that were normally state-owned enterprises. The supply and distribution of goods in rural areas was under the control of the Supply and Marketing Cooperatives. Regional protectionism characterized this system. The retailers were only allowed to buy from wholesalers within the dictated region; supplies from elsewhere were brought in only as a very last resort.

Since 1979, the central government has introduced a series of reforms in the distribution systems: enterprises from non-commercial systems, such as production enterprises, as well as private and collective enterprises, were gradually allowed to participate in the distribution and retailing of consumer goods. By the late eighties, the distribution and retailing of household electrical appliances could be handled by different types of companies, for example, distribution of Domestic Appliances (DAPs) from

Philips in Shanghai was handled by a company under the Agricultural Bureau.

Foreign Participation in Distribution and Retailing

Before 1991, access to China's consumer market was restricted to domestic enterprises. Foreign companies were not allowed to set up direct retail outlets. All foreign manufactured consumer goods had to be imported by the Foreign Trade Corporations, subject to high tariffs and licensing requirements where applicable.

Another alternative was to set up a manufacturing plant either in the form of a contract manufacturing/joint venture or wholly-owned venture. It might be possible to distribute part of the production in China if a domestic sales right was granted, as consumer goods were not considered priority projects. Export to China or setting up manufacturing plant there usually met with many obstacles.

China decided to open up the retail sector to foreigners in 1992. The policy statement (Document No. 5) issued by the Communist Party of China and the State Council on 16 June 1992 titled "Decision To Accelerate Development of Tertiary Industries," urged the provincial and local authorities to take bolder measures to utilise foreign capital know-how and technology and develop distribution channels (State Council Office, PRC, 1992).

Following this, in October 1992, the State Council announced that a maximum of two large-scale joint-venture department stores would be allowed to operate in six cities and five Special Economic Zones (SEZs) on a trial basis. The six cities are Beijing, Shanghai, Tianjin, Dalian, Qingdao, Guangzhou, and the SEZs are Shenzhen, Xiamen, Zhuhai, Shantou and Hainan.[1] These joint-venture department stores must be approved by central government (*Hong Kong Economic Journal*, 21 March 1993). They are allowed to sell a full range of merchandise and enjoy import and export rights. They can import goods for sale, limited to general merchandise, with a value not exceeding 30% of their annual total turnover and must balance their foreign exchange needs (Hong Kong Trade Development Council, 1994).

Up to January 1998, 18 large-scale joint-venture department stores have been approved by the State Council. Some of the examples are Beijing Yansha Shopping City (a joint venture between Friendship Commercial

Enterprise Group, a state-owned corporation under the Commercial Corporations under the commercial system, and Sin Cheng (Holdings) Pte Ltd from Singapore, and Yaohan in Pudong Shanghai (a joint venture between Yaohan International of Japan and Shanghai Number One Department Store). Details of the 18 large-scale joint-venture projects are shown in Table 1. From the table, you may see that four joint-venture projects have been approved for Shanghai. This is partly because Pudong can be considered a new development zone, where special preferential treatment is given to promote foreign investment. Moreover, the so-called foreign partners of the two joint venture projects are Chinese enterprises from Hong Kong. China Resources Enterprises Group was set up by the Ministry of Foreign Trade and Economic Cooperation (MOFTEC) in Hong Kong. Shanghai Industries is the window company of the Shanghai municipal government in Hong Kong. As the joint venture partners are mainly from Asia, i.e., Singapore, Japan, Malaysia, Thailand and Hong Kong, there is a new policy directive that, in order to gain more advanced know-how and management skills in retailing, future joint venture should focus on big North American, European and Japanese department stores or groups.

In addition to the above, the local government can approve joint-venture retailing projects on a smaller scale. Joint venture retailing projects approved under this category will not have import rights. Examples are Sincere, Shui Hing, Carrefour, Printemps, and Isetan (Shanghai), Seibu (Shenzhen), and Park'N Shop (East China and Shanghai).

Another objective of the No. 5 Document is to encourage state enterprises to set up service subsidiaries so that excess staff and workers in the state enterprises can be redeployed. As a result, many newly set up tertiary industry organizations (TIOs) have entered the wholesale and distributing sector. With more and more collective and private players entering the industry, the distribution system in China is undergoing great changes. In a move to streamline the government structure, the Ministry of Materials and Equipment (in charge of the supply of raw materials and equipment to industrial organizations) and the Ministry of Commerce (in charge of distribution of commodities to consumers) were combined to form the Ministry of Internal Domestic Trade in March 1993 (*South China Morning Post*, 16 March 1993). In November 1993, the Central Committee of the China Communist Party decided to establish a Socialist Market Economic Structure (*China Economic News*, 29 November 1993). The monopolistic state-owned distribution system was broken down further. In order to

Table 1

18 Sino-Foreign Retail Joint Venture Projects Approved by the State Council (up to January 1998)

City	Chinese Party	Partners
Beijing	Makro*	China National Native Produce and Animal By-Products Import and Export Corp.
		SHV Makro N.V. (Holland)
Beijing	Hua Tang Yokado*	China National Sugar and Wine Group Corp.
		Itochu (China) Holding Co. Ltd. (Japan)
		Itochu Co. Ltd. (Japan)
		Ito-Yokado Co. Ltd. (Japan)
Beijing	Sun Dong An Plaza Co. Ltd.	Beijing Dong An Group
		Sun Hung Kai (Hong Kong)
Beijing	Yansha Youyi Department Store	Beijing Youyi Commercial Corp.
		Sin Cheng Holdings PTE Ltd. (Singapore)
Dalian, Liaoning Province	Dalian International Commerce and Trade Building	Dalian Market
		Nichii-Jusco Society (Japan)
Guangzhou, Guangdong Province	Hualian Broadway Co.	Provincial Sugar, Tobacco, and Spirits Group Corp.
		Broadway Development Co. (Hong Kong)
Guangzhou	Tianhe Commercial Plaza	Guangzhou Jiajing Commercial Trade Co.
		Hong Kong Chia Tai International Co.
Qingdao, Shandong Province	Parkson No. 1 Department Store	Qingdao No. 1 Department Store
		The Lion Group (Malaysia)
Qingdao	Qingdao Jusco Co. Ltd.	Qingdao Supply and Sales Cooperative
		Jusco Group (Japan)

Table 1 (Cont'd)

City	Chinese Party	Partners
Shanghai	Shanghai Jusco Co. Ltd.	Shanghai Hua Yue Commercial Co. Shanghai Shenhua Industry Co. China International Trust and Investment Corp. (Hong Kong) Jusco Group (Japan)
Shanghai	Shanghai No. 1 Yaohan Department Store ("Next Age")	Shanghai No. 1 Department Store Yaohan International Group (Hong Kong) Yaohan Co. (Japan)
Shanghai	Shanghai Orient Shopping Centre	Shanghai First Department Store (Group) Corp. Hong Kong Shanghai Industrial Holdings Co. Ltd.
Shanghai	Shanghai Runhua	Hualian Group (Shanghai) Hong Kong China Resources Group
Shantou, Guangdong Province	Golden Silver Island Commercial Center	Tianjin Hualian Shantou Jinsha Trading Co. Shantou Travel Group Chen Shixian, an ethnic Chinese Thai national
Shenzhen, Guangdong Province	Shenzhen Wal-Mart Supercenter	Shenzhen International Trust and Investment Co. Wal-Mart China Co. (Hong Kong)
Tianjin	Tianjin Chia Tai International Commerce Building	Tianjin Lida Group Corp. Chia Tai Group (Thailand)
Tianjin	Tianjin Huaxin Mansions	Hualian Commercial Group (Tianjin) Shun Tak Group (Hong Kong)
Wuhan, Hubei Province	Lailai Center Department Store	

Source: PRC Ministry of Internal Trade.
* Chain store.

support the application to rejoin GATT/WTO, Ministry of Internal Trade officials revealed that foreign investors would be given the green light to do wholesale business (*China Daily Business Weekly*, 11–17 December 1993, p. 1). (For more details of the reforms of distribution and retailing in China, please refer to Tseng, et al., 1994.)

Different Channels Used by Foreign Companies To Access China's Consumer Market

As mentioned above, before 1991, foreign companies wishing to access China's consumer market could only do so through export or local manufacturing. With the reforms in 1992 permitting limited foreign participation, more channels are available now. The following is a summary of the channels foreign companies may use to access the consumer market in China.

Through Duty Free Organizations

Consumer goods may be imported through the China National Duty free Merchandise Corporation which is responsible for the import, distribution and retailing of consumer goods in various retail outlets in key international airports, ferry ports (Guangzhou, Shenzhen and Zhuhai), railways stations (Guangzhou and Shenzhen) and duty-free stores for diplomats and returning overseas Chinese or their relations spending hard currency in China, or through China Travel Service in Hong Kong (A company under the Overseas Chinese Office of the State Council) for consumer durables such as colour televisions and motorcycles for overseas Chinese (including Taiwanese) entitled to import one item every year for their relatives in China. Overseas Chinese may purchase a voucher for the particular item in Hong Kong and the voucher may be stamped at any port of entry by Chinese customs for duty free purposes and delivery may be taken in any major city. However, since 1994, this privilege for overseas Chinese (except Taiwanese) has been abolished.

Export through Trading Organizations in Hong Kong or China Who Possess an Import License

Many foreign consumer goods manufacturers who do not have manufacturing facilities in China go through this channel to bring their product into the

China market. For high value product such as Cognac or electrical appliances, which carry high import duties, the foreign companies usually use trading organizations in Hong Kong that are able to negotiate a lower tariff, or other means such as unofficial channels to import the products to one of the SEZs and then distribute to other parts of China. Many state-owned department stores, wholesalers and distributors will approach the offices of the trading organizations in SEZs instead of Foreign Trade Corporations to purchase the goods, to avoid paying the high tariff.

Through the Hong Kong Trade Development Council's (HKTDC) Promotion in Department Stores

The HKTDC has been active in organizing in-store exhibitions, "Hong Kong Showcase," with department stores in China. During the promotion period, participating manufacturers can, under the management of the respective department store, sell their products both wholesale and retail. HKTDC will provide marketing and promotional services, including advertising, product display and counter design. The first event was held in May 1989, jointly organized with the Nanfang Building Department Store in Guangzhou. The promotion lasted for two years. Since then, HKTDC has organized similar events in coastal cities such as Shanghai, Beijing, Dalian, Shenyang, Tianjin and inland cities such as Wuxi, Wuhan, Zhengzhou, Nanjing, Chongqing, Harbin and Hangzhou. HKTDC is now focusing on other inland cities and is planning to hold similar events in Chengdu, Changsha and Qingdao, as by now Hong Kong businessmen are quite familiar with the coastal cities. The promotional period is now adjusted to about three months. Participating manufactures can take this opportunity to see whether their products are acceptable in the China market and then decide whether to rent a counter in the store.

Through Exclusive Counters in Department Stores

Consumer goods manufacturers or suppliers may sell their products through special counters in department stores. They may directly rent a counter in the department store by signing a contract with the store permitting the store to manage the sales activities or alternatively, instead of paying rent for the counter, the supplier may sell the merchandise to the store with a discount built into the agreement. One example is Goldlion, a

Hong Kong-based manufacturer and retailer of upmarket men's accessories. It operates 460 Goldlion counters in major cities and urban areas such as Guangzhou, Tianjin, Shanghai, Beijing, Xi'an and Shenzhen. It sells its merchandise to the stores with a 20% discount built into the agreement (Davies, 1994).

Through Formation of Joint Venture Retailing Outlets

A wholly-owned or Sino-foreign joint venture manufacturer may set up another joint venture retailing outlet with a domestic company that has a shop in a prime location and possesses a retailing licence.

Foreign companies without manufacturing facilities in China may also set up joint venture retailing outlets with companies under former commercial systems. For example, Park'N Shop's parent company, Watson's Group, formed a joint venture with Zhuhai Development Store Group to set up a supermarket in Zhuhai.

By Granting Franchise to Local Mainland Retailers

Franchising is still a relatively new concept in China. It is sometimes very difficult to convince the Chinese to pay you royalties for "soft technology" such as ideas in store decoration, management and marketing know-how. Many international fast food groups generally use "franchising" as a form of market entry in the internationalization of their operation. However, they have to modify their strategy in China. For example, McDonald's first restaurant in Beijing is in the form of a joint venture.

Franchising can be translated as "specially allowed business" (*texujing-ying*) in Chinese. It is sometimes mixed up with the term *liansuodian* or "chain store" (U.S. Foreign and Commercial Service in Beijing, 1994). Franchising does not have a legal definition in China. Franchising operations can be established in China under three legal areas, the Equity Joint Venture Law, the Cooperative (or Contractual) Joint Venture Law and licensing legislation (U.S. Foreign and Commercial Service in Beijing, 1994).

Because of the unfamiliarity of the business environment and structure in China, Western companies usually find it very difficult to directly "franchise" a domestic company in China. Moreover, these companies are not familiar with the environment in China and their corporate cultures do not allow executives to enter into any contract that is not legally binding.

For the reasons mentioned above, Western companies usually franchise the operation to Hong Kong or Taiwanese companies. These companies then "franchise" or set up joint ventures in China. One example is Walt Disney's franchise of children's apparel awarded to a Taiwanese company was then granted to local mainland retailers. The Taiwanese company provides Walt Disney products as well as store decoration and marketing and management know-how. The retailers sell the franchised products exclusively. Other examples are Giordano, Benetton, Crocodile and Bossini Stores. Another interesting example is Printemps of Paris, which franchised their name and departmental operations to Topforms, a listed company in Hong Kong. Topforms then set up joint venture department stores in Huaihai Zhonglu, a prime shopping area in Shanghai, with the Yimin Department Store Group, a listed company on the Shanghai Stock Exchange.

Chain Stores

Chain stores or *liansuodian* is the latest form of officially promoted retail operation in China. Restaurants, fast food outlets, supermarkets, convenience stores, jewellery shops, photo finishing shops, speciality boutiques, and optical shops are seen as businesses that it is feasible to develop into chain stores or *liansuo jingying* in China. Due to rapid urbanization and changing life style in major cities, as well as to improve operational efficiency, the small staple and non-staple food stores including wet markets under the commercial system have embarked on major reforms, and many supermarket/retail outlets in the form of chain stores are being set up. For example, by 1995 there were 21 supermarket groups (with centralized purchasing, packaging and distribution centres) in Shanghai with 700 retail outlets. The Shanghai municipal government has set a target of more than 1,000 chain stores outlets in Shanghai by the year 2000, with four to five big supermarket groups, each with more than 100 big retail outlets (*Jiefang Daily China Economic News*, 8 January 1996). As chain stores have great coverage in the distribution of products, foreign consumer goods manufacturers should explore the feasibility of distributing their products through this channel and should start to establish business contacts and *guanxi* with potential big chain store operators.

Foreign companies can also set up chain stores themselves. Several Hong Kong companies have recently announced plans to establish joint venture chain stores in China; examples include Fotomax photofinishing shops, Hong Kong Optical, City Chain, and Fortei Boutique. It is important to note that to date there is still no central body to issue a retail license to enable a company to operate chain stores in the whole of China. The operator needs to make separate application with different joint venture partners in different cities.

Supermarket/Hypermarket

Foreign investors can also engage in supermarket operations, which involve retail sales of foodstuffs and small household items. In the past, entry was usually in the form of a joint venture located in hotels for foreign visitors. Today, foreign investors can form joint ventures with corporations under commercial systems that own shops in strategic locations convenient for domestic customers.

For example, A.S. Watson Group (Hutchison Whampoa), parent company of Park'N Shop, established a joint venture called Park'N Shop Shanghai Ltd. (PNSS) with Lu Wan Non-Staple Food Company. The first store opened in Quxi Lu, Lu Wan District on 15 October 1994. By December 1995, Park'N Shop had ten stores in Shanghai.

In addition to supermarkets, hyperstores and big discount shops can also be set up by joint venture in China. For example, Carrefour from France has concluded a joint venture agreement with Shanghai Lian Hua Supermarket Co. Ltd. and is planning to set up its first store in Quyang Road, Shanghai. Wal-Mart Store Inc., a U.S.-based discount retailer, set up stores in Shenzhen.

Department Stores

As mentioned before, foreign investors may engage in large-scale projects in 11 cities subject to State Council approval. They may also engage in smaller scale department store projects (less than US$30 million investment) without import and export rights.

Property Development Projects

Foreign companies engaged in development of commercial/office/shopping complexes, in particular for projects in prime urban locations, upon completion of the projects can either, in conjunction with local partners, lease the space to local retailers, or indirectly engage in retailing business, utilizing the licence of their joint venture partners. Examples include Henderson, Hang Lung and Hysan in Shanghai's Xujiahui district and Ryoden's Shanghai Square projects.

Direct Marketing

Foreign companies became involved in direct marketing, for examples Avon, Mary Kay and Amway. However, credit cards are not so popular in China and also Government policy does not encourage these types of activities and severe restrictions were imposed on direct selling in 1998. Since then the foreign companies have become involved in retailing and franchising.

Wholesaling

In China, officially, foreign companies are not allowed to engaged in wholesale activities. Foreign investment in the Retailing Provisions (issued by State Council in November 1992) does not specify what is retailing and what exactly is meant by "wholesale." If you treat "wholesaling" as retailing in bulk orders, then you are getting into the grey area of the law; in China, if the law does not specifically prohibit it, the chances are that you can get away with it.

At present, foreign companies may engage in "retailing in bulk quantity" through the following channels.

International Fashion Centre Located in Panyu Organized by the HKTDC

The International Fashion Centre located in Panyu was organized by the HKTDC to assist Hong Kong garment manufacturers distributing their products in China. The HKTDC plans to develop the Centre into a national distribution centre for garments in China. The Centre accommodates shops, showrooms, meeting rooms and warehousing facilities under one roof. Hong Kong garment manufacturers can also make use of the promotional expertise of HKTDC to build up their product image.

Industrial Park with Distribution Facilities Developed by Li and Fung Development (China) Ltd.

Manufacturers in light industrial products can make use of the industrial park also located in Panyu developed by Li and Fung Development (China) Ltd. Foreign companies can make use of this for manufacturing and distributing bulk orders at the same time.

International Merchandise Mart (IMM)

IMM is situated in Shanghai Yaohan Nanfang Shangcheng in Mei Long District, on the outskirts of Shanghai. This is a large-scale distribution centre set up by Yaohan that opened in 1994. It is similar to that already operating in Singapore (joint venture between the Trade Development Board of Singapore and Yaohan for distribution of goods for ASEAN). In addition to wholesales, IMM also carries out retail business. Foreign companies may use this for the distribution of their goods in China, especially for the Yangtze Delta region.

Problems and Practices

Payment Terms

Long payment terms are very popular in China. Often the retailer owes the distributor and the distributor owes the manufacturers or the importers. Therefore, foreign companies must have effective means for dealing with cash flow problems. The majority of wholesalers do not have the resources to provide credit facilities, therefore they prefer consignment arrangements. Long payment periods (e.g., 150 days instead of the usual 60 days) are widely practised. Foreign companies have few options but to agree to this arrangement. Moreover, companies should be very careful to select wholesalers that are economically viable.

Geographic Differences

China is a big country comprising provinces that are at different stages of economic development. It would be very costly for a company to set up a retail network in China. The purchasing power of people in the coastal provinces is much higher than that in the interior provinces. It has been a usual practice for companies to go to the cities with higher income first, hoping that they can explore other cities later. However, companies should also note that customers differ in buying behaviour from city to city. The author was involved in a study on consumer behaviour in three cities in 1993. The three most developed cities, Guangzhou, Shanghai and Beijing, were included in the study. It was found that consumers' preferences are, in order: imported foreign brands, joint venture-made foreign brands, and local brands. Yet consumers in these areas differ in some aspects. Consumers in Guangzhou are more westernized and more ready to accept new things, due to the proximity to Hong Kong. Moreover, they are the wealthiest group of customers in China, and so are more selective in purchasing goods. Shanghai consumers appear to be more "calculating." Although they perceive that foreign brands are of better quality, they cannot accept the immense difference in price. They also like to examine the product carefully before making any decision. Beijing consumers are very emotional and quite receptive to advertising messages. Companies should adapt their marketing strategies accordingly.

Different cities also have different styles of dealing with foreign companies. Shanghai has been reported as the city that holds the best cooperative attitude to overseas investors. Perhaps this is because Shanghai was among the first cities opened to foreign businessmen, and because the leaders in the municipal government are young, open-minded and energetic. In Beijing, everything must go by the book, and so there is no alternative for foreign investors but to follow the regulations. There is one good point about this at least: companies can get a clear direction as to what course to follow. In the South, the central government is remote, and control is lax. Thus, companies may find difficulties sometimes in discovering what is feasible and what is not.

Availability of Market Information

Market information is vital for business success. A company cannot formulate its strategies without knowing the needs of the consumers and the strategies of competitors. Unfortunately, there are not many published materials on China that can be used. Neither is there any organization like the Trade Promotion Board that can provide assistance to foreign businessmen. Companies wanting to explore the China market must usually gather some primary information rather than rely mostly on secondary data.

Philips is a good example. When they first planned to enter the China market, they used a very primitive method of sourcing the appropriate retailers to handle their electrical appliances. They bought a map of the targeted city; then they traced all the department stores shown on the map and visited them one by one. They observed the environment, the traffic, the atmosphere of the store, and the buying behaviour of the customers, and they talked to the employees working there. They evaluated all these factors and then made their decisions. It turned out to be an effective approach of selecting retailers. The way to obtain sales figures is also unique in China. As China is still a developing country, staffs in the stores often do not realize the importance of the sales figures and thus do not treat them as highly confidential. Therefore, if one can show a sincere attitude when asking for sales information, they may be willing to release it. The author has carried out consultancy research in China and has copies of the prices of various products in the stores and has taken photographs of the display, without being interrupted. When the stores are not busy, you may engage in a friendly conversation with the staff and obtain a lot of market information.

Logistical Problems

The transportation infrastructure in China is not yet well developed and it makes the physical movement of goods inefficient. The highway system is not comprehensive as it links only the few coastal cities, and most distributors must use railways for long-distance movement. However, the rail system is closely controlled and priority is often given to goods that are still under tight central government control such as coal and agricultural products. Distributors are left to fight for the remaining space and those who enjoy a good relationship with the rail office can have better services. Therefore, it is better for companies to use the governmental centralized distribution system rather than set up their own in some provinces. Philips Inc. is using a dual system for the distribution of its products. In the big cities, which are linked by highways, it sets up its network; in other provinces, it uses the governmental centralized system.

Warehousing is another problem that companies must address. Although space is usually available, it is usually not in good condition and the protection for goods is minimal. Thus, many companies choose to build their own warehouses and handle their own products. Companies can also select domestic independent distributors who have experience in handing particular kinds of goods.

Relationships

Guanxi (relationship) is the key for business success in China. Companies with good *guanxi* with some government officials can enjoy many advantages like speedy processing of documents and ready approval of permits. However, one should be very cautious. It is too simple to think that there is only one clique with whom to establish *guanxi* in China. Having good *guanxi* with one clique who may be the enemy of another, and this can cause trouble. There are no rules in building *guanxi*. Hiring someone who knows the Chinese market well may be the best solution. The *guanxi* phenomenon can also be applied to managing retailers. A company can enjoy many privileges if it has a good relationship with its retailers. For instance, because of its good relationship with the retailers in Tianjin, General Foods has been able to get better shelf positions than Nestle. Staffs in the department stores were willing to push Nestle's products to the back. Similarly, through personal influence, Philips was able to have its promotion posters placed in prominent positions in Jing Pin Shang She (a big department store situated in Nanjing Road in Shanghai). There are many ways to establish good *guanxi* with retailers. Incentives to the staff are one of the methods. Visiting them frequently and showing trust and a sincere attitude are two additional factors that can win the hearts of the staff in the stores.

Staffing

The focus group study carried out by the author also revealed that Chinese consumers rely heavily on suggestions by retailers in making their purchase decisions. It appears that consumers often do not know exactly what to look for when choosing products. The reliability and the believability of the sales message very much depend on the product knowledge of the salesperson. Therefore, it is very important to train salespeople to know the products they are selling, as well as to teach them a service quality concept. Hence, it is advisable for companies to conduct training courses for salespeople to make sure that the salesperson knows the products and has the right attitude towards consumers. However, it is advisable to bear in mind that transforming attitudes is not possible overnight. It should be considered a long-term investment.

For those using the "make" route, the setting up of a well qualified marketing team is the major problem. As China is a newly open economy, the marketing concept is a new phenomenon. It is therefore difficult to recruit people who have a marketing background. According to the general manager of Honghton (China) Co. Ltd., whom the author interviewed, marketing staff recruited in China do not really possess the "marketing concept," but only adopt the "product concept" in selling the goods: they believe that a good product would speak for itself. Moreover, they rely only on past sales contacts rather than on adopting more innovative ways of attracting customers.

Differences in attitudes are true not only of consumers but also of employees in different parts of China. Many managers reported that the junior level staffs in the North are easier to manage than those in the South. Perhaps those in the South are more exposed to the Hong Kong culture, and thus have more job opportunities, thus increasing the turnover rate of employees.

Table 2
Contracts Signed with Foreign Companies Investing in China

	1990	1991	1992
Number of Project	7,371	12,086	48,858
Sum of Investment (US$ billions)	12.08	19.58	69.43

Source: *Statistical Yearbook of China*, 1993, p. 647.

In addition to the problems mentioned above, it can be disastrous for retailers to position their merchandise beyond the reach of consumers. It was reported recently that Printemps in Shanghai made a big loss because the merchandise were too high profile. The share price of their parent company, Topform, was reduced by more than half. It was also reported that 20 outlets of Giordano had been closed down. The actual reason was not revealed, but it may have been criticism of Premier Li Peng that appeared in *Next Magazine*, owned by the Giordano boss (*South China Morning Post*, 10 April 1996).

Implication of Theories

Much of the literature on international business has taken on a manufacturing perspective, often implicit rather than explicit (Buckley, et al., 1992). Theory on internationalization of firms proposed at Uppsala is no exception. The sample firms used in the empirical studies are all manufacturers. The internationalization process relates to different stages through which a company may pass as it develops into foreign markets, normally beginning with (a) direct/ad hoc exporting, moving on to (b) active exporting and/or licensing, to (c) active exporting, licensing and joint equity investment in foreign manufacturing, and to (d) full-scale multinational marketing and production (Root, 1994). Figure 1 illustrates the typical sequence a company is believed to follow as it internationalizes.

There is evidence from a number of studies to support this stage model: Johanson and Wiedersheim (1975) and Johanson and Vahlne (1977) found that Swedish firms expanded abroad in small steps, the typical pattern extending from exporting via an agent to the establishment of a sales subsidiary and, finally, to production abroad. Buckley and others (Buckley, 1983, 1988) in studies of U.K. small firm first time investors and small Continental European investors in U.K. found that only 15% of the combined sample of companies omitted the exporting phase in route to foreign manufacturing; and of these, one half were prevented from exporting by the

Figure 1
The Internationalization Process

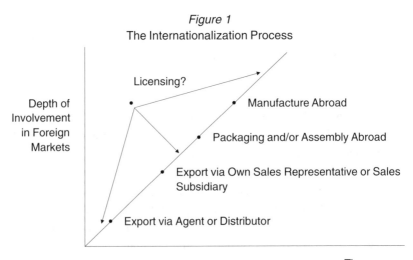

Depth of
Involvement
in Foreign
Markets

Licensing?

Manufacture Abroad

Packaging and/or Assembly Abroad

Export via Own Sales Representative or Sales
Subsidiary

Export via Agent or Distributor

Time

nature of the product — transport costs or a high service element effectively excluded exporting.

Services are different from goods in terms of intangibility and inseparability. Sampson and Snape (1985) categorize services according to their tradability, proposing that "Separated" services, or those that do not require direct contact between supplier and consumer, are the only services that can be exported, distinct from those that demand movement of factors of production to the consumer (e.g., repair services) or movement of the consumer to factors of production (e.g., tourism) (Buckley, et al., 1992). For some services such as data communication, or creative work for advertisement design, exporting or subcontracting is possible. But for retailers, as retailing is a type of service that requires interaction with the customers, export is not possible. As there is no opportunity for the retailer to acquire foreign market knowledge through export, the risk involved is very much higher.

Suggestion for Future Research

As mentioned above, consumer product manufacturing and retailing are different. It will be valuable to look into what sort of strategy manufacturers and retailers may adopt when entering the China market. As mentioned before, Giordano and Printemps encountered problems in their operation in China. Up to the time of writing this chapter, the problems encountered by Giordano are still unknown. One of the problems Printemps encountered was that the positioning of the merchandise was too high. One solution is to focus on the general merchandise and encourage customers to make bulk purchases. This is what Carrefour and Wal-Mart are trying to achieve in China. In the West, the stores usually provide a big car park to facilitate customers using a car for bulk purchase. However, in China, private ownership of car is still very low. Foreign retailers need to adapt their strategy accordingly. However, exactly what strategy foreign retailers need to adopt is a challenge to the retailers as well as to researchers in this field.

Notes

1. In July 1999 overseas investors were allowed to establish joint retail sales outlets in the capitals of all provinces and a number of other cities.
2. Wal-Mart Store Inc. initially teamed up with C. P. Pokphand Co., a Hong

Kong listed affiliate of the Charoen Pokphand Group (CP Group), a pioneer among foreign investors in China with major interests in agriculture and motorcycle production. CP was expected to help Wal-Mart with regulatory details of business in China; Wal-Mart would provide expertise in operating a huge warehouse style discount store. However, the joint venture was not without problems, according to the *Asian Wall Street Journal* (11 January 1996, p. 1 and p. 5), and the two companies ended their venture and are now going their separate ways in China's retail market. Under the terms of dissolution, Wal-Mart is keeping the Shenzhen venture while CP group will take over the rest of the venture's holdings in Shanghai and Shenyang.

14

Consumer Behaviour in Retail Services: The Use of Time in Hong Kong and China*

Henry C. Steele

Introduction

The 1990s has been characterized by a period of major political and economic change in the global economy. New consumers and emerging markets, which promise much for the future, present international marketers with new opportunities and challenges. Emphasis on strategic implications and of competition in different country markets must not obscure the realities of the pervasive and enduring power of culture in shaping consumer behaviour. Although rising living standards, economic prosperity, global technologies and communications will tend toward convergence among cultures, some elements will be lasting. Environmental assessments and monitoring can assist in understanding which cultural elements predominate and for which there may be a need for local modification of the marketing programme. Such cultural sensitivity will benefit a firm in gaining market access and in achieving a better match between suppliers and customers.

Cultural values will be manifested in basic consumption patterns, of who buys, what and where it is bought, and frequency of purchase, which

* An earlier version of this chapter appeared in Antonio and Steele, 1996.

are established by cultural values. Although culture may be viewed as a totality, it is also understood that at the same time some individual elements of a culture may have more direct influence. The more complete the proposed marketing involvement, or the more unique the product, the more the need to study each cultural element (Cateora, 1996). One element that permeates so much of society and gives strong cultural identity is language. Through language effective communication is possible between members of a society. In addition to formal verbal language, Hall (1960) identified the use of five different silent languages: time, space, material possessions, friendship patterns, and agreement across culture. Time has a different meaning in each culture and has been described by Hall (1983). When evaluating the business environment, and understanding consumer behaviour, temporal aspects should be studied and appreciated. People experience time in different ways, and have different attitudes towards time.

In recent years, a number of studies have been undertaken as the relevance of time has become widely recognized in explaining consumer behaviour. Theoretical and empirical investigations on situational influences on time behaviour have been conducted (Feldman and Hornik, 1981; Graham, 1981; Hendrix, Kinnear and Taylor, 1983; Jacoby et al., 1976; Hornik, 1984; Kelly and McGrath, 1988; Nicosia and Mayer, 1976; Schary, 1971; Usunier and Valetta-Florence, 1994). In the context of adoption and diffusion of innovation (Rogers, 1962) and in segmenting markets (Morello, 1989), time has been treated as the dependent variable. Previous studies have examined expenditure and consumption patterns in relation to time usage and time allocation. Traditionally, studies have used the concept of clock time to determine consumer allocation of time within a fixed amount of available time. Such time budget studies were described by Sorokin, (1943). Time budget studies are considered inadequate for explaining behaviour in the consuming of services. A more innovative idea of "social time" is proposed by Robert Lauer (1981) who suggested that social time, unlike clock time, recognizes that consumer activities take place in the context of the social environment.

Concept of Social Time

Social time, unlike clock time, recognizes that an individual's behaviour takes place in a social temporal environment. Societies have their own social time, a time when events are to take place, a pace at which they are to be accomplished, and rules and customs of human behaviour and inter-action with respect to temporality. Lewis and Weigert (1981) view social time as involving rhythms or cycles of time or changes in social processes, the daily round, with its sequence between darkness and light providing the basis for social temporal activities. The weekly routine provides another temporal structure in which the weekend may be a dominant temporal marker, and the year may be denoted by the passage of seasons. Three different concepts of time have been considered: mechanical (or clock) time, natural time, and social time. Natural time is determined by changes and rhythms in nature, the farmer's year is marked by the seasons, there is a time for planting and a time for harvesting. The social time concept applies to the relationship of human and social activity. Time is perceived, "with reference to our own action and interaction; or with reference to events in our social environment and in the society at large" (Gronmo, 1989). Social time will be influenced by both mechanical time and natural time, but these influences will differ between societies. In modern societies, social time will be more influenced by the use of clock time in order to coordinate labour and communication processes (Zerubavel, 1982). Social time is important in all societies, social life being influenced more by either mechanical time or natural time. Authors discussing the nature of time and of the temporal dimensions of human activities and social processes have agreed on the legitimacy of the concept of social time. Since social time is always closely related to these social processes, for the newcomer to a country, after language problems, the general pace of social life and the punctuality of others may present the greatest difficulties. Indeed lack of punctuality may demonstrate status and be a symbol of success (Levine and Wolff, 1985). Social time reflects how people think and feel about time. "A social time system is a comprehensive framework that encompasses rules, standards, practices and customs of human behaviour and interaction with respect to temporality" (Anderson and Venkatesan, 1994).

A social time framework for exploring the temporal dimensions of consumer behaviour has been proposed by Anderson and Venkatesan (1985a and 1985b), which appears suitable in explaining time use phenom-enon by consumers in service settings. The framework is based on the conceptual model of Lauer (1981), which consists of temporal pattern, temporal orientation, and temporal perspective. In addition, the concepts of interactional structures of Lewis and Weigert (1981) are applicable to the conceptual framework as all are interrelated and have a direct influence on time allocation, time perception and the level of satisfaction with a particular service encounter.

The concept of "time pattern" views the time system consisting of three broad constructs, namely: temporal pattern, temporal orientation, and temporal perspective. Temporal pattern involves five elements, which relate to how time is perceived and used, namely: periodicity, timing, duration, tempo and sequence. The study of consumer patterns in terms of these five dimensions helps us to go beyond the time budget studies in understanding consumers' time system and explaining their behaviour. The dimensions will be explained in the context of the research findings, including the concept of temporal perspective based on regularity of socio-temporal sequence of daily activities.

Cross Cultural Social Time Study

A cross-cultural research design was used to collect information on how time is used in a cross-cultural setting. Based on the studies of Venkatesan et al. (1991) and Anderson and Venkatesan (1994) of the temporal pattern dimensions of consumer behaviour use is made of the social time framework described. The data is focused on temporal pattern and temporal perspective of selective retail services transactions in Hong Kong in comparison with Guangzhou and Beijing, the People's Republic of China. The rapid economic progress of China is well known but income, attitudes and life styles are very different between Guangzhou, Beijing and Hong Kong. For most people in Hong Kong the pace of life is very fast, time is very important and leisure time is at a premium. It would be expected that there would be major differences between people's time perceptions between Guangzhou, Beijing and Hong Kong with the relative isolation of China over four decades and the very different regimes under which the Chinese speaking communities have developed. With the economic reform programmes well in place, and Guangzhou showing the greatest degree of industrialization and economic benefits, it may be that as China moves ahead to recover from lost time, there will be a narrowing of the differences in the temporal patterns of consumer behaviour between Hong Kong and its counterparts in mainland China. The recent results of the Beijing studies are compared with the findings reported for Hong Kong and Guangzhou.

This study is the first to examine the temporal patterns of consuming of retail services in the Chinese communities and provides a cross-cultural study applying the concept of social time. Findings are presented for temporal pattern and orientation, and are limited to selected consumer retail services, namely: supermarket, convenience store, traditional grocery, restaurant, laundry/dry cleaning, and hairdressing services.

Characteristics of Respondents

As shown in Table 1, respondents come from households of small average size, although in Hong Kong 27% of households had six or more than six persons, the modal number was four persons per household in both Hong Kong and Guangzhou and three persons in Beijing. The "one child" policy in China has had a dramatic effect on reducing the number of large households (i.e., five or more persons). In Hong Kong there has also been a rapid reduction in household size, but this has more to do with rising prosperity and consequent reduction in the birth rate. The very high cost of housing in Hong Kong reduces the number of one-person households and children do not usually leave the family home before marriage. Even after marriage it may still be necessary to live with parents, both in Hong Kong and China due to housing shortages. Three generations living in one household are still common, with elderly parents being the responsibility of the children. Hong Kong is witnessing an increase in single-person households, with 2% of the sample living alone, which does contrast with the number of single-person households in Guangzhou (6.9%).

Shopping is normally considered the responsibility of the mother/wife in Hong Kong and Guangzhou, although the father/husband alone or husband and wife together are, on occasions, reported having responsibility for shopping in Hong Kong and Guangzhou respectively. Beijing respondents displayed a rather different pattern where the highest number of responses gave shopping as a joint husband and wife responsibility. With regard to the responsibility for household finances, in Hong Kong the mother/wife is most likely to have full responsibility, and if not it will be the father/husband. In Beijing the situation is very different, in most households both husband and wife have joint responsibility and if not the mother/wife will be responsible. Guangzhou people take a middle road for household finances with more joint responsibility by both husband and wife than in Hong Kong, but, with more either husband/father or wife/mother taking sole

Table 1
Characteristics of the Respondents

	Hong Kong		Guangzhou		Beijing	
	N	%	N	%	N	%
Household size						
1	6	2.0	23	6.9	5	1.5
2	31	10.1	27	8.1	43	13.0
3	45	14.7	98	29.3	157	47.6
4	85	27.7	136	40.6	84	25.5
5	57	18.6	43	12.8	34	10.3
6	50	16.3	5	1.5	5	1.5
7	15	4.9	2	0.6	—	—
8	12	3.9	1	0.3	1	0.3
9	4	1.3	—	—	1	0.3
10	2	0.6	—	—	—	—
Total	307		335		330	
Average household size	4.5		3.5		3.4	
Sex						
Male	128	39.7	168	48.8	165	50.0
Female	194	60.3	176	51.2	165	50.0
Total	322		344		330	
Member responsible for household shopping						
Single household	8	2.5	26	8.6	5	1.5
Husband and wife	40	12.4	50	16.6	139	42.1
Father	21	6.5	11	3.7	13	3.9
Mother	189	58.7	159	52.8	115	34.8
Daughter/Sister	19	5.9	4	1.3	3	0.9
Son/Brother	8	2.5	2	0.7	3	0.9
Housemaid	2	0.6	—	—	1	0.3
Whole family	35	10.9	49	16.3	51	15.3
Total	322		301		330	
Member responsible for household finance						
Single household	8	2.5	26	8.6	5	1.5
Husband and wife	50	15.5	82	27.0	157	47.6
Father	75	23.3	54	17.8	35	10.6
Mother	150	46.6	114	37.5	98	29.7
Daughter/Sister	17	5.3	2	0.7	1	0.3
Son/Brother	12	3.7	1	0.3	3	0.9
Whole family	10	3.1	25	8.2	31	9.4
Total	322		304		330	

responsibility than in Beijing. Taking care of the family is much more likely to be a shared responsibility between husband and wife in China.

A major difference in the three groups of respondents is in stated average annual household income, which for Hong Kong is HK$239,000 whereas in Guangzhou average income is RMB28,000 (HK$26,500) and in Beijing RMB18,000 (HK$17,000). However, in terms of purchasing power, the differences are much less due to state provision and subsidy in China whereas many households in Hong Kong have high mortgage and rental payments. Published figures have led some analysts to erroneously conclude that households in China do not have sufficient disposable income to purchase luxury products and consumer durables. Families in China seldom pay a significant amount in rent and transportation. Food and medical expenses are often covered by the state or work unit and there is a disproportionately high disposable income with a saving rate of about 35%. In Purchasing Power Parity (PPP) terms the per capita GDP of China is more than five times greater than the US dollar value would suggest. For Hong Kong, its PPP is almost identical to the US dollar value (*Asiaweek*, 1996). There are rising expectations among China's consumers. In the 1970s, the desired durables were a bicycle, a sewing machine and an electric fan. By the 1980s, consumer aspirations were for a television, a washing machine and a refrigerator. The three icons of affluence in the 1990s are a VCR, a motorcycle and a telephone. A survey of household ownership of durables in Guangzhou showed 98% had a television, 85% owned a washing machine, 76% owned a refrigerator and 44% had a VCR (Tong, 1995).

If concern with time and keeping schedules is indicative of keeping an appointment calendar or of the number of timepieces owned, there are significant differences between Hong Kong and China (Table 2). The differences between Guangzhou and Beijing are less marked in terms of the number of watches owned and in the frequency of wearing a watch. 86% in Hong Kong wear watches all the time, 78% in Guangzhou and 74% in Beijing. The average number of watches owned in Beijing is 1.8 and in Guangzhou 2.0 per person, significantly less than ownership in Hong Kong. The need to arrange and schedule a large number of activities dictates a greater need to maintain an appointment calendar in Hong Kong (51%). In Guangzhou only 18% kept an appointment calendar, but more people (33%) kept an appointment calendar in Beijing.

Table 2
Time Perspective of the Respondents

Place	Hong Kong	Guangzhou	Beijing
Keeping appointment calendar to schedule activities			
Yes	51.0%	18.1%	32.7%
No	49.0%	81.9%	67.3%
Number of watches owned by the respondents			
0	1	9	12
1	114	141	148
2	87	113	115
3	67	48	36
4 or 5	37	26	14
6 or more	15	6	4
Total respondents	321	343	329
Average number of watches owned	2.5	2.0	1.8
	HG*	HB*	GB*
Significance	<0.1%	<0.1%	<5.0%

* HG = Hong Kong and Guangzhou; HB = Hong Kong and Beijing; GB = Guangzhou and Beijing.

Periodicity

Various rhythms of social life are referred to as periodicity and are measured by the frequency with which retail services are utilized. Fixed working time violates the preferred periodicity, but nevertheless, visits to retail service establishments recur at regular intervals. These patterns of frequency of visits will vary across cultures. Supermarket visits in Hong Kong may take a once or twice weekly pattern whereas in China there is a daily cycle for shopping, especially for fresh meat, fish and vegetables. In Western countries daily cycles have become extended into weekly or monthly ones following the introduction of hypermarkets, packaged and frozen food, the widespread availability of personal transport and of freezer ownership.

During the 1980s, there was an increase in the number of supermarkets in Hong Kong with a large shift in share of business from traditional outlets. Supermarkets and convenience stores are more recent innovations in China. In Hong Kong, 61% of respondents visit a supermarket weekly or more frequently, whereas in Guangzhou and Beijing the corresponding figures

Table 3
Frequency of Using Services

Place	Hong Kong	Guangzhou	Beijing
		(Percentage)	
Total sample size	322	344	330
Frequency of going to supermarket			
Daily	4.3	1.7	4.2
More than once a week	32.0	10.8	11.8
About once a week	24.2	11.0	17.3
About every 1–2 weeks	17.7	16.0	16.1
About every 3–4 weeks	11.8	20.6	12.7
About every 1–3 months	6.5	18.0	9.1
About every 4–6 months	2.5	7.0	8.8
At least once a year	0.9	5.2	4.8
Less than once a year/Never visit	—	9.6	15.1
	HG	HB	GB
Significance	<0.1	<0.1	<0.1
Frequency of going to 24 hours/convenience store			
Daily	4.0	2.0	9.4
More than once a week	23.6	11.9	18.2
About once a week	16.1	7.8	8.5
About every 1–2 weeks	18.3	7.6	6.7
About every 3–4 weeks	17.1	6.1	3.9
About every 1–3 months	8.1	4.7	3.9
About every 4–6 months	7.1	2.6	3.0
At least once a year	1.6	4.7	4.8
Less than once a year/Never visit	4.0	52.7	41.5
	HG	HB	GB
Significance	<0.1	<0.1	<0.1
Frequency of going to Chinese grocery store			
Daily	3.7	17.7	21.8
More than once a week	11.2	39.2	38.8
About once a week	9.9	15.4	15.8
About every 1–2 weeks	11.8	9.6	9.7
About every 3–4 weeks	13.4	6.4	8.2
About every 1–3 months	15.2	2.6	2.4
About every 4–6 months	13.0	3.2	1.2
At least once a year	7.5	2.6	1.2
Less than once a year/Never visit	14.3	3.2	0.9
	HG	HB	GB
Significance	<0.1	<0.1	<0.1

Table 3 (Cont'd)

Place	Hong Kong	Guangzhou	Beijing
		(Percentage)	
Frequency of going to restaurant			
Daily	8.1	1.7	1.2
More than once a week	27.0	11.0	4.2
About once a week	20.2	9.0	4.2
About every 1–2 weeks	13.7	15.7	0.4
About every 3–4 weeks	11.8	21.8	0.4
About every 1–3 months	11.2	19.8	15.2
About every 4–6 months	5.0	9.0	10.0
At least once a year	1.6	7.3	14.2
Less than once a year/Never visit	1.6	4.7	35.1
	HG	HB	GB
Significance	<0.1	<0.1	<0.1
Frequency of going to laundry/dry cleaner			
Daily	—	0.6	0
More than once a week	0.6	0.9	0.2
About once a week	2.5	1.5	0.8
About every 1–2 weeks	7.1	1.5	0.8
About every 3–4 weeks	5.0	1.7	0.1
About every 1–3 months	12.4	1.5	0.5
About every 4–6 months	11.2	2.3	0
At least once a year	19.6	13.1	13.9
Less than once a year/Never visit	41.6	77.1	66.7
	HG	HB	GB
Significance	<0.1	<0.1	<5.0
Frequency of going to hairdresser or beauty salon			
Daily	0.3	0.6	0
More than once a week	0.9	2.3	1.2
About once a week	1.9	3.8	3.6
About every 1–2 weeks	5.0	7.0	6.1
About every 3–4 weeks	20.8	34.3	25.2
About every 1–3 months	37.9	23.8	23.9
About every 4–6 months	23.0	10.5	10.6
At least once a year	5.6	6.7	7.0
Less than once a year/Never visit	4.7	11.1	22.5
	HG	HB	GB
Significance	<0.1	<0.1	<1.0

are 23% and 33%. Although virtually all respondents in Hong Kong visited a supermarket at least every six months, in Guangzhou 15% and in Beijing 20% never visit or visit less frequently than every six months. In contrast, continuing use of the traditional grocery store is seen in China with visits weekly or more frequently by 73% of respondents in Guangzhou and 77% in Beijing. The widespread occurrence of 24 hours convenience stores and the maturation of supermarkets are reflected in the comparable figure of only 24% in Hong Kong.

Consumer affluence, availability and the cultural characteristic among Chinese for taking meals together with family or friends is shown by the high frequency of visits to restaurants. In Hong Kong, it is normal to eat out with friends after work before returning home in the evening, and Sunday is the family day for eating out. Over 55% visited restaurants weekly or more frequently — the modal value is more than once a week. In Guangzhou, eating out is increasingly important, restaurants are once again flourishing to meet the demand of an increasingly prosperous population. In Guangzhou, 21% eat out once a week or more often, which is in contrast to Beijing where the corresponding figure is only 9%.

Frequencies of visits to the hairdresser or beauty salon are greater in Guangzhou and Beijing than Hong Kong. The numbers of making visits every 3-4 weeks or more frequently are 48% in Guangzhou, 36% in Beijing and 29% in Hong Kong. Visits to laundry/dry cleaners are more frequent in Hong Kong.

The frequency of visits demonstrates some contrasts between Hong Kong and mainland China. The change to a socialist market economy has produced a rise in living standards and dramatic changes to China's infrastructure affecting retailing and consumer shopping habits. There is still a lot of catching up to do, Guangzhou and Beijing show the continuing dominance of traditional outlets, but supermarkets and convenience stores are rapidly gaining ground. One can expect the frequency of visits to the newer forms of retail outlet to increase at the expense of traditional ones. As one would anticipate there are more similarities between Guangzhou and Beijing with Hong Kong exemplifying the contrast. However, it is Beijing which provides the contrast for frequency of visits to restaurants. An explanation may be the cultural differences between Cantonese and Beijing people. Cantonese cuisine is widely recognized and appreciated throughout the world. Beijing people whilst preferring their own style of Chinese cuisine are more likely to indulge in home cooking than in eating out.

Duration

The time spent on an activity is one measure of its meaning for the individual, and will determine the priority given to that activity and its interrelationship with other activities. An individual's perception of how long an activity will or does take is affected by a number of situational and personal variables. For example, if shopping is an enjoyable activity, it will be perceived to have been of shorter duration than if shopping is disliked. Investigations have been made into the relationship between actual waiting time and perceived waiting time (Hornik, 1984; Maister, 1985). A fixed waiting period is perceived to be longer when it occurs during the pre-process, or post-process rather than during the in-process phase of the service encounter (Dube, Leclerc and Schmitt, 1991). However, evidence suggests that the mean estimates of waiting time given by a sample is remarkably close to the actual mean waiting time and gives support for the use of clock time as a measure of duration of activities within a social time context (Hui and Zhou, 1993).

Time spent in the retail service encounter is separated into three components, time spent actually engaging in the service transaction, time spent waiting, and elapsed time, which includes time spent waiting for service, time spent in the transaction and travelling time to and from the retail service location. Visits to the restaurant, hairdresser and to the supermarket take up more time. Waiting times are longer at the restaurant and hairdresser. When elapsed time is longer, there will be more need to plan visits carefully and it is more likely to be regarded as a major activity.

There are many similarities among the three cities studied, for example the time components measured for duration of service at the supermarket, convenience store, restaurant and hairdresser/beauty salon. In China, longer time is spent in the service interaction at the traditional store and at the laundry/dry cleaner, and less time is spent in the hairdresser/beauty salon. Waiting times are more consistent except that longer waiting time is shown in China at the traditional grocery store, laundry/dry cleaner, and less waiting time at the hairdresser/beauty salon than for Hong Kong.

The convenience store is more convenient than the traditional grocery store in Hong Kong, but not so in China where the distribution of convenience stores is less. The opening hours of convenience stores are also less in China, the 7-Eleven Group is more likely to open at 7 a.m. and close

Table 4
Duration of Service

	Hong Kong	Guang-zhou	Bei-jing	Sign. (HG)	Sign. (HB)	Sign. (GB)
	(Time in Mean Minutes)			(Percentage)		
Waiting time at service						
Supermarket	8.3	7.5	6.5		<5.0	
24 hours/Convenience store	4.8	5.8	4.5			
Chinese grocery store	3.5	5.6	6.5	<0.1	<0.1	
Restaurant	20.6	16.7	17.0	<0.1	<5.0	
Laundry/Dry cleaner	1.4	8.6	7.0	<0.1	<0.1	
Hairdresser/Beauty salon	18.1	16.5	16.5			
Time spent at service						
Supermarket	22.6	34.4	41.3	<0.1	<0.1	<1.0
24 hours/Convenience store	7.8	13.9	10.1	<0.1	<0.1	<0.1
Chinese grocery store	5.2	10.8	15.0	<0.1	<0.1	<0.1
Restaurant	85.8	99.9	90.8	<0.1	<0.1	<1.0
Laundry/Dry cleaner	5.8	12.6	13.0	<0.1	<0.1	
Hairdresser/Beauty salon	71.4	55.3	59.1	<0.1	<0.1	
Elapsed time at service						
Supermarket	39.3	63.8	73.8	<0.1	<0.1	<1.0
24 hours/Convenience store	22.5	29.8	20.8	<0.1		<0.1
Chinese grocery store	17.4	21.8	27.5	<0.1	<0.1	<0.1
Restaurant	115.0	128.3	128.9	<0.1	<0.1	
Laundry/Dry cleaner	19.8	35.8	30.7	<0.1	<0.1	<5.0
Hairdresser/Beauty salon	103.6	76.6	84.9	<0.1	<0.1	<5.0

at 11 p.m., which is unlike in Hong Kong where convenience stores are open continuously 24 hours per day.

It is indicative that people in China spend more time in the supermarket and also have a longer elapsed time for the visit. In China, there are fewer supermarkets, so a visit requires more travelling time and consequently more effort. In Hong Kong, each housing development has its own Wellcome or Park'N Shop supermarket. A visit to a restaurant requires a special effort if the total elapsed time is indicative, and restaurants will be chosen selectively. The same logic would appear to support visits in Hong Kong to the hairdresser/beauty salon, but in China it is not such a special occasion. Time spent is less on each occasion but visits to the hairdresser are more frequent.

Timing

For the service encounter to be successful, transactions need to be timed to coincide with those of the vendor, although responsibility for adjusting timing has often been left to the buyer. However, service providers have become more flexible either by becoming more synchronized to preferences of consumers and adjusting opening hours, or through the use of technology and telecommunications eliminating the need for a personal encounter between buyer and seller.

There are similar tendencies among the three groups of respondents, which could be in line with the similarity of cultures — some flexibility is lost in city life due to the need for many people to have fixed working hours and days of the week. In Hong Kong, professionals and those working in offices of international organizations will normally work a five-day week, whereas those working for local companies, especially in manufacturing firms will have a six-day working week. At the time the study was undertaken in Guangzhou, the People's Republic of China had a six-day working week, but during 1995 a five-day working week was officially introduced.

Visiting on the same day of the week applies more to supermarkets and restaurants but differences are evident. In Beijing, there are more respondents visiting grocery stores and supermarkets on the same day, and the popularity of using the restaurant is not evident in Beijing, is less pervasive in Guangzhou but is a strong behavioural factor in Hong Kong. The significance of the visit to the restaurant on both the same day of week and same time of day can be seen for Hong Kong people. The majority of visits are made on Sunday, a key family occasion and important temporal marker in the weekly cycle of activities.

The monthly calendar has little impact on timing of visits to retail services included in the survey, although visits on the same day of the month are more prevalent in China, especially in Beijing for use of the beauty salon, grocery store and supermarket. For visits to the beauty salon they may coincide with a monthly cycle whereas the frequency of visits is less than once a month in Hong Kong. The regularity of visits by time of day is more pronounced, 40% in Hong Kong and 30% in Guangzhou go to the restaurant at the same time of day. Across all three locations 18% to 27% visited the hairdresser/beauty salon at the same time of day, as did 19% to 25% of those visiting the supermarket. In China, high percentages visited the grocery store and convenience store at the same time of day compared with Hong Kong people. In Guangzhou and Beijing, timing of visits to retail services show greater regularity, which may be due to self time being less precious and that the pace of life and demands on time are more under an individual's control than in Hong Kong. As a consequence, arrangements in Hong Kong are more susceptible to unplanned changes, thus limiting temporal synchronization.

The popular days for visiting the supermarket although not shown are Sunday in Guangzhou, Saturday in Beijing and both Saturday and Sunday in Hong Kong. In Hong Kong (81%) and Guangzhou (74%) the popular day for visiting the restaurant is Sunday with Saturday as the second most popular day. A similar pattern is not discernible in Beijing with fewer

Table 5

Timing

	Hong Kong	Guang-zhou	Bei-jing	Sign. (HG)	Sign. (HB)	Sign. (GB)
		(Percentage)				
Visiting on the same day of week						
Supermarket	12.1	17.5	17.8		<5.0	
24 hours/Convenience store	4.0	4.8	7.2	<0.1		
Chinese grocery store	3.2	10.9	19.8	<0.1	<0.1	<1.0
Restaurant	28.0	11.8	5.2	<0.1	<0.1	<1.0
Laundry/Dry cleaner	2.0	4.9	4.1	<0.1		
Hairdresser/Beauty salon	8.1	8.1	12.6			
Visiting on the same date of month						
Supermarket	0.9	3.6	5.4	<0.1	<0.1	
24 hours/Convenience store	0.9	1.6	2.8			
Chinese grocery store	0.6	4.1	4.9	<0.1	<0.1	
Restaurant	1.6	2.9	3.5			
Laundry/Dry cleaner	0	4.9	1.3	<0.1	<5.0	<5.0
Hairdresser/Beauty salon	0.9	4.0	9.2	<0.1	<0.1	<1.0
Visiting at the same time of day						
Supermarket	19.3	24.5	22.3			
24 hours/Convenience store	9.4	16.1	13.1			
Chinese grocery store	4.2	16.9	25.3	<0.1	<0.1	<1.0
Restaurant	39.8	29.8	13.7	<0.1	<0.1	<0.1
Laundry/Dry cleaner	3.0	12.4	5.5	<0.1		<5.0
Hairdresser/Beauty salon	18.0	27.4	18.8			<1.0

people eating out at restaurants and a more dispersed pattern, although weekends are more popular for visits than weekdays. More persons in Beijing say they visit the grocery store on the same day, and here again, although there is an inclination towards Sundays (43%), other days are popular, except Tuesday and Thursday. Visits to the hairdresser/beauty salon cluster around the weekend in all three cities. Friday is almost as popular a day to visit the beauty salon as Saturday and Sunday in both Guangzhou and Beijing, although the latter shows a wider choice of days. In Hong Kong, Saturday is the most popular choice of day to visit the hairdresser.

There are few respondents claiming to visit retail services on the same day of the month, and no apparent pattern is discernible. For example, it is found that Beijing has the highest number claming to visit hairdresser/ beauty salons on the same day of the month. The choice of day is spread across the month with a slight clustering towards the beginning and middle of the month.

As for time of day, people appear more active in the afternoon in all locations, shopping if done at the same time of day is done in the afternoon — including visits to convenience stores in Guangzhou. In Hong Kong (57%) and Beijing (62%), regular visits to convenience stores are mainly concentrated in the evenings. In Guangzhou and Hong Kong, the popular regular time for eating at a restaurant is in the morning, which would be for Cantonese "yum cha" on Sundays. In Hong Kong, 64% of regular visits to the restaurant are made in the morning, and the equivalent percentage in Guangzhou is 57%. In Beijing, the time to visit a restaurant is in the evening when 58% of regular visits are made. Although afternoon is the most popular regular time to visit the hairdresser/beauty salon in Guangzhou, evenings are equally popular; and are also popular to a lesser extent in Beijing, but are not chosen by Hong Kong people.

Sequence

For most retail services the consumer will have freedom to determine the sequence of visits, for example whether to visit the dry cleaner, before or after visiting the supermarket. A visit to the hairdresser/beauty salon may require a prior appointment in which case the visits to other retail service providers could have to be fitted in around the appointment. These other visits would be "embedded" activities fitted in with the major activity of visiting the hairdresser. The concept of time "embeddedness" is important in understanding the sequence of consumer service acts and has been measured by whether the activity is a major activity of one that is embedded in another social act.

There are parallels between Hong Kong and Guangzhou in treating visits to similar service providers as a major activity, for example going to a restaurant for a meal. Visits to retail stores are generally not considered major activities and may be "embedded" in other more important activities. In Beijing this was not the case and respondents in Beijing have a smaller repertoire of activities or less time constraints or pressure and that the degree of planning of activities and their sequential pattern is less problematical than for respondents living in Guangzhou or Hong Kong (Table 6).

Table 6
Time Embeddedness (Treat the Visit as a Major Activity)

	Hong Kong	Guang- zhou	Bei- jing	Sign. (HG)	Sign. (HB)	Sign. (GB)
	(Percentage)					
Supermarket	34.1	28.4	60.7		<0.1	<0.1
24 hours/Convenience store	25.9	21.5	58.9		<0.1	<0.1
Chiense grocery store	31.6	22.2	72.9	<1.0	<0.1	<0.1
Restaurant	60.9	58.5	86.7		<0.1	<0.1
Laundry/Dry cleaner	42.2	48.6	86.8		<0.1	<0.1
Hairdresser/Beauty salon	68.2	60.8	87.4	<5.0	<0.1	<0.1

Tempo

The perceived passage of time will differ between urban and rural life and from city to city. A tempo that is perceived as either too fast or too slow will be perceived negatively by consumers. In the study no direct measure of tempo was identified and can therefore be inferred only. It is suggested that the pace of city life is getting faster. Hong Kong's pace of life is considered fast, but to someone used to life in Beijing, the pace of life in Guangzhou will be considered fast. Time pressures result in service providers having to match the pace of life of consumers by providing for 24 hours a day, seven days a week service. In Hong Kong, petrol filling stations and restaurants

Table 7
Temporal Activities

	Hong Kong	Guang-zhou	Bei-jing	Sign. (HG)	Sign. (HB)	Sign. (GB)
	(Percentage)					
Awake at the same time everyday	66.6	75.2	88.8	<5.0	<0.1	<0.1
Awake to a preset alarm or radio	62.5	40.8	42.6	<0.1	<0.1	
Schedule some time for personal activities	49.1	70.3	82.4	<0.1	<0.1	<0.1
Leave home at the same time everyday	53.1	65.0	77.3	<0.1	<0.1	<0.1
Schedule an exact time for lunch	56.6	70.3	81.2	<0.1	<0.1	<0.1
Eat dinner at the same time everyday	46.3	66.2	57.9	<0.1	<1.0	<5.0
Go to bed at a planned time	23.4	51.6	50.3	<0.1	<0.1	
Usually wear a watch	86.3	78.4	74.8	<1.0	<0.1	
Use appointment calendar to schedule activities	50.9	18.1	32.7	<0.1	<0.1	<0.1
(The following percentages only include those respondents who use an appointment calender)						
Your appointment calender has the day divided into hours	29.8	46.8	23.1	<5.0		<1.0
Record the beginning time of future activities	63.6	62.9	39.8		<0.1	<1.0
Record the expected finishing time of future activities	19.2	35.5	27.8	<5.0		

stay open all night and 7-Eleven convenience stores have become well established in every corner of the territory. For foreign visitors to Hong Kong the "being rushed" tempo can be felt in almost every service encounter from having a meal in a Chinese restaurant, or hiring a taxi to entering or exiting a lift.

Temporal Perspective

The temporal perspective indicates the extent to which there is a need to plan and schedule the day's activities, and respondents will be guided by the daily work routine, the nature of their employment and the time pressures of the employment and of social and family life. The use of an alarm clock is more prevalent in Hong Kong, whereas the daily schedule of awakening, leaving home, having lunch, returning home to dinner and going to bed at the same time is more characteristic of China. Hong Kong people do not plan on going to bed at the same time. It may not be just work pressures, but social pressures, availability of entertainment, meeting friends in restaurants and travelling time involved in getting from the centrally located business and leisure attractions to far flung housing estates. However, Hong Kong people are less likely to schedule some time for personal activities, whereas in Guangzhou and Beijing time will be programmed for personal activities, and Beijing people are more likely to use an appointment calendar. Beijing is unlike Hong Kong where a record of the exact time is made rather than the actively merely recorded.

Conclusions

Studies conducted using the concept of social time do show significant differences in temporal pattern and perspective between Guangzhou, Beijing and Hong Kong in consuming of retail services. An analysis of the social time system as part of cultural assessment may demonstrate temporal dimensions of consumer behaviour that will require localized marketing.

Some similarities are shown between Beijing and Guangzhou, with Hong Kong providing the contrasting experience. Improved living standards, the growth and modernization of the China economy are likely to produce more convergence of social time systems. Findings show that there is little similarity between temporal pattern and temporal perspective between Hong Kong and China. It may be postulated that some similarity should be evident from the common Chinese cultural heritage and in temporal pattern as this can be seen in visits to the restaurant by Cantonese people. There is a danger of treating all Chinese consumers as culturally similar. Local adaptation will still be necessary to take account of regional differences and of the differential patterns of regional growth and exposure to external environmental influences. The temporal analysis indicates the future direction of some of these changes. Global communications and media will assist in the push toward cultural convergence, but for China this is a long way ahead. The change to a socialist market economy where businesses have to compete to survive will increase time pressures on people in China both as employees and as consumers. Temporal patterns and orientation of consumers in China are likely to become more akin to those of their Hong Kong counterparts.

From the studies undertaken it would seem that further temporal studies are worthwhile and that there is, as yet, limited understanding of the temporal dynamics of consumer behaviour. More understanding of temporal dynamics will guide businesses in matching goods and service offerings and will enable their strategies to correspond to the requirements of different market segments.

Section IV
China International Business

15

Market-Based Financial Accounting Standards in the People's Republic of China: A Point of No Return

Richard A. Maschmeyer and Michael D. DeCelles

Introduction

With the recent and ongoing development of accounting and auditing standards, the People's Republic of China (PRC) has reached an important plateau in its effort to transform the country's economic system from a purely socialistic model to one with a significant market orientation. The process has not been without setbacks but its momentum, once established, has to date not been seriously challenged. Even so, institutionalization via formal legislation of internationally acceptable accounting standards is an event of considerable importance not only within the PRC but also to the world as a whole. Consequently, the purpose of this chapter is to review and analyse recent accounting changes that have occurred in the PRC. Discussion will include development of an economic and political context within which readers may more fully appreciate the dramatic nature of these accounting changes and a brief of the existing legal and regulatory hierarchy for PRC accounting standards. The chapter will also detail recent PRC financial accounting-related legislation and assess the impact that this legislation will have upon both the PRC economy and its foreign trading/investing partners. Finally, analysis of the direction that the ongoing reform process in China is likely to take will be presented.

On the Development of Market-Oriented Accounting Standards in the PRC

While an often far from perfect process, the historical development of market-oriented internationally accepted accounting principles has tended to be a function of the decisions made based upon the information generated. This gradual, ad hoc development of specific standards has been influenced in large measure by the identification of inadequacies in existing accounting systems as perceived by the information users. For example, in market-based economies, the information needs of investors and creditors has provided the overwhelming impetus for change and progress.

In contrast, from the founding of the PRC in 1949 through the subsequent three decades, private investors and creditors were virtually non-existent. Subsequent to the final phase of the nationalization of private firms in 1958, the dominant share of the PRC's gross industrial output value was generated by state-owned enterprises (SOEs) with the remainder contributed by village and township enterprises (VTEs). Consequently, the accounting system developed during the nationalization period was quite different from analogous systems in market-based economy. For instance, in market economies, largely discrete, broad based accounting sub-systems evolved to serve the needs of largely discrete user groups (i.e., investor/ creditors, corporate management, government bureaucrats, etc.). Given the predominance of state-owned enterprises and the absence of a capital market, China's accounting system needed only to provide vertical information for central planning and stewardship requirements. So, instead of focusing on the breadth of resource allocation and market related issues at the micro level, the pre-reform accounting system was used to strengthen the planning and control over the enterprises under various administrative departments and to provide information to the state for macroeconomic decisions.

Given the information needs of the centrally planned economy, China's pre-reform accounting system was fund management oriented. That is, the accounting system was based on the circulation and turnover of funds. As shown in Figure 1, the application of funds was identified within three categories: fixed assets, current assets, and specific assets.

Likewise, the sources of funds were identified in three categories: fixed fund source, current fund source, and the specific fund source. The fund framework requires that total assets equal total sources and the assets of

Figure 1
A Simplified Balance Sheet

Fund Application	RMB (000s)	Fund Source	RMB (000s)
Fixed Assets		Fixed Fund Source	
Original Cost	12,000	State Fixed Fund	4,000
Less: Depreciation	–2000	Enterprise Fixed Fund	3,500
		Fixed Loan Fund	2,500
Subtotal	10,000	Subtotal	10,000
Current Assets		Current Fund Source	
Stock	3,000	State Current Fund	14,000
Accounts Receivable	12,000	Enterprise Current Fund	6,000
Cash and Bank Balance	9,000	Current Loan Funds	4,000
Subtotal	24,000	Subtotal	24,000
Special Purpose Assets		Special Fund Source	
Bank Deposit	10,000	State Special Fund	8,000
Assets — Special Fund	9,000	Enterprise Special Fund	6,000
		Special Fund Loans	5,000
Subtotal	19,000	Subtotal	19,000
Total Fund Application	53,000	Total Fund Source	53,000

each category equal the sources of the corresponding category. The purpose of the fund oriented accounting system was to show the application and source of funds in an enterprise, ensure that specific funds were used for their designated purposes and to allow the function of fund management to penetrate all levels of economic activity through the control, supply and allocation of funds (Wang and Qian, 1987). To effect the consolidation of information from micro to macro levels, a uniform chart of accounts was prescribed by the Ministry of Finance. These accounting charts were very precise, as was the strict format advocated for the preparation of balance sheets and income statements (Tang, Chow and Cooper, 1994).

The last seventeen years of economic reforms has had a profound effect on the structure and operating processes of the PRC industrial sector, which, in turn, has influenced significant changes to the accounting system. Evolving from a command economy, significant economic inputs are now realized from a broad spectrum of business organizations. This is illustrated by Table 1, which shows the relative shares of gross industrial output value by ownership. The data clearly shows a shift of economic activity away from SOEs to VTEs with a concomitant rise in individual proprietor businesses (IPBs) and foreign investment enterprises (FIEs) from near zero to substantial percentages.

This shift away from SOEs was accompanied by several factors, which, in turn, fuelled the general need for reforming accounting practices. First, China's government authorities appear to have accepted the premise that "profit" is the principal criterion by which enterprises should be measured to achieve the goal of strengthening the nation's economic base. Thus, in order to inject a stronger element of economic reality into the Chinese economy, the price setting mechanism gradually shifted away from state regulatory authorities to market forces.

Table 1
Proportionate Gross Output Value of Industry in China by Ownership

Year	SOEs	VTEs	IPBs	FIEs
1980	0.7598	0.2352	0.0002	0.0048
1985	0.6486	0.3208	0.0185	0.0121
1990	0.5461	0.3562	0.0539	0.0438
1992	0.5152	0.3507	0.058	0.0761
1994	0.3734	0.3772	0.1009	0.1485
1995	0.3397	0.3659	0.1286	0.1658

Source: *China Statistical Yearbook*, 1996.

By 1992, in fact, some 80–90% of product prices from all enterprises were determined by the market. Secondly, decisions over enterprise operations were being decentralized and enterprise profit was accepted as the decision making criterion for resource allocations. This new domestic business environment required a broader, more objective financial measurement process for effective management decisions at the enterprise level. Finally, PRC authorities recognized the desirability of foreign investments to develop the national economy. However, an accountability system, capable of measuring the investor's financial position and progress, was recognized as a precondition by foreign firms considering long-term investments in China. The development of China's stock markets had a similar effect, particularly with respect to foreign investors. For example, foreign underwriters had difficulty interpreting the financial reports prepared under China's antiquated accounting practices (Duckworth and Leung, 1991). All of these factors were intrinsically linked with the development of accounting practises consistent with a market-oriented economy.

An apparent purpose of China's economic reforms is to restructure all industrial enterprises to a point at which they are operating on a self-support, market-based competitive basis, regardless of their ownership type (Xinhua, 1992). Following these objectives, China's authorities realize that information systems must be coordinated with the structural and procedural changes that have taken place in the business sector. Consequently, during the mid to late 1980s, a series of acts and regulations were promulgated to initiate the reform of PRC accounting. However, the latest set of accounting regulations appear to be a significant step in the overall restructuring of business sector accounting that will be more aligned with the continued homogenization of China's enterprise system (Ge, Fang and Li, 1993). Before addressing the specific accounting laws and regulations, an overview of the new accounting system in the PRC will be presented.

Hierarchy of the PRC Accounting Regulations

As presently formulated, the authoritative source for financial accounting and reporting practices for business enterprises operating in China consists of four hierarchical levels. As show in Figure 2, the Accounting Law of the PRC (hereinafter "Accounting Law") is the highest source of authority for China's accounting system. The second, and perhaps the most significant level, is the Accounting Standards for Business Enterprises (hereinafter "Basic Standards"). The third level of authority within the PRC accounting system is the Applied Specific Accounting Standards (hereinafter "Applied Standards") and the final source of PRC accounting regulations is the Accounting Systems by Industries (hereinafter "Accounting Systems"). Each of these cohesive levels will now be discussed.

The Accounting Law

The promulgation of the Accounting Law demonstrated the start of a new era of legalization and standardization of accounting in China. Initially adopted by the National People's Congress in 1985, the law was subsequently modified in late 1993. The Accounting Law charges the

Figure 2

A Hierarchy of Accounting Guidelines for Enterprises Operating in the PRC

Accounting Law	First Level
Basic Standards	Second Level
Applied Standards	Third Level
Accounting Systems	Fourth Level

Ministry of Finance with the responsibility of regulating accounting and reporting practices nationwide. The Accounting Law also specifies the responsibilities, duties and rights of all enterprise directors, controllers and accountants regarding accounting matters, and describes the relationships between these participants. In addition, the Accounting Law provides an ethical code with which to influence the actions of accountants operating within the country. The presence of an ethical code is particularly important inasmuch as numerous challenges are virtually certain to occur during the transition from a planned to market economy. The following are some of the Accounting Law's more important ethical features (*People's Daily*, 1993):

- emphasis on the independence of accountants in the performance of their duties;
- establishment of a mechanism by which to settle theoretical disputes;
- establishment of disciplinary measures to be taken against individuals who violate accounting regulations.

As a final item of note, the 1993 revision of the Accounting Law extended the legal scope of the legislation from state-owned enterprises to all enterprises and units operating in China, irrespective of the form of ownership.

The Basic Accounting Standards

Similar in intent to the U.S. Financial Accounting Standards Board's (FASBs) Statements of Financial Accounting Concepts, the PRC's Basic Accounting Standards provide a conceptual framework which serves as a basis for the development of applied accounting standards for more specific accounting topics. Effective 1 July 1993, the specific purpose of the Basic Standards is stated in the first article as follows (Ministry of Finance, 1992):

> The Accounting Standards for Business Enterprises are promulgated pursuant to the development needs of the socialist market economy, to standardize the accounting systems, and thus to improve the quality of accounting information.

The Basic Accounting Standards include 63 articles which articulate the specific objectives of PRC accounting and discusses the related concepts, principles and elements upon which financial accounting practices are to be based. Although the concepts, principles and elements had never been formally codified within China, it is important to note that most of the items identified in the Basic Standards have consistently been utilized in Chinese accounting both prior and subsequent to the formation of the PRC. However, the PRC's currently far more decentralized economy dictates that it is now substantially more important for accounting standards to be issued in as consistent a manner as possible in order to satisfy the demands of a much wider array of information users.

As shown in Table 2, the assumptions, principles, accounting elements and financial statements advocated in the Basic Standards are relatively compatible with the framework offered by the FASB. The Basic Standards are not, however, a duplication of Western standards nor do they represent a mere compilation of prior PRC practices. Rather, the Basic Standards attempt to capture the current state of the PRC's transition to a socialist market economy and, at the same time, strives for compatibility with acceptable international accounting practices. For a complete interpretation of China's conceptual framework of accounting as compared to the FASBs framework, see Davidson, Gelardi and Li (1996).

An Analysis of the Basic Standards

Despite the general degree of conformity between Western and PRC reform accounting practices, some variations of principles/practices between the

Table 2
The PRC's Conceptual Framework of Accounting

Objectives
1. To meet the macroeconomic management needs of the state
2. For external parties to assess the enterprise's financial position and operating results
3. To strengthen internal management of the enterprise

Assumptions	**Basic Principles**
1. Accounting entity	*Qualitative*
2. Going concern	1. Trueness
3. Periodicity	2. Relevance
4. Monetary unit	3. Uniformity
Elements of Accounting	4. Consistency
1. Assets	5. Timeliness
2. Liabilities	6. Clearness
3. Owners' equity	7. Materiality
4. Revenues	8. Accrual basis
5. Expenses	*Recognition and Measurement*
6. Profit and loss	*Concepts*
Financial Reports	9. Matching principle
1. Balance sheet	10. Prudence
2. Profit and loss statement	11. Historical costs
3. Statement of changes in financial position (cash flow statement is optional)*	12. Separation of capital expenditures from revenue expenditures

* The Applied Standards exposure draft requires the cash flow statement.

two persist and merit attention. It will likely prove useful, consequently, to provide a contrasting analysis between the Basic Standards and the FASB's conceptual framework. Toward that end, emphasis will be placed on highlighting major PRC accounting principles that have altered in such a way as to enhance compatibility with international norms. Emphasis will also be provided for PRC principles/practices, which continue to differ from international norms. Any comparison between the FASB conceptual framework and the Basic Standards must be tempered by the lack of definition or specificity offered in the Basic Standards. For example, assets are broadly defined as "economic resources which are measurable in monetary amounts and which are owned or controlled by an enterprise" and the entity to be accounted for is specified as simply the enterprise with no definition. While the Basic Standards do include several assumptions about the monetary unit, there is no mention of an assumption of a stable monetary unit.

Also, limited notions of the materiality concept are mentioned, but cost-benefit and specific industry constraints are not mentioned. Although the phrase "contingent liabilities" is not directly expressed in the Basic Standards, Article 36 does says (Ministry of Finance, 1992):

> All current liabilities should be recorded according to the amount actually incurred. When a liability has already been incurred but its amount still must be estimated, the estimation must be done reasonably.

One can only assume that the operational definitions of "actually incurred" and "done reasonably" will be specified in the Applied Standards. Taking into consideration the lack of specificity and definitions in the Basic Standards, the more significant changes China's accounting system has undergone to enhance conformity with international standards will now be presented.

Relative Conformance to U.S. Accounting Practices

Our intent is to discuss only the more pertinent issues portrayed in Table 3. One of the most significant changes relates to an omission from the standards. In the first draft of the Basic Standards, "legitimacy" was included as one of the qualitative characteristics. Legitimacy infers that accounting practices should follow government regulations. However, legitimacy was deleted from the Basic Standards' final version, implying that government regulations cannot override financial accounting and reporting as outlined by the Basic Standards. For example, government tax regulations limit the amount of bad debt and business entertainment expense an enterprise can claim each year. The new standards allow the enterprises to recognize the full amount of these incurred expenses for financial reporting purposes, regardless of the legal tax limitations. In the past, the recognition of bad debts was limited by the necessity of a lengthy and highly uncertain court approval process. As such, any bad debts eventually recognized were accounted for by the direct write-off method. The Basic Standards signal a major shift from the past by permitting the allowance method for bad debts. This results in a net realizable accounts receivable on the balance sheet as well as conforming to the matching principle for income determination purposes.

Table 3

New Elements of Conformance with U.S. Accounting Conventions
and Practices

Item of Change	The Essence of the Change
Accounting for bad debts	The allowance method is now acceptable
Accounting for capital leases	Capital leases require capitalization and a corresponding recognition of a liability, but no mentioning of present value
Depreciation	Accelerated depreciation methods are now acceptable, if pre-approved
Inventory	Lifo is now acceptable as an inventory costing method
Equity section of the balance sheet	The equity side of the balance sheet is now separated between creditor equity and owner equity
Administrative expense	Now recognized as a period expense rather than a product cost for manufacturing firms
Balance sheet classifications	Assets and liabilities are now classified in a manner that is consistent with U.S. practices
Profit and loss statement format	A multi-step profit and loss statement approach is now required
Required financial statements	A balance sheet, profit and loss statement and a cash flow statement are now required
Legitimacy	This concept was deleted at the exposure draft stage. The concept inferred that accounting practices should follow government regulations, accounting treatments can now differ from regulations

The Basic Standards also allow enterprises to use accelerated depreciation methods when the methods conform to the enterprise's respective Accounting System regulations. Prior to the Basic Standards, the state mandated the use of the straight-line depreciation method. Enterprise managers have long argued for higher straight-line depreciation rates or the option of an accelerated depreciation method to retain additional funds for more timely production development purposes.

The Basic Standards appear to provide similar revenue recognition principles to that of the FASB. On the expense side, the Basic Standards require a greater conformance to Western accounting than was prescribed under the old accounting regulations. In the past, administrative expenses of manufacturing firms were capitalized as a product cost. Article 49 of the Basic Standards clearly changes this position by stating (Ministry of Finance, 1992):

> Administrative expenses and financial expenses incurred by an enterprise's administrative departments for organizing and administering production and business activities, as well as purchases expenses and sales expenses incurred for sales and services offered should be treated as period expenses and charged directly to the profits and losses account of the current fiscal year.

This charge will enhance conformance to the matching principle and will prevent the previous understatements of losses during periods of low productivity or temporary plant closures.

The Basic Standards require the presentation of three financial statements: the statement of assets and liabilities (i.e., the balance sheet), the profit and loss statement, and the statement of changes in financial position. Interestingly, the Basic Standards allow the cash flow statement as an alternative, but the relevant exposure draft of the Applied Standards requires the cash flow statement. Notes to the financial statements and other supplemental information required to explain the financial statement are also prescribed.

The overall structure of the new balance sheet represents a significant change in PRC accounting, the nature of which can best be illustrated by a review of the pre-1979 PRC balance sheet presentation. Westerners generally have a misconception about pre-1979 PRC state-sector accounting. That is, many Westerners assume fund accounting is synonymous with non-profit (and governmental) accounting. Thus, fund accounting is assumed to have no profit measurement motive and expenditures, rather than expenses based on consumption, are recognized as incurred. The term "fund" accounting, as used to describe earlier PRC accounting, was correctly interpreted as simply a method of controlling the use of funds. Although not a predominant attribute of a state-owned enterprise's performance evaluation, profit (or surplus) was measured on the basis of accrual accounting, including the recognition of depreciation. Thus, the basic accounting equation in China, formulated on the basis of accounting control, was Fund Usages = Fund Sources. Compared to the equation utilized in the West, i.e., Assets = Liabilities + Owners' Equity, the Chinese version did not make a distinction between funds borrowed by and funds invested in enterprises. While the left sides of both equations represent the resources of an enterprise, China's lack of distinction between debt and equity was arguably consistent with their totally centralized economy. Inasmuch as the state was ultimately the sole source of funds for state-owned enterprises, the legal rights of the state were identical whether the funds were considered to have been loaned to or invested in individual enterprises.

With the dramatic increase in stock companies, joint ventures and other forms of privatized companies as well as a dramatic rise in bank loans as sources of operating funds, a clear distinction between borrowed and invested funds was necessary for the broader array of decisions and decision makers. Hence, the reformed PRC accounting standards mandate offsetting assets on the balance sheet with clearly delineated liability and owners' equity sections.

For its part, the format for the profit/loss statement is required to follow a multi-step presentation. Specifically, total enterprise profit/loss must be broken down into the following distinct components: operational profits, investment profits and other non-operational profits. The distinction between these three profit components is not well defined in the Basic Standards. Operational profits are simply defined as operational revenues minus operational costs, period expenses, and taxes. Investment profits include all gains, losses, revenues and expenses resulting from investments. Non-operational profits appears to be a catch-all for all revenues, gains, losses, and expenses that do not meet the definition of operational or investment profits. As the exposure drafts suggest, the Applied Standards will likely provide greater clarity on the profit and loss statement components.

Another development in PRC accounting directly related to the change from a planned to market economy involves the importance of a cash flow statement. Just as PRC accounting under a planned economy disregarded an allowance for uncollectable receivables on the theory that defaults were not possible, the concept of liquidity was similarly deemed not particularly important under pre-1979 PRC accounting. That is, even though Chinese banks were a primary source of enterprises' current funds, all defaults on such loans were absorbed by the government. As a practical matter, consequently, the sources and uses of an enterprise's cash were largely irrelevant to the decision makers. If more cash was needed, enterprises simply obtained it from banks, which, in turn, passed any resulting bad debts on to the government.

In contrast, however, liquidity and cash flow information are very important to investors and creditors in market-based economies. This is obviously the case for Chinese stock companies, but it is also true for SOEs and VTEs as they attempt to become more responsive to the economic reality of competing in a market-based economy. In recognition of this, the Basic Standards will likely be revised to require the cash flow statement from all enterprises.

Divergence from U.S. Accounting Conventions

Taking into consideration the characteristics that are unique to the Chinese business environment, the Basic Standards also include requirements that differ from those practised by the U.S. Table 4 illustrates the major differences between the Basic Standards and the FASB's conceptual framework, some of which will now be discussed in greater depth.

The obvious divergence from the FASB's micro approach is China's continuing emphasis on providing information that meets the macroeconomic management needs of the state. While private investment, both domestic and foreign, has increased rapidly in the past decade, the government remains the predominant equity party of enterprises in the PRC. Thus, the primary objective of providing information to meet the macro-management

Table 4
Differences in Accounting between the PRC and the U.S.

Accounting Item	The PRC's Accounting Treatment
Accounting objectives	Primarily concerned with serving the China's macro-economic needs
Lower of cost or market	The lower of cost or market convention is not acceptable for inventories or marketable securities
Intangible assets	The capitalization of specified internally generated developmental costs is acceptable for patents.
The composition of the owner equity section	Comprised of the following four components: (1) Invested capital, (2) Capital reserve, (3) Surplus reserve and (4) Undistributed capital
Reimbursements	Provides guidance on the accounting treatment of reimbursements for enterprise losses
Cost Accounting	The Basic Standards include accounting guidance on cost accounting issues

needs of the state appears consistent with the current overall structure of China's enterprises.

Intangible asset costs are defined more broadly by the Basic Standards than by the FASB or the International Accounting Standards. Whereas the FASB limits the capitalized cost of intangibles to acquisition costs and expenditures to prepare the intangible asset for use, the Basic Standards also include any expenditures incurred during the internal development of an intangible asset. Thus, all costs associated with self-developed patents are capitalized under the Basic Standards rather than expensed (Adhikari and Wang, 1995, p. 29).

As a reflection of China's current transitional status, the Basic Standards provide both similar and dissimilar owners' equity characteristics in comparison with the FASB's model. The Basic Standards define owners' equity as the residual claim that investors have on the enterprise's net assets and is comprised of invested capital, capital reserves, surplus reserves and undistributed profits. The composition of the owners' equity section is designed to accommodate the different ownership types operating in the PRC. For example, the invested capital section is defined as the capital fund actually invested in the enterprise, whether in the form of cash, physical goods or other assets and is accounted for at the amount actually invested. It is important to note, however, that an exception to this rule is provided for stock companies whose invested capital is to be accounted for at par value. In addition, appropriations provided by the state (except those that are otherwise regulated) are separately identified as government investments. The capital reserve section includes stock premiums, legal re-valuations of assets, the value of gifts or donated assets, and exchange rate gains or losses. A surplus reserve section refers to the reserve fund set up from accumulated enterprise profits to cover possible losses in the future. Currently, regulations for the implementation of the surplus reserve fund are limited to stock companies. For these companies, 10% of their annual after-tax profit is mandated for accumulation in this fund. Increases beyond this level are at the discretion of the enterprise's board of directors. Equity associated with possible future losses is to be accumulated each year until the total amount reaches 50% of the company's total book value of assets. An additional 5% of a stock company's after-tax profit is accumulated for employee welfare benefits. The undistributed profit section is designated for the accumulated amount of profit reserved for future distribution or profit not yet distributed. Losses not covered by government subsidies are to be accumulated in a contra account as an overall reduction in owners' equity.

The Principle of Prudence (Conservatism)

The trend towards internationalization of accounting continues around the world, but one of the more controversial issues is the principle of prudence (or conservatism, for FASB purposes). Even among Western countries the principal is not universally defined and adopted. The International Accounting Standards Committee (1994, p. 44) defines prudence in the following way:

> Prudence is the inclusion of a degree of caution in the exercise of the judgements needed in making estimates required under conditions of uncertainty, such that assets or income are not overstated and liabilities or expenses are not overstated.

The relative adoption of the principle by individual countries is a function of that country's specific conditions and environment. Some argue that the treatment of bad debts, inventory costing methods, the costing of marketable securities, the accounting for warranties and depreciation methods all present issues that may fall under the definition of "prudence."

Article 18 of the Basic Standards simply provides the following general statement: "The principle of prudence should be followed in reasonably determining the possible loss and expense." With little guidance from the Finance Ministry to date, there are mixed interpretations from Chinese academics as to how broad the principle of prudence should be interpreted. The Basic Standards explicitly allow for accelerated depreciation, the lifo inventory method and the allowance method for bad debts. The Basic Standards do not mention the lower of cost or market (LCM) convention, but explicitly requires that both inventory and marketable securities should be recorded according to their actual cost at the time of purchase and that any subsequent reporting of these assets will be on the basis of their original costs. Thus, Lou and Zhang (1992) interpret Article 18 to mean that, under appropriate circumstances, the principle of prudence can be applied to accounting for bad debts and depreciation of plant assets, but the LCM convention cannot be applied to inventory or marketable securities.

Chinese accounting theory has long rejected the principle of prudence (or conservatism), but previous arguments for rejection were usually ideologically based. Today, however, there is a persuasive practical argument for not allowing the LCM convention. The past inefficiencies of state-owned enterprises have resulted in huge build-ups of obsolete and damaged inventories that cannot be sold. If the LCM method were put into practice, tremendous losses would be reported by many state enterprises around the country. Because this would have a significant impact on government revenues, these losses must be absorbed gradually. Once the losses are fully absorbed, LCM should be a more salient convention for true and relevant financial reporting. Overall, the inclusion of the prudence principle, as interpreted in the Basic Standards, represents a significant breakthrough for improved accounting transparency in the PRC.

Applied Standards

As the name implies, Applied Standards involve the application of the Basic Standards to individual accounting topics. Currently being developed by a team of Chinese accounting specialists and professors aided by consultation with an international accounting firm, a set of Applied Standards are expected to be promulgated. At the same time, the expectation is that a set of revised Basic Standards will also be issued. Table 5 provides the titles and issue dates of the Applied Standards exposure drafts. A review of the exposure draft list suggests that many of the un- certainties or ambiguities associated with the Basic Standards will likely be clarified by the Applied Standards. Initially, the new Applied Standards will only apply to the largest SOEs (approximately 100) as well as all companies listed on China's stock exchanges. At the conclusion of the trial period and after appropriate modifications, the standards will be implemented nationwide.

Accounting Systems by Industry

The final sources of PRC accounting practices are the Accounting Systems by Industry. Focusing on 13 industries, the intent of the Accounting Systems is to formulate accounting systems specific to these industries. The designated industry categories for which the Accounting Systems apply are provided in Table 6. Enterprises must follow the Accounting Systems for which they belong, except in two situations. First, foreign investment enterprises must follow the accounting practices stipulated in the Accounting System for Foreign Investment Enterprises that was promulgated in 1992.

Table 5

Exposure Drafts of the Applied Standards

No. Topic	Date of Exposure Draft	No. Topic	Date of Exposure Draft
1. Accounts payable, notes payable and bonds payable	02/14/94	16. Revenue	07/12/95
2. Receivables	07/06/94	17. Foreign currency translation	07/12/95
3. Inventories	07/06/94	18. Accounting for income taxes	07/12/95
4. Investments	07/06/94	19. Consolidated financial statements	07/12/95
5. Capitalization of borrowing costs	07/06/94	20. Accounting policies and changes in accounting policies and estimates	07/12/95
6. Balance sheet	07/06/94	21. Events after the balance sheet date	09/27/95
7. Profit and loss statement	07/06/94	22. Employee benefits	09/27/95
8. Fixed assets	04/21/95	23. Donation and government grants	09/27/95
9. Intangible assets	04/21/95	24. Contingencies and commitments	09/27/95
10. Owners' equity	04/21/95	25. Disclosure of related party relationships and related party transactions	09/27/95
11. Construction contracts	04/21/95	26. Liquidation accounting	09/27/95
12. Research and development	04/21/95	27. Leases	01/04/96
13. Cash flow statement	04/21/95	28. Futures	01/04/96
14. Basic banking business	04/21/95	29. Business combinations	01/04/96
15. Deferred assets	07/12/95	30. Non-monetary transactions	01/04/96

And second, because of their specific characteristics, stock companies must follow the Accounting System for Experimental Stock Companies promulgated in 1992.

Somewhat controversially, the Ministry of Finance issued the Accounting Systems in late 1992, over four years prior to the issuance of the Applied Standards. For a more consistent flow, one would argue that the Applied Standards should have been issued prior to the development of the Accounting Systems. The Ministry of Finance has offered three reasons for this apparent inconsistency. First, since uniform accounting systems from different industries were already in existence from the pre-reform era and developing the Applied Standards involving issues that were not covered under the old systems would take three to four years, the Ministry argued that it was more expedient to make consolidations and adjustments to the old systems to fit the newly designated industry classifications. Second, the Ministry argued that it would be better to have the enterprises reporting under the 13 new classifications than the more than 70 uniform accounting systems (Swanz, 1995, p. 43) in effect prior to 1992 while the Applied Standards were being developed. And finally, since only certain aspects of the old accounting systems would require revision, the new Accounting Systems would likely be more readily accepted by practitioners already accustomed to the old systems.

The PRC approach to industry specific accounting issues is far more specialized than Western approaches to the same problem. Western systems generally assume that the preponderance of accounting for a given enterprise is the same regardless of the nature of the particular industry within which the enterprise falls. Given that, the Western approach to accounting standards for industry specific problems tend toward narrow treatments focusing only on those aspects of the overall accounting process which are different for a particular industry. Consequently, developing entire accounting systems for so large a number of general industries must surely result in significant redundancy. Given the PRC's stated rationales for its decision, however, it is our hope that such redundancy is merely being accepted in the short-term in order to enhance acceptance of the accounting reforms. Theoretically, the Accounting Systems should have been designed on the basis of the Applied Standards, otherwise the likelihood of contradictions is present. But like all systems, revisions will take place in the future and with these changes redundancies can be eliminated and inconsistencies can be corrected.

Table 6

Accounting Systems by Industry Categories

1. Manufacturing and mining
2. Retail and wholesale
3. Agriculture
4. Railway transportation
5. Other transportation
6. Post and telecommunications
7. Civil aviation
8. Finance
9. Insurance
10. Real estate development
11. Construction
12. Tourism, catering and service
13. Foreign economic cooperative enterprises

Maximizing Compatibility of Auditing System with PRC Economic Conditions

As a premise for the following discussion, it is the case that appropriate accounting standards and guidelines are a necessary but not sufficient condition to insure effective financial accounting in China. Beyond such reliable accounting standards, that is, an auditing system that is compatible with the environment in which it must function is also necessary. In the case of China, furthermore, several state initiatives undertaken in recent years do provide evidence that some progress has been achieved in putting an effective auditing system into place. Such progress has not, however, been completely uniform, with the result that some areas related to the compatibility between PRC financial accounting standards and its auditing system require further attention.

While previous rules and regulations had been issued during the reform period, it was not until 1994 that the first law was enacted on auditing-related issues. The Law of Certified Public Accountants, effective January 1994, defined and specified the overall business of CPAs in China. The law defined CPAs and CPA firms and provided details on the CPA's scope of business, the rules for conducting CPA-related business, and the legal responsibilities of CPAs and CPA firms. The law also detailed the role of the Chinese Institute of Certified Public Accountants (CICPA), China's professional accounting association. The first law enacted on governmental auditing was the Law on Auditing in the PRC, effective January 1995. This law detailed the organizational structure of governmental auditing, the jurisdiction and obligations of the participating organizational units, the general principles and practices of governmental auditing and associated legal responsibilities.

The first set of Independent Auditing Standards became effective on 1 January 1996 and the second set of Standards became effective 1 January 1997. The Independent Auditing Standards consist of three levels of specificity:

- Basic Auditing Standards;
- Detailed Auditing Standards and Practice Guidelines; and
- Professional Guidelines

After reviewing the Independent Auditing Standards, the authors believe it is safe to assert that China has consistently sought out common ground with international auditing standards on major issues while occasionally reserving differences on relatively minor ones. The promulgation of detailed auditing standards pertaining to China's professional auditing sector represents a significant contribution to the ultimate success of the developing accounting system. While lacking in practical importance under a centralized economy, a credible auditing system is crucial for a broader base of users that require more transparent financial reporting in a market-based economy.

Future Challenges to PRC Financial Accounting

While China has achieved significant progress towards the development of an accounting and auditing system that are intended to serve their information needs, several issues remain which may restrict the rate of future progress. These challenges include: (1) assessing whether the developing accounting system meets the information requirements of the primary report users, (2) ensuring the existence of a sufficient number of accounting professionals with the expertise needed to implement the sophisticated level of the new accounting system and (3) reforming the legal system to support the development of accounting. A brief discussion of these challenges follows.

Who Are the Dominant Report Users?

Originally, the PRC had hoped to have its Applied Standards issued by July 1996. The standards were subsequently deferred, however, until late 1996 and are now delayed until mid-1997 or later. The delay is due in part to the ongoing dispute over the general orientation of China's accounting system with respect to whether the system should be harmonized with international standards or whether it should be more reflective of the information requirements of the domestic economy? That is, should China allow the development of its accounting system to evolve from the experiences of other developed countries or should China allow its own environment to guide accounting development on the basis of its own characteristics and sequence of cultural, socioeconomic and political events?

This argument is not limited to the academics and professionals of China. Rather, this dilemma is faced by most developing countries, particularly when the country's economy is in a transition from a centrally planned to market-based economy? As Riahi-Belkaoui emphasizes (1994):

> The economic planning route chosen by most developing countries in the context of a mixed economy is motivated by several variables. The most important variable is related to the market-failure argument. The imperfection of structure and operations of markets in developing countries, with the results of distorted prices and inequities, renders the market concept an inefficient tool for economic development in these countries.

Yet, the primary objective of China's Basic Accounting Standards is to provide information for macroeconomic decisions from a market-based (e.g., investor/creditor) accounting model that is in harmony with U.S. accounting conventions where capital markets dominate the economic activity. Briston (1978) has expressed his dissatisfaction with the influence that both the United Kingdom and the United States have had on the development of accounting systems in less developed countries. In this regard, Briston suggests that each "country should not be encouraged to harmonize the structure and specifications of its accounting/information system, but advised that each should create a system which is more appropriate to its own requirements."

As Samuels (1990) suggests, the user needs approach to the development of accounting guidelines has a good deal of merit. However, a difficulty implicit in relying on the user needs approach is the potential for different users to have different information requirements. The question is:

Which users' needs dominate? The challenge for China is to determine whether their developing market-based accounting system is compatible with their primary objective of providing information for macroeconomic decisions at the state level. In addition, the question exists as to whether market-based information will prove sufficient decision making input for the supervisory administrative agencies that continue to have significant influence over the majority of China's enterprises.

The accounting demands of a country generally embrace the broad areas of enterprise accounting, government accounting and macro (or national) accounting. In most capitalist countries, "where the efficient allocation of a nation's resources is presumed to be achievable by the invisible operation of the market-price mechanism and not by national planners, the need to regulate the economy" comes from statistical sources beyond the enterprise reports (Wallace, 1990). In these countries, usually three independent accounting systems exist: enterprise accounting, governmental accounting and macro (national) accounting. Some systems in continental Europe and in other central planning countries, uniform national accounting is followed. Thus, the national income accounts and national balance sheet are comparable to the enterprises' income statements and balance sheets. Implicitly, then, if the primary accounting objective included in China's Basic Accounting Standards is to "meet the macroeconomic needs of the state," an integration of macro-accounting and micro-accounting will be required. This integration requires a strong degree of uniformity at the micro level, yet the Basic Accounting Standards and the exposure drafts of the Applied Standards allow flexibility on various accounting treatments. These are major issues that relate to the relevance of information to each user group. Among the questions raised in this regard are the following. Can a single accounting system, as China has suggested, provide relevant information to each of the user groups identified in the objectives statement of the Basic Standards? The answers to these questions in China are yet to be provided. It is clear, however, that the PRC accounting system will require assessment and adjustment to ensure the information provided meets the needs of the dominant users.

Quantity and Quality of Accounting Professionals

Due to the rapid rise in demand for both financial accounting and auditing services in China, a severe strain has been imposed upon the supply of qualified professional accountants in the country. For example, in 1996, the PRC State Council mandated that CPA audits be conducted annually for all enterprises operating in China by the year 2000. The number of FIEs in China already numbers 200,000, however, and are expected to increase at the rate of 10% per year. While audits of FIEs are required, only 60% of these are currently having their financial statement audited. In addition, of the current 300,000 plus state-owned enterprises in China, only approximately 10% are now being audited (Ding, 1966). By the end of 1995 there were only 53,000 professional auditors practising in China. Faced which such an overwhelming shortfall, the CICPA has developed a plan to increase the number of professional auditors by 20,000 to 25,000 individuals by the year 2000. Even should such an optimistic goal be achieved, the shortfall of professional accountants will still be significant.

Beyond the quantitative shortfall, problems exist with respect to the qualitative level of expertise for all parties involved in accounting. Given the upgraded sophistication of the new accounting and auditing standards, it is questionable whether most of China's accounting professionals possess the experience and training to implement the recently enacted standards. In recognition of this problem, the CICPA has endorsed several policies to upgrade the quality of accounting professionals. Closing the quantity and quality gap of professional accountants represents a significant challenge to China's accounting community.

Legal Issues

Another area of concern relates to China's undeveloped legal system. Criminal laws seem to be well entrenched, but property and commercial law is not well defined. As Sinha (1995) aptly notes:

> The problem for the legal profession in China is a very tricky one. They have to walk the tightrope of reforming the process without appearing to be meddling in the internal affairs of China. Without legal reform, development of accounting in China will not be very effective.

In late 1994 the Ministry of Justice, in conjunction with the World Bank, initiated a programme to develop the legal system such that it will be able to coordinate with Western-style legal systems. This development is of particular interest to multinational and joint venture companies. When attained, the reformed legal system will be a positive ingredient for further investment from abroad.

Conclusion

Any reasonable assessment of China's efforts to reform its accounting processes in accordance with their economic transformation from a planned to market basis can only conclude that significant progress has been achieved toward that goal. This development is particularly praiseworthy when the psychological nature of the reform is considered. That is, to cast aside the psychological security of a highly centralized and planned economy in order to take up the volcanic eruptions characteristic of market economies is an act whose difficulty should not be understated. And, faced with such a daunting task, China has pragmatically faced up to the deficiencies of its previous accounting system and has resolutely moved to remedy those deficiencies. There is no question about the fact that the PRC has, in a remarkably short period of time, taken great strides toward the development of an accounting system that is compatible with a market-based economy.

16

Impact of PRC's Tax System and Trade Policy Reform on Foreign Direct Investment

Daniel Kam-tong Li, Gordon R. Walker
and T. K. P. Leung

Introduction

In 1995, the total import and export volumes of foreign-invested enterprises (FIEs) in the People's Republic of China (PRC) reached US$109.8 billion, showing a growth of 25% from 1994 and representing 39% of the total value of imported and exported commodities in the whole nation. As intended by China's open door policy — "the bracing wind through the open door" — the pace of economic development was accelerated by foreign direct investment (FDI) (Jia, 1994). During the last two years, the business operations of FIEs employed over 16 million staff and workers with large amounts of fixed asset investment. The average annual amount of fixed asset investment represented 18% of the national total and the industrial output generated amounted to 13% of total national industrial output. During 1995, FDI in the PRC grew tremendously in volume and in scale. There were 37,126 newly established FIEs in 1995 with capital investment amounting to US$37.7 billion, reflecting a growth of 12% from 1994 and reaching an all-time historical record.

The statistical data indicates that FDI is playing an increasingly important role in the development of the PRC's national economy. Thus, since 1994, the PRC has implemented a series of major economic reform measures to improve the business environment and shift the national economic structure (including regulatory frameworks) toward international norms. The reform measures are mainly in such key areas as taxation, foreign exchange, finance and foreign trade and are aimed at achieving the following objectives:

- to accelerate the transition from the old economic system to a socialist market economic system in order to maintain and further attract FDI;
- to dovetail the economic system into the international economy by closer compliance with international norms of economic and trade, (e.g., for joining the World Trade Organization (WTO), successor to the GATT);
- to standardize economic activities and regulatory frameworks to produce a more lenient business environment and efficient trading mechanisms which favour fair market competition, optimal allocation of resources and rapid development of the economy.

The reform of the taxation system with effect from 1 January 1994, is a conspicuous structural reform which comprises the following four aspects:

1. The Reform of Turnover Tax

Revenue from turnover taxes has always accounted for close to 85% of total tax revenue in the PRC. Hence, turnover tax reform is a key component of tax reform. As of 1 January 1994, the Industrial and Commercial Consolidated Tax (ICCT) with tax rates ranging from 1.5% to 66% was abolished. In place of ICCT, three new turnover taxes, comprising Value-Added Tax (VAT), Business Tax and Consumption Tax have been introduced. As is the case in developed and Western countries, VAT is revenue neutral and operates to broaden the tax base thereby facilitating long-term economic development. VAT is intended to eliminate weaknesses present in the old taxation system and to provide an engine for a steadily increasing source of revenue.

2. The Reform of Domestic Enterprise Income Tax

Prior to the introduction of the open door policy in 1978, all enterprises were owned by the state (see Rohwer, 1995, ch. 7 for a good account). Under the planned socialist economy, state-owned enterprises (SOEs) largely turned their operating incomes over to the state in the form of profits. The tax revenue was a small proportion of total state revenue. The revenues and expenditures of SOEs were tightly controlled and monitored by the central government in the manner known as the "big pot" socialist wealth distribution system. Since 1978, in order to facilitate the transition from the old economic system to a socialist market economic system, SOEs have gradually assumed business management in- dependence. Further, business structures have gradually splintered into complicated forms such as Sino-foreign joint ventures, FIE's publicly-owned corporations, sole proprietorships and so on. To cope with such change in business structures, the ICCT was introduced over 30 different tax items. As of 1 January 1994, the ICCT was abolished and was replaced by the Enterprise Income Tax, which is directed at establishing an equitable tax system regardless of ownership or nationality.

3. The Reform of Individual Income Tax

The reform of Individual Income Tax (IIT) aims at unifying the Individual Income Tax Law applicable to foreigners promulgated in 1980 and the Individual Income Adjustment Tax Law applicable to Chinese nationals promulgated in 1986. Under the unified IIT, discrimination between foreigner and Chinese nationals is eliminated and the tax burden for local Chinese nationals will be lightened while the tax liabilities for most foreigners will increase. The reform has also introduced a progressive tax rate structure, with progressive marginal rate ranging from 5% to 45%, in order to achieve equitable income distribution.

4. The Reform of Local Taxes

Reform in this area has codified and adjusted such local taxes as Land Value Appreciation Tax, Vehicle License Tax, and Stamp Duty. However, the reforms have placed strong emphasis on unification goals rather than the adjustment of tax burdens. Local tax reform has introduced some new tax items, which in the long run could supply a neutral and stable revenue source for local governments while most inappropriate tax items have been abolished.

The Post-Reform Taxes Chargeable on Foreign-Invested Enterprises and Foreign Individuals

Under the post-reform taxation system, FIEs established in the PRC prior to 1 January 1994 will be eligible for a refund of increased tax burdens (as a result of the introduction of such new tax items as VAT, Consumption Tax,

Business Tax and the like) for a grace period of five years. In a nutshell, FIEs and foreign individuals will be subject to the following taxes: Value-Added Tax, Business Tax, Consumption Tax, Income Tax on Enterprises with Foreign Investment and Foreign Enterprises, Individual Income Tax, Stamp Duty, Land Value Appreciation Tax, Vehicle License Plate Tax, Urban Real Estate Tax, Slaughter Tax and Resources Tax.

The Most Recent Round of Tax and Trade Policy Reforms

The most recent round of tax modification includes the "Import Tariff Reduction" (down from an average rate of 35.9% to 23% with effect from 1 April 1996) and the "Reduction of Refund for VAT Paid on Inputs for Exports" (down by 3% and 5% with effect from 1 July 1995 and 1 January 1996 respectively). PRC has also introduced complementary trade policy reforms aimed at tax evasion and smuggling, namely, the "Modification of the Administrative Measures on Processing Trade," which launched the "Customs Duty Security System" as from 1 April 1996. These are discussed below.

The Reduction of Import Tariffs and the Achievement of Tax Reform

As part of its strategy to join the WTO, successor to the GATT, the PRC has been gradually reducing import tariffs since 1991 to a targeted level of 15% by the year 2000. This is the general level of import tariffs in developing countries around the world seeking a free trade system in alignment with the international norm. On 19 November 1995, Chairman Jiang Zemin of the PRC announced at the Asia-Pacific Economic Cooperation (APEC) conference held in Osaka, Japan that the PRC would reduce import tariff rates by no less than 30% in 1996 (*ACLR*, 1996). In fulfilment of the objective set by the Fourteenth National People's Congress of the Communist Party of China to establish a socialist market economic system from 1994 onwards, a new tax system based upon VAT has been established which has largely achieved:

- the unification of tax law with a fair tax obligation;
- a stable transition from the old tax system as a result of, on the whole, no additional tax burdens on enterprises;

- the cancellation of all tax exemptions and tax reductions granted on a temporary basis or by reasons of particular industry difficulties. In general, tax system reforms during 1994 to 1995 were successful with benefits outweighing adverse effects.

The Reduction of Refund for VAT Paid on Inputs for Export

In order to generate sufficient revenue to meet growing needs for public expenditure and infrastructure facilities, the State Taxation Bureau made two announcements about the "Reduction of Refund for VAT Paid on Inputs for Exports", resulting in reductions of 3% (down from 17% to 14%) and 5% (down from 14% to 9%) with effect from 1 July 1995 and 1 January 1996 respectively. These two reductions brought about a significant adverse impact on foreign multinational corporations (FMNCs) engaged in exporting. On 26 December 1995, subsequent to Chairman Jiang Zemin's announcement, the State Council promulgated new tax and trade reforms which took effect on 1 April 1996. These are known as "The Adjustment and Perfection of Import and Export Taxation" and "The Modification of the Administrative Measures on Processing Trade." Under these reforms, the average customs tariff rate will be reduced by 36% (down from 35.9% to 23%) for 4,962 trade items. As a result, existing tax exemptions and reduction policies for FDI enterprises will be cancelled gradually. The rate of refund for "Value-Added Tax Paid on Inputs for Exports" will also be lowered. For example, in the case of industrial products produced from processing using agricultural products as raw materials, the tax refund rate will be reduced by 4% (down from 10% to 6%). For other goods subject to VAT at a rate of 17%, the tax refund rate will be reduced by 5% (down from 14% to 9%).

The Reform of Processing Trade Policy

As to the "Modification of the Administrative Measures on Processing Trade," a "Customs Duty Security System" (CDSS) has been introduced (fully effective 1 July 1996) to prevent tax evasion and smuggling. Under the CDSS, a "Customs Duty Security Account" with the Bank of China will be required for every processing trade contract to safeguard the state's interests as well as those of foreign and local investors.

The Implications for Foreign Direct Investments in the PRC

Taxes have a significant impact on multinational corporations (MNCs) in areas such as FDI decision-making, capital structure planning, exchange risk management (Li et al., 1996b, p. 228) and the like. Hence, MNCs should be alive to the benefits and burdens of the PRC's new tax system and trade policy reforms. Consider, for example, the following possible adverse consequences:

- MNCs profit margins from export sales will be reduced as a consequence of the "Reduction of Refund for VAT Paid on Inputs for Exports";
- MNCs may experience cash flow problems as a result of delays in input VAT refunds for exports; and
- some industries, such as the automobile industry, may lose their industrial protection due to the reduction of import tariffs and the relative strength of Renminbi (RMB) due to foreign exchange rate reform (Li et al., 1996b, p. 228).

The data implies that the new reforms will have significant implications for FDI in the PRC. In general, the reforms will affect MNC's returns on investment, cash flows and their strategic, behavioural and economic motives for FDI in the PRC. This chapter attempts to assess some implications of the reforms.

The Reduction of Import Tariffs

It is sometimes assumed that the PRC's tax revenues from import tariffs are high on account of the high rate of import tariffs, and that there will be a corresponding sharp decline in tax revenues as a consequence of the reduction of average import tariff rate from 35.9% to 23%. Both assumptions are misplaced. The statistical data from the GATT shows that the outcome is otherwise. According to the GATT's statistical data, the PRC's overall nominal rate of import tariff in 1994 was 36.4%, but the actual amount of import tariff revenue was only equivalent to 3% of the total amount of imports (Chan, 1996). The main reasons for this phenomenon are tax evasion and preferential tax treatment of FIEs. Further, the percentage of tariff revenue to total state tax revenue shows a declining trend since 1986. By 1994 the percentage declined to as low as 5.94%. Table 1 shows this trend.

Table 1
Total State Tax Revenue and Total Tariff Revenue for the Period 1986 to 1994

Year	Total State Tax Revenue (Million RMB)	Tariff Revenue (Million RMB)	Tariff Revenue to Total State Revenue (%)
1986	209.073	15.162	7.25
1987	214.036	14.237	6.65
1988	239.047	15.502	6.48
1989	272.740	18.154	6.66
1990	282.186	15.901	5.63
1991	299.017	18.728	6.26
1992	312.155	21.500	6.89
1993	425.530	25.647	5.97
1994	479.758	28.511	5.94

Source: *Statistical Yearbook of China*, 1995.

In comparison with other countries, the PRC's situation is poor. For example, although South Korea's overall nominal rate of import tariff in 1994 was as low as 10%, the actual amount collected was equivalent to 5% of total imports (H. C. Lam, 1995). In PRC, it is the existence of tax evasion, smuggling and excessive policy-related tax exemptions granted to MNCs and SOEs with businesses under industrial protection that explains the different position. We do not expect a sharp decline in state tax revenue as a result of the reduction of import tariffs. Rather, revenues should increase due to the effectiveness of the new CDSS in the prevention of smuggling and tax evasion, the reduction of refunds for VAT paid on inputs for exports and the cancellation of numerous preferential import tariff exemptions and concessions.

Long Term Beneficial Effects to the National Economy and FDIs in the PRC

Subsequent to Chairman Jiang Zemin's announcement on the substantial reduction of import tariffs at the APEC conference held in Osaka, Japan on 19 November 1995, the PRC has reduced the average rate of import tariffs by 36% (down from 35.9% to 23%) for 4,962 items with effect from 1 April 1996. The PRC has also announced that further reductions within the coming four years are planned which will bring the overall average tariff rate down to 15%, which is the level of the international norm for a free trade system.

The underlying objectives of these reforms can be explained by various long-term national economic benefits to the PRC and advantages to MNCs. These are detailed below:

- the reforms facilitate the PRC joining the WTO.
- expansion of International Trade:
  The further elimination of trade barriers with major trading partners by aligning rates of import tariffs should result in a further expansion of international trade. Prior to the tax reduction, the PRC's average import tariff rate was as high as 35.9%, more than double the 15% generally adopted in developing countries around the world.
- fairer Domestic Business Environment:
  The reforms should expedite the establishment of a fairer domestic business environment and trading mechanisms that favour fair market competition, optimal allocation of resources and the rapid development of the economy.
- stimulate Product Competitiveness:
  Tariff reduction is conducive to healthy competition by providing a level playing field.
- reduce Excessive Tax Exemptions and Reductions:
  The reforms are intended to eliminate negative effects brought about by the old tax system with its high import tariff rates and excessive tax exemptions or reductions granted to foreign enterprises. The old system did not comply with prevailing international practice and deviated from the principle of non-discrimination.
- increase in Tax Revenue and Cutback of Tax Evasion and Smuggling Activities:
  Total tax revenue should increase as a result of the cutback of tax evasion and smuggling activities. This is because the reduction of import tariffs will result in higher opportunity costs for smuggling activities and tax evasion. As a result, tax evasion and smuggling activities will become less attractive.
- beneficial Effects to Manufacturing Industries and Infrastructure Developments:
  The reduction of import tariffs will be advantageous to manufactur-

ing industries and domestic infrastructure development, which rely heavily on imported raw materials and equipment since supplies of domestic raw materials cannot always meet demand. The reduction of import tariffs will contribute to cost cutting and the enhancement of raw materials supply.

Rationale for the Import Tariff Reduction

The PRC's import tariff reductions adhere to the following four principles which should contribute to the maintenance of the PRC's competitive edge as a production base for FDI, expedite further economic and trade development and facilitate the transition from a planned economy to a socialist market economy.

- Protection of Nascent Industries and Those with Comparative Advantages:
  Industries with comparative advantages in production resources and capacity (such as labour cost advantages) will enjoy larger tariff reductions for their imported raw materials and assembly parts. For example, the tariffs for men's suits, trousers, and overcoats made of wool and fibres have been reduced by 43.75% (down from 80% to 45%). For leather garments and handbags, the reduction is 35.7% (down from 70% to 45%). On the other hand, for industrial protection purposes, the tariff cuts for some industries (for example, automobiles, railway or tramway locomotives) are comparatively small (see *Trade Watch*, various issues; *People's Republic of China Tax Update*, September 1995).

- Stimulate Production:
  In general, import tariffs on raw materials and equipment for manufacturing industries have been reduced by a relatively larger percentage than those for finished goods. For example, the tariff cut of 30% on television assembly parts is relatively larger than that for manufactured television sets, which have a 23% cut. Tariffs on plastic raw materials are reduced by 42.9% whereas manufactured plastic products merely enjoy a 28.6% tariff cut.

- Stimulate Advanced Technology Transfers:
  Tariff reductions for the import of advanced technological hardware and software are the most dramatic. This has been done with

a view to encouraging technology transfers. For example, import tariffs on advanced technological products are generally below 15% (tariffs for aircraft, spacecraft, and parts thereof are as low as 2% to 5.5%). Tariff reductions for integrated circuits with advanced and new technologies are as high as 60%. The tariff for nuclear reactors has been slashed by 55.56%.

- Conformity with the National Industrial Policy:
Heftier tariff reductions have been applied to raw materials and equipment designated for underdeveloped industrial sectors given top priority in national industrial policy, e.g., energy, infrastructure facilities, transport, raw material, advanced technologies. Here, the rates of import tariff are generally below 15%.

Implications for FDI in the PRC

- Preferential Treatments in Import Tariff Exemptions and Reductions for FDI Enterprises' Exports will be Cancelled:
To attract FDI, the PRC has offered numerous preferential treatments in import tariff exemptions and concessions to FDI enterprises for their imported raw materials and production equipment. The PRC's current policy is intended to gradually remove these exemptions as a means of offsetting potential declines in tax revenue due to reduction of import tariffs. It is also aimed at establishing a tax system with a broader tax base and lower tariff rates within the framework of a standardized and fair tariff policy.

The greatest impact will be on those new FDI enterprises set up after 1 January 1996. These enterprises will be subject to the new policy immediately (no privilege of any import tariff exemption and reduction). This means that their export costs will rise accordingly. Existing FDI enterprises set up prior to 1 January 1996 will be granted a grace period of one to two years to enjoy the preferential treatments in import tariff exemptions and concessions; however, adverse effects on the profit margin of their exports will emerge in the longer run.

- The Reduction of Refund for VAT Paid on Inputs for Exports:
As a remedial measure to prevent potential decline in state tax revenues due to tariff cuts, the PRC has further reduced the refund of VAT paid on inputs for exports of FDI enterprises by 5% (down

from 14% to 9%) as from 1 January 1996. Previously, as a precautionary measure, a reduction of 3% (down from 17% to 14%) had been introduced as from 1 July 1995. Hence, FDI enterprises face a further decline in profit margins.

- Cancellation of Import Tariff Exemptions for Production Equipment used in Export Processing Trade:

  In December 1995, the State Council promulgated a tariff-free preferential treatment for production equipment imported by FDI enterprises for use in export processing. This measure was intended to prevent a decline in state tax revenues and narrow the gap between SOEs and FDI enterprises. As a consequence of the reforms, FDI capital investment will generally rise by 30% to 40%, namely, 17% VAT for imports plus import tariffs of about 20%. In turn, this will result in rising production costs in terms of written-off depreciation. As to return on investment, pay back periods will be prolonged thereby requiring a downward adjustment in the required rate of return. Note here that the PRC's statistical data indicates that the export processing trade amounted to US$133.2 billion in 1995 (an increase of 27.5% compared with 1994), and accounted for 47.5% of total foreign trade. The portion of export processing trade by FDI enterprises in 1995 was US$79.12 billion or 59.4% of the total amount of US$133.2 billion. Hence, import tariffs will have severe impact on FDI.

- FDI Enterprises' Participation in Domestic Industrial Sectors favoured by the PRC's Industrial Policy:

  To induce foreign investment to underdeveloped industrial sectors, a number of industrial sectors have been given top development priority by way of bigger import tariff cuts pursuant to the PRC's industrial policy. To obtain this investment incentive, some FDI enterprises may enter into these priority sectors, i.e., infrastructure facilities, energy, advanced technology, transport and raw materials. Thus, FDI will gradually shift from labour-intensive production sectors to high priority sectors. As a consequence, foreign investors will be faced with extra capital investments, longer pay back periods and added business risks for higher returns.

- FDI Enterprises' Sales of Products on the Domestic Market:

  FDI enterprises are required to pay all import tariffs and import VAT for their domestic sales. They can take the advantages of product and factor market imperfections, as advocated by the theory of industrial organization, deriving from reduced import tariffs. But they still must confront the added business risks of the PRC such as the higher rate of doubtful debts under current macroeconomic modification, unfamiliar business customs and practices, lengthy legal proceedings for business disputes, extra capital investments, insufficient professional and legal advice, changing regulatory frameworks and practices of accounting and taxation.

The Reduction of Refund of VAT Paid on Inputs for Exports

Purposes of the Reduction of Refund for VAT Paid on Inputs for Exports

This is a remedial measure for the reduction of import tariffs with a view to maintaining state tax revenues. It also supplements national industrial policy, which gives top priority to underdeveloped industries such as energy, infrastructure facilities, transportation and advanced technologies. Such a trimming down of investment incentives for exports should effectively channel FDI to priority sectors where import tariffs have been heavily cut. Table 2 shows the distribution and trend of FDI in the PRC for the period 1992 to 1994 and indicate that FDI weightings in the export-oriented manufacturing sector and public utilities, land and property sectors were the highest, i.e., 87.3% (56.2% plus 31.1%) in 1992 and 82.9% (53.7% plus 29.2%) in 1994. By contrast, weightings in the top priority sectors of national industrial policy were the lowest, e.g., 2.5% in the energy, post and transportation sector and 0.3% in the advanced technology and scientific research sector in 1994.

General Features of VAT

VAT is a part of the spectrum of the new Turnover (Sales) Taxes introduced as from 1 January 1994 to replace the former ICCT on gross domestic sales, with tax rates ranging from 1.5% to 66%. The Turnover Tax consists of VAT, Consumption Tax and Business Tax (Shih et al., 1995).

VAT is leviable on the selling or importation of goods, or in the provision of processing, repairing and replacement services in the PRC. Normally, export goods are exempt from VAT in the form of the "Refund

Table 2
Distribution and Trends of Contracted Value of FDIs
for the Period 1992 to 1994

	1992	1994
Manufacturing (export oriented)	56.2	53.7
Land and property and public utilities	31.1	29.2
Construction and building	3.2	2.9
Energy, post and transportation	2.6	2.5
Restaurant and storage	2.5	3.7
Agriculture	1.2	1.2
Health, sport and welfare	0.7	2.4
Education, culture and arts	0.2	0.7
Advanced technology and scientific research	0.1	0.3
Finance and insurance	0	0.5
Others	2.2	2.9
Total	100%	100%

Source: *Almanac of China's Foreign Economic Relations and Trade*, various issues.

for VAT Paid on Inputs." VAT operates at a basic rate of 17% and a lower rate of 13%. The lower rate of 13% is applicable to taxpayers selling or importing certain specified items as regulated by the State Council from time to time, e.g., agricultural products, coal gas, books, chemical fertilizers, heating equipment and air conditioning (*People's Republic of China Tax Update*, September 1995).

The leviable rate of 6% is applied to "Small Taxpayers" with no deductions or credits allowed. The criteria for Small Taxpayers are as follows:

- taxpayers engaged in the production or provision of taxable services, and taxpayers engaged principally in the production of goods or provision of taxable services but also in wholesale or retail of goods, are recognized as Small Taxpayers if the annual sales amount subject to VAT is below RMB 1 million.
- for those engaged in wholesaling or retailing of goods, taxpayers are recognized as Small Taxpayers, if the annual taxable sales amount is below RMB 1.8 million.

- regardless of the above-mentioned threshold, those who do not often have taxable activities are treated as Small Taxpayers (*People's Republic of China Tax Update*, September 1995).

The Tax Refund for VAT Paid on Inputs for Exports

Under the "Provisional Regulations on Value-Added Tax" promulgated by the State Council in 1994, exported goods except those prohibited from export by the state (such as musk, copper, copper alloys, platinum, crude oil, and sugar) are subject to a zero rate and entitled to a tax refund for VAT paid on inputs.

Two Reductions of Tax Refund for VAT Paid on Inputs for Exports

There have been two Reductions of Tax Refund for VAT Paid on Inputs for Exports on 1 July 1995 and 1 January 1996 by 3% and 5% respectively which have had a significant impact on FDI enterprises. Currently, the specific tax refund rates after the reductions are as follows:

- 5% (i.e., 13% minus 3% and further minus 5%) for industrial products produced or processed from agricultural raw materials and for other goods which are subject to the 13% VAT rate; and
- 9% (i.e., 17% minus 3% and further minus 5%) for goods that are subject to 17% VAT rate.

The main purpose of this reduction of VAT refund for exports is to compensate for reduced import tariffs. Hence, total state tax revenue can be maintained without a substantial decline.

Impact on FDI

The new policy for reduction of refund for VAT has caused considerable concern for exporting enterprises. Listed below are the main implications:

- Lower Profit Margin and Rise of Product Cost:
  Export product costs will rise by RMB 0.75 for every export sale of US$1 in the event that 1% reduction of refund for VAT-Exports takes place. The two earlier reductions on 1 July 1995 and 1 January

1996 by 3% and 5% respectively were a shock to all export enterprises. Since 1995, due to world economic recession, the marginal profits of most export businesses have gradually declined. In general, export commodities of the PRC can be classified into three broad categories in terms of profitability, namely: 33%, which is profitable (with the privilege of industrial protection and preferential treatment); 33%, which is marginally profitable and 33%, which is unprofitable. The reduction of refund for VAT-Exports will put export enterprises in an awkward position. Where they cannot raise the selling price to compensate for the reduced refund for VAT-Exports, then, those enterprises that are marginally profitable will suffer loss and those that are unprofitable will suffer a further decline in profit margins.

- Cash Flow Problems Due to the Delay in Refund of VAT-Exports from State Tax Bureau:

  In November 1995, completed refund payments of VAT-Exports by the State Tax Bureau to export enterprises had been made up to February, 1995. This shows a nine-month (March to November, 1995) delay in refund payments. The official estimated amount of overdue refund payments as of 30 June 1996 was RMB 60 billion. It is estimated that such an overdue amount for the year 1995 as at 1 July 1996 would far exceed the total annual 1995 operating profits of exporting enterprises. This means that amounts equivalent to total cash inflows for the 1995 annual profits of exporting enterprises are tied up in the delayed refund process (Cheng, 1996).

- Potential Detriment to Bank Credit Rating:

  Official estimates indicate that the ratio of "Export Amount" to "Amount of Overdue Refund Payment for VAT-Export" is US$1 to RMB 1. To avoid the two reductions in VAT-Export Refund by 3% as from 1 July 1995 and by 5% as from 1 January 1996, most export enterprises expedited their export sales before these two dates. The result is that part of their export sales orders in 1996 were completed in advance in 1995, thereby necessitating additional investment in working capital (because of Accounts/Bills Receivable with longer credit terms and increases in Accounts/Bills Payable). As a consequence, most export enterprises experienced a shortage of cash and decline of sales in 1996. In turn, their bank credit ratings (the canons of good lending such as Character, Capital, Capability, Purpose,

Amount, Repayment, Term and Security) were undermined by contracted cash flows.

Reform of Export Processing Trade and the Customs Duty Security System (CDSS)

The Economic Role of the Export Processing Trade

Since the launching of the open door policy and economic reform in late 1978, the export processing trade has been one of the top priority industries in the PRC. In 1995, the total volume of the export processing trade was US$133.28 billion, accounting for some 47.5% of the total value of imports and exports which amounted to US$280.85 billion. This shows a notable growth compared with the figures for 1981 when the total value of imports and exports amounted to US$44.02 billion and when the export processing trade merely accounted for 5.6% of the total of US$2.48 billion. Thus, the export processing trade plays a vitally important role in the PRC's economic policy of opening up to the outside world.

Reasons for Reform of the Export Processing Trade

As the export processing trade is a top priority industrial sector, the PRC's policy has always been to make it as flexible as possible in order to attract FDI. Basically, all declared imported raw materials and parts for export processing trade purposes are not levied any tariffs for their reexport in the form of finished goods or work in progress after processing in the PRC. As a remedial measure to address deficiencies in the old export processing trade system, the PRC has implemented the CDSS in the following three phases:

Phase 1   On 27 November 1995, the trial implementation of the CDSS was launched in three pilot cities with flourishing export processing activities, namely: Dongguan city in Guangdong province; Suzhou city in Jiangsu province and Ningbo city in Zhejiang province;

Phase 2   On 1 April 1996, the trial implementation of the CDSS was extended to a further 25 cities with thriving activities in export processing trade;

Phase 3   On 1 July 1996, the CDSS was fully implemented throughout PRC.

The following are the main deficiencies of the old export processing
trade system, which gave rise to the reforms contained in the CDSS:

- Cash Flow Pressures on Export Processing Enterprises:
  Under the old export processing trade system, export processing
  enterprises were required to deposit a sum equivalent to 10–20% of
  the tariff value of the raw materials or parts with Customs which
  was refunded as long as the raw materials or parts were reexported
  after processing. Under the CDSS, enterprises are merely required
  to open a Customs Duty Security Account (CDS A/C) at a designated Bank of China branch office without the requirement of a
  security deposit. In other words, the account is purely nominal. A
  handling charge of RMB 100 is debited to every transaction.
- Loopholes for Fraudulent Activities:
  There were loopholes under the old system for such fraudulent
  activities as tax evasion, smuggling activities, re-sales of imported
  raw materials, under-declaring the imports, over-declaring of exports, overstating wastage, re-sales of processed goods on the
  domestic market without official approval and the like. Such
  fraudulent activities caused loss of state tax revenues, disruption of
  normal production and operations, unfair competition and adversely
  affected law-abiding enterprises. There were reportedly 465 major
  cases of smuggling via the processing trade tracked down by the
  Customs Investigations in 1994. The value of goods in these cases
  accounted for 61% of the total value of all smuggling cases.
- Monitoring and Control Problems:
  As the export processing trade is thriving throughout the PRC, it is
  difficult for Customs to carry out centralized monitoring and control
  over the bonded raw materials of widely dispersed export processing enterprises. Under the CDSS, the human resources of the Bank
  of China can be utilized for closer supervision.

Operating Procedures of the Old Export Processing Trade System

The operating procedures of the Old Export Processing Trade System prior
to the reform (namely, the introduction of the Custom Duty Security System) were as follows:

Step 1   Export processing trade enterprises submitted their processing contracts to the subordinate department of the Ministry of Foreign Trade and Economic Cooperation (MOFTEC) for examination and approval;

Step 2   Submission of contract already approved by MOFTEC to Customs for reexamination and filing;

Step 3   Issuance by Customs of the "Processing Trade Handbook" to the export processing trade enterprise;

Step 4   (a) The export processing trade enterprises imported the required raw materials and parts for the contracted processing with Customs declaration as to varieties and quantities; and
(b) Simultaneously, deposited a sum equivalent to 10–20% of the import tariff value of the imported raw materials and parts at Customs;

Step 5   (a) Application to Customs for verification of the reexport of imported raw materials and parts after export processing;
(b) Application for refund of the Customs deposit.

The New Export Processing Trade Policy — The CDSS

The goal of the State Council in the new CDSS is to improve the monitoring and control of the export processing trade. Through the cooperation and interplay of Customs, the Bank of China and other local authorities for the CDSS, it is anticipated that evasion of tax, smuggling and other fraudulent activities will be prevented or minimized.

CDSS Operating Procedures

The following are the operating procedures of the CDSS:

Step 1   The export processing enterprises submit their processing trade contracts to a subordinate department of the MOFTEC for examination and approval. To guard against fraudulent activities such as smuggling and tax evasion through the well-known device of "Enterprises of Three Noes" (no factory, no processing equipment and no workers), the MOFTEC office examines the contract and checks actual production prerequisites in full detail, (i.e., operational conditions and capacity as indicated by plant and equipment, workers etc);

Step 2   The submission of the contract already approved by MOFTEC to Customs for the contract details to be inputted into Customs' computer network whereupon the export processing enterprise obtains a printout of the "Basic Fact Sheet for the Contract";

Step 3   After Customs' reexamination of the contracts, a Customs Duty Security Account Opening Memo is issued to the enterprise which stipulates an amount equivalent to the value of the raw materials to be imported for the contracted processing. With the approval of this Memo, the exporting processing enterprise can then apply to open a CDS A/C at a designated branch of the Bank of China;

Step 4   (a) Upon presentation of the CDS A/C Opening Memo, the Bank of China will open the CDS A/C for the enterprise;
(b) Simultaneously, the Bank of China will issue a CDS A/C Registration Notice to the enterprise;

Step 5   The enterprise presents the "CDS A/C Registration Notice" to Customs for the issuance of the Processing Trade Handbook;

Step 6   (a) The enterprise proceeds to import the required raw materials and parts for the contracted processing with a Customs declaration on the varieties and quantities;
(b) When the processed products are exported within the stipulated time, the enterprise then applies for Customs' verification of the exports by the presentation of a CDS A/C Registration Notice within one month;
(c) After verification of the exports, Customs will issue a CDS A/C Cancellation Memo to the enterprise for its application for cancellation of the CDS A/C.

The Penalties

The penalties for breach of the new CDSS are severe. The following are the penalties for the most common breaches:

- Re-sales of the Imported Raw Materials on the Domestic Market: Where the enterprise sells the imported raw materials of the contracted processing on the domestic market without payment of the required import tariff, the Bank of China will directly debit the processing enterprise's normal bank account for the unpaid tariff amount as stated in the demand notes issued by the Customs.

- Malpractice:
  As a penalty for malpractice by a processing enterprise (smuggling, tax evasion, under-declaring imports, over-declaring exports), MOFTEC will revoke the enterprise's right to engage in export processing trade. Also, Customs will sue the enterprise and refuse to handle any new export processing contracts.

- Delay in Application for Cancellation of the CDS A/C:
  The Bank of China will not open further CDS A/Cs for new processing contracts for those enterprises who fail to apply to Customs for cancellation of the CDS A/C of the previous contract within the stipulated period.

Implications For FDI

The following lists the salient implications for FDI export processing enterprises:

- Effect on Cash Flows:
  Under the new CDSS, the CDS A/C opened at a designated Bank of China Branch is of a nominal nature. Unlike the old system with the deposit requirement of a sum equivalent to 10–20% of the import tariff, the processing enterprise is not required to deposit any cash into the CDS A/C. The enterprise only pays a handling charge of RMB 100 for every transaction on a contract by contract basis. Thus, enterprises are relieved of a cash pressure.

- Severe Penalties:
  Under the old system, export processing enterprises were lax in tallying the export volume of the processed goods with the imported raw materials and parts. In the worst cases, the enterprise was still allowed to continue its processing trade business with either fine or forfeiture of the deposit for tariff.

  By contrast, under the CDS A/C system, the penalties for malpractice by enterprises are severe. MOFTEC will revoke the enterprise's right to engage in export processing trade. The Bank of China and Customs will refuse to handle their CDS A/C applications and the examination of new export processing contracts. Hence,

offending enterprises will no longer be qualified for export processing trade operations (Lee, 1996b).

- Longer Processing Time:
  Under the new system, export processing enterprises have a longer
  processing time in order to go through two additional procedures,
  namely,
  - the submission of the contract already approved by MOFTEC
    to Customs or Custom's agencies for the contract details to be
    inputted into the Customs computer network; and
  - the application for opening a CDS A/C at a designated branch of
    the Bank of China.

Conclusions

In 1995 and 1996, PRC undertook intensive reforms in areas of the tax
system and processing trade, namely, the "Reduction of Import Tariffs," the
"Reduction of Refund for Value-Added Tax Paid on Inputs for Export" and
the "Reform of Processing Trade Policy with the Customs Duty Security
System." It is anticipated that the benefits of these reforms will outweigh
the adverse impacts in the long run. In the short run, the implications of
these reforms will cause considerable concern to foreign investors.

Overall, the positive effects of the reforms include:

- aligning the PRC tariff practices in with international norms;
- establishing the preconditions for joining the WTO;
- establishing a fairer domestic business environment and trading mechanisms which favour fair market competition, optimal allocation of
  resources and the healthy and rapid development of the economy;
- placing domestic enterprises and foreign-invested enterprises on the
  same level playing field;
- channelling foreign investments to such priority industrial sectors as
  energy, infrastructure facilities, transport, advanced technologies,
  raw materials etc.;
- improving monitoring and control of the export processing trade
  and countering such malpractices as smuggling, tax evasion, under-
  declaring imports, and over-declaring exports; and
- relaxing enterprises' cash flow pressures by means of the new
  Custom Duty Security Account system.

On the other hand, there are a number of adverse implications for FDI. As far as the Reduction of Import Tariffs is concerned, the adverse effects are:

- the preferential import tariff exemptions and reductions for FDI enterprises' exports will be gradually cancelled;
- the reduction of refunds for VAT for exports;
- the cancellation of import tariff exemptions for production equipment used in export processing;
- FDI enterprises' extra capital investments, added business risk and longer pay back periods for participation in domestic industrial sectors favoured by the PRC's industrial policy; and
- added business risks arising from the domestic sales of their products (higher rate of doubtful debt under current macroeconomic modification, unfamiliar business custom and practices, lengthy legal proceedings for business disputes, extra capital investments, ever changing regulatory frameworks and practices of accounting and taxation, insufficient professional and legal advice).

The adverse impacts on FDI in respect of the Reduction of Refund for Value-Added Tax Paid on Inputs for Export are mainly on the financial side, namely

- lower profit margins and rise of product costs;
- cash flow problems due to the delay in refund of VAT-Exports from the State Tax Bureau; and
- the potential detriment of bank credit status as a result of the decline of sales in 1996 and squeezed cash flow and profitability. The squeeze could be attributable to expediting 1996 sales orders into 1995. But in so doing, enterprises can avoid the double imposition of VAT-Export refund reductions of 3% as from 1 July 1995 and by 5% as from 1 January 1996. It follows, therefore, that the decline in sales and profitability in 1996 as well as cash flow problems due to the longer credit term of Accounts/Bills Receivable are largely unavoidable.

As to the Reform of Processing Trade Policy with the CDSS, the most notable impact on FDI is the imposition of severe penalties for malpractice (such as over-declaring their exports, under-declaring their imports, smuggling, tax evasion, illegal sale of processed goods on the domestic market etc). These will result in the revocation of the right to engage in the export processing trade by MOFTEC. With the introduction of the Customs Duty Security Account System, export processing enterprises will have a longer processing time for completing the additional procedures in the declaration of imported materials and the export of processed goods.

Looking Ahead

The PRC's economic achievement during the Eighth Five-Year Plan from 1991 to 1995 was excellent even though the world economy was hit by cyclical fluctuations. For instance, during the period from 1991 to 1994, the PRC achieved the highest average annual economic growth rate among major economies of the world of 11.7% while the global average stood at 1.9%. Another remarkable achievement was the successful transition of the fiscal and taxation systems. The PRC adopted a system of revenue sharing between the central and local governments. The new taxation system utilized VAT as the key means to broaden and stabilize the source of tax revenue. It also put income tax for foreigners and nationals on a better footing by unifying the Enterprise Income Tax and the Individual Income Tax.

Under the Eighth Five-Year Plan, the PRC undertook a range of reforms in the areas of foreign exchange, fiscal policy, taxation, banking, foreign trade, planning and enterprise in 1994 which strengthened the functions of such regulatory tools as tax rates, foreign exchange rates, money supply and interest rates in pursuit of the macro-economic modification. All economic reform measures implemented during the Eighth Five-Year Plan period demonstrate that the PRC is making good progress in replacing direct economic control by means of mandatory executive orders with indirect control by economic means and unambiguous regulatory frameworks.

In September 1995, the State Council promulgated the Ninth Five-Year Plan and Long-Term Targets for the Year 2010, both of which aimed at achieving the transition from a planned economy to a socialist market economy, thereby affirming the open market policy in order to boost the confidence of foreign investors. The Long-Term Targets and the Ninth Five-Year Plan outline the overall targets for the period from 1996 to 2010 and the blueprint for economic development and reform over the next five years from 1996 to 2000 respectively. The taxation and foreign exchange system reforms will be the spearhead of the PRC's market-opening policy. They also form key components of the strategy for reform and development of other industrial sectors given top priority under national industrial policy, e.g., agricultural, machine-building, electronics, construction, petrochemical, automobile and the tertiary sector (banking, insurance, legal services, information, consultancy, tourism and the like).

Following the basic frameworks and principles of the Ninth Five-Year Plan, the most likely implementation strategies and tactics adopted by PRC to tackle the potential economic problems and the adverse impacts on FDIs arising from the tax system and trade policy reforms are as follows:

Selective Relaxation of Import Restriction by Means of Lower Tariff and Removal of Import Quota

Under the Eighth Five-Year Plan, the Chinese government's economic reform strategy included goals such as full alignment with the global economy, internationalization of RMB and fulfilment of the requirements of Article 8 of the International Monetary Fund Agreement. On 25 December 1993, the State Council promulgated a "Notice for Further Reform of Foreign Exchange Control System" which stated that the realization of full exchangeability of RMB was the ultimate goal for the foreign exchange control system. Subsequently, on 1 January 1994, the PRC replaced the fixed and managed exchange rate system of the RMB with a floating exchange rate system. The move constituted an important step in China's economic reform process.

Under the fixed exchange rate system the RMB continuously devalued during the 1980s. The criteria for these devaluations were noticeably different from those adopted by most Western and developed countries. Western and developed countries will typically devalue their currencies on the basis of such factors as growth in money supply, government deficits, domestic wage levels, financing-level trends and changes in productivity. By contrast, the only criterion adopted by the Chinese government to determine the degree of devaluation of RMB was the cost of exports in terms of RMB for exchanging one US dollar thereby allowing a profit margin for export business. For example, in January 1981 the exchange rate of RMB was Yuan 1.52/US$1. The cost of exports rose in January and October 1985 and the exchange rate was devalued to RMB 2.79/US$1 and RMB 3.21/US$1 respectively. In June 1986, the exchange rate was further devalued to RMB 3.73/US$1, and remained unchanged until December 1989. The main purpose of the criterion was industrial protection for export business.

Under the fixed exchange rate system, export business, especially those of state-owned enterprises, were protected by the devaluation of RMB. Under the floating exchange rate system, the devaluation practice has been abolished as of January 1981. In turn, export-oriented enterprises lost the industrial protection provided by RMB devaluation. This posed a new business risk to those FDIs with export orientation. To mitigate the adverse impact, the PRC selectively relaxed import restrictions, for example, higher import quota and reduction of customs duties on raw materials to those industries whose export business relied heavily on imported raw materials. Otherwise, there would be a drastic change in industrial structure as a result of the elimination of less competitive export business resulting in an added business risk to foreign investors.

Gradually Extending National Taxation and Import Treatment to Foreign Direct Investment

In 1996, the operating deficit of SOEs further declined reaching RMB 69 billion, a deficit growth of 45% from 1995. This was attributable to foreign exchange reform and the preferential treatment enjoyed by FIEs resulting from the removal of industrial protection to export-oriented SOEs previously granted under the fixed exchange rate system and unequal competition between SOEs and FIEs. As a consequence, the products of SOEs lost certain competitive advantages. In turn, the value of unsold inventory of finished products for the year ended 31 December, 1996 was as high as RMB 8 billion representing a growth of 17% from 1995, taking the accumulated value to RMB 540 billion which was 3.53 times the value of the national total annual export turnover in 1996 of RMB 153 billion.

As a remedial measure, the PRC will accelerate the pace of reform in the SOEs. The most viable solution would be the extension of national treatment to FIEs thereby enabling SOEs to compete on an equal footing. The PRC will gradually remove the preferential policy for attracting foreign capital, such as the preferential tariff rate, enterprise and individual income taxes concession. However, for those underdeveloped industries with high priority under national industrial policy such as energy, infrastructure facilities, transportation, advanced technologies and raw material, China will still implement the preferential treatment policy to attract foreign capital.

Financial System Reform via Subsidies as a Supplementary Measure to Tax Reform

With the exception of 1985, the PRC has always been in financial disequilibrium since the introduction of economic reform in 1978. Statistical data shows that ever since 1980 there has been a continuous growth in the state financial deficit. The deficit has accelerated from RMB 12.75 billion in 1980 to RMB 63.801 billion in 1994. The budgeted deficit for 1995 was RMB 66.68 billion. The notable items in the deficit are the "Subsidy to State-Owned Enterprises" and the "Commodity Price Subsidy" (for agriculture products, meat, coal and petroleum products etc.), accounting for 11.64% (6.27% plus 5.37%) of the total deficit in 1995 and 31.99% (19.7% plus 12.29%) in 1989 (Y. C. Lau, 1995). Table 3 shows the details.

Table 3
Subsidy to State-Owned Enterprises and Commodity Price Subsidy
for the Period 1986 to 1995

Year	Subsidy to State-Owned Enterprises for Their Deficit		Commodity Price Subsidy	
	RMB Million	Percentage to State Total Expenditure	RMB Million	Percentage to State Total Expenditure
1986	32.478	13.94	25.748	11.05
1987	37.643	15.37	29.460	12.03
1988	44.646	16.50	31.682	11.71
1989	59.888	19.70	37.355	12.29
1990	57.888	16.77	38.080	11.03
1991	51.024	13.38	37.377	9.80
1992	44.496	10.14	32.164	7.33
1993	41.129	7.78	29.930	5.66
1994	36.346	6.24	31.277	5.37
1995	39.850	6.27	34.141	5.37

Source: *Statistical Yearbook of China*, 1995.
Figure for 1995 is estimated.

In this regard, it is likely that the PRC will intensify the reform of SOEs and improve the situation of Commodity Price Subsidy in order to gradually mitigate or phase out these two subsidies rather than relying on the further imposition of tax.

Improve the Administration of Tax Imposition by Provincial/ Local Governments

As a means to reinforce the commitment of local authorities to economic reform, the central government has delegated authority with a high degree of autonomy to local governments enabling them to impose "Taxes for Special Purposes" and "Taxes Other Than Collected by State Administration of Taxation," e.g., Urban Maintenance and Construction Tax, Fixed Assets Investment Direction Tax, Land Value Appreciation Tax, etc., according to their peculiar situations (Y. P. Lau, 1995). However, as revealed in Table 4, local governments' abuse of tax imposition autonomy was substantial and imposed a heavy tax burden on enterprises. The item "Unbudgeted Tax Revenue" in 1992 as contained in Table 4 is an obvious example of local governments' abuse of local taxes. It was nearly equivalent (97.74%, RMB 385.492 billion) to the "State Total Budgeted Revenue" (RMB 394.414 billion, exclusive of overseas loans).

Even though FDI enterprises can be exempted from most of these taxes, the SOEs tax burden will give rise to a state subsidy for their deficits. In turn, the state's financial deficit will be transferred to FDI enterprises in the form of cancellation of preferential tax treatments and tax concessions. It is likely that the PRC will attempt to rectify this problem by rigorous monitoring and control.

Modification of Penalties for Malpractice in the Export Processing Trade

A survey has revealed that FDI enterprises are concerned about the penalties for malpractice in the Export Processing Trade, which may result in the revocation of their right to operate by MOFTEC. Owners and top management of export processing trade enterprises are concerned about their administrative or operative employees' unwitting mistakes in such malpractices as over-declaring the exports and under-declaring the imports, which may result in the revocation of operating rights by MOFTEC. It

Table 4
State Budgeted Revenue and Unbudgeted Tax Revenue Collected by
Local Government for the Period 1982 to 1993

Year	State Budgeted Revenue* (RMB Billion)	Unbudgeted Tax Revenue Collected by Local Government	
		RMB Billion	% to State Budgeted Tax Revenue
1982	108.394	80.274	74.06
1983	121.116	96.768	79.90
1984	146.705	118.848	81.01
1985	183.716	153.003	83.28
1986	218.452	173.731	79.53
1987	226.242	202.880	89.67
1988	248.941	227.000	91.19
1989	280.381	265.883	94.83
1990	313.434	270.864	86.42
1991	343.075	324.331	94.54
1992	394.414	385.492	97.74
1993	473.030	143.254	30.28

Source: *Statistical Year Book of China*, 1994.
* Excluding Cash Inflow from Overseas Loan.

would be sensible to expect a favourable response from China to foreign investors' requests for lightening penalties, for example, allowed a warning for two to three minor malpractices with a reasonable fine. The PRC's response will be critical for reinforcing foreign investors' confidence in their investments.

Longer Grace Periods for Future Reforms

The FDI decisions of MNCs result from a complex process motivated by strategy, behavioural, and economic considerations. The empirical evidence shows that the PRC's reform measures have always been carried into effect with very short lead times resulting in a shock to foreign MNC's initial capital budgeting, working capital, profitability, return on investment and performance evaluation. For example, the average notice period for the above reform measures was as short as three months. It is disadvantageous for exporting enterprises to accept sales orders with production schedules or delivery periods longer than three months due to the potential for further reductions of VAT refunds. Some FDI enterprises may have to pay the unbudgeted additional equipment cost of 30% to 40%, namely 17% import VAT plus import tariff of about 20% for production equipment (with delivery periods of longer than three months), which were ordered prior to the promulgation of the "Cancellation of Import Tariff Exemption for Production Equipment to be Engaged for Export Processing." Thus, longer grace periods for reforms would be beneficial to SOEs and foreign investors (Lee, 1996a). It seems reasonable to suggest that PRC will mitigate the potential impacts by allowing longer grace periods for reform in the future.

Expedite the Refund for VAT Paid on Inputs for Exports and Shorten the Processing Time for Customs Duty Security Processing System

The official estimated amount of overdue refund payments for VAT-Exports as at 30 June 1996 was RMB 60 billion with nine months delay. This far exceeds the annual operating profit of all exporting enterprises in 1995. Also, the additional processing time for the CDSS is one to two days. In both cases, export enterprises will suffer heavy cash flow pressures. Thus, it seems justifiable for the PRC to expedite its five-year computerization plan by shortening it to three years. The total amount of investment required is US$1.2 billion for 85,000 computer sets to be installed in 30,000 branches of the State Tax Bureau. It is expected that tax evasion activities could then be effectively prevented. In 1994, the State Tax Bureau tracked down innumerable tax evasion activities valued at US$2.1 billion, representing an increase by 60% as compared with 1993. With computerization, the delay in refunds of VAT-Export and the processing time of the CDSS would be greatly improved.

17

Development of Foreign Technology Imports in China

Zeng Dao-xian, Oliver H. M. Yau,
and Raymond P.M. Chow

In today's world of fast advancement in science and technology, developing countries wanting to achieve rapid economic growth must make full use of opportunities from the evolution of the world's science, technology and economic developments. A developing country must utilize not only its domestic capabilities but also resources available internationally, especially in the acquisition of foreign technologies, capital and expertise. Since its founding in 1949, the People's Republic of China (PRC) has followed this philosophy and acquired a significant amount of new technologies and advanced equipment from overseas for its capital reconstruction. This pushed the development of its economy to a new frontier towards achieving the ultimate goal of building a comprehensive industrial structure.

From the macro-perspective, there exists a tremendous gap in technology between China and developed countries. Up to now, China is still a technology importing country. Its limited financial resources, combined with weaknesses in its economic and technological systems and the shortage of qualified personnel and an underdeveloped market, etc., have substantially restricted China in its technology transfers. As such, the acquired technologies were, relatively speaking, significantly more advanced than the technological foundation in China. In many cases, such advanced technologies could not merge well enough with the local technological and economic environments. As a result, some projects could not be put into profitable production and generate economic benefits rapidly. Under the conventional planned economic system, China's technology imports were a part of the central or regional government's investment activities. To a great extent, such investment decisions were guided by the bureaucratic behaviour of the ruling officers, which intensified the level of risk associated with these investments.

The purpose of this chapter is to take a systematic view on the development of technology imports in China over the past several decades, with the aim to map out the path taken in each stage of the development and the effects of the acquisition efforts, and to make an attempt to suggest possible future directions. Our findings are based primarily on extensive literature review on technology imports with special reference to those relevant articles written by Chinese analysts. Moreover, many of our comments in this chapter were drawn from personal interviews of managers of selected firms in China in 1995 and 1996. Given the scope of this chapter, the view taken here is macro in nature. Thus, it might not effectively describe the specific developments of some particular industries. However, it is evident that changes in the past few decades have been enormous, and further development toward more intensified technology transfers can be envisaged.

A Development Path

Due to its fundamental weakness in technology and economy, China was forced to take progressive steps in its technology imports, starting from complete plants, essential equipment and turnkey projects, to licensing, consultancy, technical services, or a combination of these various modes (Table 1).

Since 1950, the total value of China's technology and equipment imports has amounted to US$600 billion. Approximately 70% of this value was comprised of about 10,000 projects that were financed with foreign exchange by the central government. The majority of these projects were related to industries such as energy, transportation, and raw materials etc., and the large core projects were related to the electrical, machinery and textile industries. Others projects financed by foreign exchange were retained in the ministerial, provincial, municipal governments and the enterprises level for technology reform, including production technology advancement, improvement in product quality and diversification, reduction of raw material consumption, and energy savings, etc.

Table 1
Methods Used for Technology Imports by China

1. Complete plant, essential equipment, turnkey

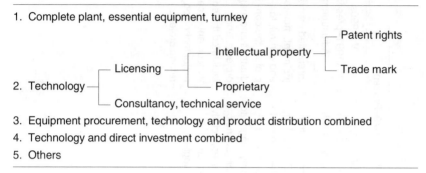

3. Equipment procurement, technology and product distribution combined
4. Technology and direct investment combined
5. Others

Following the rugged path of the country's economic development, technology imports in China have gone through two stages of development. The migration through these two distinct stages clearly signifies the evolution from a highly centralized planning and control system to a more "simplified and decentralized" structure.

Stage One (1950–1978)

This stage started from the founding of the country to the period prior to the beginning of economic reforms (1950–1978; Table 2). The most salient characteristics in China's technology imports in this stage can be summarized as follows:

1. Mainly imports of complete plants by those newly established large-scale enterprises;
2. Sources of foreign exchange funds came mainly from foreign exchange reserves of the central government and cross-country trade credits; basically no foreign capital was used in technology and equipment imports;
3. Project management and its implementation that include negotiation and contract signing, were primarily the responsibility of the relevant ministerial departments in the central government level.

Stage One can further be subdivided into three phases, the 1950s, 1960s and 1970s, each with its own unique characteristics (Table 2).

Table 2

Characteristics of the Different Stage in China's Technology Imports

Stage	Stage One (1950–1978)			Stage Two (1979–Present)	
Phase	I. 1950s (1950–1959) Start Up	II. 1960s (1963–1968) Change Course	III. 1970s (1973–1978) Recovery	IV. 1980s (1979–1990) Rapid Growth	V. 1990s (1991–present) Adjustment
Background	In the initial stage, focused on the recovery and development of the economy, put emphasis on developing heavy industries, established a foundation for industrialization and also modernized its national defense	Sino-Soviet relationship deteriorated, Russia unilaterally terminated the various transfer contracts; PRC began to develop technology trades with countries other than USA; counteracted the economic dislocation (1958–1960) and need to improve the conditions of agriculture, light industry and textile industry; intensified technology imports on chemical and textile	Technology imports greatly affected by the Cultural Revolution; to restore economic development, the government approved two technology import schemes to strengthen the fundamental industries and to support agricultural and basic needs	Implemented the Open Door policy, and direction set to do well in local economy; began to focus on technology imports, especially production technologies	Intensified macro adjustment, monitoring and control, to protect the core industries and major projects, and facilitated the advancement of certain major technology reform projects

Technology imports by industry	Energy (36.8%, in which electro-power 29.4%); machinery (23.1%); metallurgy (22.9%); chemical (5.6%); others (11.6%)	Metallurgy (31.7%); chemical (28.1%); textile (11.7%); machinery (10.9%); others include petroleum, electro-power, light industry, etc.	Focused on the fundamental industries (energy, transportation, communication, raw materials, 43.2%); chemical fertilizer, agricultural chemical and feed production and machines to support the agriculture needs, also machinery, electronic and military applications, etc.	Continued to focus on the fundamental industries, and at the same time moved toward the aims of advanced technologies, high market share and economic benefits
Methods used	Mainly complete plant (89.3%); others include technical drawings, technical data, foreign specialists	Mainly complete plant (96.6%)	48 large-scale complete-set import projects, amounted to US$ 88 billion; began to use licensing, export credit, co-op production and development, etc.	Adopted licensing, consultancy and technical services, co-production and other methods; encouraged technology combined with equipment and direct investment arrangements	Also encouraged use of enterprises' own financial resources and induced direct foreign investment and joint ventures for technology imports

Table 2 (Cont'd)

Stage	Stage One (1950–1978)		Stage Two (1979–Present)		
Phase	I. 1950s (1950–1959) Start Up	II. 1960s (1963–1968) Change Course	III. 1970s (1973–1978) Recovery	IV. 1980s (1979–1990) Rapid Growth	V. 1990s (1991–present) Adjustment
Sources	The then Soviet Union and the Eastern Block	Japan, Federal Republic of Germany, England, France, Italy, etc. — 11 countries	Japan, Federal Republic of Germany, England, France, USA, Holland, Switzerland, Sweden, etc. — over 10 countries	Japan, Federal Republic of Germany, England, France, USA, Holland, Switzerland, Sweden, etc. — over 30 countries	Multi-dimensional
Number of projects	448	84	1,500	7,000 (central government fund)	1,356 (1991–1993)
Total amount	US$ 2.7 billion	US$ 0.3 billion	US$ 11.8 billion	US$ 17 billion (central) US$ 13 billion (regional)	Approx. US$ 16 billion
Effects	1. Filled the technology gaps; established machinery, metallurgy, synthesized materials industries	1. Intensified the modernization of the textile, chemical, metallurgy, machinery industries	1. Major technology import projects in the early stage greatly enhanced the agricultural and industrial development	1. Expedited technology imports and new product development, pushed enterprises reform and human resources development, improved export competitiveness, induced significant changes in economy	1. Ensured the progression of the essential industries and major technology reform projects

Effects	2. Improved the industry structure; developed cities with distinguished features all over China 3. Human resources development; built basic foundation for industrialization	2. Technology import plan affected by the Cultural Revolution; only 1/3 of contracts completed	2. Underestimation to the destruction of national economy by the Cultural Revolution, excessive scale and speed of imports, implementation difficulties, etc. lead to forced adjustment and loss	2. Duplicated and low-level technology imports; inadequate essential technologies; incomplete absorption and diffusion, affected overall economic benefits	2. Ratio of "software" imports using licensing, consultation and technical services, co-production, etc. increased to over 30%
Macro-management	Central planning, central control, external affairs centrally handled	Central planning and control; tightly scrutinized approval process	Central planning and control; tightly scrutinized approval process	Gradually enlarged the project establishment, review and approval at the regional, departmental and enterprise level; began to explore scientific macro-management and supervisory method	Continued to explore systems for structural reforms and effective macro-management schemes

Phase I (1950–1959) — Start Up

In this start-up phase, focusing on the recovery and development of its economy, China made initial efforts to build a foundation for industrialization and modernization of its national defense. The emphasis was on developing heavy industries, primarily in the energy, machinery, metallurgy, and chemical segments. In this phase, foreign technologies mainly in the form of complete plants were transferred from the then Soviet Union and Eastern Block. Such transfers were managed under a central planning and control mechanism.

Through such initial efforts, China succeeded in: (1) filling the technology gaps and establishing the machinery, metallurgy, and synthesized materials industries; (2) improving the industry structures and developing industrial cities with distinguished features all over China; (3) developing their human resources and building a basic foundation for industrialization.

Phase II (1963–1968) — Change Course

As a result of the deterioration of Sino-Soviet relationship, China began to develop technology trade with countries other than the USA. During this phase, the primary focus was to counteract the economic dislocation experienced in the period from 1958 to 1960. The Chinese authorities saw the needs to improve the conditions of agriculture, light industry and textile industry, and to intensify technology imports for the chemical and textile sectors. Technologies transferred were almost solely through complete plant acquisitions, with the majority in the metallurgy, chemical, textile and machinery industries. Project management continued to be under central planning and control with tightly scrutinized approval processes.

While intensified modernization of some industries was achieved, the Chinese technology import plan was greatly affected by the Cultural Revolution. As a result, only one third of the technology contracts could be completed.

Phase III (1973–1978) — Recovery

To restore economic development after the Cultural Revolution, the Chinese government approved two technology import schemes to speed up the technology transfer process in order to strengthen the fundamental industries and to support the country's agricultural and basic needs. Acquisition methods and sources of technology suppliers became more diversified. While complete plant projects still dominated the economy, new means like licensing, co-production, and other transfer methods began to be adopted. A wider scope and industry coverage were also observed. Central planning and control with a tightly scrutinized approval process continued to be applied during this period.

Those major technology import projects implemented in the early stage of this period greatly enhanced agricultural and industrial developments in the country. However, underestimation of the impact of the Cultural Revolution, the excessive scale and speed of imports, implementation difficulties etc., led to forced adjustment and losses.

Stage Two (1979–Present)

This stage covers the period since the beginning of economic reforms in 1979 to the present day. Based on the experience learned from the technology imports performed in Stage One, activities in this stage continued to be administered with a more open architecture, emphasizing "focus on technologies." Different channels of imports were used, demand for economic benefits were increased, and new ways to import foreign technologies were called for by the intensified structural and system reforms. The most distinctive characteristics of this stage are:

- Methods used for acquisition of foreign technologies became more flexible and varied. The state began to control complete plant imports and turned to the use of licensing, consultation, technical services, and cooperative production etc., with more emphasis on the import of "software" technologies.
- Project management and control were gradually moved from the central planning system to a process of autonomous decision making at the departmental, regional and enterprise levels. Authorization for project initiation, review and approval were passed on to the respective levels, based on the size of the projects and the various sources of foreign exchange funds utilized.
- Modes of cooperation and sources of foreign exchange funds were also extended. Various kinds of technology were imported through government loans, export credit, cooperative production, leasing,

compensation trade, and foreign direct investments (including equity joint ventures and cooperative ventures). Foreign direct investments had the fastest growth rate in this particular stage.

- Country sourcing of foreign technologies also became more diversified. The sources of origin for the imported technologies expanded to over 30 countries and districts.

- While the focus was on core industries and key projects, particular attention was also given to incorporate medium and small-sized enterprises in the technology reform. During the period from 1983 to 1985 (three years after the sixth Five-year Plan), which was the peak period for large-scale foreign technology imports and enterprise reform since the founding of the country, China expended US$40 billion and signed off on 4,450 such projects.

- China aggressively searched for new directions to manifest the macro-level control and supervision of technology imports, with an attempt to change from direct control via administrative orders to the use of legal, taxation and credit control systems as the guiding principles and controlling mechanisms.

Stage Two can be further subdivided into two phases that encompass the 1980s and 1990s (Table 2), both exhibited significant growth over the periods in Stage One.

Phase IV (1979–1990) — Rapid Growth

As an integral part of the economic reforms, China implemented the open door policy and set its direction to do well in local economy. They began to put more emphasis on technology imports, especially acquisition of production technologies. Apart from those fundamental industries, i.e., energy, transportation, communication and raw materials, China also directed its technology imports efforts toward its agricultural needs. The focus was on technologies for chemical fertilizers, agricultural chemicals and feed production and machines to support agricultural development. Technologies for machinery, electronics and military applications were also included.

During this phase, China widely adopted licensing, consultancy and technical services, coproduction as well as other methods, to acquire the needed technologies from more than 30 countries. Acquisitions in the form of technology combined with equipment and direct investment arrangements were encouraged. To enhance the technology import process, China gradually released some of the project establishment, review and approval responsibilities to the regional, departmental and enterprise levels.

Noticeable improvements were achieved, including expedited technology imports and new product development; strengthened enterprise reform and human resources development; improved export competitiveness; and significant changes in the economy. Even so, there were duplication of imports, imports of low- level technologies, and inadequate import of technologies that were essential to the enhancement of local industries. The absorption and diffusion of acquired technologies were less than satisfactory. All these inversely affected the overall economic benefits the country had planned to achieve through technology imports.

Phase V (1991–Present) — Adjustment

To curb the overheated economy, China intensified its macro adjustment efforts and introduced various monitoring and control measures in order to protect the core industries and those major projects earmarked by the central government. Special efforts were made to facilitate the advancement of certain major technology reform projects. During the early stage of this phase, China continued to focus on the fundamental industries and, at the same time, aimed at progressing towards advanced technologies, high market share, and economic benefits.

The sources for the technologies were multi-dimensional and various methods for their acquisition were used. Apart from those methods utilized in Phase IV, China also encouraged the enterprises to use their own financial resources for technology imports. At the same time, they induced more direct foreign investments and joint ventures. While retaining some administrative control over technology imports, China continued to explore systems for structural reforms and effective macro-management schemes.

Efforts were directed to focus on ensuring the progression of the essential industries and the major technology reform projects. The ratio of "software" imports had increased through the use of licensing, consultancy, technical services and co-production.

Review of Technology Import Projects

Details of the foreign technology imports for the 45-year period from 1950 to 1994 are summarized in Tables 3 to 6. Table 3 shows the number of major projects and their values. The period from 1979 to 1990 marked a rapid increase in technology importation projects since the economic reforms in China. The average number of projects and values per year reached 358.5 and US$2.11 billion respectively. The period from 1991 to 1995 saw a further increase with many state-invested large-scale projects that were concluded in the early years of the Eighth Five-Year Plan (1991–1995). The year 1995 saw the greatest growth in technology imports in China. During this year, China signed 3,629 technology and equipment import contracts, with a total value of over US$13 billion covering 10% of the total import volume. Better availability of sources of funds, improved autonomy of decision making, and large infrastructure improvement projects are some of the underlying reasons that caused an import boom.

Table 3

Major Technology Import Projects — No. of Projects and Value

	No. of Projects		Amount (US$ billion)	
	Total	Average/year	Total	Average/year
1950–1959	229	22.9	(1.701)*	
1963–1968	55	9.2	0.266	0.044
1971–1978	242	30.2	7.788	0.973
1979–1990	4,302	358.5	25.326	2.111
1991–1995	5,429	1,085.8	33.298	6.660
Total	10,257		66.678	

Sources: *People's Republic of China — 40 Years of Technology Imports (1950–1990),* Wen Wei Press, 1992; *Almanac of China's Foreign Economic Relations and Trade,* 1990/91, 1991/92, 1992/93, 1993/94, 1994/95, 1995/96 and 1996/97.
* In billion Rouble, not included in the total sum.

Major projects by acquisition methods are shown in Table 4. While licensing (31.2%) and complete plant (34.1%) take up the majority in terms of the number of contracts, complete plant outweights all other methods in value terms (74%). In general, the technology contents of such import projects were relatively low, averaging only about 5% on the total values of

Table 4

Major Technology Import Projects (1960–1995) by Acquisition Methods
(amounts in US$ billion)

Method	No. of Contracts	% of Total	Total Value	% of Total	Technology as % of Total*
Licensing	3,124	31.2	6.20	9.3	9.13
Consultancy and technical service	565	5.6	1.61	2.4	16.63
Co-production	268	2.7	3.07	4.6	1.67
Complete plant	3,422	34.1	49.33	74.0	4.86
Essential equipment	2,634	26.3	6.44	9.7	3.07
Others	15	0.1	0.03	0.0	
Total	10,028	100.0	66.68	100.0	5.22

these contracts. While the year 1995 marked a significant increase in the import of technology, the majority of the projects are still in the form of complete plants and essential equipment that accounted for 2,913 (80.3%) and US$11.27 billion (86.5%) in total number and contract value respectively. This indicates that their imports are still very much hardware dominated.

Table 5a shows the major projects by industry, with the industrial segment leading in both technology-dominated and equipment-dominated contracts for the period from 1960 through 1990. During this period, the industrial sector led both in terms of number of projects and in contract value terms. Table 5b shows the sector allocation of technology import contracts from 1991 to 1995. During this period, the machinery and electronic sector took up the majority in number of contracts (46.5%). In terms of contract value, both the machinery and electronic sector and the energy sector occupied the major shares (23.3% and 24.7% respectively).

Table 6 shows the major projects by exporting country. For the period from 1960 through 1990, Japan, Germany and the USA were the major suppliers. The U.S. outweighed all the others in technology-dominated contracts and Japan led the way in equipment-dominated contracts, both in the number of contracts and in value terms. For the period from 1960 to 1995, Japan, Germany and the USA remain the major suppliers, leading both in the number of contracts as well as in contract value terms.

Table 5a

Major Technology Import Projects — Percentage Breakdown by Industry
(1960–1990)

Industry	Technology (a)		Equipment (b)		Total	
	% No.	% Value	% No.	% Value	% No.	% Value
Agricultural and fishery	0.4	0.1	0.3	0.1	0.3	0.1
Industrial	97.1	98.3	88.5	96.4	93.2	96.7
Geological	0.3	0.3	0.1	0.1	0.2	0.1
Transportation and communication	1.2	1.0	9.0	2.8	4.9	2.5
Environmental	0.7	0.1	0.5	0.3	0.6	0.2
Banking and insurance	0.1	0.1	0.0	0.0	—	—
Others	0.2	0.1	1.6	0.3	0.8	0.2
Total	100	100	100	100	100	100

Source: Same as Table 3.
(a) Technology = Technology-dominated contracts;
(b) Equipment = Equipment-dominated contracts.

Table 5b

Major Technology Import Projects — by Industry (1991–1995)

Industry	No. of Contracts	% of No. of Contracts	Contract Value (US$ billion)	% of Contract Value
Machinery and electronic	2,522	46.5	7.775	23.3
Energy	361	6.6	8.218	24.7
Communication and transportation	609	11.2	3.008	9.0
Metallurgy and nonferrous metals	266	4.9	3.591	10.8
Petrochemical	506	9.3	7.435	22.3
Light industry and textile	291	5.4	1.207	3.6
Others	874	16.1	2.068	6.2
Total	5,429		33.302	

Source: Same as Table 3.

Table 6
Major Technology Import Projects by Country (1960–1995)

	Technology (a)		Equipment (b)		Total (1960–1995)	
	No.	Value (US$ billion)	No.	Value (US$ billion)	No.	Value (US$ billion)
Japan	513	6.698	666	10.000	2,106	17.087
Germany	497	6.699	331	5.297	1,500	10.837
USA	636	18.134	318	2.676	2,016	9.294
Italy	82	1.759	140	2.055	531	6.238
France	103	4.242	96	2.295	342	5.197
Former USSR	8	0.269	20	1.232	37	2.633
Russia (91–95)					305	1.387
England	163	3.845	113	1.371	401	3.008
Spain	7	4.573	3	0.263	70	1.679
Canada	39	0.535	79	0.670	219	1.565

Source: Same as Table 3.
(a) Technology = Technology-dominated contracts, 1960–1990;
(b) Equipment = Equipment-dominated contracts, 1960–1990.

Achievements and Problems

As indicated in Table 2, technology imports for China, especially those large-scale imports since the launch of its economic reforms, have fostered the growth of the national economy and its technological advancement. The following achievements have been observed:

- improved the overall level of science and technology;
- strengthened the technological foundation of the enterprises;
- sped up the technology advancement;
- improved the economic benefits of the firms as well as the country;
- enhanced its self-developing capability;
- improved product quality and diversification;
- strengthened the competitiveness of China-made products in the international market, resulting in a rapid growth of exports;
- cherished its vision and changed the concepts of the people towards market economy;

- developed qualified human resources in various fields ready for the furtherance of foreign economic and technological co-production operations;
- bustled the domestic market and improved the living standards of the people.

Technology importation is a very complicated strategy that affects various factors of production in the economic system. In China, its impact, together with the serious effects of the former planned economy system, have posed many problems that need to be solved. These problems can be reflected in the following two contradicting facets:

1. Enterprises have depended too much on the advanced level of the technologies and ignored the practical situation in China in the course of technology transfer. This has caused the establishment of enterprises incapable of commercializing potential products using the imported technologies;

2. Enterprises put undue emphasis on short-term economic benefits and neglected the level and structure of technologies required to succeed. Hence, there is an imbalance in the proportion of imported software and hardware with imports of small-scale and low-grade technologies and excessive duplicate imports is a common phenomenon.

Without doubt, these problems have greatly affected the overall economic benefits of both the enterprises and China as a whole. Under the economic reform and the open door policy, China needs to charter its path leading to more successful future technology imports as these imports will continue to play a very important role in the development of China's economy.

Path for Future Development

Based on what has happened since 1978, it is obvious that technology imports in China will continue to keep pace with the country's economic development. As described previously, though China has made considerable achievement through technology imports, the problem of lagging behind overall in the level of technology is not yet totally resolved. The economy as a whole is not growing as rapidly as anticipated. Under the current situation, directed by the macro-adjustment practices, technology imports in China could be significantly affected by the following factors.

Current Transformation of the State-Owned Enterprises

In the process of the transformation of the state-owned enterprises, certain Chinese enterprises will become operationally independent and autonomous. They will be responsible for and in control of losses and profits. Such corporations, together with those under the "three-form of investments" (joint ventures, foreign ventures and cooperation enterprises) will be the most active participants in foreign technology transfers. However, in the short run, some of these enterprises might not have the capability to raise large amounts of capital quickly. It will be beneficial for them to gain rapid economic benefits by taking on short-term technology import projects that are low in risk and investment but fast in generating returns. In such a case, to protect their own interests, foreign technology suppliers might not want to transfer the most advanced technologies to China for two reasons. Firstly, these Chinese enterprises are not likely to have the ability either to modernize their technologies or the capability to develop new products. Secondly, other small companies would not have the prerequisites to draw in foreign capital and technologies.

For enterprises that are energy-related and considered to be integral parts of the major industries, such as mining, petroleum, and transportation, the state will continue to assume ownership and responsibility for the management of operations. Hence, these enterprises will continue to operate under the state planning mechanism. To meet the production and operational needs, they might still need to acquire some advanced foreign technologies, using traditional methods like purchase of a complete plant, essential equipment or outright purchase of technology. Such acquisitions would be most likely long-term in nature, focusing on building an industry foundation for the overall economic benefits of the country. To avoid over reliance on foreign suppliers, "technology-trade combined" or "technology-investment combined" form of acquisition would be minimal.

Market Development

Despite technological and capital limitations, opening up the market would be deemed to be a viable approach to attract foreign technologies. To a certain extent, China has already opened up a portion of its domestic market for foreign investment and technologies. Active participation in the "three-form of investment" has also directly led to the development of the Chinese market. However, as restricted by its technological and financial limitations, China has found that the role of market development has been led mostly by foreign parties. As such, technology reforms and business directions to be taken by local enterprises would still be somewhat limited. On the other hand, as the market continues to develop with considerable general economic growth and increases in consumption expenditures, demand for products of higher quality will increase rapidly. This would undoubtedly induce the inward transfer of more advanced technologies to improve quality and to increase the varieties of locally produced goods. Competitiveness of products made in China in the international market would eventually be improved. This thus leads China's exports to be further enhanced. The dynamism of demand and supply would generate a continuous stream of technology imports, spinning in an upward direction.

Conclusion

Technology importation is a very complicated strategy that involves various factors of production in the economic system. Its impact on the economy can be seen only in the long run. Since 1949, China has taken a rather systematic approach in handling technology imports. It has gone through various stages progressively, from a closed economy to a socialist market economy of today. While it will continue to focus on the development of its fundamental industries, it also emphasizes the facilitation of the advancement of major technology reform projects. Overall, the volume of technology imports in China will continue to exhibit very pronounced fluctuations from time to time, but such activities will not stop completely, despite the major problems as stated above that still need to be resolved.

To understand technology transfer to China further, we feel that it is necessary to conduct more in-depth case study on various aspects of technology transfer in specific industries with specific methods of transfer. With the huge number of technology transfer transactions implemented in the past decades, we could explore the factors that distinguish successful and unsuccessful transfers. Technology transfer has been shown to be of immense importance to firms in China. The same would apply to foreign firms that are willing or considering to transfer their technologies to China.

Studies of this nature are important and of practical significance for both the technology recipients and suppliers.

In a recent study performed by the authors, the following factors were identified as significant in affecting the level of success of technology acquisitions: (1) organization factors; (2) adaptive capacity of the firm; (3) technology buying strategy; (4) behavioural characteristics of the technology recipient and supplier relationship; (5) nature of the technology; (6) characteristics of the agreement; (7) external market environment; and (8) government legislation and support. Further effort is necessary to develop a comprehensive model that incorporates the above factors for facilitating strategies for development and success assurance. We trust that this model will be useful for firms with the intention to be involved in technology transfers in China.

18

Buying International Technology for New Product Development: An Analysis of Success of Firms in China

Oliver H. M. Yau, Kwaku Atuahene-Gima and
Raymond P. M. Chow

Introduction

Buying external technology through licensing is an important method of new product development (NPD) for firms in developed and developing countries. While several studies in the literature on technology marketing have explored the determinants of the decision to buy technology through licensing, an understanding of the characteristics and factors associated with its successful use in the NPD process is still lacking. Such an understanding is important for both buyer and seller firms, particularly for those in emerging economies, to balance the available prescriptions for firms to buy external technology with the reality that many fail in their use of such technology. This chapter investigates the factors leading to the success and failure of firms in China using licensing from unaffiliated foreign firms. We will identify the following five factors and discuss their influence on these firms' performance:

- the absorptive capacity of the buying firm,
- the technology buying strategy adopted,
- behavioural characteristics of the technology buyer-seller relationship,
- the nature of the technology and agreement, and
- the market and legislative environment.

Background

Many firms acquire external technology through licensing as an alternative or supplement to internal R&D for new product and process development (NPD) (Gold, 1987; Clark et. al., 1989; Friar and Horwitch, 1985; Mansfield, 1988). The lack of attention to external sources of technology in the NPD process gives an unrepresentative view of the development and implementation of effective marketing strategy (Wind and Mahajan, 1988). Atuahene-Gima (1992) explored the conceptual limitations of the internal NPD approach and the conditions under which firms adopt technology licensing as an external alternative to internal R&D.

Technology licensing is a contractual agreement by which a firm buys the rights to product, process and management technology from another firm for the payment of royalty or other compensation. Unlike a pure market-based transaction, buying technology through licensing is a market relational exchange. It is a form of strategic alliance, in view of the nature of payment, the seller's continued interest in the use of the technology and the use of pooled assets such as patents and designs (Borys and Jemison, 1989). Buying technology through licensing appears to be a better option for resource-constrained firms, particularly for those in developing countries. It offers a relatively speedy, flexible, safe and cheap way to acquire new products in comparison with internal R&D (Atuahene-Gima, 1992, 1993a; Lowe and Crawford, 1983; Gold, 1987). It can also serve as a viable tool for accomplishing product development and technical renewal in small firms (Svensson, 1984, p. 184).

Technology licensing has been shown to be of immense importance to Chinese firms (Yin, 1992). Recent data showed that it accounted for 38% and 19% of all technology inflows into China in 1994 and 1995 respectively (*Almanac of China's Foreign Economic Relations and Trade*, 1995/96, and 1996/97). Breakdowns of technology import contracts of China by mode of import, by number of contract and by contract value for 1986 to 1995 are shown in Appendices I and II. Since the implementation of economic reforms and the open door policy, there was continuous inflow of foreign technologies. The period from 1991 to 1995 saw significant increase of technology import contracts, with many state-invested large scale projects that were concluded in the early years of the Eighth Five-Year Plan (1991–1995). Better availability of sources of funds, improved autonomy of decision making, and large infrastructure improvement projects are some of the underlying reasons that caused the import boom.

Several studies have examined technology licensing as a selling strategy (Carstairs and Welch, 1982; Contractor, 1981; Atuahene-Gima, 1992, 1993a, 1993b; Gold, 1982, 1987; Killing, 1978, Lowe and Crawford, 1983; Weinrauch and Langlois, 1987; Welch, 1985). However, these studies provide little evidence of the factors that affect the successful acquisition and exploitation of external technology for NPD.

A few attempts have been made to explore to fill this gap (Yin, 1992; Svensson, 1984; Atuahene-Gima, 1933c). However, certain conceptual and methodological limitations attenuated their findings. The first limitation relates to the measure of successful performance. These attempts have failed to develop measures for success empirically and as such ignored a firm's explicit objectives and expectations in buying technology. Second, they did not provide good reasons for selecting variables that are likely to affect performance of technology licensing (Svensson, 1984; Atuahene-Gima, 1993c). Last but not the least, they overlooked some important interaction and environmental variables. Hence, the objective of this chapter is to present findings of a study that takes into account some of these limitations.

Figure 1 shows a conceptual model of successful buying of external technology, in which performance is treated as the criterion variable and the following eight factors as predictor variables:

- organizational factors;
- absorptive capacity of the firm;
- technology buying strategy;
- behavioural characteristics of the technology recipient and supplier relationship;
- nature of the technology;
- characteristics of the agreement;
- external market environment; and
- government legislation and support.

The model is based on the rationale that in China, the use of external technology for new product development exhibits some characteristics leading to successful performance of the licensing firms. Furthermore, it incorporates several theoretical frameworks. First, the transaction costs analysis was used to explain that firms engage in technology licensing

Figure 1
A Conceptual Model of Successful Buying and Use of External Technology

when internal R&D is seen as costly and inefficient (Williamson, 1975). Strategic behaviour that indicated firms had acquired external technology to improve competitive positions contributes as the second major input to the model (Porter, 1985). Interaction theory (Svensson, 1984; Welch, 1985) which emphasizes the importance of buyer-seller relationships serves as the third framework while the eclectic framework (Atuahene-Gima, 1992) explains the importance of the above factors along with managerial perceptions and characteristics.

Methodology[1]

We employed a two-stage research design to test the model. In the first stage, we conducted five in-depth interviews with selected firms in the Pearl River Delta area to explore the following topics:

- the strategic role of external technology in their NPD efforts;
- definition and measure of success and failure of licensed technology;
- internal and external factors that drive or hinder the acquisition and successful use of external technology for NPD; and
- the technology acquisition process and its management and orientation.

The specific objective of this stage is to uncover factors that may not be available in the literature. To determine the most likely potential respondents is the second stage of the study. In the third stage, we focus in the design and test of an instrument for data collection. The outcome of this phase is a more refined conceptual framework of successful use of licensed technology.

In the second stage, we carried out a cross-sectional survey of firms across various industries in China. In-depth personal interviews with managers involved in the technology acquisition projects were conducted. The objective of this stage is to identify factors generalizable across industries. We successfully interviewed 23 firms (including the five interviewed in the first stage) in diverse industries. Of these firms, eight (34.8%) were in the machinery industry, six (26.1%) in light industry, four (17.4%) in electronics, two (8.7%) in pharmaceutical, and three (13.0%) in other business. In terms of company type, fourteen (60.9%) were state-owned, four (17.4%) public share-owned, four (17.4%) joint ventures, and one (4.3%) collectively-owned. Geographically, nine (39.1%) firms were located in Beijing, nine (39.1%) in Shanghai, and five (21.7%) in the Pearl River Delta area. Regarding the method of technology acquisition, eleven (47.8%) used outright purchase, and seven (30.4%) were under licensing, four (17.4%) were tied to the transfer of technology with the joint venture arrangement, and one (4.3%) under a cooperative agreement. A profile of the firms is shown in Appendix 3.

We conducted in-depth interviews using in a structured questionnaire. Usually more than one member of the management team of a firm attended the interview, and in most cases representatives from various departments participated and provided supplemental insights from the perspective of their respective functions. Apart from background information on the firms, we also discussed topics such as the absorptive capacity of the buying firm, the technology buying strategy adopted, behavioural characteristics of the relationship between technology buyers and sellers, the nature of the technology and agreement, and the market and legislative environments.

Findings

Acquisition of foreign technology is a very complex process in China. It encompasses factors internal to a firm itself (i.e., firm competence), government direction and support, as well as other external factors (e.g., environmental factors, customer support, local supplies, and supplier relationship). Figure 2 illustrates a typical technology acquisition process that a state-owned enterprise in China has to go through in their import of foreign technology. It serves as a road map for the rest of the chapter.

The rest of this chapter gives a detail description of these factors identified in Figure 1.

Organizational Factors (The Technology Recipient)

"Organizational factors" refer to conditions internal to a firm that might probably affect the effectiveness of the transfer of foreign technologies. Such factors may include elements relating to the firm's management system, autonomous power, and firm size etc.

Management System

An adequate management system that matches the new technology requirements has been identified as a crucial variable for the success of a technology transfer. The new technology requires changes in the hardware of the factory while advanced technology requires a suitable management system to match it. To Chinese firms, some of these management concepts such as quality control system and production planning and control are almost new. Consequently, Chinese managers have to be trained to handle the technology that is transferred (De Bruijn and Jia, 1993).

Buying foreign technologies can be considered as a shortcut to technology change in a firm. It has many characteristics of technology innovation that is a process initiated by demand-pull and technology information push. On the one hand, technology innovation process needs to be well managed to develop effectively. On the other hand, it affects the firm's structure and its management process if these two are to be effectively adapted to each other (Wang, 1994).

Figure 2
The Foreign Technology Acquisition Process

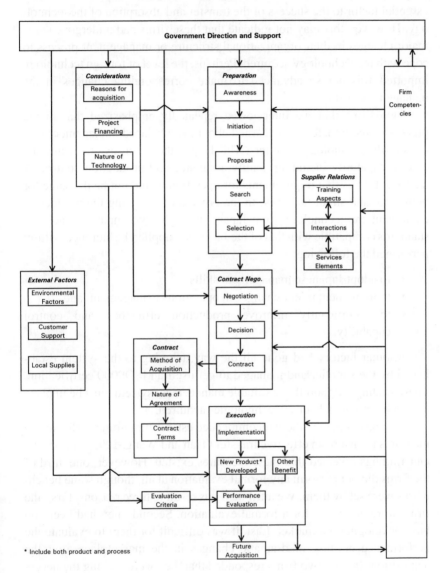

* Include both product and process

Some managers told us that strong management leadership and persistency in putting the acquired technologies into productive applications is an essential factor to the success of the transfer and absorption of the technology. However, this may not indicate that these firms had undergone some major changes in their organizational structure or management process to cope with the technology acquired. Perhaps, the level of foreign technology imported was not so advanced to make corresponding changes in the management system.

Two firms that we interviewed repeatedly emphasized that in the process of the transfer, they learned about the advanced management systems of the technology suppliers. This helped them improve their internal control capability including quality assurance and production control. A manager told us that requirements for operation would not be the same for both large and small factories. In the process of acquiring the production equipment and technology from Japan, although it was unable to achieve standards compatible with that of the Japanese supplier, he had successfully performed the following:

- to adopt Japanese management skills;
- to implement major changes in operations management; and
- to significantly improve production efficiency and control capability.

Another factory had gone all the way adhering to the system established by the supplier and managed to get itself an ISO9000 certification. These findings support that a suitable management system must be in place to match with the advanced technologies acquired.

Several Chinese authors recommended establishing some performance measures to ensure an effective transfer (Tian and Wang, 1992; Cai, 1991). Our findings revealed that these measures existed. However, one third of the firms did not perform any formal evaluation at all, though some benchmarks were set by them. We attributed this result to three reasons. First, the firms were not ready for a formal evaluation. Second, they had been too busy developing the market. Last, it was difficult for them to evaluate the performance because of dramatic changes in the marketplace after the acquisition. In fact, two firms responded that they were making the necessary preparation for the evaluation of performance; and one of them told us that they are arranging to invite specialists in the field to conduct an evaluation.

Our findings indicated that in many instances, a formal evaluation was initiated and carried out by the supervising government organization of the firms after the completion of the transfer. Firms with a "top-down" project have to carry out the "State Project Acceptance Checking" which is an overall evaluation of the performance of the project against the approval granted. They set very specific objectives and criteria for the performance evaluation. Some of these objectives are as follows:

- to ensure production capacity is met;
- to ensure product quality meeting standards set; and
- to realize economic benefits.

Criteria identified include the following:

- production volume;
- quality of products made in comparison with that of the imported;
- increased product varieties; and
- economic benefits, such as unit production cost, selling price and recovery of cost of investment.

Two factories did mention market share as one of the evaluation criteria while a leading goods factory included brand image as an important element.

Autonomous Power

The "top-down" approach in technology acquisition is prevailing in China. The supervising government unit is responsible for importing technology and for assuming its economic risk. The firm, however, is responsible for implementing but takes no position in the outcome.

From a micro perspective, if a firm is given sufficient independent capability to launch "bottom-up" project, the transfer will be more successful (Odagawa, 1990). The opinion is consistent with Wang (1994) who argued that firms should have autonomous power to make investment decisions and the practices in gaining approval for technology renovation projects were inappropriate. This implies that state-owned factories that are completely controlled by the state and have not the discretion in sales, organization of departments, and so forth are doomed to fail. Despite the small sample size, we made some interesting observations in relation to this argument. Initiating a technology transfer themselves, firms appear to have higher level of autonomous power to make investment decisions. However, many of them needed to rely on their supervising bureau and/or its import and export corporation for some reasons. First, they are inexperienced in conducting the supplier and technology searches and in contract negotiations. Second, they need the endorsement from the supervising unit to secure the necessary bank loans to finance the investment. Third, they may require foreign exchange facilitation for their imports. If any of these reasons prevails, they would have limited autonomy although they took control of the process and were responsible for the outcomes.

Almost all firms declared that their acquisitions were successful. Surprisingly, firms that were assigned the responsibility for the implementation of technology transfers by the respective supervising government units ("top-down" mode) were found to have performed well. This was mainly because their managers were mostly given the chance to participate to search and select technology and suppliers in the preparation phase of the transfer. A manager said, "We were given almost a free hand to choose suppliers and products, although the supervising bureau was involved in the selection and negotiation process." This indicates that regardless of a "top-down" or "bottom-up" management approach used in the transfer, timing and the magnitude of a firm's involvement in the acquisition process would be more important than the level of autonomous power in investment decisions.

The relationship between the management of a firm and the relevant government organization, including the supervising unit of the firm and other administrative agents, would be a critical success factor for the effective implementation of technology transfer. A technology transfer does not simply involve the Chinese recipient and the foreign technology supplier. In most cases, it may require the support from other local firms and government agents. For example, the technology recipient may need to build a new plant to house the new production equipment together with the foreign technology transferred. Hence, the involvement of local instruction firms and utilities supplying agents would undoubtedly be required.

Some firms indicated to us that the ability of their management in securing the cooperation and mobilizing the support of these agents was extremely beneficial to successful transfers. Supporting agents mostly fall under a different line of organizational supervision. The relationship that management of the technology recipient has established with such supportive units is therefore of significant importance.

Firm Size

Yin (1992) used the size of the recipient firms, measured in volume of sales, as a covariate in his study. He postulated that the gain on technology transfer increased with firm size because larger firms generally had a wider spectrum of managerial and technical resources for assistance during the transfer. However, results of this study showed that this variable was not significantly relevant.

Firms that we studied ranged from medium size second class to large size first class enterprises, with a few small size operations. Our findings do not appear to conform to those of Yin (1992). Despite their incapability to select appropriate technologies and suppliers, smaller firms could rely on the support of the supervising government units to bring together the relevant foreign technology suppliers. The appropriate selection of the technology and suppliers, combined with the readiness and potential of the market, would be a more crucial factor than the size of the operations in successful transfers of technology.

Absorptive Capacity of the Firm

This refers to a firm's ability to search for, acquire and exploit external technology to the advantage of both itself and technology suppliers. Several indicators can serve to explain this construct. They are R&D capability, manufacturing and marketing capability, firm size, prior experience and managerial factors (Atuahene-Gima, 1992; Gold, 1975, 1982; Yin, 1992). These include assessment and selection of technology, search efforts, ability to localize production, sufficiency of funds, involvement of local R&D, matching technology with local needs, quality of staff and government assistance. The following sections are devoted to explain these indictors.

Adequate Assessment and Selection of Technology

Inadequate assessment and improper selection of technology had been identified as one of the reasons for failure in some of the technology transfer projects in China (Xiao and Chen, 1988; Liu, 1994).

Interestingly, all firms involved in technology acquisition out of their own initiatives claimed that they had conducted market research. This includes market surveys to understand customers' needs and to assess market potential before submitting their proposal to the higher-level government organization for approval. A tool-making factory even told us that they worked together very closely with their essential customers on a feasibility study of transferring a new powder metallurgy process. The key customers provided them with usage and material consumption data to substantiate the proposal of the firm. Another machine-tool factory said that they looked 15 to 20 years ahead and assessed the needs of the automobile industry in China. Result of the investigation encouraged their factory to upgrade their production through acquisition of advanced foreign technology.

A proper assessment of the market potential is another success factor for new product development projects. Firms in this study confirmed its importance. Their effective assessment of the market situation was a major contribution to their success.

Search Efforts

Although most Chinese technology recipients and foreign technology suppliers are anxiously looking for partners, it is difficult for them to select the right partner due to their lack of mutual understanding (De Bruijn and Jia, 1993). The inability of China and its firms to select the appropriate technologies in the international market had created some strategic problems because of inadequate exposure and experience in such activities (Kang, 1992).

Searching for foreign technology suppliers was a substantial problem for the Chinese parties before China implemented the economic reform and open door policy especially in the 1970s. However, as imports of foreign equipment increased and foreign companies established their representative and sales offices in China, effectiveness of such search effort gradually improved. Chinese firms had become aware of the availability of foreign technologies through trade shows, exhibitions and other technology exchange activities. We also found middlemen in Hong Kong and overseas Chinese playing an important role in facilitating the exchange.

The firms we interviewed used a combination of the following means to gain awareness and build contacts with the potential foreign technology suppliers:

- trade shows and exhibitions held in China and overseas;
- technical exchange organized by the industry or the relevant government agents;
- visits to the factories of the same industry in China, especially those that have acquired foreign equipment and/or technologies;
- overseas investigation trips, usually organized by the supervising government units;
- adversary or consultation provided by specialists in the field, for example the research institutes of related industry;
- business contacts and middlemen in Hong Kong and overseas originated from related departments of the supervising government agents;
- survey of users of imported equipment/system to explore opportunities that firm could act as a local vendor for supply of parts or components, and at the same time identify foreign manufacturers currently supplying such items;
- customer visits;
- maintaining an information centre within the enterprise that collect and analyze industry information from local and international sources; and
- relying on the supervising government unit to do the search for them.

Comments from these firms show that the more direct their involvement in the preparation phase, the more likely that they have less problems and conflicts in the negotiation and implementation stages. Of course, firms that are capable of doing the supplier search on its own tend to be more involved in the contract negotiation and hence take better control of the entire transfer process. They know what they want, and how to get it. However, the time involved in the search, the subsequent selection and the eventual contract negotiations are long, laborious, and intensive. A manager from an electronics factory told us that they spent over a year, while the instrument producer said it only took them less than half a year to complete the entire acquisition cycle. The size of the project and the complexity of the technology acquired would undoubtedly have some bearing on the amount of efforts that both the technology recipient and the supplier have to put in.

Ability to Localize Production

The gaps in the level of technology between the firms and the newly acquired assets had significant impact on the firm's ability to localize the production. As a result, continuous reliance on the foreign suppliers for raw materials, parts and components greatly affected their capability in the adoption and diffusion of the technology transferred, and also their ability to develop new products (Hsiang, 1991).

With the exception of the instrument factory, the TV glass tube factory and the elevator company, firms that we interviewed did not mention localization or potential for localization as a criterion for selecting foreign technologies. In fact, only a few of them used the degree of localization as a criterion to evaluate the performance of their acquisition projects. This finding is not consistent with those mentioned in the literature (Cai, 1991).

The instrument factory that mentioned potential for future localization as one of their selection criteria also told us that they were very cautious in their localization process. They said they would not blindly localize their production just for lowering the cost in the expense of product quality. They cited the example of their Xi'an competitor that used the same acquired foreign technology from the same supplier, took much more aggressive steps in localization and ended up with many quality problems. The firm repeatedly emphasized their quality principle and said they would rather pay more for the imported materials. They justified this argument by saying that their customers demanded high reliability of the instrument installed. These customers were industrial users, like petrochemical, power plants and steelmaking factories etc. that could not afford to stop their productions at anyone time. Any stop in production would cost them millions of dollars each day so that the firms had to make sure that their end customers had full confidence in using the instruments they supplied. Firms requested to ensure that their instruments once installed could last for at least five years without any problem.

Some firms attributed that the use of local materials is an important criterion in the selection of technology and supplier. The TV glass tube factory emphasized that the technology supplier had to comply with such criterion and to guarantee that the technology transferred should be able to produce products meeting the stipulated quality standards using the local materials specified by the recipient. For such firms, localization is an important process to ensure the ultimate success of the project. To promote and expedite the localization process, the elevator company established a localization department to plan and coordinate all related activities. Eventually it achieved an 80% localization rate, the most important success measure of the acquisition project.

Apparently not all new technologies require the use of high quality imported raw materials. A pharmaceutical factory made an interesting remark: "Because of the newly acquired technology, quality of raw materials to be used would be less demanding, and yet they could manufacture the same product with higher quality in terms of consistency and uniformity." When operated with the old technology, although they used higher quality imported raw materials, they were only able to manufacture products of lower quality, yield rate and output efficiency. In this case, the use of acquired technology actually helped them to cut down the amount of raw materials imported and hence foreign exchange funds.

There are some differences in motives between the macroeconomics and microeconomics objective settings. At the government level, firms build up the local production base and become technologically independent as quickly as possible, hence would attempt to opt for very high degree of localization. On the other hand, firms might be aiming for fast economic returns to support their own operations and growth. When "up-stream" local suppliers cannot provide the needed items in either availability or quality, they would naturally continue to count on foreign suppliers to satisfy their production needs. Some firms told us that although the bank loans financing the projects were arranged by the supervising government agents, they were still responsible for repayment and interest. In many cases, this exerted tremendous pressure on the firms to seek short-term quick returns on their investments.

Sufficiency of Funds

Significant imbalance between the allocation of funds for hardware importation and the lack of post acquisition activities had greatly affected the firms' ability in the development of diffusing new product and process (Hsiang, 1991). This could be a reason for China to eventually open itself up for more foreign investments, in the form of joint ventures and other ventures.

Most firms interviewed did not seem to have experienced major difficulties in obtaining funds to finance their technology acquisition projects.

Many managed to secure local bank loans arranged or supported by their respective supervising government units. The instrument factory even obtained an interest free UNDP loan for that purpose. However, the amount of funds available did limit the level of technologies imported. For example, the TV equipment factory mentioned that the Japanese supplier did recommend installing fully automatic chip inserters to reduce possible human errors. The firm that took an alternative approach without such automatic machines in the first attempt commented, "This could save us some money and could better utilize our labour force." However, it eventually acquired some automatic machines to improve their production efficiency and effectiveness in the second round.

Some of the less successful firms might have faced the problem of insufficient funds that hindered their technology advancement. The refrigerator factory told us that they were forced to start with low investment and acquired a lower level technology with a less than optimum output capacity. Quality of their products, although received relatively good acceptance in the initial period, became less competitive as various imported and JV brands entered the market. Unless they put in substantial investment to upgrade their technology and production capacity, they would face an extremely difficult situation as their competitiveness become weaker day after day.

Involvement of Local R&D

Many Chinese analysts also identified the lack of involvement of the local R&D organizations as one of the major limitations for more effective adoption, diffusion and development. According to Hsiang (1991), a survey of 220 enterprises conducted by the China National Science Commission revealed that only 2% of them had worked together with local R&D organizations on adoption and diffusion of the technology transferred.

Almost all firms told us that factory managers and chief engineers are key players in the acquisition process. Only two TV equipment factories and a machine tool company had their representatives from their R&D department participated in the acquisition process. Under the former planned economy system in China, only large corporations had the financial ability to own their in-house research and development establishments. Thus, they would include their R&D personnel in the process. On the contrary, smaller firms might have to count on themselves or the service of the industry research institutes to provide R&D support. Their engineers would assume the role of change agents and used the foreign technologies acquired to develop new products for the local market. If this trend continue to develop and expand, these industry research institutes would become manufacturers themselves and might soon become competitors in the market for products and technologies, instead of being pure service providers to support the industry.

Matching Technology with Local Needs

Low capability of firms to select the suitable technology and adjust to local conditions is perceived as a major handicap in technology transfer (Kang and Yang, 1992). The lack of skills to acquire the "core" technology leading to a series of duplication of imported technology is another. Thus, matching technology with real needs serves as an important requirement for technology transfer (Odagawa, 1990). Results of our survey fall very much in line with the proposition we established. Apart from the other elements, the firms used a combination of the following criteria to select suitable technologies:

- material and utilities consumption rates;
- reliability and mature level of technology — easier for absorption;
- suitability for local conditions so that firm can handle all by itself after acquisition; no need to continuously rely on supplier;
- usage level of existing products in China;
- feed back from users;
- capability for absorption and localization;
- use of local materials;
- potential in market — size and growth;
- supplier's strength and experience in China;
- production technology suitable for firm — ability to absorb; enter into mass production quickly;
- integration with existing skills and facilities;
- provision for further technology advancement;
- product suitability for local market, e.g., consumer acceptance, quality and price.
- transfer price of the project; and
- low cost of production.

In sum, our findings indicated several implications for Chinese managers. First, technology must be able to allow local applications, absorption and diffusion effectively and efficiently. Firms must capture a potentially large and growing market for the products it produces by using the acquired technology. Second, availability of local raw material supplies and utilities could also be considered. Third, it is important to observe the physical operating requirements of the new technology and equipment, and the actual conditions of the plant in which the newly acquired technology will be used. Many workshops in China are still not operating under "weather controlled" conditions. Hence, the equipment and raw materials used with the new technology might not function properly to produce the desirable quality results. This might end up with very unhappy situations and might even render the transfer project unsuccessful.

Quality of Staff

Successful technology innovation involves enhancing the initiatives and creativity of all related employees (Wang, 1994). An important factor determining the success of a technology transfer is the quality of staff in the recipient's country. It is essential for staff of various levels to learn the new technology and to facilitate the transfer process. The problem with China is that it has too many unskilled and semi-skilled workers but a serious shortage of professionals and managers (Tsang, 1994).

Among the factors that contributed to the success of the transfer projects, about half of the firms identified leadership and involvement of their management as two crucial determinants. In particular, they mentioned behaviours such as right management decision, management attention and control, persistence of management, management working long hours together with the staff throughout the entire process, etc. as the essential attributes. Thus a manager told us, "It was because of the persistence of the factory manager that our factory was able to reduce production workers' resistance to change and successfully implemented the transfer."

Along the same lines, other successful factors are:

• hard working team;
• good sense of responsibility;
• staff felt honoured to take part in a major project;
• quality consciousness;

- discipline;
- total involvement;
- technical competent staff selected for project and training: and
- close coordination between departments.

We have found at least two areas that needed to be improved. The first is to enhance the capability of developing objective measures for performance assessment of a newly acquired technology. Several managers told us that they encountered this difficulty because of their incapability of anticipating and controlling changes in the marketplace. The second is to improve the management staff's understanding of the marketing concept. Under the planned economy system, most factories did not have the sales responsibility. They were requested to manufacture and deliver products to commercial establishments under their supervising government units, which in turn distributed the products through their networks. As such, they did not have any ideas about post-production activities. This greatly affected their understanding of consumer needs and wants and thus their ability in new product development.

Government Assistance

Government coordination and assistance facilitate absorption and adaptation of foreign technology and enhance the accumulation of local technological competence (Yin, 1992). Under the planned economy system, the government agents were usually involved in foreign technology transfer projects. However, the role played by the supervising government agents varied depending on the nature of the transfer and the status of the firms. The following functions performed by these agents were uncovered in the study:

- initiation or review and approval of the project;
- arranging bank loans and foreign exchange funding;
- directed or supported the contract negotiation, especially on commercial terms; bringing in the experience obtained from other foreign economic contract negotiations;
- monitoring of macro issues against policies set; and
- making "duty-free" arrangement for the imported items.

Therefore, it seems that these agents played dual roles. On the one hand, they acted as the clearing house for the acquisition projects with an aim to control the money spent and to ensure that the projects were justified. On the other hand, they assisted firms in the technology and supplier search, the selection process and the contract negotiation. In some cases, they even provided translation and interpretation services, and acted as an information centre for those firms that needed technical data.

Active participation of government agents, especially in the preparation phase, contributed to the success of the transfer. A manager of the mainframe equipment factory told us his experience, "Before the launch of the project, our supervising government unit summoned representatives from selected factories to perform two activities: a market study and a technology/supplier search. Under its guidance, a working team was formed to identify the most suitable technologies and potential suppliers before they proceeded to the vendor selection phase. Meanwhile, the unit called for a meeting of factories that could supply the needed components to provide a 'complete set menu (support)' to us."

In fact, these "up-stream" factories also needed to acquire some foreign technologies in order to enhance their capabilities to produce the supportive parts and components. Such a master project involving multilevel participation would be difficult to accomplish without active coordination of the government.

Another manager from a tool-making factory also mentioned that the government's active involvement and decision to develop the auto industry affected significantly the success of the technology transfer. The growth of the industry positively affected the demand on the products they made.

Technology Buying Strategy

This construct pertains to a firm's approach to planning for buying technology, sources of information, search effort, types of technology sought, types of markets and products developed with a technology-, and strategic-orientation. In fact, existing literature has showed that the lack of proactive licensing strategy is a major cause of conflicts in the technology licensing process (Corsairs and Welch, 1982; Weinrauch and Langlois, 1987) and failure (Svensson, 1984).

Dynamic Technology Transfer Process

The product quality and efficiency required to export products and be highly competitive in the internal market can only be achieved by using equipment and production methods which are transferred to the Chinese firms from abroad. However, the current industrial infrastructure in China is not geared to adopting the most advanced technology. Therefore, many joint ventures develop what are called "dynamic" technology transfer arrangements (De Bruijn and Jia, 1993). This means that older technologies are first transferred to form a basic structure and then upgraded in the future in a number of steps. For firms in China acquiring foreign technology through licensing, it seems a logical approach by taking on such a dynamic technology transfer process to ensure long-term success, given their technological and infrastructure limitations. However, we also found that some firms would like to see the dynamic process in a joint venture rather than licensing. They considered this more effective in getting foreign partners more committed in feeding them with the latest technology in the long run.

Some of the firms interviewed engaged in more than one technology transfer projects, but only a few of them worked with the same supplier again in their subsequent acquisitions. Thus we are unable to ensure whether firms did plan for a dynamic technology transfer at the outset, or simply took up additional items or more advanced models as they built up their confidence while moving up along the learning curve. One thing for sure is that firms would have the intent to progress further in their technology advancement after their initial acquisition. One of them mentioned that they had a long-term agreement or understanding with the technology supplier whereby the latter would have the obligation to continue to upgrade the technology of the Chinese party. Some added that for future acquisitions, their firm would request the technology supplier to continuously keep their firms in advanced technological status for a specified period.

Realistic Approach

Watanabe (1993) pointed out the Japanese side generally claimed that the Chinese were not willing to introduce technology in a realistic manner in stages and irritated the Japanese with their demands for the latest technology at the very outset. To a certain extent, this ties in with the need for a dynamic technology transfer process as discussed in the section above.

In this study, we collected the following comments that are quite relevant to this particular issue:

- only limited funds were allocated to the project;
- difficult to get government approval for import of similar technology, if another firm had acquired the technology before — symptom of "duplicate import"; and
- if other type of technology is available, but has already been acquired by another factory, the firm has to take on a different type instead.

Although firms have limited financial resources, they have been directed by the government to acquire only the "new and advanced" technologies that are beyond their means to acquire. Thus, this leads firms to demand for the latest technology at the very outset despite technology suppliers' recommendation to transfer by stages.

For high-technology products and products with short life cycles such as micro-electronics and computer software, it is logical that the technology recipients would aim for the most advanced technology if at all possible. For example, the elevator company emphasized the need to enter the market with high-end products for their elevator control systems, otherwise they would not be able to cope with the fast development in the industry, as new systems and designs would become available in as short as every five years. The overall objective is to upgrade the technology level in China, if they start at a relatively low end, it would almost be impossible for them to catch up in a long time.

Over-Emphasis on Price Negotiation

It is natural for the technology recipient to try to negotiate for the lowest possible price; however, such strategy might result in some adverse effects on the transfer. Many Chinese and foreign analysts pointed out that among the key problems involved in technology transfer is a lack of understanding of the extreme importance of software. Yabucchi (1986) noted that some Chinese factories could see no need at all to provide for operating guidance when purchasing equipment and simply refused to pay money for software. He even pointed out that in some negotiations, the Chinese have had Japanese corporations submit separate prices for equipment and the related software and then foregone the software, citing budget constraints.

Almost all the firms visited told us that their acquisition projects included both equipment and technology, which appeared to be the common approach taken by these firms that are successful in the transfer of foreign technologies. Many of them highlighted that what they had acquired was a complete production line. The TV equipment factory emphasized that their project was a "complete-set" import covering both software and hardware, including product technology and design, equipment, and production process skills. Complete-knock-down (CKD) parts were also included in the initial stage to get themselves started.

On the other side of the spectrum, the fuel injection equipment factory told us that they only acquired the technology from the supplier, without any equipment. The transfer included product drawings, product technical standards, production technology, together with some tools made by the supplier. This is by far the only example that we came across with that is "software heavy" technology transfer.

Price negotiation would be one of the major topics in any commercial transaction including the transfer of technology. One would therefore expect that price would definitely be an essential criterion in the selection of technology. While most of the firms visited mentioned price as one of the selection criteria, few of them put price as the most crucial element in the entire selection profile. Although the interviewees were not asked to rank the importance of the selection criteria they used, it was noticed that many respondents named price as the last or almost the last element mentioned, if they did mention price at all. In fact, factors relating to the technology itself were usually the first mentioned during the discussions. Apparently for most firms, price is an important but may not be the most important criterion affecting their selection.

It may be of interest to note that in only a few cases (two only in fact), the firms commented high price was one of the problems they encountered in the negotiation phase of the acquisition process.

Competition among Suppliers

Yin (1992) proposed that competition among technology suppliers is favourable to recipients for better choice, better deals, and better assistance and service from suppliers. However, the results of this study show that this variable was not significantly relevant.

It is a commonly used negotiation tactics that the buyer would invite he quotes from several close competitors so that they can seek the most favourable offer. Most of the firms visited mentioned that they did use such tactics during their supplier search and negotiation. In fact, the auto glass factory we visited said they usually invited all the potential suppliers to meet with them at the same time, in separate meetings, and conducted price negotiation in turn until the most attractive offer was selected. They commented that this approach was effective and they could always achieve what they wanted. On the other hand, the fuel injection equipment factory said they had no choice but to accept the terms set by the supplier since the latter was the only qualified supplier they could get hold of at that time.

Behavioural Characteristics of the Technology Recipient and Supplier Relationship

This refers to attributes of the licensee-licensor relationship during the acquisition and use of the technology. It includes commitment, cooperation, information sharing, the level of interdependency, conflict resolution processes, coordination mechanism, and trust (Gold, 1982; Svensson, 1984; Weinrauch and Langlois, 1987; Welch, 1985). The underlying attributes include: cultural factors, trust and relationship, interaction, understanding and agreement, training, and consultants.

Cultural Factors

Management of technology transfer is complicated not only because it is a combination of technical matters, capital and personnel, but also because it is influenced by the different cultures and social systems (De Bruijn and Jia, 1993). Such would include various qualitative variables as management philosophies, organizational cultures, administrative style, and individual personalities. Johnston (1991) presented a list of problems industrial marketers have to resolve when selling to Chinese enterprises. Such obstacles can be further summarized into cultural difference and interpersonal relationships, which greatly affect the degrees of success of the sellers, but may also affect the eventual success of the transfer.

Most of the firms interviewed told us that they are satisfied with the service and support provided by the technology suppliers. Cultural difference does exist, but did not seem to have affected the effectiveness of the transfer to a great extent. There were examples of conflicts between the parties, but only a few of them related cultural difference to be the source of such conflicts. The instrument factory criticized the "great nation chauvinism" attitude of the management of the technology supplier and said such attitude did not give comfortable feelings. They did, however, comment that implementation of the transfer was smooth due very much to the strong cooperation between both parties, especially at the technicians' level. They did not recall having any argument with the supplier, not even in the negotiation phase.

The TV equipment factory pointed out that the difference in working habits and management style had led to some personality clash between Chinese workers and on-site team leaders assigned by the technology supplier. The task oriented supervisory style of the foreign team-leaders was not accustomed to by the local workers and hence the dispute. Higher level of management involvement was called for to resolve the difference. The foreign leadership style was some sort of a culture shock to the technology recipient, but they took it positively and praised highly the good working attitude of the foreign staff assigned to work with them. "It was a good internal clean up," commented the chief engineer. They further expressed that they counted on the foreign technology supplier to build up a foundation for their management skills. They have seen the results and recognized the benefits achieved.

Trust and Relationship

Technology is an intangible product and can only be successfully transferred if the conditions of the two sides involved mesh. Most technology transfer takes place from person to person and therefore mutual trust and eager cooperation are essential (Odagawa, 1990). To ensure a long-term success, Tian and Wang (1992) expressed that a sense of partnership between the transferor and the recipient was an important prerequisite, instead of a mere seller-buyer relationship, as technology transfer is an extended process. Undoubtedly, there would be difficult situations, but such could be resolved if both parties handle the obstacles with a sense of mutual trust, flexibility, and a sense of responsibility.

Our study findings fall very much in line with the proposition established. Most of the firms visited said they have good relationship with the technology suppliers, and at least one of them mentioned that there is strong mutual trust between the two parties. The beer factory said they considered relationship extremely important as they need to induce some foreign investment in the future and they viewed the technology supplier as a preferred partner for further cooperation. In fact, several firms indicated to us that because of the satisfactory transfers and good relationships, the foreign technology suppliers approached them to establish manufacturing joint ventures in China.

The machine tool factory took a somewhat different approach to strengthen the bonding with the technology supplier. Right from the beginning, they agreed to jointly develop the China market. The supplier assigned a sales representative to work with them, and together with the representative from the machine tool works they called on potential customers jointly to promote the full line of products made by them. If the sale calls for a product model that the machine tool works produced, the order would be handled by the Chinese party. If a more advanced model was needed, the U.S. party would supply it from its head office through the machine tool works with local supports. In certain cases, with the provision of needed technical drawings and specifications by the U.S. party, the Chinese party could produce it locally in their workshop. This cooperative arrangement has worked well and developed into a joint venture arrangement. This is an evidence of cooperation that has led to mutual benefits and a long-term relationship.

Relationships would sometimes be more readily observable at the level where interactions are intensive. Many firms told us that they have established good working relationship with foreign specialists and technicians assigned to transfer projects. Because of such relationship, they managed to acquire many skills not stipulated in the technical document. Many of these skills were tacit in nature and could only be learned on the job for quite some time. Apparently, firms that recognized the importance of this experience and expertise of foreign specialists became very patient in building up a good relationship so that more tacit knowledge and experience would eventually be obtained.

A fuel injection equipment factory had a different experience. They reckoned that the European technology supplier was rigid, inflexible, and thus untrustworthy. They believed that the foreign supplier set very harsh terms to take advantage of the situation that they had no alternative but to rely totally on the supplier.

Some authors do not believe that friendly relationship would lead to commercial deals or trade cooperations (Yabuuchi, 1986). However, our findings provide further evidence that their proposition does not receive support.

Interaction

Transfer of technology always requires close interaction and exchange of personnel of the parties concerned (Tsang, 1994). Firms in this study took available opportunities to build a working relationship with their suppliers. Opportunities, which include technical discussions, training at both locations and on-site installation works, could enhance interactions and facilitate exchanges. As indicated in the section above, firms tried very hard to earn the support of, and interact with, foreign specialists. Apparently, such effort paid off well, as most firms had successfully learnt a lot of practical skills from foreign technicians through these close contacts and interactions. Some of them even maintained active exchanges with foreign specialists and continuously obtained their technical advice after the transfers.

The machine tool works even took a more aggressive approach to tighten the relationship with the technology supplier. They had established an annual technical exchange programme with the supplier, whereby specialists of both parties would meet and discuss the latest technology development, and exchange technical information relating to modifications and improvements to products. They regarded the programme as one of the best clauses in the technology transfer agreement as such practice had enabled them to elevate their technological level and booster their new product development capability. As such, they had excelled local competitors in terms of quality and features.

Understanding and Agreement

To secure a successful technology transfer, many authors (Tian and Wang, 1992) have emphasized that understanding the scope of the transfer and having it agreed upon by both parties are necessary. The scope includes the following items:

- specific details of the technology to be transferred;
- goals that the technology supplier wants to achieve in the transfer process;

- ultimate goals of the technology recipient in acquiring the technology;
- willingness of the supplier in transferring the technology; and
- level of ease of the transfer.

In effect, a thorough analysis of the project work design is another important and prerequisite step leading to a scrupulous specification of each element in the transfer process.

Although common goals are always stipulated in the transfer contract, the respective ultimate goals of the technology supplier and the technology recipient may not be consistent. This may affect the ultimate long-term success of firms involved in technology transfers.

Most firms complained that technology suppliers were unwilling to transfer the most advanced technologies to them in order to avoid the creation of possible future competitors in the market. Although sympathetic on the supplier, they were not at all satisfied with the arrangement made. A fuel injection equipment factory criticized that the German technology supplier was reluctant to expand the type of technologies to be transferred. They wanted to acquire the needed technologies to develop eventually their own products for the whole diesel engines market in China. However, the German supplier held that they would only provide them with the technology for the production of accessories for their engine models. The ultimate goal of the Chinese firm was to master the product development techniques and become technically independent. This was obviously not in the best interest of the technology supplier.

Contrary to the above, there were cases in which technology suppliers and recipients appeared to share a common goal or have an empathic understanding of the scope of the transfers. For examples, a technology supplier was willing to share its research data with a turbine generator factory and to help the latter develop its own advanced models. As previously mentioned, the machine tool works and its technology supplier agreed to develop the China market is another good example of long-term cooperation. The practice not only produced positive results for both parties, but also expedited the migration into a more formal joint venture operation. In this transfer, the technology supplier also agreed to provide the Chinese party with the latest technology whenever a new product is introduced. This helped to keep the Chinese technology recipient always in line with the most updated technology that is the ultimate goal of the foreign technology acquisition strategy.

Training

"Training is one of the key success factors." Many Chinese and foreign analysts made this remark. The poor absorptive capacity of China implies that when foreign firms are considering to transfer technology to China, they should make sure that they are able to implement extensive training programmes for the local Chinese (Tsang, 1994). On training, Tian and Wang (1992) expressed the need for a systematic approach that would include training objectives, detailed training plan, and evaluation of the effectiveness of the programme.

Obviously training is an essential element in all technology transfers. All firms in the sample expressed that training was covered in the process. However, the level and mode of training might differ depending on the complexity of the transfer. Most firms told us that training provided by technology suppliers was mainly related to production process techniques and equipment operations, taken place in both the supplier's location or on-site in the recipient's workshop. Evidently, such training programmes were structured and well-planned. In most cases, details of the training provided were stipulated in the transfer contract, including the type of training, duration, place and expenses.

While the general approach to training was the same, there were differences in the methods used. To improve communication effectiveness, the instrument factory arranged for their engineers to attend foreign language classes before they sent them overseas for training. The engineers thus trained would become the trainers for other technicians after their return from the training programmes. The firm commented that this arrangement was very effective, as their engineers would be able to communicate directly with foreign specialists without using an interpreter with a technical background. Speaking from their experience, the other instrument factory said they encountered some communication difficulties due to language barrier.

In the case of the TV equipment factory that we previously mentioned, they took the approach to assign their local technicians to work under the direct supervision of the foreign team leaders and workshop supervisors. Thus, it acquired and adopted the production management and quality control skills of the technology supplier, and significantly improved their internal control capability. Further, as the firm was guaranteed to meet the designed production capacity, it was crucial that its workers know how to do it.

As far as training effectiveness is concerned, we found the following comments in the study:

- engineers trained by the technology supplier became the trainers for the others;
- sufficient training provided;
- trainees carefully selected and well experienced;
- managed to master the relevant skills, including both tacit and non-tacit knowledge essential to the production techniques;
- technology supplier did not hold back any technical knowledge;
- firm also acquired and adopted the production management and quality control skills; and
- specialists sent in by supplier were all very experienced.

However, some firms appear to have the following problems:

- specialists sent in by supplier were not technically competent enough; and
- language barrier created some communication difficulties.

Consultants

Effective use of on-site consultants is another success factor during the start-up stage. This has been the cause of some friction because both technology suppliers and recipients view the functions of a consultant differently. Thus, the degree to which agreement on the consulting functions can be reached is regarded as a good indicator of successful cooperation between the parties (Schnepp, Von Glinow and Bhambri, 1990).

While not all firms specifically commented on the effectiveness of their on-site consultants, the positive feedback on the training provided may indicate their satisfaction of the services rendered by technology suppliers. On the other hand, some firms highlighted that the off-site consultation service should be included as a contract term. The tools making factory told us that they continued to rely on the supplier to provide computer software servicing and upgrade support. The leather goods factory required the supplier to provide continually new product designs to maintain a leadership position. The fuel injection equipment factory periodically sent products to the technology supplier for inspection and suggestion on improvements.

Some technology suppliers continue to provide certain level of consultation service, even after the completion of the contract. In the case of the refrigerator factory, representatives from the supplier visited every year and provided some consultation support. Obviously, the technology suppliers use such strategies to maintain good relationship with the recipients, which turn out to be mutually beneficial to both parties.

Effective use of consultant service is an essential element for the success of firms that aimed at gaining access to the international market. This is particularly true for some specialized products. A pharmaceutical company hired a U.S. consultant to help build a production line to meet the Good Manufacturing Practice (GMP) requirements, which is a prerequisite for product acceptance in the international market of the pharmaceutical industry. The consultant provided all the necessary training, plant layout and design assistance, and GMP audits. As GMP was a totally new concept to the firm, outside consultation was extremely important to ensure that their production management and products could meet the required international standards.

Nature of the Technology

This refers to the form or type of technology licensed. It is a criterion for any technology import project, in which the technology is advanced and appropriate for digestion and absorption. It is often interpreted as the state-of-the-art technology or realistically more advanced than the level currently available, but not so advanced that the Chinese enterprises cannot assimilate it easily (Davenport, 1987). Inadequate assessment and selection of technology have been identified as problems of technology imports in China (Liu, 1994).

Product Selection

Product selection is of paramount importance to the success of a technology transfer. Foreign technology acquired may be used to fulfill a variety of objectives such as to improve existing products, to extend the existing product lines, to broaden the portfolio of product offerings, and to change the scope of business. Sometimes, these objectives are determined by some macro-policies directed from supervising authorities. For example, a firm may want to acquire foreign technology to provide parts locally to support a new industry earmarked for development by the state. However, these objectives are derived from micro-internal goals generated by firms on their own initiative and for their benefits.

Product selection, identified as a major problem in technology transfer, should meet with market objectives under the market constraints (De Bruijn and Jia, 1993). In effect, our findings confirm this proposition. Firms in the study seemed to be able to manage this pre-transfer process well through effective use of market and/or industry surveys. Managers of two TV equipment factories indicated that they conducted comprehensive market studies by the firm itself or under the direction of the supervising government unit. By identifying popular brands and models in the domestic and international markets, they generated a list of products and their respective manufacturers to facilitate the product selection process. This process is not as resources demanding under the planned economy system because of the tightly integrated industry structure and the intensive involvement of government organizations that laid down the direction for the technology transfers.

Identifying data on product technology is very difficult for the Chinese party. China has its own set of technical standards. Chinese engineers who translate the specifications into the Chinese language must verify all technical data. The problem may be complicated when the foreign party cannot provide a complete set of technical data, detailed specifications or drawings of components, especially when the product has a high proportion of purchased components.

This exercise is extremely time consuming and technical labour intensive, but is an essential element of the technology transfer process. Some firms acknowledged the difficulties they encountered. A manufacturer of hydraulic components took the approach to transcribe the technical document in stages. It did not produce all models and put them on the market right away. Instead, it worked together with its customers and developed products suitable for each customer using the technology acquired. Such effort can be viewed as a positive contribution to its success in the absorption and diffusion of the technology acquired, despite spending several years to translate and reconciliate with the established national standards.

Through this process, the firm managed to integrate the technology with the needs of the market.

Type of Technology

From the supplier's perspective, the level of the transferred technology has a negative impact on the probability of a successful transfer. That is, the lower the level of the transferred technology, the higher is the probability of success. Various levels of technology transfer can be referred to as "composite technology," "technology spanning diverse sectors," and "management technology" etc. (Odagawa, 1990). However, Chinese firms frequently interpret "advanced technology" as the state-of-the-art although many of them have a limited ability to adopt even the early 1980s technology (Davenport, 1987). Furthermore, China authorities had even openly criticized foreign companies for passing on obsolete technology (Barnett, 1985; Ma, 1985) and demanded that advanced technology be transferred to China (Crowell, 1986).

Two companies in the study indicated that the unwillingness of foreign suppliers to transfer the most advanced technology and top-of-the-line products as one of the major problems they encountered in the negotiation process. They criticized that foreign companies, in both cases Japanese suppliers, were very conservative and had the misconception that Chinese firms would not be able to absorb and master the advanced technology at that time. However, the TV factory mentioned that the capability of absorption and localization was one of the criteria for selecting the technology acquired. While other firms did not indicate it as a hurdle in the negotiation process, some expressed their understanding of such a situation and believed that foreign suppliers would tend not to transfer the best technology. Even if the suppliers did, they would demand unaffordably high price for recipient firms.

Matching Local Conditions

The technology transferred must suit the specific local conditions (Tian and Wang, 1992; Wang, 1994; Yabuuchi, 1986). In this study, we have found consistent findings. A factory that produced automatic process control instruments told us that the mature nature of the technology was the most important criterion for acquiring technology. It said that the more mature it was, the easier it would be for them to absorb and diffuse the technology.

Level of Sophistication

In understanding modes of international technology transfer, Tsang (1994) has successfully identified three factors, technology characteristics, the characteristics of the receiving country, and the transferor. Technology consists of two types of technical know-how, namely non-tacit and tacit. The former is embodied in designs, specifications, and drawings while the latter is an individual's personal knowledge. Tacit know-how requires close human interaction and is therefore difficult to transfer in codified form alone. The proportion of tacit know-how embodied in a technology is closely related to its age and level of sophistication.

Like most developing countries, China is anxious to acquire the latest, state-of-the-art technologies. Such an approach creates difficulties of its own. By definition, the more sophisticated an imported item, the more difficult it is to assimilate into the local economy. The inevitable technology gap not only creates sharp conflicts with existing modes of production, but also prevents smooth transition from one to the other (Yokata, 1987).

However, firms in the sample did not seem to have faced this problem. The following appears to be the possible explanations:

- most of them were already in the trade for many years prior to the implementation of the project;
- they had the fundamental skills and knowledge of the technology;
- the technologies imported served the purpose of upgrading their existing product and/or production process;
- the technologies transferred were not the most advanced technologies that the suppliers had;
- some firms took a progressive approach in the transfer by first engaging themselves in SKD/CKD assembly process of the less sophisticated products and then moved onto a more automated production process for more advanced models.

Characteristics of the Agreement

This construct refers to the restrictions or conditions imposed on the licensee by the agreement, such as entry and exit conditions, grant-back provisions and level of royalty payments (Atuahene-Gima, 1993c; Svensson, 1984; Yin, 1992).

Compensation

De Bruijn and Jia (1993) viewed compensation for the technology and the procedures for remittance of earnings as two sensitive issues. The first issue is the price for the technology to be supplied. There is a conflict of interest between the partners. The Chinese complain that foreign technologies are always over-priced because foreign suppliers believed that their technologies are very advanced and expensive to develop. The second issue is the transfer of profits in hard currency. The first issue may be applicable in almost all forms of technology transfer including transfer through licensing. However, the second issue may be more related to joint ventures, unless the terms in the transfer contracts include also compensation based on the future sales and/or earnings of the local technology recipients.

In relation to price negotiation, the common approach taken by Chinese firms is to approach several potential foreign suppliers that are interested in transferring technology and in participating in project discussions with an aim to select the best offer. In some cases, price is the most critical selection criterion, especially when the offered technologies are similar and meet the needs of the recipients. In other cases, firms manage to get what seemed to them a reasonable price in the negotiation. Two factories even adopted a close-bid approach with which they were very satisfied. To obtain the best price, a factory may negotiate with several potential suppliers simultaneously. Very often, the appearance of other aggressive competitors may force suppliers to cut the offer down to a more reasonable price. However, this approach may lengthen the negotiation process to a year or more to finish.

However, firms may not involve in price negotiation. Either they have no knowledge and experience of comparing prices to enable them to chose the best deal, or negotiations were not conducted by them but by their supervising agents.

Most firms indicated that foreign exchange payments were arranged through the Import and Export Corporation under the supervising government agents or the related organization. Only authorized firms could involve in foreign trade transactions under the planned economy system before the economic reforms. Except for one firm, no firm in the sample made any specific comment regarding disputes with the foreign suppliers on this issue. However, some told us that they still had outstanding local currency payments not yet settled with the Import and Export Corporation, due mainly to the problem of exchange rate difference resulting from the appreciation of foreign currencies against Renminbi in the past periods. This has little to do with the technology suppliers.

Understanding and Agreement on Contract Terms

A contract is the most important working document that guides or governs the behaviour of the parties concerned. Firms interviewed paid much attention to the terms and conditions of the agreement and in some cases, rendered much stress and frustrations to both sides, especially in the contract negotiation phase. However, once agreed the transfer process would move much faster in most cases. For example, a factory commented that the contract negotiation was tough and that the technology supplier did not give in at all. "They fought for every inch of land," said the Chief Engineer of the factory. However, when implementing the technology transfer, the supplier was very cooperative and serious. They did anything as long as it was their responsibility. They even took the initiative to involve in work that was the responsibilities of the recipient. Hence, this had led to a success transfer and resulted in follow-on transfers. In this study, we only found a few incidents with major dispute on the terms and conditions of the contract.

Misunderstanding between technology suppliers and recipients is detrimental to the success of technology transfers. It occurs for a number of reasons. For example, when signing an agreement, the Chinese party may assume that all technologies relevant to the product to be manufactured will be transferred (Schnepp, Von Glinow and Bhambri, 1990).

While most firms expressed that they had good working relations with the technology suppliers, one factory encountered a different experience. Firstly, they found that there were some problems with the equipment supplied. However, the supplier demanded extra labour and traveling expenses to bring the engineers in to perform the necessary repairs. Secondly, representatives sent by the technology supplier were not technically competent enough to rectify the problems. Thirdly, there was apparent misunderstanding of royalty payment calculations. Consequently, the factory refused to pay any royalty to the supplier. The root of the problem, as the factory perceived, is that contract terms were not clearly defined. For example, expenses relating to equipment repair and living expenses for technicians sent to the supplier's factory for training had not been stipulated in the contract. Both parties should be responsible for the oversight. On the Chinese party's side, the oversight may be due to the inexperience of the negotiator of the Import and Export Corporation who represented the factory in the contract negotiation, or the incapability of the Corporation to effectively use commercial terms to cover its technical requirements. However, the equipment supplier, serving as a middleman for the technology supplier, also had the responsibility to remind the Chinese party of possible incurrence of costs relating to training and repair. Otherwise, the supplier would be accused of "not trustworthy" and this will become an obstacle of future cooperation.

To eliminate such problems for any future acquisitions, the firm said they would need to sort out the details on price and technical specifications directly with the original equipment manufacturer instead of through the middleman, and would demand that technical training be provided by the original equipment manufacturer.

Contractual or Technical Restrictions

The possibility of the technology recipient becoming a competitor is a general concern of a technology supplier. Such an occurrence is a negative indicator of further cooperation, since it will affect the supplier-recipient relationship adversely and may damage the supplier's competitive advantage. Schnepp, Von Glinow and Bhambri (1990) commented that loss of technology by leakage to third party Chinese enterprises is still a risk to be reckoned with and competition from companies outside the technology transfer project remains a possibility. It could be due to this and other related concerns that the technology suppliers imposed certain contractual or technical restrictions in the transfer agreement, and such restrictions could eventually limit the level of success of the transfer process and the technology recipient's ability to develop its own new products and process improvements.

While these appear to be legitimate concerns in the supplier's perspective, not all recipients would agree to the restrictions set. The fuel injection equipment factory was particularly upset about this. They commented that the technology supplier, recognizing the fact that the firm had no choice but to acquire the technology from them, took advantage of the situation and set very harsh terms, such as export restrictions, confidentiality and etc. The firm was unable to convince the supplier to accept the standard terms set by the Chinese government on foreign technology transfers.

There was a general criticism made by the foreign suppliers that the Chinese technology buyers seek guarantees in terms of the finished products which are difficult or impossible to make, especially when the recipient insisted on using the existing equipment wherever possible. In some cases, the technology suppliers concerned were asked to achieve quality standards even higher than those adopted in their home country (Yabuuchi, 1986). Some of the firms we visited told us that this was one of the requirements they demanded the supplier to comply with. Instead of making such a guarantee in the contract, the suppliers of the TV equipment factory and the fuel injection equipment factory arranged to provide training and technical assistance to the firms to ensure that the workers of these factories know how to produce the products using the technologies transferred. In the case of the fuel injection equipment factory, the supplier also agreed that the firm could ask for additional training if that provided was not sufficient. Such alternative arrangement obviously met with the satisfaction of the firms as both of them commented that the training provided was sufficient and effective.

External Market Environment

Strategic behaviour explanation for technology licensing suggests that the environment plays a major role in performance (Porter, 1985). Both technological and market competitive forces as well as government legislative environment have been found to impact on success (Atuahene-Gima 1993c; Yin, 1992).

Intensity of Market Competition

Several important external environmental factors would have impact on the success of a transfer project. In his empirical analysis, Yin (1992) proposed that the intensity of competition could be positively relate to the performance of an international technology transfer. The more competitive the market, the more a firm will want to gain competitive advantages by introducing and using foreign technology. His finding indicated that market competition explained the two economic variables, marginal change of sales growth and marginal change of profitability, better than the two technological variables, the level of absorption and the level of diffusion.

Several managers mentioned competition as an important factor. One suggested that they must compete on quality, brand name and service. The other indicated that they must try to maintain their market share by stabilizing the prices offered especially when competitors are coming. Likewise, a manager commented that the opening up of the China market attracted domestic and foreign competition, pressing them to introduce new designs to keep themselves ahead of the others. As can be expected, factories making specialized line of products could gain better competitive advantages over suppliers of the general models.

Most firms commented that changes in the market environment, especially the size, growth and potential of the domestic market, attributed to the success in introducing and using the acquired technologies. In addition, the fast development of an industry could create large demand of items that firms in that industry produce. In many cases, as there are still relatively few local suppliers producing quality products, the market demand in general still exceeds supplies and thus forming a seller's market. This is distinctly observable in the "upstream" suppliers of accessories and components, such as the instruments and machine tools factories supporting the mainframe equipment and machinery manufacturers.

Duplication of Imported Technology

Many Chinese analysts expressed the opinion that the impact of technology transfer was severely limited largely due to excessive duplication of imported technology. Kang and Yang (1992) attributed this problem to the lack of coordination at the macro level while Hsiang (1991) criticized that the excessive capacity greatly affected the ability to further diffuse technology and localize production. Regarding it as a major difficulty, Schnepp, Von Glinow and Bhambri (1990) commented that the emergence of excessive capacity was due to poor quality control and product design. It appears therefore that excessive duplication of imported technology is a significant factor causing a high intensity of market competition.

Only a manager in all the firms we interviewed indicated that duplicate imports had been a problem to them. Since a similar production line had been acquired in Xi'an under the supervision of the same Ministry, he had a difficult time in getting the approval in acquiring the technology. Thus, through a survey, he first confirmed that a huge domestic demand could not be totally satisfied by the Xi'an factory. Then he focused the effort on enhancing quality and service and eventually gained a significant market share.

Other firms also indicated that before the acquisition they had conducted market studies to identify the needs of the customers, to assess the market potential, and to evaluate the suitability of the technologies. Duplication of imported technologies, on the one hand, might be a concern that the government might consider if the market competition created was beneficial to the growth and advancement of each individual firm and the industry as a whole. A manager mentioned that the market in China is so big that not any single factory would be able to satisfy all the needs and there are geographic limitations hindering effective distribution coverage by anyone firm alone. Under the market economy system, each enterprise would have to consider factors such as its own development needs, the geographic considerations, current and future market potentials and competitions, in order to determine its own technology acquisition direction.

Government Legislation and Support

On top of the other environmental factors, government legislative environment has been found to impact on success (Atuahene-Gima, 1993c; Yin, 1992). In the case of China, government involvement is imperative due particularly to the influence of the former planned economy.

Government Support

Chinese law specified that a government organization must be responsible for managing every business unit (Schnepp, Von Glinow and Bhambri, 1990). In their studies, the authors noted the following supports provided to a local subsidiary by the supervising corporation: (1) finding local sources of components; (2) meeting foreign exchange problems; and (3) getting tax exemption on imported components.

Literature indicates that the state should create an economic environment in traditional industrial sectors to provide incentives and capabilities for enterprises to launch technology innovation process (Wang, 1994).

Reducing tax to allow enterprises to finance activities relating technology innovations can achieve this. Government assistance in boosting both technological absorption and diffusion competence is a part of the national economic plan (Yin, 1992). To achieve this, the state provides the investment capital in particular foreign currency, the needed human resources (skilled workers and engineers) and coordination.

Almost all firms gave positive comments on the role of government in the acquisition process. Supports provided by the supervising government agents might differ depending on the timing, magnitude of the project, and background of the firms. The following is a list of supports provided:

- financial supports, including loans, foreign exchange availability, duty-free privilege;
- project negotiation, ranging from translation service, technical data collection, search for technologies and suppliers, to full contract negotiation service;
- the municipal government acted as the leader of the project and pulled together resources of all the supportive units to ensure that the plant be built according to plan; and
- the municipal government acted against the view of the ministerial authority and supported the acquisition project although it was considered as a "duplicate import."

In fact, many firms highlighted that government support is a major factor to the overall success of technology acquisition. The government has provided the right direction to help specific industries to meet market demand and to facilitate growth. For examples, a manager mentioned that the development of the local automobile industry facilitated the introduction of tools-making techniques. A hydraulic component factory remarked that the aggressive promotion of the excavator manufacturing industry also set a smooth path for the development of machine component units that in turn encouraged the advancement of indirectly related industries.

Supports from Other Local Firms

On the problems in Japan-China technology transfer, Yabuuchi (1986) pointed out that it is indispensable that a comprehensive plan involving the development of peripheral industries be worked out in order that the introduction of new technology could be successful, since some technology transfer requires that importation of necessary parts and raw materials in light of their absence in China. Likewise, Yokota (1987) noted that assimilation could not take place without greater Chinese efforts to develop the supportive network necessary to sustain advanced technology integration.

Many managers acquired foreign technologies with the intention to produce peripheral components to support the core industry promoted by the government. A firm in the sample wanted to raise the level of manufacturing technology for excavators. Because of the economic reforms, there was a huge demand for construction machines such as excavators. The old machines they had were mostly models of the 1950s and 1960s, which could not cope with the work requirements any more. To satisfy the local demands and to improve the manufacturing capability of the country, a comprehensive plan that included technologies for the essential elements such as diesel engines, pump motors and hydraulic components was developed. This eventually became a good example showing how peripheral industries were integrated to build up a local supportive network to achieve the ultimate objective of a developed and highly self-sufficient industry.

Localization

Relating to local supports, localization is another essential factor leading to the success of technology transfer (De Bruijn and Jia, 1993). The objectives of localization are multifold. The first objective is to replace as many imported components as possible and as soon as feasible. The second is to reduce the cost of investment to an acceptable level, while the last objective is to improve the country's international balance of payments by reducing the amount of foreign payments.

Localization would be achieved by technology recipients through various means such as licenzing. There are problems faced by both recipients and suppliers in localization. From the recipient's perspective, Chinese factories have to realize the localization in time before foreign firms phase out components of the products transferred. From the supplier's perspective, the concern for a high-tech producer is that the required inputs may not be available in China (Tsang, 1994). Even if they are available, local suppliers may not be able to deliver on time and the product quality may fail to meet the stringent standards demanded by high-tech production.

In many cases, the localization process is handled under the state's consolidated planning efforts. While firms took various approaches and achieved different levels of success in their localization efforts, many move forward with a great deal of caution. They made use of local materials only when quality standards did not suffer. A manager commented that it is necessary for his firm to focus on quality to maintain their competitive edge. Thus, he would not blindly localize production just for lowering cost and at the expense of quality. Another manager from the instruments factory mentioned that their products are all used by customers engaging in a sensitive production control process, so he needed to make sure that his customers had full confidence in their products. Furthermore, he trusted that customers would prefer to pay a higher price for a more reliable piece of instrument. Hence, quality is an important determinant to the success of technology transfer.

Conclusion

This chapter has suggested several critical success factors for the acquisition of technology. These include timing and magnitude of a firm's involvement in the acquisition process, correct assessment of the market potential, matching technology with real needs, mutual trust and intensive interactions between the firm and the technology supplier. Depending on the nature of the transfer and the status of the firm, the role played by the supervising government organization varied. A comprehensive development plan set by the government targeted at a specific industry appears to be essential for forecasting the market potential and growth, and for enlarging the supportive network to sustain advancement of the overall technology-base.

At a pure pragmatic level, findings of this study have some important implications for various stakeholders involved in the acquisition process. From the technology recipient's perspective, firms with the following characteristics may tend to be more successful in the transfer of imported technologies:

- to have strong management leadership and persistency throughout the whole process, set very specific objectives and criteria to monitor and evaluate the performance of the project;
- conduct a detailed market survey to assess the needs of the customers and the market potential;

- build strong relationship and connection with the relevant government organization and be given a chance to participate very early in the preparation phase of the project;
- direct involvement in search and selection of technology and supplier;
- match technology with real needs of the firm and the market;
- adopt a realistic approach and implement the acquisition process in successive phases that match with the growth and development of the firm;
- take cautious steps in the localization process as quality is most important in the long run;
- provide adequate training to the staff to enhance their capability to absorb the skills and techniques to operate the new technologies acquired;
- maintain close contacts and interactions with the technology supplier to keep themselves up-to-date on technological development in the field;
- to have sufficient funds available to support the needs of the entire project to carry the firm over to the final implementation of the technology acquired.

From the perspective of the technology supplier, successful transfer of technologies may require the foreign firm to:

- demonstrate strong cooperation and willingness to help the staff of the technology recipient at all levels to ensure smooth transfer;
- maintain close contacts and interactions with the technology recipient to keep them up-to-date on technological development in the field; this may lead to development of further cooperation opportunities in the long run;
- provide structured and well-planned training programmes to the staff of the technology recipient;
- realize the importance of off-site consultation, and provide adequate support along this line;
- provide adequate support to the recipient firm in their localization efforts.

In the host country, the government plays a very important role in the technology transfer process through several activities. In the first place, it has to create a market environment and set clear directions for the firms to participate. Secondly, it should adopt a comprehensive industry development planning orientation to integrate local and foreign technologies so as to enlarge the overall technology base. Thirdly, financial and technical supports should be provided to facilitate the absorption and implementation of the technologies acquired. Fourthly, a supportive network should be created whereby firms acquiring foreign technologies can obtain the needed local resources and materials to match the needs of the new technologies.

Note

1. This study was an empirical investigation into the factors that affect the success and failure of firms in China in using technology acquired through/ from foreign unaffiliated firms. We confined the scope of this study to technologies acquired through licensing. However, after an in-depth investigation it became apparent that we need to widen the scope of the investigation to cover other different modes by which technologies are being transferred to China. Assistance from the Hong Kong branch of Xinhua News Agency and the cooperation of the Municipal Economic Commissions of Shanghai and Beijing made it possible for us to conduct a reasonably sized survey.

   One limitation of our study is that firms that experienced extreme difficulties or failure in their technology acquisition tended not to entertain survey or interview of this nature. Thus, our findings are primarily based on input from firms that are successful in their acquisition process.

Appendix I
Mode of Technology Import Contracts of China: 1986–1995 (Number of Contract)

		1995	1994	1993	1992	1991	1990	1989	1988	1987	1986
No. of Contract	Licensing	677	169	200	166	116	101	96	169		
	Consultancy	15	22	12	18	8	9	14	27		
	Technical Service	22	14	17	18	10	5	13	19		
	Co-production	2	5	12	11	8	12	11	10		
	Complete Plant	1,355	195	194	166	86	71	194	138		
	Essential Equipment	1,558	38	53	116	131	34		70		
	Others		1	5	9	0	0	0	4		
	Total	3,629	444	493	504	359	232	328	437	581	744
Change over prior year (%)	Licensing	>200%	−15.5%	20.5%	43.1%	14.9%	5.2%	−43.2%			
	Consultancy	−31.8%	83.3%	−33.3%	125.0%	−11.1%	−35.7%	−48.1%			
	Technical Service	57.1%	−17.6%	−5.6%	80.0%	100.0%	−61.5%	−31.6%			
	Co-production	−60.0%	−58.3%	9.1%	37.5%	−33.3%	9.1%	10.0%			
	Complete Plant	>200%	0.5%	16.9%	93.0%	21.1%	−45.9%	−6.7%			
	Essential Equipment	>200%	−28.3%	−54.3%	−11.5%	>200%					
	Others	−100.0%	−80.0%	−44.4%							
	Total	>200%	−9.9%	−2.2%	40.4%	54.7%	−29.3%	−24.9%	−24.8%	−21.9%	18.9%
% of total number	Licensing	18.7%	38.1%	40.6%	32.9%	32.3%	43.5%	29.3%	38.7%		
	Consultancy	0.4%	5.0%	2.4%	3.6%	2.2%	3.9%	4.3%	6.2%		
	Technical Service	0.6%	3.2%	3.4%	3.6%	2.8%	2.2%	4.0%	4.3%		
	Co-production	0.1%	1.1%	2.4%	2.2%	2.2%	5.2%	3.4%	2.3%		
	Complete Plant	37.3%	43.9%	39.4%	32.9%	24.0%	30.6%	59.1%	31.6%		
	Essential Equipment	42.9%	8.6%	10.8%	23.0%	36.5%	14.7%	0.0%	16.0%		
	Others	0.0%	0.2%	1.0%	1.8%	0.0%	0.0%	0.0%	0.9%		
	Total	100.0%	100.0%	100.0%	100.0%	100.0%	100.0%	100.0%	100.0%	100.0%	100.0%

Source: *Almanac of China's Foreign Economic Relations and Trade*, 1987–1996/97.

Appendix II

Mode of Technology Import Contracts of China: 1986–1995 (Contract Value in US$ million)

		1995	1994	1993	1992	1991	1990	1989	1988	1987	1986
Contract Value (US$ million)	Licensing	1,474	390	448	604	478	227	148	477		
	Consultancy	112	22	17	31	4	5	6	14		
	Technical Service	199	66	19	118	13	3	38	28		
	Co-production	1	3	186	1,108	53	538	7	10		
	Complete Plant	9,089	3,519	5,112	4,308	2,570	395	2,724	2,865		
	Essential Equipment	2,159	106	262	393	341	106	0	154		
	Others			5	29	0	0	0	1		
	Total	13,033	4,106	6,049	6,591	3,459	1,274	2,923	3,549	2,980	4,460
Change over prior year (%)	Licensing	>200%	−12.9%	−25.8%	26.4%	110.6%	53.4%	−69.0%			
	Consultancy	>200%	29.4%	−45.2%	>200%	−20.0%	−16.7%	−57.1%			
	Technical Service	>200%	>200%	−83.9%	>200%	>200%	−92.1%	35.7%			
	Co-production	−80.0%	−98.4%	−83.2%	>200%	−90.1%	>200%	−30.0%			
	Complete Plant	158.3%	−31.2%	18.7%	67.6%	>200%	−81.6%	−9.8%			
	Essential Equipment	>200%	−59.5%	−33.3%	15.2%	>200%					
	Others	>200%	−100.0%	−82.8%							
	Total	>200%	−32.1%	−8.2%	90.5%	171.5%	−56.4%	−17.6%	19.1%	−33.2%	50.7%
% of total value	Licensing	11.3%	9.5%	7.4%	9.2%	13.8%	17.8%	5.1%	13.4%		
	Consultancy	0.9%	0.5%	0.3%	0.5%	0.1%	0.4%	0.2%	0.4%		
	Technical Service	1.5%	1.6%	0.3%	1.8%	0.4%	0.2%	1.3%	0.8%		
	Co-production	0.0%	0.1%	3.1%	16.8%	1.5%	42.2%	0.2%	0.3%		
	Complete Plant	69.7%	85.7%	84.5%	65.4%	74.3%	31.0%	93.2%	80.7%		
	Essential Equipment	16.6%	2.6%	4.3%	6.0%	9.9%	8.3%	0.0%	4.3%		
	Others	0.0%	0.0%	0.1%	0.4%	0.0%	0.0%	0.0%	0.0%		
	Total	100.0%	100.0%	100.0%	100.0%	100.0%	100.0%	100.0%	100.0%	100.0%	100.0%

Source: *Almanac of China's Foreign Economic Relations and Trade, 1987–1996/97.*

Appendix III
Profile of Firms Interviewed

Company	Location	Industry	Major Products	Method of Technology Acquisition
1.	Beijing	Electronics	TV camera, recorders	Licensing
2.	Beijing	Electronics	Television	Outright Purchase
3.	Beijing	Machinery	Industrial process control instruments	Licensing
4.	Beijing	Machinery	Pressure gauges and special gauges	Outright Purchase
5.	Beijing	Light Industry	Measuring and cutting tools	Outright Purchase
6.	Beijing	Light Industry	Leather goods	Outright Purchase
7.	Beijing	Machinery	Reducers	Licensing
8.	Beijing	Machinery	Fuel injection pumps and nozzles	Licensing
9.	Beijing	Metallurgy	Powder metallurgy materials	Licensing
10.	Foshan	Textile	Polyester chips and fibre	Outright Purchase
11.	Guangzhou	Beverage	Beer	Outright Purchase
12.	Shanghai	Electronics	Integrate circuits	Joint Venture
13.	Shanghai	Light Industry	Photo copier	Joint Venture
14.	Shanghai	Light Industry	TV glass picture tube bulbs	Outright Purchase
15.	Shanghai	Light Industry	Refrigerators, air-conditioners	Outright Purchase
16.	Shanghai	Machinery	Elevators and escalators	Joint Venture
17.	Shanghai	Machinery	Grinding machines, precision instruments	Licensing
18.	Shanghai	Machinery	Turbine generators	Outright Purchase
19.	Shanghai	Medical	Pharmaceutical products	Outright Purchase
20.	Shanghai	Medical	Pharmaceutical products	Outright Purchase
21.	Shenzhen	Electronics	Industrial testing service	Joint Venture
22.	Shenzhen	Light Industry	Glass products	Licensing
23.	Shenzhen	Machinery	Silicon steel plates	Cooperative Venture

19

Entry Strategies of Multinational Companies in China's Pharma Market: A Case in Competitive Positioning*

Gert Bruche

Introduction

Over the last two decades modern competitive analysis has developed a set of propositions and frameworks which can be applied to real world situations in order to better understand the evolution of industries and markets, the basis of competitive advantage and the relationship between the former and company performance (see for example Oster, 1990; Porter, 1980, 1985, 1991; Ghemawat, 1991; D'Aveni, 1994). In this chapter I attempt to apply some of the concepts of competitive analysis to the "case" of the entry strategies of multinational pharmaceutical companies (MPCs) in China during the period 1980–1996/2000. It is hoped that the analysis can serve a dual function: It may help to enrich some of the conceptual frameworks with practical examples and thus prove their utility in analyzing real world situations; it should "inform practice" in providing managers and industry experts interested in China with a basis for reflecting their entry strategies and the factors and circumstances that may have led or will lead to the acquisition of strategic market positions.

The following questions will be guiding the analysis:

---

* An earlier version of this chapter appeared in Antonio and Steele, 1996.

1. Why have MPCs entered China, what are the underlying "entry drivers"?
2. Which were the different "modes of entry," how did they change over time and which competitive implications did they have?
3. Which implications did the timing of entry have on competitive position?
4. Which other factors facilitated (or will facilitate) success in the Chinese pharma market and helped incumbents to maintain once acquired competitive positions?

In trying to research the entry process into a particular industry or country market, one has to address the question whether to rely on a "snapshot" in time by using a cross-sectional perspective and collect as much as possible "hard" statistical data or whether to go for a historical analysis which implies necessarily a "softer" approach. Tellis and Golder have argued in their recent study of market pioneering that "cross-sectional databases cannot provide the same perspective, because a matrix of numbers loses the richness of history while introducing potentially serious biases" (Tellis and Golder, 1996, p. 67). In addition, it can be argued that the research of a particular industry or market in China must cope with an extremely "ambiguous" environment which results from the emergent and often transitory nature of China's institutions as well as with a notorious lack of reliable data in almost all areas. For the mentioned reasons this chapter relies on a historical perspective and a number of "soft" sources: the long-time personal work experience of the author in China,[1] a large number of newspaper and trade journal articles (of which only a small part is quoted in this chapter), a number of industry reports (like for example Yu and Chen, 1996) and seminar contributions and numerous talks with managers and staff of pharma companies. A certain "ambiguity" in the findings and conclusions is partly due to the ambiguous and volatile environment, and partly due to the way in which the information and data were collected.

Industry Drivers of China Market Entry

"Billion-Consumer Dream Tempts the Pharma Giants,"[2] "Western Drug Companies Rushing into China,"[3] "China's Pharmaceutical Output Ranking the World's Second"[4] — these are some examples for headlines of press articles in 1994, which comment on an unprecedented wave of direct investment by MPCs in China. After a first period of gradual engagement of a limited number of MPCs (lasting from about 1980 until 1990) the years 1991/1992 brought a decisive turnaround. A large number of new joint venture projects have been set on track, were contracted or completed in only five years (1991–1995); a number of new exporters of drugs have entered the China market at the same time.[5] By the time of writing this chapter, it can now be said that in a second period starting around 1991/1992 the multinational pharmaceutical industry will have by and large completed its entry into China. It will take until 2000 that all planned ventures to become operational and the full impact of the entry will be played out in the market. For an overview of major MPCs that have entered the market, see Appendix.

The obvious first question to ask is: Why did MPCs enter the Chinese pharma market at all? And what are the major drivers of the massive entry process between 1992 and 1994/95? Apart from many special, "idiosyncratic" reasons which may eventually lead to the entry "decision" (which is often more a series of gradual, small decision rather than one big one), four major drivers can be identified: cost (particularly R&D cost), maturing of the key pharmaceutical markets, a (temporary?) bright outlook for China's market potential, and a kind of "herd instinct" or "me-too" or "missing the train" syndrome. Cost and market maturing could be classified as "push" factors, market attraction and "herd instinct" as "pull" factors.

The multinational pharmaceutical industry[6] is a research-based industry which markets "scienceware products."[7] Since the thalidomide disaster in the 1960s, regulatory requirements for the approval of new drugs have become more and more demanding and restrictive all over the world. As a result, the average development time for new drugs has increased to some 12 years, which in turn has greatly raised the cost of R&D — to some US\$194 million per new drug, taking into account failures and risk-adjusted cost of capital (US Congress 1993, 328; see also the much higher figure in James, 1994, p. 17)). Since patent protection periods in the U.S., Europe and Japan have stayed more or less unchanged; the effective (high revenue) market life of innovative drugs has shortened to some 6 to 10 years. An increasingly intense global competition has further eroded the "strategic window" (Abell, 1978) of premium revenues for innovative drugs. For all these reasons, MPCs are under an ever-increasing pressure to seek global market presence in order to spread the R&D cost over as many markets as possible.

Although there is pressure for global market exploitation, MPCs do not go randomly for all national markets, but prioritize and sequence their market entry (or market penetration) activities. Assuming that resources are limited and that MPCs consider expected returns (sales potential vs. expected marketing cost) there will be a "macro entry order across markets" (Mascarenhas, 1992). MPCs will strive to first introduce their products to the large pharma markets of the developed world; the pharma markets in developing countries will tend to be neglected and substantial entry commitments will often be considered not justified in view of the limited market potential, the uncertainties and the difficult operating conditions. Starting from the mid to end 1980s the pharma markets in the advanced Western countries (and recently also the Japanese pharmaceutical market) have come under increasing pressure from various fronts: health regulators, insurance providers, generic imitators, big institutional buyers, and pharma wholesalers; and the United States saw the emergence of a new system of "Managed Care," which is predicted to substantially erode industry profits by the end of the 1990s (James, 1994; McGahan, 1994). Market growth rates of between 10–15% in the 1970s and the early 1980s have came down to 4–5% or to temporary market stagnation in some countries.[8] Under increasing pressure to look for growth opportunities elsewhere, MPCs have started to screen the "Rest of the World (ROW)" more actively in order to identify future growth opportunities in the "emerging pharma markets" of developing countries.

Among the developing countries in the ROW China got an increasing attention for a number of reasons, some of which are given as follows:

- China has a potentially very large market in terms of population;
- an upsurge in pharmaceutical imports from 1992 onwards;
- the emergence of stories about sales success of certain pioneering joint ventures;
- China further moves towards a capitalist free market system.

The argument that China must be a large (pharma-) market because of the sheer size of its population is a myth that does not hold up in reality. Nevertheless, it stimulates fantasies of pharma managers along lines as the following: "if we sell only one pack for 14 RMB to 1 % of the people in China, it amounts to 20 million US dollar!" Although sales projections are normally not done in such a simple way, there is clearly a temptation to base sales scenarios and projections for China on large numbers of patients while "forgetting" or de-emphasizing the restricting conditions like limited purchasing power, restricted hospital budgets, limited distribution capacities, limited access of patients to treatment, and limited health and quality consciousness.

The most important stimulant of a positive market entry decision was probably the large jump in pharmaceutical imports between 1991 and 1992, the publication of optimistic pharma market projections by several consulting companies in 1993, and a number of very upbeat comments of managers and experts on the market.[9] At around the same time some of the larger pharma ventures achieved for the first time substantial sales, a fact that was passed around through reports in the industry's special newsletters or through word of mouth (particularly Xi'an Janssen, Bristol-Myers Squibb, Shanghai and SmithKline Beecham, Tianjin). As these events increased the perceived attractiveness of the China market in the head-quarters of MPCs and their respective regional organizations, the many reports on delegation visits, market survey activities and ongoing negotiations of a number of MPCs triggered another reason for a China engagement: "If they are there we must also be there." Finally, after Deng's "tour to the south" in early 1992 the Western media and public opinion settled on the assumption that China's opening to the outside world cannot be turned back anymore; therefore the (political) risk of an investment in China was now perceived much lower than in the 1980s and during the difficult post-Tian'anmen period.[10]

Although the market entry of MPCs is clearly driven by the intent to establish a strategic market position to sell into China, Chinese officials have occasionally proposed other reasons for an engagement of MPCs in China. They have tended to praise China as a location for drug production because of its cheap labour costs and preferential conditions ; as a source for leads in the drug discovery process (based on herbal medicine); or as a location for cheap and/or faster drug development. Generally these propositions exaggerate the importance or value of China as a "factor market" for the multinational pharmaceutical industry. As mentioned before, the pharmaceutical business is a "scienceware industry" which is dependent on a high-tech, information-rich and "proprietary" environment for conducting R&D as well as for the production of the more sophisticated drug substances; and as drug substance production is usually capital intensive, strategies based on (substance) cost advantages are rare. All these conditions do not support the proposition that the entry of MPCs into China was to any relevant extent related to factor market conditions.

The Evolution of the Modes of Entry

After the review of the "why" of market entry we now turn to the "how" of the entry process: the "mode" of entry. Before we discuss the modes of entry used by MPCs in China, it is useful to make a general distinction between a "sales entry approach" and a "strategic entry approach" (Root, 1994, chapter 2). The former aims at a short-term exploitation of market opportunities without much control over marketing, and the latter is geared towards the build-up of a long-term market position including the acquisition of first hand market intelligence, direct customer access, and control over marketing. The multinational pharmaceutical industry enters the China market with the aim to build permanent long-term market position, i.e., it uses the "strategic entry approach." There are, however, also examples for a "sales entry approach." The leading export product in 1995, the "brain enhancer" Cerebrolysin with sales of more than US$35 million CIF, was exported by EBEWE, a 75%-subsidiary of BASF via trade agents without visible activities to secure this business in the longer term; moreover, many of the smaller Hong Kong or Taiwanese export or repackaging ventures in China's pharma market take a more short-term sales approach as well. Nevertheless, in the following discussion we consider only the prevailing approach which aims at establishing a permanent, strong market position.

International market entry modes are conventionally described as a sequence of modes with increasing degrees of (capital) risks and (management) control: from indirect exporting, via direct exporting, various contractual arrangements (e.g., licensing for partly or fully local production) to production under part (JV) or full ownership of the market entrant (Root, 1994; Jeannet and Hennesey, 1995). Taking the two dimensions (risk and control) into consideration the principal modes of the entry process of the multinational pharmaceutical industry into China is shown in Figure 1.

In the early stage of the first entry period (1982 to about 1987), two major modes of entry can be distinguished: mode 1, the export of finished drugs via a Hong Kong-based sales and marketing subsidiary (export-led entry); mode 2, the "skipping" of the export stage by directly entering into (equity) joint venture agreements for the local production (i.e.,

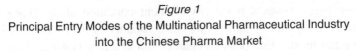

Figure 1
Principal Entry Modes of the Multinational Pharmaceutical Industry
into the Chinese Pharma Market

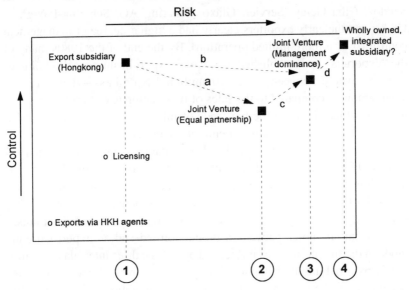

pharmaceutical formulation of imported active ingredients) of some of the MPC's drugs (production-led entry). Both entry modes correspond to the concept of a "strategic entry" mentioned above in that they imply a high degree of control over operations, allow for direct customer access and for the building up of a base for the collection of market information. Other entry modes like for instance the use of Hong Kong trade agents without its own subsidiary presence can also be observed, but they have usually been used for a "sales entry approach" and consequently did not lead to the establishment of strategic positions.

A production-led entry (mode 2) was chosen by a few companies only. Among them are Otsuka from Japan, some pharma companies from the Nordic countries (Kabivitrum, Astra, Leo), Bristol-Myers Squibb and SmithKline from the U.S. and Janssen (Belgium, subsidiary of Johnson & Johnson, USA). One characteristic of these early joint ventures is that they were concluded under the clear guiding principle of "equal partnership" which usually meant that the foreign and the Chinese parties shared management rights. (Whether the foreign partner liked this or not is not relevant here, it was a basic environment condition at the time). The export-led entry mode (mode 1) was taken mainly by the Swiss MPCs and some other mostly European companies (for instance Hoffman la Roche, Sandoz, Ciba Geigy, Servier, Glaxo, Schering AG, Schering-Plough — USA); and the early exporters clearly had a higher degree of management control (over a more limited operation). By the end of the 1980s many of the "exporters" had established a "sizable" export business (sales volumes were anywhere between 2 and 10 million US dollars — these are still small amounts compared to the sales of these companies in major country markets which figure in the hundreds of millions or even billions of US dollars). Three of the export-led entrants (Ciba Geigy, Glaxo and Pfizer) went from the export stage into local formulation ventures between 1987 and 1990 (which is reflected in Figure 1: route a). Since during this time the prevailing concept and the approval practice of the Chinese government was still oriented towards partnership and joint management control, they concluded the same type of ventures as the early production-led entrants.

The initial choice between a production-led and an export-led entry mode in the first period was influenced by at least three interrelated factors: the firms' "risk taking behaviour," their management structure, and their perception of the (China) market. The China operations of exporters like Roche, Sandoz, Glaxo, Schering AG and Schering-Plough were Hong Kong and mostly under the decentralized control of their Hong Kong general managers or the regional directors in charge of Asia. They had first hand experience with an extremely risky operating environment and had a rather sober view of the (uncertain) market potential which needed to be developed step by step. Moreover, they often employed Hong Kong Chinese managers who by and large were looking for short- or medium-term sales results rather than being concerned with strategic position. The "middle management perspective" together with the other factors favoured a concentration on exports and the (bottom-up) build-up of demand through marketing and sales forces; it implied a "de-prioritization" of the production task.

The few companies which went directly for a production-led entry (which implied a higher risk exposure in terms of capital investment) were driven by a different perspective. Top management tended to be actively involved which implied a different attitude towards risk taking and market information. For a CEO to support a comparatively "small" but high risk investment like a joint venture in China is definitely less of a personal career risk than for a middle manager who is in charge of a region or even of only one country. China was seen as a potentially very large, politically controlled market with serious supply shortages (of higher quality drugs). It was assumed that if one only provided locally formulated high quality drugs, selling was more of a "logistical" task — and even if there were problems and risks involved, the potential size of China's market was worth the risk of the comparatively small investment needed to establish a local formulation factory. An example for the "early visionary type" of CEO-driven JVs is the story of Johnson & Johnsons' JV by its subsidiary Janssen, which was established under the leadership and personal tutelage of Dr. Paul Janssen, the founder and CEO of the Belgium company (Ball, 1996).

The two primary entry modes implied at least initially a very different focus of attention of the respective companies. The early joint ventures were often struggling with their partners and busy to get their (production) operations going at all; the exporters focused their efforts on the gradual build-up of sales (which required above all the putting in place of suitable hospital sales promotion teams). The heavy "entrance fee" which the joint venture pioneers had to pay for their decision to choose a production-led entry mode in a highly uncertain market environment shall be illustrated below by the case of the Sino-Swed Pharmaceutical Corporation (SSPC) JV in Wuxi; admittedly this case belongs to the category of the more extreme ones.

As early as 1981/1982 a consortium of Swedish and Danish pharma companies (Astra, Kabivitrum, Pharmacia, Ferrosan, Leo supported by Swedfund, the Swedish development assistance organization) went into negotiations with China's State Pharmaceutical Administration (SPAC) which runs most of the pharma factories as well as the (top level of the) distribution network. A joint venture contract was signed in September 1982 with the foreign and the Chinese side each taking up 50% of the equity. The pharmaceutical formulation factory under the name of SSPC was to be established in Wuxi (a secondary pharmaceutical market at that time, but only a few hours train ride from the major pharmaceutical centre of Shanghai). It took a full five years (!) and enormous (not planned for) extra cost (the details of which will remain unknown) until the factory could start production in September 1987. The foreign companies had already paid a hefty "fine" for this early production-led entry, but the story does not end here.

The Swedish partners in the JV had somehow assumed that once the factory turns out goods it would just deliver them to the five class I wholesale drug distribution stations in China, which were after all under the umbrella of its JV partner organization (SPAC).[11] Marketing (in the sense of demand creation) was largely considered as unnecessary. This "production view" quickly turned out to be an outdated (if ever adequate) perspective. As a result of decentralizing reforms, China's local distribution stations (class II and III stations) had become more independent from their wholesaling superiors (class I stations); moreover, hospitals could be less and less simply forced to buy what was offered to them. Although class I stations bought SSPC's entire production in the years 1988 and 1989, they were soon building up stocks and were unable to sell them through the system. Finally they requested the return of goods to SSPC to get back their money. In the end a massive destruction of goods which had run out of shelf live had to take place (in Shanghai alone goods for RMB 1 million had to be burned towards the end of 1989).

As a reaction to the behaviour of the Chinese government during the Tian'anmen Incident, the Swedish president and the five other foreign staff of SSPC left China in late summer 1989, leaving the JV entirely to Chinese control. Initial attempts of the Nordic side to liquidate the JV were given up and eventually the Chinese side took full management control of the JV. Under Chinese management the JV changed its course from 1990 onwards. Some 12 branch offices throughout the country were established, more than 100 sales staff were recruited, a large number of commercial distribution partners (class II stations) were contracted and an aggressive incentive scheme was started. This massive switch to a "marketing orientation" (ironically implemented by Chinese managers normally said to be not market oriented) led to a massive expansion of sales from some 23 million RMB in 1989 to 278 million RMB in 1993. Swedish experts came back in 1993, but to date the Swedish side has not managed to get back the degree of control of the JV, which they had had before 1989. In 1994 Astra started to pull out of the JV and built its own separate unit.

Around 1986 the early "exporters" like Roche or Glaxo began to realize that the Chinese pharma market was gradually turning from a mainly centrally-managed and supply-driven system to a more and more demand-driven market in which hospitals choose which drugs to buy and which not. The pure sales-driven approach of dealing with distributors and "pushing" goods into hospitals (a large share of which would be contracted at the annual Guangzhou fair) had therefore to be complemented by the creation of "pull" at the hospital level. This required the build-up of local hospital promotion teams which was first done in a rather experimental phase around the years 1987–1990. The "exporters" maintained their head offices in Hong Kong and the sales forces were run from Hong Kong with the help of Hong Kong or other overseas Chinese. For lack of a suitable institutional structure (pure promotion JVs were/are legally not possible, liaison offices were/are not entitled to do direct sales promotion) many of these teams were operated in various "semi-legal" or at least unconventional ways.

Whilst three of the early "exporters" had already decided towards the end of the 1980s to secure their export businesses through the establishment of a formulation joint venture (Ciba Geigy, Glaxo, Pfizer), starting in 1991/1992 after the end of the post-Tian'anmen recession most of the remaining companies of the group of export-led entrants completed their entry process through contracting JVs (see Figure 1, route b). The differences in the new joint venture contracts in the second period were subtle, but nevertheless important. Due to the Tian'anmen Incident and the accompanying recession, the amount of newly contracted foreign direct investment had decreased significantly in 1989 and 1990 — generally and also in the pharma sector. This led to a (temporary) increase in the bargaining power of MPCs vis-à-vis their potential joint venture partners and the Chinese approval authorities. Having learnt from the mistakes, problems and suffering of the early joint ventures as well as using the changed power balance, the new joint venture contracts usually provided for higher equity shares for the foreign partners and a clear assignment of management rights to the foreign party. In some cases the requirement of management rights was a criterion for the partner choice, i.e., MPCs would not be prepared to contract with partners who demanded equal equity shares. Some companies, like for instance Schering AG from Germany, concluded joint venture contracts with partners from outside the pharmaceutical industry which were essentially looking for "portfolio investments" only with neither interest nor capability to manage the JV.

At around the same time a "second entry wave" was building up, initiated by many MPCs which so far had conducted only small scale export activities or which had not been engaged in China at all. They now "rushed" to China to secure a position in the market (see Figure 1, entry path 3). Most of them tried to initiate or increase their export activities whilst at the same time negotiating joint ventures. Exporting was seen by those companies as a short-term interim measure while the real entry would be achieved through the formulation joint venture, i.e., exports were just a stop-gap measure (or exploitation of an opportunity or a kind of "test-marketing"), not a strategic entry as such. The JVs concluded by new entrants between 1991 and 1996 reflect the above-mentioned trend towards foreign manage- ment control (see also Appendix). Meanwhile, many of the earlier JVs also raised the foreign equity share usually at the occasion of needed capital increases, e.g., Bristol-Myers Squibb from originally 50 to 58 per cent, Ciba Geigy from originally 50 to 60 per cent, Glaxo, Chongqing from 50 to 90 per cent (see Figure 1: route 2c).

With the Chinese pharma market becoming more transparent and with more (expatriate and local) managerial expertise and experience available, which can be tapped by new entrants, the rationale for MPCs to use (mainland) Chinese (industry) partners when entering the market becomes less and less compelling. Therefore, new MPCs, which wish to enter the Chinese pharma market, would probably opt today for full management control in the form of a Wholly-Owned Foreign Enterprise (WOFE) if this was possible and feasible (see Figure 1; entry path 4). A number of MPCs that already have JVs would theoretically like to switch to this form as well (see Figure 1, route d). However, the prevailing restrictions on WOFE (high reexport commitment, high technology transfer component) will limit this option to a few exceptional cases (Astra, Farmitalia in Wuxi) as long as the existing regulations are not changed. In view of the attempts by the Chinese government to tighten the approval and control of foreign ventures (*CBM Research*, 1996) such an option seems to be not possible at least in the second period of the entry process up to about the year 2000.

Are There Time-Based Competitive Advantages?

In order to discuss the order of "entry" into the Chinese pharmaceutical market we have to define what constitutes a successful entry. For the purpose of this analysis, a market entry shall be defined as the achievement of a substantial market/sales presence regardless of whether these sales are sourced from a local manufacturing venture or are in the form of finished goods exports. "Substantial" shall mean here a total sales of at least 1–2 million US dollar per annun in the 1980s and of greater than 3 million US dollar after 1992; it also means that sales not be one time hits or spot sales, but should be "embedded" in a longer term market presence. Based on these definitions, the following list of entrants has been compiled (based on Appendix and material from unpublished sources).

First Period 1982–1990: The Early Movers (15 companies). a) Subgroup of pioneers: Otsuka (Japan), BMS (USA), SmithKline (US-UK), SSPC (Astra, Kabivitrum, Pharmacia, Ferrosan, Leo — counted as two in terms of the surviving companies Astra and Kabiparmacia), Janssen (Belgium resp. J&J, USA), Pfizer (USA). b) Other early movers: Glaxo (UK), Merck, Sharp & Dohme, Roche (Switzerland), Ciba-Geigy (Switzerland), Sandoz (Switzerland), Servier (France), Schering AG (Germany), Schering-Plough (US), Takeda (Japan). The dividing line between "pioneers" and "other early movers" is somewhat arbitrary.

Second Period 1991–1996/2000: The Followers (31 companies). These companies have completed their entry process already or will complete it by the year 2000 at the latest. Many of the companies that have been categorized as followers started limited sales activities in China, made investment decisions or concluded JV contracts already before 1991. Their annual sales amounts (based on a multiyear perspective) are estimated, however, to have been until this time below the threshold mentioned above or occasionally higher sales fell again below the threshold so that in this sense they had not yet completed the entry process in the first period.

Potential Advantages of Early Movers

Early mover advantages in the sense of time-based competitive advantages can arise from many sources. A review of the potential sources (Lieberman/ Montgomery, 1991, 1988) and its application to the case of the entry process of the multinational pharmaceutical industry into the Chinese pharma market clearly yields among many not so important ones five aspects which constitute very relevant sources of advantage:

- the preemption of "space" in the perception of prospective buyers;
- the preemption of positions in China's drug distribution system;
- the acquisition of government approvals which are not available to followers or late movers any more;
- learning-based advantages (in cost or operating effectiveness); and
- availability of asset leverage.

The phenomenon that market pioneers or early entrants are able to acquire (scarce) space or positioning in the perception of prospective buyers has been shown in the history of many of the world's leading brands (Wuster, 1987). The early movers' messages stand alone and are noticeable, whilst those of later entrants tend to crowd each other out. Moreover, the early movers are usually able to define the position not only of the product but of the whole product category in the prospective buyers' mind.[12] In China, being a "tabula rasa" for Western branded drugs in the 1980s has been a very important, if not the most important, early mover advantage. Early movers could also use the very cheap rates for television advertising reach audiences in the order of 400 million viewers. In the late 1980s and the beginning 1990s, more than 60% of TV-advertising in China was devoted to pharmaceuticals. Company names like Bristol-Myers Squibb, Xi'an-Janssen and SmithKline Beecham have become "household names" for Chinese doctors and also for the broad public. Contac, a cough remedy sold by SKB was established as one of the first major Western medicine brands with Chinese consumers through extensive TV-advertising. Xi'an-Janssen established the anti-histamin Hismanal in the same way in the minds not only of doctors, but also of the broad public. In some instances, even such special drugs as anti-epileptics were advertised to a broad TV audience. Moreover, senior experts and doctors were willing to spend time on clinical trials, in reviewing of and publishing on early movers drugs even if they were often rather old and well-known drugs in the West.

Starting in 1992/1993 television advertising rates rose substantially, and advertising slots tended to become much shorter and any new advertisements had to cope with the increasing "noise levels." In February 1995 an Advertising Law (Riley, 1995) with very restrictive conditions for pharmaceuticals was enacted, thus effectively ending the period of liberal direct-to-consumer advertising which was so well used by a number of the early movers and excluding a repeat of a similar approach by the followers.

China's drug distribution system, another scarce resource for market entrants, has evolved from an essentially three-tiered nationwide government controlled system into a fragmented structure in which a large number of local or regional companies which are still owned by government units, but act rather independently and compete among each other at local or regional level (see Chen, 1993; Shum, 1994; Zwisler, 1995). Early movers have built up relationships with most of the stronger distributors and represent already a large share of their sales. Even if these relationships are not formally "exclusive" for certain product categories, the strong relationships and economic leverage of established suppliers (e.g., in the form of a threat of changing the distributor) form a barrier for later entrants or leave only the less efficient distributors to them. Moreover, there may be considerable switching cost for the distributor.

Another scarce resource is the myriad of government approvals for operating in the Chinese pharma market. Early movers obtained drug registration for imported as well as locally manufactured drugs in an environment which was still less regulated and crowded; although the relevant "Drug Administration Law" was already enacted in 1985, the implementing regulations followed much later.[13] With respect to the approval of registration for imported drugs, procedures have clearly become more elaborate since 1990/1991 and rejection rates have kept rising.[14] Approvals for JVs have actually been liberalized (which for some time gave followers entering between 1991–1994 some advantage), but it is now very likely that late followers will have to face more stringent demands, for instance, concerning the reexport requirement or the technology transfer content in JV contracts (*CBM Research*, 1996). Another scarce resource could be suitable partners for JVs, especially in the more developed coastal areas of China or approval of JVs in the more favourite locations like Beijing or Shanghai which are already "crowded" with pharma JVs and where the authorities may not be so interested as in earlier years when every foreign investment was very much welcome.

Organizing operations (countrywide management, production, sales forces, information systems, distributor relations etc.) in a country the size of China which lacks institutional structures, has a hypertroph bureaucracy and no real "models" of how to do things is a major learning process with unavoidable (costly) trials and errors. Early movers like Xi'an-Janssen or Bristol-Myers Squibb, Shanghai have worked their way through this "maze" and accumulated organizational know-how which is "stored" in structures and behaviour influencing rules as well as "embodied" in their key personnel. As long as this organizational experience can be kept proprietary and the organizations keep adapting to environment changes (this argument will be elaborated), it constitutes an early mover advantage over competitors entering the market later. Related to the above-mentioned aspect is the well-known concept of the learning curve. An early entrant into China's pharma market may be able to maintain an efficiency advantage over later rivals: the efficient handling of a countrywide distribution system involves significant learning effects; the management of large sales forces is also open to significant cost efficiencies inter alia through the time consuming build-up of proprietary market information systems.

The pioneers and early movers have built-up positions (company image, distribution agreements, relationships with hospitals through a large sales force, for example) which provide them with the ability to shared economies in the case of new, additional product introductions in the same therapeutic indications or in related market segments i.e., they can leverage assets built in the early phase of market entry. Most early movers like Janssen, Bristol-Myers Squibb or SmithKline Beecham built their China business originally on one or two products, which usually accounted for over 70 or 80% of sales. In a second phase when followers are trying to establish themselves with their first products in the market, most of the early movers are introducing a whole range of additional products based on the established position. Apart from the asset leverage which makes these product launches more efficient and/or more effective, they create in this way economies of scope not (yet) available to the followers.

Potential Advantages of Followers

Followers on the other hand may be able to capitalize on early mover's investments in many areas. Of particular relevance in the case of the Chinese pharma market are to be the following aspects:

- the substantial investments of early movers into buyer education (i.e., into the education of other transaction partners including JV partners);
- the investments of early movers into staff training;
- the avoidance of early movers strategic errors.

By the mid-eighties when the first more serious attempts at marketing foreign drugs in China were started, Chinese distributors, hospitals, doctors and patients were used to the workings of a state-controlled drug supply system. People were used to extremely low priced generic drugs with little regard to pharmaceutical quality and a low level of drug action know-how. Early movers had to spend large amounts of money over extended periods on symposia, conferences, delegation visits, scientific material and enter-tainment in order to convince buyers of the necessity for higher performing drugs, of the need to accept a price level of sometimes 10 to 20 times of the one for local generic drugs, to promote the concepts of pharmaceutical quality and to understand gradually the sophistication of modern clinical trials. All these efforts have resulted in a much better understanding of what modern drugs are and eased the way for new drugs into the market. In this way late movers can catch a "free ride" on the early movers' investments. The "educational investments" extend, however, not only to end-users of pharmaceuticals in China (doctors and patients), but also to distributors (with whom newcomers can now deal in an easier way than the early movers could) or to Chinese joint venture partners who have learnt to some extent from the failures and problems of the early ventures. This much improved environment is certainly one of the reasons for the results of a study which shows (across industry sectors) that later entrants in the China market have generally experienced a much faster break-even of their investments than the earlier entrants (EIU, 1995c).

The large "wave" of JV contracts concluded in the years 1992–1995 will further increase the pressure in the markets for Chinese managers and sales staff. The recruitment, training and "adjustment" to modern company practices of Chinese personnel are among the most important, difficult and costly aspects of operating in China (Shum, 1995b). Since the early 1990s the early mover and pioneer company Xi'an-Janssen for example has annual job turnover rates of over 20%. It is very obvious that later movers are tapping this pool of qualified manpower by offering better salaries or other incentives and are in this way able to exploit the investments of pioneering firms.

Early movers made a lot of strategic mistakes which they were almost bound to make given the extreme uncertainty of an emerging pharma market like China. Strategic errors (as seen from today's perspective) were for instance made by the Swedish company consortium Kabivitrum, Astra, Leo which created in the mid-eighties the Sino-Swed Pharmaceutical Corporation (SSPC) in Wuxi (see the story given above). Strategic errors (as seen from today's perspective) were the choice of Wuxi as a location (at least considering the conditions prevailing in the 1980s) and the assumption that with the top level of China's pharma distribution corporation as a JV partner a massive investment into the marketing of the JV products would not be necessary (in other words the view that China was a "distribution push market" only). Another strategic error was the choice by Glaxo to go for a joint venture in Chongqing which is far away from the major regional pharmaceutical markets. The careful observation of Bristol-Myers Squibb's experiment with direct to hospital distribution gives or will give later entrants information which may prevent them from strategic errors in setting up their distribution strategies.

The Product–Market Fit

There are a number of reasons other than the mode and timing of entry which are conventionally assumed or which may be suggested to explain why certain pharma companies like for instance Roche, Janssen (Johnson & Johnson) or Bristol-Myers Squibb entered the Chinese pharmaceutical market successfully in the sense of establishing a strong competitive position in their various market segments. Two other major factors shall be explored here: the product-market fit and a number of organizational behavioural traits.

The pharma industry is a very "product-oriented" industry. One of the dominant "frames" of pharma managers for interpreting success is to attribute it to a particular good "fit" between product (offering) and market demand. What are now the special dimensions of "fit" under Chinese conditions? Until about 1994/1995 two characteristics of the Chinese pharma market were particularly relevant for assessing the product–market fit from the point of view of MPCs. First, the existing local Chinese pharma companies supplied the market generally with low price, low quality products (often generic imitations of Western drugs from the 1960s or 1970s, frequently produced under insufficient quality control and with rather poor packaging). Second, more than 90% of the pharmaceuticals in China were and still are dispensed through hospitals and pharmacies. Apart from the pure medical evaluation of the utility of a drug, hospitals in China had and have a strong interest in the income from drugs. The very low base incomes of doctors are complemented by varying bonuses which in turn depend on cash profits of the hospitals. The latter depend to a large part on the cash profits derived from dispensing drugs: In the early 90s in a survey of 20 large hospitals, the author found that 30–50% of the hospital cash profits were derived from drug dispensing (Bruche, 1994). Until the start of major health care reforms in 1994/1995, hospital doctors were relatively unconstrained to prescribe whatever they considered good for the patient and good for their "business."

As long as the above-mentioned conditions prevailed, hospitals had a strong incentive to adopt higher priced imported or JV drugs (as long as they could convince the work units which acted as "insurers" to cover drug expenses — or the patients and their relatives to pay for them private-ly). Additional conditions which may have favoured the acceptance of a drug were: within acceptable price range (super expensive treatments would be confined to a very small group of high cadres or the few rich people who could afford them); advantage compared to locally available drugs; "selling points" easy to understand/promote; and frequent indication with the potential to become a "money spinner" for the hospital. From the point of view of MPCs one additional aspect needed to be taken into consideration: Since patent protection was not available, products which were difficult to generically imitate and/or which lend itself for positioning as "brands" with end-users were generally more promising than products without those properties.

Can we now say that the availability of "ideal" products is a major factor which explains why certain companies succeeded in establishing a strong position? The entry of MPCs especially in the first entry period was accomplished not with the latest innovative breakthrough products (they played only a marginal role), but with established products which were in many cases in an advanced stage of the product life cycle in Western countries. Almost all major successful JV or exported products in the market could be matched by often several similar products for the same indications which had either already occasionally been imported into China in smaller quantities or were available elsewhere in the world. It can therefore be concluded that the product-market fit in a wider sense was a necessary precondition for success, but it does not explain at least for the period under review why many companies with similar — sometimes even better — products did not succeed.

Whilst this line of argument holds for the period 1982 till the mid-1990s, it shall not be denied that product-market fit may become much more important in the future. The reason for this are the significant changes on the demand as well as on the supply side. On the demand side, we observe a far-reaching reform of the Chinese health care system and of the way drugs will be prescribed, dispensed and reimbursed; the essence of the reform is cost-containment mainly through restricting the freedom of doctors and hospitals in prescribing reimbursable drugs and perhaps the introduction of a stronger division of drugs for prescription and freely available "over-the counter" (OTC)-drugs (Shum, 1996; Wheatley, 1996; Zimmerman, 1996). On the supply side, we observe that in the mid-1990s all relevant market segments are now already served with at least some

MPC-drugs and a gradual "overcrowding" (similar to the situation in the more advanced Western pharmaceutical markets) is taking place. In this situation, product-market fit based on a much more sophisticated market research, particular product benefits and precise positioning will certainly gain in importance (Gao, 1996; Swanson, 1996). However, the author still believes that even in the years to come, apart from a few very outstanding innovative substances product-market fit will still be not more than a basic necessary condition for achieving a strategic market position. This situation may change once the patent protection for pharmaceutical substances introduced in January 1993 will have an impact in the market, which should not be expected before the year 2000.[15]

Organizational Behaviour and Competencies

There are a number of MPCs which entered early into JV negotiations but failed to conclude a contract or which achieved exports already before 1990 but were not able to maintain their position. Some of them have entered China in a second major attempt in the second entry period starting after 1990 but others have not completed entry so far. The mode of entry, early mover advantages, or the lack of a product-market fit are not sufficient to explain their failure nor to explain success in establishing competitive positions; other factors must play a role. It is suggested here that at least three other factors can be identified that have contributed to success: managerial persistence, financial commitment, permanent learning/adaptation.[16] These factors have been selected from a potentially "endless" list of specific circumstances (which may also include sheer "luck" as an important element) that may also explain success or failure.

Managerial persistence can be an important prerequisite for competitive success. As Tellis and Golder have convincingly shown for the competitive domain of product categories, successful products are the fruit of small, incremental innovations in design, manufacturing, and marketing over many years (1996, p. 69). In a comparable way, competitive success in a large, "distant" and "ambiguous" environment like the Chinese pharma market is usually not the result of one right "breakthrough" decision (although wrong decisions can "abort" the entry process). Entering such a market and establishing a viable competitive position is more like tilling a slow growing plant which needs permanent attention, protection against cold and stormy weather or parasites as well as occasional adding of fertilizer. In order to bring managerial persistence to bear fruit, several preconditions must exist: The backing-up of the local managers through an understanding headquarters which works on the assumption that local conditions can only be understood by the local managers; the selection of expatriate managers which are ready and capable to take on the hardship of the position for extended periods; a reasonable way of managing the rotation of managers which ensures that "persistence" (based on a growing know-how base) is maintained despite occasional changes in the expatriate management. The persistence in overcoming obstacles, in "sticking it out" for years and even decades is certainly one of the major reasons for the relative success of companies like Janssen and Roche; the lack of it (reflected in frequent changes of emphasis or very different levels of commitment) is one of the reasons why a number of companies which had entered China in the first phase already but have not (yet) succeeded in this period (examples are Organon, Hoechst, Bayer).

Because the establishment of a pharma JV in the first period required persistence over many years against great odds, companies involved needed to commit finances to last through this struggle. Although there are only sketchy data available, one can safely assume that virtually without exception the early JVs were loss-making operations for many years and the original expectations which may have been included in the financial calculations for the feasibility study almost never materialized. Even for today it can be safely assumed that few China operations of pharma companies have achieved a break even or yield significant annual profits (EIU, 1995a; *AWSJ*, 1995). An exception are, of course, some of those companies which confine their activities to exports and which have achieved substantial export volumes (example is EBEWE); they did, however not yet achieve a strong strategic position and are therefore not considered here.

If there is one constant in China and also in China's pharma market it is change. The far-reaching changes of the health care environment starting around 1994 and the sudden wave of new pharma JVs after 1990/1991 are a case in point. Even in the first period environment changes for MPCs have been permanent and often radical.[17] What makes the Chinese pharma market so outstanding is not the changes as such — pharmaceutical companies are faced with rapid environment changes also in the major developed pharma markets of the world (James, 1994). The particular characteristic of the Chinese pharma market is rather the speed and often

erratic nature of changes which is inter alia due to a "hypergrowth" environment combined with a very low level of institutional and legal infrastructure. In such an environment MPCs — early movers or followers alike —
can only maintain a once created strategic market position through constant
organizational learning and adaptation ("adaptability").

Adaptability, the capability to constantly "unlearn" those routines that
were created for environment situations that have become outdated, to
constantly explore the best ways and means to cope with emerging new
environments and to implement the needed changes is a "soft" organizational competence. It is influenced by many circumstances some of which
shall be mentioned here as particularly relevant for pharma ventures. First,
adaptability tends to be improved through "closeness" of senior management to key regional pharma markets in China (like Shanghai, or Beijing/
North-East); operations with senior managers (expatriate and Chinese)
working out of Hong Kong and leaving China's "sales regions" to low level
sales managers has tended to weaken adaptability as those having extremely centralized structures. Second, since China's pharma environment is
very "politicized" and market access and to some extent maintaining positions depends on political authorizations and approvals, closeness to
regulators in Beijing is a second prerequisite for adaptability. It is probably
due to these two reasons why the JV operations of Glaxo located in a
secondary market (Chongqing, Sichuan) became a failure (so far) and why
Janssen has moved its headquarters from Xi'an (the original JV site) to
Beijing. Adaptability therefore is one key requirement, which is particularly difficult to achieve for companies that opt for a "hinterland" location.

Last but not least, it is the availability of suitable managers which is
most decisive for adaptability. The expatriates which in many cases still run
the MPCs' China operations as general managers need, in addition to the
normal prerequisites for such positions, particular behavioural characteristics: a strong ability to tolerate ambiguity and frustration, an open probing
mind and eventually a basic sympathy (or empathy) with the Chinese
culture. In addition to the availability of suitable expatriate managers,
adaptability depends very much on the company's ability to nurture a core
of open minded, capable and loyal mainland Chinese managers. Due to the
scarcity of qualified mainland Chinese pharma managers, the latter requirement was certainly only available to a limited group of MPCs. In the mid-
term future with a rapid increase in competitive intensity, it is probably
going to become one of the most decisive factors for a continued defense of

competitive positions which have been acquired under different environment conditions.

Conclusions

Based on an analysis of the drivers of entry of MPCs into the Chinese pharma market this chapter set out to explore the factors for success in the sense of the acquisition of strategic market positions. It was shown that the entry of MPCs into this market was and is driven by a combination of push (cost and market maturing) and pull factors (market potential and "herd instinct"). Two periods of entry can be distinguished: The first period when pioneers and early movers went into a largely undeveloped market (1980–1990); the second period during which a large number of followers rushed into China and started to compete in an increasingly restrictive (demand side) and crowded (supply side) market. The second period started at the end of the post-Tian'anmen recession in about 1991 and is still going on at the time of this writing (1996). It is estimated that this second period of the entry process will come to a conclusion at around the year 2000 when all the ventures which are currently still in the preparatory or build-up phase are impacting the market (and when all the ongoing health care reforms will largely be implemented).

In looking at the potential factors that may have contributed to success or failure in building up strategic competitive positions, four aspects have been considered: mode of entry, timing of entry, product–market fit, organizational resources and competencies. If we look at competitive positions and strong overall sales results, it is quite clear that early movers are in the leading positions in most markets. Whilst early production-led entrants may have had a chance for deeper market penetration in an earlier phase, the difficult operating environment, the higher chance for "strategic errors" and the stronger management restrictions have meant in some (if not all) cases that the strong market position was "bought" at a very high price. Export-led entrants of the first phase which entered into JVs in the second period might not have reached the depth of market penetration with their products, but they had avoided some strategic errors, taken advantage of less management restrictions in the newer JV contracts, achieved or will achieve shorter JV build-up periods in a more supportive environment and on the whole had saved cost in comparison to the early production-led entrants. There are also a number of export-led entrants which did not succeed in establishing a viable market position in the first period, some of them have dropped out altogether while others have decided to enter into joint ventures in the second period. The difference in success of the production-led as well as the export-led entrants compared to the (temporary) failure of a number of companies in the first phase is most likely due to organizational-behavioural factors: lack of managerial persistence (sometimes also due to the loss of a key Chinese manager), lack of financial resources, and lack of adaptability. In few cases the products per se can be seen as the reasons for success or failure.

In the second period 1991–2000 the conditions are changing. Early movers who have completed their entry process will now have to defend their positions against the "onslaught" of the large number of followers which have come or will come onto the market. Basically they have to do this in two complementary ways. The first is the protection and exploitation of early mover advantages, which largely comes down to "asset protection" and various types of "asset leverage." One of the most important assets that need to be protected (against "poaching") is the key managerial personnel of the ventures; asset leverage concerns a series of measure like for instance the rapid introduction of more products, deepening the outreach to more customers, using the information lead to develop superior logistics etc. The second way of defending position is through ensuring sufficient organizational adaptability in order to cope successfully with the ongoing rapid environment changes (or in other words to avoid the well-known phenomenon of "incumbent inertia").

Followers need a more offensive strategic posture. Apart from some advantages, which basically will save cost (see above), many of them will have to fight an uphill battle. They can try to exploit the early mover investments into management education by poaching good managers from the existing ventures (which will however be difficult and does not necessarily promise success), they can try to exploit the weaknesses of the early movers (lack of adaptability for example) or they can go for less competitive areas (product-wise or region-wise). However, the most important change is that they will have to rely on product positioning and the demonstration of benefits and advantages over existing MPC products in the market. In other words, whilst product-market fit was a less important competitive dimension in the first period, it will become a key dimension in the competitive battles of the coming years.

As a final thought I want to address a different question, which was not a topic in this chapter: What in all this will be the role of the local Chinese pharmaceutical industry (for a description of the industry see Yu and Chen, 1996). I believe that under the given circumstances of a massive entry of the multinational pharmaceutical industry into China (and as long as the government does not change the trend which seems difficult to do) there is only a limited role left for Chinese pharma companies not associated with JVs. The Chinese pharmaceutical companies will partly go out of business, or partly consolidate into larger units. A few big Chinese pharma companies will survive and dominate the (important) market for generic pharmaceuticals. Whether the declared government intention to develop selected Chinese pharmaceutical companies into research-based multinational players can be realized remains to be seen. Certainly this will not take place in this millennium.

Notes

1. The author was General Manager of Schering AG's operations in Hong Kong and China for five years until 1991. After leaving Schering in 1994 he continued to advise pharmaceutical companies on China and Asia strategy issues. Since 1994 he has been Professor of International Management at the Fachhhochschule für Wirtschaft Berlin.

2. *South China Morning Post*, 4 April 1994.

3. *Financial Times*, 2 February 1994, p. 5.

4. *China Chemical Reporter*, 25 October 1994.

5. Perhaps typical for the roller-coaster ride nature of doing business in China the investment wave had not yet petered out when a strong disillusionment set in — mainly triggered by plans and first measures of the Chinese government to contain escalating drug costs in China's health care bill (the envisaged new system of drug reimbursement was pioneered in China's most important regional drug market, Shanghai). See for instance EIU, 1995a, 1995b; *AWSJ*, 1995.

6. The global MPI is composed of several strategic groups. The major strategic groups are: Research-based companies selling ethical pharmaceuticals (i.e., drugs which are usually delivered on prescription through medical doctors); companies selling primarily OTC (over-the-counter) drugs which are usually sold in pharmacies and drug stores without prescription and for which direct to consumer advertising is a main element of marketing communication (often alongside promotion to doctors); generic drug makers, i.e., companies concentrating primarily on the imitation of off-patent drugs. MPCs are typically

research-based and engaged in the ethical market, but they may also conduct OTC-operations and generic activities at the same time. Stand-alone OTC and particularly generic drug makers tend to be less global and often of only regional, national or local importance. For more detailed analyses of the global pharma industry see the articles in Lonsert et al., 1995; McGahan, 1994 and Chow, 1996.

7. See Albach, 1995, pp. 2–6 for an attempt to define "scienceware products."

8. Meanwhile it seems that the developed countries' pharma market growth is bouncing back. The growth rate of the world pharma market in 1995 was back to some 8% (IMS, 1996).

9. See for example *Pharmasearch International*, 1993.

10. An example of the upbeat press reports at that time is "When China Wakes: A Survey of China," *Economist*, 28 November 1992, pp. 11–18. For a later evaluation of this "turning point in history" see for instance Willy Wo-Lap Lam's comment on Deng's *nanxun* ("imperial tour of the south") in early 1992: "From this stage onwards, the country was irrevocably committed to a quasi-capitalistic path." Willy Wo-Lap Lam, 1995, p. 2.

11. For a short description of the distribution system see Zwisler, 1995.

12. Famous examples are "Aspirin," "Cola" and "Tempo" (paper handkerchiefs).

13. Implementing regulations for the law were issued in 1988 and 1990.

14. Whereas in 1990/1991 the rejection rates may have been in the order of 20–40% it had gone up to 50–70% by 1995.

15. The interim "Administrative Protection Regulation" for pharmaceuticals is applicable to a limited number of products only and is therefore considered to be of only limited relevance for a certain time period (see Shum, July 1995).

16. These factors are — among others — frequently mentioned as general requirements of doing (long-term) business in China. They also reflect the 10 years of general management and consulting experience of the author in China. Two other often quoted factors for doing successful business in China — "cultural adaptation/understanding," "relationships" (*guanxi*) — have not been explicitly mentioned because they are assumed to result from the combination of "managerial persistence" and "adaptivity."

17. For example, the far-reaching changes in the distribution system — see Zwisler, 1995, the constant changes in regulations, in enforcement of drug registration regulations, in the approval of JVs, in drug import procedures and generally in the handling of the foreign exchange issue.

Appendix

Activities of Multinational Pharmaceutical Companies in China — Status 1996

Company, Home Country	Type of Activity	Manufacturing Venture					Additional Comments	Est'd Year of Entry
		Location	Investment US$	Equity Shares	Contract	Start Operation		
Ajinomoto, Japan	E						Among top 10 exporters 1995	(1991)
Allergan, US	E, M							(1993)
Amgen, US		Zhejiang						(1992)
Astra, Sweden	M, E	#1 Wuxi #2 Wuxi	See Kabi 18 mn	See Kabi 100%	See Kabi 1994	See Kabi 1996	Established new JV independent from SSPC (see Kabi Pharmacia). Gradual transfer.	1987
Baker-Norton, US	M	Kunming	8 mn	50%	1992	1994	Has another small JV in Beijing	1992
Baxter Healthcare, US	M	Guangzhou		95:5%	1993	1997		1993
Bayer, Germany	E, M	Beijing	30 mn		1994	1998	Research cooperation: Chinese herbs	1994
Beauford Ipsen, France	M	Tianjin	20 mn	75:25%	1996	1998		1996
Boehringer-Ingelheim, Germany	L, M	Shanghai	25 mn		1995	1999		1992
Bristol-Myers Squibb, US	M, E	Shanghai	30 mn	(50:50)% 58:42%	1987	1993	Among top 5 pharma JV in China 1995. Among top 10 exporters	(1985)
Ciba Geigy, Switzerland (Novartis)	E, M	Beijing	21 mn	(50:50)% 60:40%	1987	1993	Serious start-up problems. Under wholly owned holding company.	1985
Daiichi, Japan	E						Wholly owned subsidiary in 1995 for clinical research	(1991)
EBEWE, Austria	E						75% subsidiary of BASF Pharma. #1 exporter 1994/95	1991
Elli Lilly, US	M	Suzhou	28 mn	90:10%	1995	1998		1995

Appendix (Cont'd)

Company, Home Country	Type of Activity	Manufacturing Venture					Additional Comments	Est'd Year of Entry
		Location	Investment US$	Equity Shares	Contract	Start Operation		
Farmitalia, Italy	E, M	Wuxi	20 mn	100%		1996	Subsidiary of Kabi Pharmacia	(1992)
Fresenius, Germany	M	Beijing	12.5 mn	60:40%	1994	1995	Another small injection systems JV in Ningbo	1994
Fujisawa, Japan	E						Among top 10 exporters 1995	1992
Glaxo, U.K.	E, M	Chongqing	10 mn	50:50% (90:10)%	1988	1991	Among top 10 exporters 1995. Weak JV, used as base for export business.	(1986)
Hoechst, Germany	E, M	Shijia-zhuang	25 mn	50:50%	1994	1996	Shanghai JV with subsidiaries (Behringwerke, Copley); Wholly owned holding co. Among top 10 exporters 1995	(1991)
Johnson & Johnson (Janssen), US	M	Xi'an / Shanghai	48 mn / 30 mn	52:48% / 90:10%	1985 / 1995	1989 / 1996	No. 1 pharma JV 1995. Established by Janssen (Belgium). Janssen acquired by J&J	1985
Kabi Pharmacia, Sweden (Sino-Swed-Pharma Corporation)	M	Wuxi	21 mn	50:50%	1982	1987	Former consortium of nordic companies; meanwhile consolidated through acquisitions and withdrawal. Among top 5 JVs 1995. Global merger with Upjohn 1995	1982
Kyowa Hakko, Japan	E							(1992)
Lederle (American Home), US	M	Suzhou	16 mn	90:10%		1994		1994
Madaus, Germany	E							1992
Meiji Seika, Japan	E, M							n.a.
Merck, Sharp & Dohme US	E, M	Beijing / Hangzhou	12 mn / 26 mn	75:25%	1994	1994	Another manufacturing JV planned in Shenzhen. Among top 10 exporters 1995	(1986)

Company, Home Country	Type of Activity	Manufacturing Venture					Additional Comments	Est'd Year of Entry
		Location	Investment US$	Equity Shares	Contract	Start Operation		
Nycomed, Norway	E, M	Shanghai	23 mn	60:40% (80:20)%	1994	1998	Started on preliminary basis with repackaging/labelling in 1995	1991
Organon, Netherlands	M	Nanjing	2 mn	51:49%	1992	1994	Subsidiary of AKZO. Mainly intrauterine devices	1992
Otsuka, Japan	M	Tianjin Guangzhou	30 mn 16 mn	50:50% 50:50%	1980 1993	1984 1995	First pharma JV in China. Originally high re-export share from China	1980
Pfizer, US	L, E, M	Nanjing Dalian	50 mn	67:33%	1990 1989	1992	Raw material plant Among top 5 pharma JV. (JV under discussion since 1983!)	(1984)
Pharmaz. Fabrik Evers, Germany	E						Among top 10 exporters in 1995	(1993)
Rhone-Poulenc-Rohrer, France	E, M	Qingzhou Beijing	7 mn	75:25% 90:10%	1994 1995	1996 1998	JV by subsidiary Dermik	1994
Roche, Switzerland	E, M	Shanghai	30 mn	70:30%	1993	1996	Among top 10 exporters 1995. In total four JVs in China with 110 mn investment	(1985)
Sandoz, Switzerland (Novartis)	E, L						PLA licence partner factory in Tianjin. Among top 10 exporters 1995. Merger with Ciba Geigy 1996 to form Novartis	(1988)
Schering, Germany	E, M	Guangzhou	18 mn	92:8%	1992	1995		1989
Schwartz, Germany	E, M	Zhuhai	9 mn	85:15%	1996	1997		(1995)
Schering-Plough, US	E, M	Shanghai	37 mn	55:45%	1994	1996		1988

Appendix (Cont'd)

Company, Home Country	Type of Activity	Manufacturing Venture					Additional Comments	Est'd Year of Entry
		Location	Investment US$	Equity Shares	Contract	Start Operation		
Servier, France	E, L						PLA licence partner factory in Tianjin	1988
SmithKline Beecham, US	M	Tianjin Shanghai	18 mn 17 mn	55:45%	1994 1995	1987	Among top 5 pharma JVs 1995	1984
Sterling Drug, US (abandoned)	M	Shanghai	7 mn		1993		Sterling bought by SKB, venture diverted to SKB's Tianjin facility	—
Takeka, Japan	L, M	Tianjin	26 mn	75:25%	1992	1996	Liaison office Beijing 1982. Licence production = repackaging (form of export)	(1986)
Tanabe, Japan	M	Tianjin	6 mn	50:50%	1993			1993
Upjohn, US	E, M	Suzhou	35 mn	75:25%	1994	1996	Global merger with Kabi Pharmacia 1995	(1992)
Wellcome, U.K.	E						Acquired by Glaxo in 1995	—
Yamanouchi, Japan	E, M	Shenyang	30 mn	80:20%	1994	1996		(1992)
Zeneca, U.K.	E, C	Beijing			1994	1995	The first "service JV" in the pharma sector	(1994)

Sources: The data have been compiled by the author over a longer period from various articles, information services and numerous talks with China pharma exports and China pharma company managers.

Technical Note: The data reflect the situation as of spring 1996. They represent factual data or best possible estimates. The "entry" dates in the last column are in case of "export-led entries" (see article) partly based on estimates of the author which is indicated by inserting the figures in brackets; in case of "production-led entries" the JV contract date has been used as indicator for the entry date.

* E = Export, M = Manufacturing venture, L = Licence cooperation, C = Consultancy JV.

References

Abell, Derek F. (1978), "Strategic Windows," *Journal of Marketing*, July, 21–26.
ACLR (1996), 1, B-3.
Adhikari, A., and Wang, S. (1995), "Accounting for China," *Management Accounting* (U.S.), April, 27–32.
Albach, Horst (1995), "Global Competitive Strategies for Science Ware Products," Discussion Paper FS IV 95-13. Wissenschaftszentrum Berlin.
Allinson, Robert E. (1989), "An Overview of the Chinese Mind," in Robert E. Allinson (ed.), *Understanding the Chinese Mind: The Philosophical Roots*. Hong Kong: Oxford University Press.
Almanac of China's Foreign Economic Relations and Trade (1990/91, 1991/92, 1992/93, 1993/94, 1994/95, 1995/96, and 1996/97). Beijing: China Social Publishing.
Alston, J. P. (1989), "Wa, Guanxi and Inhwa: Management Principles in Japan, China and Korea," *Business Horizons*, March–April, 26–31.
Anderson, Bevelee B., and Venkatesan, M. (1994), "Temporal Dimension of Consuming Behaviour Across Cultures," in Salah S. Hassan and Roger D. Blackwell (eds.), *Global Marketing: Perspectives and Cases*, 178–193. Fort Worth, Tex.: The Dryden Press.
Anderson, M. (1984), *Madison Avenue in Asia: Politics and Transnational Advertising*. Ratherford, N.J.: Farleigh-Dickinson University Press.
Antonio, Nelson S., and Steele, Henry C. (eds.) (1996), *Second South China International Business Symposium on "Decision Making, Market Development, Information and Technology: Managing International Business in the Twenty First Century" — Proceedings and Papers*, Volume I, November, Macau.
Art, Robert C., and Gu, Minkang (1995), "China Incorporated: The First Corporation Law of the People's Republic of China," *The Yale Journal of International Law*, 20(2), Summer, 286.
Asian Business (1992), November, 63.
Asiaweek (1993), "History's Movers: Why the Communist Party Is China's Most Valuable Asset," July 21.
Asiaweek (1996), "Business: The Bottom Line," 22(44), November 1, 57.

Atuahene-Gima, K. (1992), "Inward Technology Licensing as an Alternative to Internal R & D: A Conceptual Framework," *Journal of Product Innovation Management*, 9(2), 156–167.

Atuahene-Gima, K. (1993a), "Buying Technology for Product Development in Smaller Firms," *Industrial Marketing Management*, 22, 223–232.

Atuahene-Gima, K. (1993b), "Determinants of Inward Technology Licensing Intentions: An Empirical Analysis of Australian Engineering Firms," *Journal of Product Innovation Management*, 10(2), 230–240.

Atuahene-Gima, K. (1993c), "An Exploration of the Factors Affecting Inward Technology Licensing Performance," *Journal of Global Marketing*, 7(1), 25–46.

Atuahene-Gima, K. (1993d), "Relative Importance of Firm and Managerial Influences on International Technology Licensing Behaviour," *International Marketing Review*, 10, 4–21.

AWSJ (1995), "Drug Makers Suffer Reform Woes in China," March 13.

Bahr, S. J. (ed.) (1991), *Family Research*, Vols. 1 & 2. New York: Lexington Books.

Bakken, Borge (1993), "Crime, Juvenile Delinquency and Deterrence Policy in China," *The Australian Journal of Chinese Affairs*, 30, 29–58.

The Banker (1993a), "Follow the Leader," March, 18–19.

The Banker (1993b), "The Top 1000," July, 74–104.

The Banker (1994a), "Shanghai's Renaissance," May, 34–38.

The Banker (1994b), "The Top 100 Japanese Banks," January, 58–61.

Banker, P. (1983), "You're the Best Judge of Foreign Risks," *Harvard Business Review*, 61(2), 157–165.

Baume, C. D. L., and Gupta, J. (1991), "Japanese Banking Strategy in Europe," *European Management Journal*, 9(2), 171–175.

Bell, Michael W., Khor, Hoe Ee, and Kochhar, Kalpana (1993), *China at the Threshold of a Market Economy*, Occasional Paper No. 107, September. Washington: International Monetary Fund.

Bergtson, V. L., and Achenbaum, W. A. (eds.) (1993), *The Changing Contract Across Generations*. New York: Aldine De Gruyter.

Bernadt, T. J. (1993), "Perceptions of Parenting in Mainland China, Taiwan, and Hong Kong: Sex Differences and Societal Differences," *Developmental Psychology*, 29(1), 156–164.

Blejer, Mario I., and Szapary, Gyorgy (1990), "The Evolving Role of Tax Policy in China," *Journal of Comparative Economics*, 14(3), 452–472.

Bond, Michael Harris, and Hwang, Kwang-kuo (1986), "The Social Psychology of Chinese People," in Michael Harris Bond (ed.), *The Psychology of the Chinese People*. Hong Kong: Oxford University Press.

Borys, B., and Jemison, D. (1989), "Hybrid Arrangements as Strategic Alliances:

Theoretical Issues in Organizational Combinations," *Academy of Management Review*, 14, 234–249.

Briston, R. (1978), "The Evolution of Accounting in Developing Countries," *International Journal of Accounting, Education and Research*, 14, 105–120.

Buckley, P. J., Berkova, Z., and Newbould, G. D. (1983), *Direct Investment in the United Kingdom by Small European Firms*. Basingstoke and London: Macmillan.

Buckley, P. J., Newbould, G. D., and Thurwell, J. C. (1988), *Foreign Direct Investment by Small U.K. Firms: The Success and Failure of First Time Investors Abroad*. Basingstoke and London: Macmillan.

Buckley, P. J., Pass, C. L., and Prescott, K. (1992), "The Internationalization of Service Firms: A Comparison with the Manufacturing Sector," *Scandinavian International Business Review*, 1(1), 39–56.

Burkhardt, V. R. (1955), *Chinese Creeds and Customs*. Hong Kong: South China Morning Post Ltd.

Byrd, William (1983). *China's Financial System*. Colorado: Westview Press.

Cai, S. (1987), "Characteristics of Traditional Chinese Culture and Its Change," in Fudan University (ed.), *Re-evaluation of Traditional Chinese Culture*, 43–49. Shanghai: Shanghai People's Press.

Cai, Yue (1991), "Lun 90 niandai Guangdongsheng jishu yinjin zhanlue diaozheng de wenti (On the Problems of Strategic Alignment of Technology Import of Guangdong in the '90s)," Ji Nan University, Dec. (in Chinese).

Campbell, N. (1987), "Experiences of Western Companies in China," *Euro-Asia Business Review*, 6(3), 35–38.

Carstairs, R. T., and Welch, L. S. (1982), "Licensing and the Internationalization of Smaller Firms: Some Australian Evidence," *Management International Review*, 22(3), 33–44.

Cateora, Philip R. (1996), *International Marketing*, 9th ed., 99–101. Homewood, Ill.: Irwin.

Cavusgil, S. T., and Kaynak, E. (1982), "A Framework for Cross-Cultural Measurement of Consumer Dissatisfaction," in R. L. Day and H. K. Hunt (eds.), *New Findings on Consumer Satisfaction and Complaining*, 80–84. Bloomington: Indiana University.

CBM Research (ed.) (1996), "A Changed Attitude Towards Foreign Investment," Editorial, *China Healthcare and Pharmaceutical News*, May, 1.

Chai, J. (1992), "Consumption and Living Standards in China," *The China Quarterly*, 131, 721–749.

Chan, K. C., Cheng, Louis T. W., and Fung, Joseph K. W. *Ownership Restrictions and Stock Price Behavior in China*, BRC Papers on China. Hong Kong: Hong Kong Baptist University.

Chan, M. H. Thomas (1995), "China's Economic Growth in the 1990s," in *Doing Business in China*, Chapter 1, 1–31. Toronto: McGraw-Hill Ryerson.

Chan, Or (1996), "The Implications of Reduction of Import Tariff for Domestic Industry," *Hong Kong Economic Journal*, January 2, 34 (in Chinese).

Chan, W. T. (1963), *The Way of Lao Tsu*. New York: Bobbs-Merrill.

Chan, Wing-Tsit (1986), "Chinese Theory and Practice, with Special Reference to Humanism," in Charles A. Moore (ed.), *The Chinese Mind: Essentials of Chinese Philosophy and Culture*. Honolulu: University of Hawaii Press.

Chanda, Nayan, and Kaye, Lincoln (1993), "Circling Hawks," *Far Eastern Economic Review*, October 7.

Chang, Gene (1995), "What Caused the Hyperinflation at the Big Bang: Monetary Overhang or Structural Distortion?" *China Economic Review*, 6(1), 137–147.

Chang, T. A. M. C., and Sun, T. H. (1984), "Social and Economic Change, Intergenerational Relationships, and Family Formation in Taiwan," *Demography*, 21(4), 475–499.

Chao, C. S. (1994), "Peking's Policy of Opening Up to the Outside World," *Issues and Studies*, 12, 22–24.

Chao, Y. T. (1990), "Culture and Work Organisation: The Chinese Case", *International Journal of Psychology*, 25(5/6), 583–591.

Cheal, D. (1991), *Family and the State of Theory*. Toronto: University of Toronto Press.

Chen, Bi (1993), "The Pharmaceutical Market in China," *Scrip Reports*. PJB Publications Limited, June.

Chen, C. (1991), *The Determinants of Satisfaction with Living Arrangements for the Elderly in Taiwan*. Taiwan: The Institute of Economics, Academia Sinica.

Chen, C., and Speare, A., Jr. (1990), "The Impact of the Process of Modernization on Elderly's Living Arrangements — The Case of Taiwan," *Proceeding of the Conference on Population Change and Socioeconomic Development*, Taipei, May 8–9, 535–551 (in Chinese).

Chen, Xiangming (1985), "The One-Child Population Policy, Modernization, and the Extended Chinese Family," *Journal of Marriage and the Family*, 47, 193–202.

Cheng, B. S. (1993), *Categorizations and Chinese Organisation Behaviour*, 142–219.

Cheng, Chung-ying (1972), "Chinese Philosophy: A Characterization," in Arne Naess and Alastair Hannay (eds.), *Invitation to Chinese Philosophy: Eight Studies*. Oslo: Universitetsforlaget.

Cheng, J., and Macpherson, S. (eds.) (1995), *Development in Southern China*. Hong Kong: Longman Asia Limited.

Cheng, Te-k'un (1980), *The World of the Chinese — A Struggle for Human Unity*. Hong Kong: The Chinese University Press.

Cheng, Yee (1996), "The Reduction of Refund for Value-Added Tax Paid on Inputs for Exports and the Dilemma of Foreign-Invested Enterprises," *Hong Kong Economic Journal,* July 2, 22 (in Chinese).

Cheung, M. T., Yeung, D. W. K., and Yeung, L. Y. (1992), *The Shenzhen Stock Market.* Hong Kong: Asian Research Service.

Cheung, Yin (1996), "The Indispensable Modification of the Newly Reformed Taxation System and Public Finance Policy," *Hong Kong Economic Journal,* March 18 (in Chinese).

Ch'i, Hsi-sheng (1991), *Politics of Disillusionment: The Chinese Communist Party under Deng Xiao Ping 1978–1989.* New York: M. E. Sharpe.

The China Business Review (1996), May–June, 40–41.

China Financial Outlook (1995). The People's Bank of China.

China-Hong Kong Economic Monthly (1993), February, 36.

China Statistical Yearbook (Zhongguo tongji nianjian) (1996). Beijing: Statistical Publishing House.

China Times Weekly (1993), November 7–13.

China's Latest Economic Statistics (various issues). Hong Kong: CERD Consultants Ltd.

Chu, Bootai (1994), "The Taxation for Foreign Direct Investments," in *Handbook for Investing in People's Republic of China,* 2nd ed., 145–150. Beijing: Chung Shun Publishing (Beijing) Co. Ltd.

Chu, G. C., and Ju, Y. (1993), *The Great Wall in Ruins: Communication and Cultural Change in China.* New York: State University of New York Press.

Churchill, G. A. (1979), "A Paradigm for Developing Better Marketing Constructs," *Journal of Marketing Research,* 16, 64–73.

Clark, Gregory (1982), "Japan in Asia: A Cultural Comparison," *Asia Pacific Community,* 17, 60–70.

Clarke, Donald C. (1992), "What's Law Got to Do with It? Legal Institutions and Economic Reform in China," *UCLA Pacific Basin Law Journal,* 10(1), Fall, 43–44.

Clarke, K., Ford, D., and Saren, M. (1989), "Company Technology Strategy," *R & D Management,* 19(3), 215–229.

Coleen, T. (1985), "Foreign Bankers See China as the New Frontier," *Asian Finance,* July 15, 48–51.

Conable, Barber B., Jr., and Lampton, David M. (1992). "China: The Coming Power," *Foreign Affairs,* 5, 133–149.

Conner, Alison W. (1991), "To Get Rich is Precarious: Regulation of Private Enterprise in the People's Republic of China," *Journal of Chinese Law,* 5(1), Spring, 5–6.

Connidis, I. A. (1989), *Family Ties and Aging.* Toronto: Butterworths.

Contractor, F. J. (1981), *International Technology Licensing*. Lexington, Mass.: D.C. Heath & Co.

Crow, C. (1937), *Four Hundred Million Customers*. London: Hamish Hamilton.

Dai, H. M. (1987), "The View Point on Social Value among Young Chinese Women," *Women's Organization and Activities*, 5, 31–35.

Daniels, J. D., Krug, J., and Nigh, D. (1985), "U.S. Joint Ventures in China: Motivation and Management of Political Risk," *California Management Review*, 27(4), 46–58.

Daniels, J. D., and Radebaugh, L. H. (1989), *International Business, Environments and Operations*, 5th ed. Reading, Mass.: Addison-Wesley.

D'Aveni, Richard A. (1994), *Hypercompetition. Managing the Dynamics of Strategic Maneuvering*. New York: The Free Press.

David, Evelyn S. (1994), "A Review and Analysis of Enterprise Bankruptcy Laws in China," *Insolvency Law Journal*, 2(1), March, 175.

Davidson, R., Gelardi A., and Li, F. (1996), "Analysis of the Conceptual Framework of China's New Accounting System," *Accounting Horizons*, 10(1), March, 58–74.

Davies, K. (1994), "Foreign Investment in the Retail Sector of the People's Republic of China," *The Columbia Journal of World Business*, Fall.

Davis-Friedmann, D. (1983), "Intergenerational Inequalities and the Chinese Revolution," paper presented for the Conference on Equality and Stratification in China. Ann Arbor, Mich., August 29–30.

Davis-Friedmann, D. (1985a), "Intergenerational Equities and the Chinese Revolution," *Modern China*, 11(2), 177–201.

Davis-Friedmann, D. (1985b), *Long Lives: Chinese Elderly and the Communist Revolution*. Cambridge, Mass.: Harvard University Press.

Davis-Friedmann, D. (1985c), "Old Age Security and One-Child Campaign," in E. Croll, D. David and P. Keaue (eds.), *China's One-Child Policy*. London: Macmillan.

De Bruijn, Eric J., and Jia, Xianfeng (1993), "Transferring Technology to China by Means of Joint Ventures," *Research Technology Management*, 36(1), Jan–Feb, 17–22.

De La Torre, J., and Neckar, D. H. (1982), "Forecasting Country Political Risk," in S. Makridakis and S. Wheelwright (eds.), *The Handbook of Forecasting: A Manager's Guide*. New York: John Wiley & Sons.

Ding, Pin-Zhun (1996), "Report of the Secretariat of the CICPA," *Journal of CPA*, 6, 24–25 (in Chinese).

Dipchand, C. R., Dodds, J. C., McGraw, P., and Chen, K. (1991), "Emerging Trends in China's Financial Sector," *Asia Pacific Journal of Management*, 8(1), 35–54.

Donnithorne, Audrey (1986), *Banking and Fiscal Changes in China since Mao*, Conference on China's System Reforms, Paper No. 31. Hong Kong: Centre of Asian Studies, University of Hong Kong.

Dube, L., Leclerc, F., and Schmitt, B. H. (1991), "Consumers' Duration Estimates of Delays at Different Phases of a Service Delivery Process," paper presented at 6th John Labatt Marketing Research Seminar, Université du Québec à Montréal, Canada.

Duckworth, M., and Leung, J. (1991), "Share Offering in China Takes a Rocky Road," *The Wall Street Journal*, November 18, A11.

Dunning, J. H. (1993), *The Globalization of Business: The Challenge of the 1990s*. London: Routledge.

Economic Digest (1993), September 6 and October 24.

EIU (1995a), "Drug Money," *Business China*, January 9, 1–3.

EIU (1995b), "Measured Dose," *Business China*, January 23, 1–3.

Enderwick, P. (1990), "The International Competitiveness of Japanese Service Industries: A Cause for Concern?" *California Management Review*, 32(4), 22–27.

Far Eastern Economic Review (1992), 3 April, 55; 23 November.

Far Eastern Economic Review (1993), 19 August, 14.

Fatehi-Sedeh, K., and Safizadeh, M. H. (1989), "The Association between Political Instability and Flow of Foreign Direct Investment," *Management International Review*, 29(4), 4–13.

Fei, Hsiao-tung (1962), *Peasant Life in China: A Field Study of Country Life in the Yangtze Valley*. London: Routledge and Kegan Paul.

Feldman, Lawrence P., and Hornik, Jacob (1981), "The Use of Time: An Integrated Conceptual Model," *Journal of Consumer Research*, 7(4), March, 407–419.

Feltenstein, Andrew, and Farhadian, Ziba (1987), "Fiscal Policy, Monetary Targets and the Price Level in a Centrally Planned Economy: An Application to the Case of China," *Journal of Money, Credit and Banking*, 19(2), 136–156.

Five City Family Survey Research Group (1985), *Five City Family Survey*. Jinan: Shandong People's Publishing House.

Folsom, Ralph H., and Minan, John H. (eds.) (1989), *Law in the People's Republic of China: Commentary, Readings and Materials*, 14. Dordrecht: Martinus Nijhoff Publishers.

Foreign Bankers in China (1987), Vol. 2. Kong Yuen Publishing Company.

Forestier, K. (1988), "China Leaps into Lead in Export Processing," *Asian Business*, August, 21–28.

Frankenstein, J. (1987), "Business in China: Western and Chinese Perspectives," *Euro-Asia Business Review*, 6(1), 26–30.

Friar, J., and Horwitch, M. (1985), "The Emergence of Technology Strategy: A

New Dimension of Strategic Management," *Technology in Society*, 7, 143–178.

Fung, Yu-lan (1948), *A Short History of Chinese Philosophy*. New York: Macmillan.

Gao, Anming (1993), "Mapping New Road to Rural Reforms," *China Daily*, December 7, 1.

Gao, J. S. (1986), "From Rearing a Son for the Sake of Old Age to Economic Interdependence," *Social Science*, 11, 98–104.

Gao, Shangquan (1993), "Taking a Market-Oriented Direction and Pushing Forward in a Gradual Way — The Basic Experience of China's Economic Reform," *China Economic Review*, 4(2), 129–136.

Ge, Jiashu, Fang, Ronyi, and Li, Shaobo (1993), "The Characteristics of the Enterprise Accounting Standards and Its Relationship with the Accounting Systems for Different Industries and with the General Guideline of Finance," *Finance and Accounting Communication* (Hubei, PRC) 3, 5–10.

Glor, U. (ed.) (1994), *China: Joint Venture Companies in the Pharmaceutical Industry. Handbook*. Published jointly by Sino-Info U. Gloor and China Centre for Pharmaceutical International Exchange, Beijing, September.

Gold, B. (1975), "Alternative Strategies for Advancing a Company's Technology," *Research Management*, 18(4), 24–29.

Gold, B. (1982), "Managerial Considerations in Evaluating the Role of Licensing in Technology Development," *Managerial and Decision Economics*, 3(4), 213–217.

Gold, B. (1987), "Approaches for Accelerating Product and Process Development," *Journal of Product Innovation Management*, 4(4), 81–88.

Gold, T. B. (1989), "Urban Private Business in China," *Studies in Comparative Communism*, 22(2/3), 187–201.

Goldbery, L. G. and Saunders, A. (1980), "The Causes of U.S. Bank Expansion Overseas," *Journal of Money, Credit and Banking*, November, 630–643.

Goldstein, M. C., et al. (1983), "Social and Economic Forces Affecting Intergenerational Relations in a Third World Country: A Cautionary Tale from South Asia," *Journal of Gerontology*, 38(6), 716–724.

Graham, Robert J. (1981), "The Role of Perception of Time in Consumer Research," *Journal of Consumer Research*, 7(4), March, 335–342.

Gronmo, Sigmund (1989), "Concepts of Time: Some Implications for Consumer Research," in Thomas Srull (ed.), *Advances in Consumer Research*, Vol. 16. Provo, Utah: Association for Consumer Research.

Gu, Zhibin (1991), *China Beyond Deng: Reform in the PRC*. Jefferson, North Carolina: McFarland.

Guangdong–Hong Kong Information Daily (1994), 8 June (in Chinese).

Guangzhou Daily (1991), 15 October.

Guangzhou Daily (1993), 21 March.

Guangzhou Daily (1995), 15 September.

Hall, Edward T. (1960), "The Silent Language in Overseas Business," *Harvard Business Review*, May–June, 87–96.

Hall, Edward T. (1983), *The Dance of Life: The Other Dimension of Time*. New York: Anchor Press/Doubleday.

Hamrin, Carol Lee (1990), *China and the Challenge of the Future: Changing Political Patterns*. Boulder: Westview Press.

Hang Seng Economic Monthly, January 1994 and February 1995.

Hay, Donald, Morris, Derek, Liu, Guy, and Yao, Shujie (1994), *Economic Reform and State-Owned Enterprises in China, 1979–1987*. Oxford: Clarendon Press.

Hchu, and Yang, K. S. (1972), in Y. Y. Li and K. S. Yang (eds.), *Symposium on the Character of the Chinese*. Taipei: Institution of Ethnology, Academic Sinica (in Chinese).

Heath, Ray (1993), "Boom Continues but Watch for the Waves," *South China Morning Post*, December 21, 18.

Hendrix, Philip, Kinnear, Thomas, and Taylor, James R. (1983), *Consumers' Time Expenditures: A Behavioral Model and Empirical Test*. Boston, Mass.: Marketing Science Institute.

Hermalin, A. I., et al. (1990), "Patterns of Support among the Elderly in Taiwan and Their Policy Implication," paper prepared for the 1990 PAA Annual Meeting, Toronto, Canada, May 3–5.

Hertz, D. B., and Thomas, H. (1983), *Risk Analysis and Its Applications*. Chichester, England: Wiley.

Hill, R. (1965), "Decision Making and the Family Life Cycle," in E. Shanas and G. Streib (eds.), *Social Structure and the Family*, 113–139. Englewood Cliffs, N.J.: Prentice-Hall.

Hinton, W. (1991), *The Privatization of China: The Great Reversal*. London: Earthscan.

Ho, D. Y. F. (1972), "On the Concept of Face," *American Journal of Sociology*, 81(4), 72–78.

Ho, S. C. (1984), "Hong Kong: A Bridge to China for Foreign Investors," *Management Decision*, 22(6), 37–46.

Ho, S. C., and Lo, T. W. C. (1987), "The Service Industry in China — Problems and Prospects," *Business Horizon*, July/August, 29–37.

Hofstede, G., and Bond, M. H. (1988), "The Confucian Connection: From Cultural Roots to Economic Growth," *Organisation Dynamics*, 16(4), 4–21.

Hofstede, Geert (1991), *Cultures and Organizations: Software of the Mind*. London: McGraw-Hill.

Hong, L. K. (1987), "Potential Effects of the One-Child Policy on Gender Equality in the People's Republic of China," *Gender and Society*, 1, 317–326.

The Hong Kong Council of Social Service (ed.) (1994), *Proceedings of International Conference on Family and Community Care*. Hong Kong: The Hong Kong Council of Social Services.

Hong Kong Economic Journal, 11 May, 3 September and 27 October 1995.

Hong Kong Trade Development Council (1994), *China's Consumer Market*, August.

Honig, E., and Hershatten, G. (1988), "Personal Voice," in *Chinese Women in the 1980's*. Standford: Stanford University Press.

Hood, M. (1992), "China's Secret Crime Wave," *Sunday Morning Post*, May 31, Spectrum, 2.

Hornik, Jacob (1984), "Subjective Versus Objective Time Measures: A Note on the Perception of Time in Consumer Behaviour," *Journal of Consumer Research*, 11 June, 615–618.

Hsiang, Chinghua (1991), "Problems in Import of Technology and Their Solutions," *Gongye jingji* (Journal of Industrial Economics), October, 53–59 (in Chinese).

Hsu, F. L. K. (1947), *Under the Ancestors' Shadow: Kinship, Personality, and Social Mobility in China*. Standford: Standford University Press.

Hsu, F. L. K. (1963), *Clan, Caste, and Club*. Princeton, N.J.: Van Nostrand.

Hsu, F. L. K. (1968), "Psychological Anthropology: An Essential Defect and Its Remedy," paper presented at the 1968 annual meeting of the American Anthropologist Association, Seattle, Washington.

Hsu, F. L. K. (1970), *Americans and Chinese: Passage to Differences*, 3rd ed. Honolulu: University Press of Hawaii.

Hsu, F. L. K. (1972), "Chinese Kinship and Chinese Behavior," in P. T. Ho and T. Tsou (eds.), *China in Crisis*, Vol. 2. Chicago: University of Chicago Press.

Hu, H. C. (1944), "The Chinese Concept of Face," *American Anthropologist*, 46, January–March, 45–64.

Hu, T. W., et al. (1989), "Household Durable Goods Ownership in Tianjin, China," *The China Quarterly*, 120, 787–799.

Hu, Yebi (1995), *China's Capital Market*. Hong Kong: The Chinese University Press.

Hua, S., Zhang, X., and Lo, X. (1988), "After Ten Years' Reform in China: Retrospective, Reflection and Future Looking," *Research in Economics*, Part I, No. 8 and Part II, No. 11, 11–29.

Huanan Jingji Journal (1993), 16 December.

Huang, H. Q., et al. (1992), *Economic Development of The Pearl River Delta: A*

Retrospect and Prospects. Guangzhou: Research Center of Pearl River Delta Economic Development and Management, Zhongshan University.

Huang, Hsiao Katharine (1987), *The Government Budget and Fiscal Policy in Mainland China*. Taipei: Chung-Hua Institute for Economic Research.

Hughes, Duncan (1994), "Top Firms Rate China as Best Bet," *South China Morning Post*, November 25, 1.

Hui, Michael K. M., and Zhou, Lianxi (1993), "The Effects of Waiting Time Information on Consumers' Reactions to Delays in Services," paper presented at ASEC, Lake Louise, Alberta, Canada.

Hwang, Kwang-kuo (1990), "Modernization of the Chinese Family Business," *International Journal of Psychology*, 25, 593–618.

International Accounting Standards Committee (1994), *International Accounting Standards 1994*, 44. London: Author.

The Investment Times (1995), Vol. 375, 29 September. Shenzhen: Touzi Daobaoshe (in Chinese).

Jacoby, Jacob, Szybillo, George and Berning, Carol Kohn (1976), "Time and Consumer Behaviour: An Interdisciplinary Overview," *Journal of Consumer Research*, 2(4), March, 320–339.

James, Barrie G. (1994), "The Pharmaceutical Industry in 2000," in *Reinventing the Pharmaceutical Company. Research Report*. London: The Economist Intelligence Unit.

Jarvie, I. C., and Agassi, J. (1969), *Hong Kong: A Society in Transition*. London: Routledge & Kegan Paul.

Jeannet, Jean-Pierre, and Hennessey, H. David (1995), *Global Marketing Strategies*, 3rd ed. Boston: Houghton Mifflin Company.

Jernigan, H. L., and Jernigan, M. B. (1992), *Aging in Chinese Society: A Holistic Approach to the Experience of Aging in Taiwan and Singapore*. New York: The Haworth Press, Inc.

Jia, Wei (1994), *Chinese Foreign Investment Laws and Policies*. Westport, Conn.: Quorum Books.

Jiang, Ping (1995), "Chinese Legal Reform: Achievements, Problems and Prospects," *Journal of Chinese Law*, 9(1), Spring, 69.

Jing, T., et al. (1994), *Jingji lanpishu: 1993–94 Beijing jingji xingshi fenxi yu yuce* (Economic Blue Paper: Beijing Economic Analysis and Forecast in 1993–94). Beijing: Shoudu Shifan Daxue Chubanshe.

Johanson, J., and Vahlne, J. E. (1977), "The Internationalization Process of the Firm — A Model of Knowledge Development and Increasing Foreign Market Commitments," *Journal of International Business Studies*, 8, 23–32.

Johanson, J., and Wiedersheim, P. F. (1975), "The Internationalization of the Firm: Four Swedish Cases," *Journal of Management Studies*, 12, 305–322.

Johns, Deborah Kay (1995), "Reforming the State-Enterprise Property Relationship in the People's Republic of China: The Corporatization of State-Owned Enterprises," *Michigan Journal of International Law*, 16(3), Spring, 912.

Johnston, Wesley J. (1991), "Industrial Buying Behavior in the People's Republic of China: The Yin and Yang of Buyer-Seller Relationships in a Centrally Planned Economy," in T. Agmon and M. Von Glinow (eds.), *Technology Transfer in International Business*, 253–269. New York: Oxford University Press.

Jun, Kwang W., and Katada, Saori N. (1997), "Official Flows in China: Recent Trends and Major Characteristics," in Kui-Wai Li (ed.), *Financing China Trade and Investment*. Westport: Praeger Publishers.

Kahn, Herman (1979), *World Economic Development*. Boulder, Colorado: Westview Press.

Kallgren, J. K. (ed.) (1990), *Building a Nation — State, China after Forty Years*. Berkeley, California: Institute of East Asian Studies, University of California.

Kan, Chak-Yuen (1994), *The Emergence of the Golden Economic Triangle — Mainland China, Hong Kong and Taiwan*. Taipei: Lifework Press (in Chinese).

Kang, Rongping, and Yang, Yingchen (1992), "Xin Zhongguo jishu yinjin sishinian shuping (Review of the Last 40 Years' Technology Import in New China)," *Gongye jingji* (Journal of Industrial Economics), February, 75–81 (in Chinese).

Kelly, J. R., and McGrath, J. E. (1988), *On Time and Method*. Newbury Park, Calif.: Sage Publications.

Kendig, H. L., et. al. (1992), *Family Support for the Elderly: The International Experience*. New York: Oxford University Press.

Killing, P. J. (1978), "Diversification through Licensing," *R&D Management*, 3, 159–163.

Kim, D. D. (1986), "The Power of Commitment," *The China Business Review*, November/December, 40–43.

Kindle, I. (1982), "A Partial Theory of Chinese Consumer Behaviour: Marketing Strategy Implications," *Hong Kong Journal of Business Management*, 1, 97–109.

Kindle, T. (1985), "Chinese Consumer Behaviour: Historical Perspective Plus an Update on Communication Hypotheses," in J. Sheth and C. T. Tan (eds.), *Historical Perspectives of Consumer Behaviour*, 186–190. Singapore: National University of Singapore and Association for Consumer Behaviour.

King, A. U. C., and Myers, J. R. (1977), *Shame as an Incomplete Conception of Chinese Culture: A Study of Face*, Research Monograph. Hong Kong: H. K. Social Research Institute, The Chinese University of Hong Kong.

Kluckhohn, F. R., and Strodbeck, F. L. (1961), *Variations in Value Orientation*. Evanston, Ill.: Row, Paterson and Co.

Kobayashi, H., (1992), "Rural Economy and Distribution Problems in China," *China Newsletter*, 98, 13–20.

Kobrin, F. E. (1976), "The Fall in Household Size and the Rise of the Primary Individual in the United States," *Demography*, 13(1), 127–138.

Kobrin, F. E., and Goldscherider, C. (1982), "Family Extension or Nonfamily Living: Life Cycle, Economic and Ethnic Factors," *Western Sociological Review*, 13(1), 103–118.

Kobrin, Stephen J. (1982), *Managing Political Risk Assessment*. Berkeley: University of California Press.

Kogut, B. (1983), "Foreign Direct Investment as a Sequential Process," in C. P. Kindleberger and D. B. Audretsch (eds.), *The Multinational Corporation in the 1980s*. Cambridge, Mass.: MIT Press.

Kohut, John (1993), "China: Will the Bubble Burst?" *South China Morning Post*, May 25, 21.

Kok, Hil Fai (1996), "The Taxation Practices for Foreign Enterprises," in *The Business Environment of China*, Chapter 9, 226–290 (in Chinese). Hong Kong: Joint Publishing (H. K.) Co., Ltd.

Kornai, Janos (1986), *Contradictions and Dilemmas: Studies on the Soviet Economy and Society*. Cambridge: MIT Press.

Kwok, H. K. (1994a), "The Expectation of Shanghai Families towards Their Children in the Present Economic Reform," paper presented at the 4th National Academic Conference of Family held on 6–9 January at Guangzhou, China.

Kwok, H. K. (1994b), "Relationship between Two Generations — A Case Study in Shanghai," paper presented at the International Symposium on Family and the Young Generation held on 4–7 October at Beijing, China.

Kwok, H. K. (1994c), "The Relationship between Two Generations in the Family — A Shanghai Case," *Youth Studies* (Beijing), 194, 20–24.

Kwok, H. K. (1996a), "Adaptation in Family under Economic Reform: Cultural and Social Analysis — A Case Study of Shanghai," in Venkat Rao Pulla (ed.), *The Family: Asia Pacific Perspectives*, 186–192. Darwin, Australia: Centre for Southeast Asian Studies, Northern Territory University.

Kwok, H. K. (1996b), "The Impact of China's Economic Transition and One-Child Policy on the Social Security of the Elderly," paper presented at the 31st Annual Meeting of the Canadian Sociology and Anthropology Association, 2–5 June, Brock University, St. Catharines, Ontario, Canada.

La Barre, W. (1946), "Some Observations on Character Structure in the Orient," *Psychiatry*, 9, 215–225.

Laaksonen, Oiva (1988), *Management in China during and after Mao*. Berlin: Walter de Gruyter.

Lai, T. H., and Chen, K. J. (1980), "Historical and Demographic Perspective of the Chinese Family Size," *Chinese Journal of Sociology*, 5, 25–40 (in Chinese).

Lake, D. (1990), "Caution is the Word in Loans to China," *Asian Business*, September, 68–69.

Lam, Hang Chi (1995), "The Reduction of Import Tariff and Its Beneficial Effects for PRC's Economy," *Hong Kong Economic Journal*, April 2 (in Chinese).

Lam, Willy Wo-Lap (1995), *China after Deng Xiaoping. The Power Struggle in Beijing since Tiananmen*. Hong Kong: Professional Consultants Ltd.

Lau, S. (1993), "China's Population Policy: A Moral Critique," in Beatrice K. F. Leung and John D. Young (eds.), *Christianity in China: Foundation for Dialogue*, 266–285. Hong Kong: Centre of Asian Studies, The University of Hong Kong.

Lau, S. (1995), "Intergenerational Dependency: A Comparison of Three Cities — Beijing, Shanghai and Guangzhou," paper presented at the 30th Annual Meeting of the Canadian Sociology and Anthropology Association in Montreal, 4–7 June at University du Quebec a Montreal.

Lau, S. (1995), "Living Arrangements and Family Relationships: A Study of Three Chinese Cities — Beijing, Shanghai and Guangzhou," paper presented at VI International Conference of Asian Sociology, November 2–5, Beijing, China, 8.

Lau, S. (1996), "Changing Family Values in Present-Day Shanghai," in V. Rao Pulla (ed.), *The Family in Asia Pacific Perspectives*, 193–202. Darwin: Centre for Southeast Asian Studies, N T University Press.

Lau, S. (1996), "The Changing Pattern of Social Values in Asia during the Recent Economic Success," paper presented at the 31st Annual Meeting of the Canadian Sociology and Anthropology Association, 2–5 June, Brock University, St. Catharines, Ontario, Canada.

Lau, S. (1996), "Old-Age Support: The Case of Shanghai," in X. Chen and S. Lu (eds.), *Family and the Next Generation*. Beijing, China.

Lau, S., and Kwok, H. K. (1994), *Changing Family Values: The Case of Shanghai*. Hong Kong: Chiu Wah Press.

Lau, S., and Kwok, H. K. (1995), "Parent-Child Relationship: A Comparison of Three Cities — Beijing, Shanghai and Guangzhou," unpublished research report. Hong Kong: Lingnan College.

Lau, S., et al. (1990), "Relations among Perceived Parental Control, Warmth, Indulgence, and Family Harmony of Chinese in Mainland China," *Developmental Psychology*, 26(4), 674–677.

Lau, S. K. (1982), *Society and Politics in Hong Kong*. Hong Kong: The Chinese University Press.

Lau, S. K., and Kuan, H. C. (1988), *The Ethos of the Hong Kong Chinese*. Hong Kong: The Chinese University Press.

Lau, Yuk Ping (1995), "The Reform of Tax Collection System and the Structure of Public Finance," *The Economic and Trend of China — 1995*, Chapter 7.1, 246–249. Hong Kong: Commercial Press (in Chinese).

Lau, Yun Chong (1996), "The Expenditure Structure and Finance Policy of the State Central Government and the Local Government," *The Economic Trend of China — 1996*, Chapter 7.2, 220–223. Hong Kong: Commercial Press (in Chinese).

Lauer, Robert H. (1981), *Temporal Man: The Meaning and Uses of Social Time*. New York: Praeger.

Lee, K. H., and Lo, T. W. C. (1988), "American Businesspeople's Perceptions of Marketing and Negotiating in the PRC," *International Marketing Review*, Summer, 43–53.

Lee, Peter N. S. (1990), "Bureaucratic Corruption during the Deng Xiaoping Era," *Corruption and Reform*, 5, 29–47.

Lee, Shau Hang (1996a), " The Impacts on Foreign-Invested Enterprises Due to the Cancellation of Import Tariff Exemption for Production Equipment to be Engaged for Export Processing Trade," *Hong Kong Economic Journal*, June 1, 15 (in Chinese).

Lee, Shau Hang (1996b), "The Operating Problems of Customs Duty Security System," *Hong Kong Economic Journal*, 14 June, 22 (in Chinese).

Legge, J. (1960), *The Chinese Classics*. Hong Kong: Hong Kong University Press.

Leung, J. P., and Leung, K. (1992), "Life Satisfaction, Self-Concept, and Relationship with Parents in Adolescence," *Journal of Youth and Adolescence*, 21(6), 653–665.

Levine, Robert, and Wolff, Ellen (1985), "Social Time: The Heartbeat of Culture," *Psychology Today*, March, 28–35.

Levy, Marion J. (1965), "Aspects of the Analysis of Family Structure," in A. J. Coale, L. Fallers, M. J. Levy, D. Schneider and S. Tomkins, *Aspects of the Analysis of Family Structure*. Princeton, N.J.: Princeton University Press.

Levy, Marion J., Jr. (1955), "Contrasting Factors in the Modernization of China and Japan," in Simon Kuznets, W. E. Moore and J. Spengler (eds.), *Economic Growth: Brazil, India, and Japan*. Durham, N.C.: Duke University Press.

Levy, Marion J., Jr. (1962), "Some Aspects of 'Individualism' and the Problem of Modernization in China and Japan," *Economic Development and Cultural Change*, 10, 225–240.

Lewis, J. David, and Weigert, Andrew J. (1981), "The Structures and Meanings of Social Time," *Social Forces*, 60(2), December, 432–461.

Li, Fei (1995), *The King of Retailing: Planning and Design of Modern Stores*. Beijing: Beijing College of Economics (in Chinese).

Li, Huaizu, Gibbins, Michael, Han, Pengjie, and Luo, Sangui (1992), "Chinese

Tradition and Western Decision-Making Theory: Five Perspectives," in William C. Wedley and Nigel Campbell (eds.), *Advances in Chinese Industrial Studies*, Vol. 3. Greenwich, Connecticut: JAI Press.

Li, J. (1994), "Danwei zai shehui fenceng zhong de yiyi" (Work Units: The Implications for Social Stratification) in S. K. Lau et al., *Inequalities and Development: Social Stratification in Chinese Societies*. Hong Kong: The Chinese University Press.

Li, Ji, and Murray, Victor (1992), "Obstacles to the Development of the Field of Organizational Behavior in China," in William C. Wedley and Nigel Campbell (eds.), *Advances in Chinese Industrial Studies*, Vol. 3. Greenwich, Connecticut: JAI Press.

Li, Jing-yuan (1994), *From First to Infinitive: The Operation and Management of Chain Stores*. Beijing: China Economics Publishing (in Chinese).

Li, Kam-tong Daniel, Walker, Gordon, Fox, Mark, and Francis, Sonia (1995), "Acquisitions in the People's Republic of China: Opportunities, Constraints and Problems Faced by Foreign Investors," *Journal of International Banking Law*, 10(8), August, 361–365.

Li, Kam-tong Daniel, Walker, Gordon, Fox, Mark, Lau, Shu-keung, and Leung, T. K. P. (1996a), "Foreign Direct Investment in the PRC: Foreign Exchange Reform and Business Risk," *International Company and Commercial Law Review*, 7(7), July, 254–260.

Li, Kam-tong Daniel, Walker, Gordon, Fox, Mark, Lau, Shu-keung, and Leung, T. K. P. (1996b), "Foreign Exchange Reform in the PRC: Impact on Foreign Direct Investment and State-Owned Enterprises," *Journal of International Banking Law*, 11(6), June, 228–234.

Li, Kam-tong Daniel, Walker, Gordon, Lau, Shu-keung, and Leung, T. K. P. (1996), "Foreign Investment and the New Tariffs and Customs Regime in the PRC," *International Trade Law & Regulation*, 2(5), October, 180–188.

Li, Kui-Wai (1994), *Financial Repression and Economic Reform in China*. Westport: Praeger Publishers.

Li, Kui-Wai (1997), *Financing China Trade and Investment*. Westport: Praeger Publishers.

Li, Wei-min (1994), "A Comparative Study of Medium and Small Family Industrial Organisations in the Mainland China, Hong Kong and Taiwan," *Zhongshan Daxue Xuebao, Shekeban*, January, 52–60.

Li, Yunqi (1989), "China's Inflation: Causes, Effects and Solutions," *Asian Survey*, 29(7), 655–668.

Liao, Y. (1995), "Changes in Social Values and Educational Influence in Guangdong Province," paper presented to the International Symposium on Education and Social-Political Transitions in Asia, 29–31 May, at The University of Hong Kong.

Lieberman, Marvin B., and Montgomery, David B. (1988), "First-Mover Advantages," *Strategic Management Journal*, 9, 41–88.

Lieberman, Marvin B., and Montgomery, David B. (1991), "Strategy of Market Entry: To Pioneer or Follow?" in H. E. Glass (ed.), *Handbook of Business Strategy*, 2nd ed., 21-1–29. Boston: Warren, Gorham and Lamont.

Lin, N., and Xie, W. (1988), "Occupational Prestige in Urban China," *American Journal of Sociology*, 93, 793–832.

Lin, W. T. (1966), "Chinese Value Orientation in Hong Kong," *Sociological Analysis*, 27, 53–66.

Linda, G. M. (1988), "The Aging of Asia," *Journal of Gerontology*, 43(4), 99–113.

Linn, Gene (1993), "Climbing Back," *China Trade Report*, March.

Linn, Gene (1995), "Riding the Rollercoaster," *Asian Business*, August.

Liu, Alan P. (1992), "The 'Wenzhou Model' of Development and China's Modernization," *Asian Survey*, 32(8), 696–711.

Liu, Hu (1993), "An Account of China's Technology Import and Export in 1992," *Almanac of China's Foreign Economic Relations and Trade 1993/94*. Beijing: China Social Publishing.

Liu, Y. (1987), *Chinese Marriage and Family Studies*. Beijing: Chinese Academy of Social Sciences.

Liu, Yung-pi and Yang, Fan, (1995), "Zhu Xiaohua's Comments on China's Foreign Exchange Policy," *Wen Wei Po*, Hong Kong, 6–8 June.

Lo, C. K., Pepper, S., and Yuen, T. S. (eds.) (1995), *China Review 1995*. Hong Kong: The Chinese University Press.

Lo, T. W. C. (1986), "Foreign Investment in the Special Economic Zones: A Management Perspective," in Y. C. Jao and C. K. Leung (eds.), *China's Special Economic Zones: Policies, Problems and Prospects*, 194–200. Hong Kong: Oxford University Press.

Lo, T. W. C., and Yung, A. (1988), "Multinational Service Firms in Centrally-Planned Economies: Foreign Advertising Agencies in the PRC," *Management International Review*, 28(1), 26–33.

Locke, E. A., and Latham, G. P. (1990), *A Theory of Goal Setting and Task Performance*. Englewood Cliffs, N.J.: Prentice Hall.

Logue, B. J. (1990), "Modernization and the Status of the Elderly: Perspectives on Continuity and Change," *Journal of Cross Cultural Gerontology*, 5.

Lonsert, M., Preuss, K. J., and Kucher E. (eds.) (1995), *Handbuch Pharma-Management*. Wiesbaden: Gabler Verlag.

Loong, P. (1987), "China: Japanese Joker in the Pack," *Euromoney*, October, 137–143.

Lou, Er-xing, and Zhang, Wei-guo (1992), "A Comparative Study of China's Accounting Standards," *Accounting Research* (Beijing), 2, 5–15.

Lowe, J., and Crawford, N. K. (1983), "New Product Development and Technology Licensing for the Small Firm," *Industrial Management and Data Systems*, September, 26–29.

Lull, J., and Sun, S. W. (1988), "Agent of Modernization; Television and Urban Chinese Families," in J. Lull (ed.), *World Families Watch Television*. Newbury Park: Sage Publications.

Maister, D. H. (1985), "The Psychology of Waiting Lines," in J. A. Czepiel, M. R. Solomon and C. F. Surprenent (eds.), *The Service Encounter: Managing Employee/Customer Interaction in Service Businesses*, 113–123. Lexington: Lexington Books.

Manion, M. (1991), "Policy Implementation in the People's Republic of China: Authoritative Decisions Versus Individual Interests," *Journal of Asian Studies*, 50(2), 253–279.

Mansfield, E. (1988), "The Speed and Cost of Industrial Innovation in Japan and the United States: External vs. Internal Technology," *Management Science*, 34, 1157–1168.

Market Analysis Report (1996). China Pabst Brewery Group Company.

Martin, L. (1989), "Living Arrangements of Elderly in Fiji, Korea, Malaysia, and the Philippines," *Demography*, 26(4), 627–643.

Mascarenhas, B. (1982), "Coping with Uncertainty in International Business," *Journal of International Business Studies*, 13(2), 87–98.

Mascarenhas, Briance (1992), "Order of Entry and Performance in International Markets," *Strategic Management Journal*, 13, 499–510.

McCabe, M. (1991), "Family Relationships and Children's Personality: A Cross Cultural, Cross-Source Comparison," *British Journal of Social Psychology*, 30, 1–20.

McClelland, D. C. (1963), "Motivational Patterns in Southeast Asia with Special Reference to the Chinese Case," *Journal of Social Issues*, 19(1), 6–19.

McClelland, D. C., Atkinson, J. W., Clark, R. A., and Lowell, E. L. (1953), *The Achievement Motive*. New York: Appleton-Century-Crofts.

McGahan, Anita M. (1994), "Industry Structure and Competitive Advantage. An Outsider's Perspective on the Changes in Prescription Pharmaceuticals," *Harvard Business Review*, November–December, 115–124.

McNeal, J. M. (1969), "Consumer Satisfaction: The Measure of Marketing Effectiveness," *MSU Business Topics*, Summer, 31–36.

Meaney, C. S. (1989), "Market Reform in a Leninist system: Some Trends in the Distribution of Power, Status, and Money in Urban China," *Studies in Comparative Communism*, 22(2/3), 203–220.

Medical China Ltd. (1993), *Pharmaceutical Markets in China*, report. Hong Kong: Author.

Mei, Y. P. (1986), "The Status of the Individual in Chinese Social Thought and Practice," in Charles A. Moore (ed.), *The Chinese Mind: Essentials of Chinese Philosophy and Culture*. Honolulu: University of Hawaii Press.

Michael, R. T., et. al. (1980), "Changes in the Propensity to Live Alone," *Demography*, 17(1), 39–53.

Ming Pao (1992), March 3.

Ming Pao (1995), February 13.

Ministry of Finance, People's Republic of China (1992), *Accounting Standards for Business Enterprises*. Beijing: Publishing House of Law.

Mok, K. H. (1995), "Prosperity without Equality: An Examination of the Socio-Political Impacts of Structural Modification of Post-Mao Society," in L. Wong and S. MacPherson (eds.), *Social Change and Social Policy in Contemporary China*. Aldershot: Avebury.

Morello, Gabriele (1989), "The Time Dimension in Marketing," *Irish Marketing Review*, 1, 11–20.

Morris, C. (1956), *Varieties of Human Value*. Chicago: University of Chicago Press.

Munro, D. J. (1965), "The Yang Hsien-Chen Affair," *China Quarterly*, 22, 75–82.

Nanfang Weekend, 1 Sept. 1995.

Nathan, Andrew J. (1990), *China's Crisis: Dilemmas of Reform and Prospects for Democracy*. New York: Columbia University Press.

Naughton, Barry (1991), "Why Has Economic Reform Led to Inflation?" *American Economic Review*, 81(2), 207–211.

Neville, Robert C. (1989), "The Chinese Case in a Philosophy of World Religions," in Robert E. Allinson (ed.), *Understanding the Chinese Mind: The Philosophical Roots*. Hong Kong: Oxford University Press.

Newson, John (1996a), "Dr Doom on China Equities," *The Securities Journal*, June, 45.

Newson, John (1996b), "HSBC Asset Management on China's Equity Market," *The Securities Journal*, June, 44.

Nicosia, Francesco M., and Mayer, Robert N. (1976), "Toward a Sociology of Consumption," *Journal of Consumer Research*, 3, September, 65–75.

Nigh, D., Cho, K. R., and Krishnan, S. (1986), "The Role of Location-Related Factors in U.S. Banking Involvement Abroad: An Empirical Examination," *Journal of International Business Studies*, Fall, 59–72.

Nihon Keizai Shinbun (1993). Tokyo: Nihon Keizai Shinbunsha.

Nyaw, Mee-Kau (1997), "The Developments of Direct Foreign Investments in China," in Kui-Wai Li (ed.), *Financing China Trade and Investment*, Westport: Praeger Publishers.

Odagawa, Keisuke (1990), "Industrial Technology and Technical Transfers in China," *China Newsletter*, 89, Nov–Dec, 10–17.

O'Leary, Greg (1990), "Chinese Trade Unions and Economic Reform," *Labour-Management Relations in the Asia and Pacific Regions*. Hong Kong: University of Hong Kong, Centre of Asian Studies.

Oster, Sharon M. (1990), *Modern Competitive Analysis*. New York: Oxford University Press.

Overholt, W. H. (1982), *Political Risk*. London: Euromoney Publications.

Palmer, M. (1987), "The People's Republic of China: Some General Observations on Family Law," *Journal of Family Law*, 25, 48–54.

Parsons, J. E., and Goff, S. B. (1980), "Achievement Motivation and Values: An Alternative Perspective," in L. J. Fyans, Jr. (ed.), *Achievement Motivation, Recent Trends in Theory and Research*. New York: Plenum Press.

Parsons, P. (1993), "Marketing Revolution Hits Staid Giants," *Advertising Age*, July 10. 34.

Peebles, Gavin (1991), *Money in the People's Republic of China*. Sydney: Allen and Unwin.

Pen, Jun-chen (1992), *The Secret of Success of Chain Stores*. Taiwan: Han Yu Publishing (in Chinese).

People's Daily (1984), December 7.

People's Daily (1993), "The Accounting Law of the People's Republic of China," December 31, 5.

People's Republic of China — 40 Years of Technology Imports 1950–1990 (1992). Shanghai: Wen Wei Press (in Chinese).

Peoples' Republic of China Tax Update (1995), The Australian Society of CPAs (Hong Kong Branch), September Issue.

Perkins, Dwright H. (1986), *China: Asia's Next Economic Giant?* Seattle: University of Washington Press.

Pharmasearch International (1993), *Prospects for Multinational Pharmaceutical Corporations in China 1993–1997*. Perth, Australia.

Philips, L. (1981), "Assessment of Measurement Error in Key Informant Reports: A Methodological Note on Organizational Analysis in Marketing," *Journal of Marketing Research*, 18, 395–415.

Porter, Michael E. (1980), *Competitive Strategy: Techniques for Analyzing Industries and Competitors*. New York: The Free Press.

Porter, Michael E. (1985), *Competitive Advantage: Creating and Sustaining Superior Performance*. New York: The Free Press.

Porter, Michael E. (1991), "Towards a Dynamic Theory of Strategy," *Strategic Management Journal*, 12, 95–117.

Poynter, T. A. (1985), *Multinational Enterprises and Government Intervention.* London: Croom Helm.

Press, S., and Wilson, S. (1978), "Choosing between Logistic and Discriminant Analysis," *Journal of American Statistical Association*, 73, 699–705.

Prowse, Michael (1996), "US Can Learn from Values of Confucius," *South China Morning Post*, Business, 6.

Public Relations Journal (1993), July.

Pun, W. H. (1991), "A Study of Chinese Urban Nuclear Family," in K. Chiao (ed.), *Chinese Family and its Transition*. Hong Kong: The Chinese University Press.

Punnett, Betty Jane, and Zhao, Yasheng (1992), "Confucianism, Needs and Organizational Preferences: An Examination of Management Trainees in China," in William C. Wedley and Nigel Campbell (eds.), *Advances in Chinese Industrial Studies*, Vol. 3. Greenwich, Connecticut: JAI Press.

Pye, L. W. (1968), *The Spirit of Chinese Politics*. Cambridge, Mass.: MIT Press.

Qian, Andrew Xuefeng (1993), "Riding Two Horses: Corporatizing Enterprises and the Emerging Securities Regulatory Regime in China," *UCLA Pacific Basin Law Journal*, 12, Fall, 62–97.

Quah, S. R. (ed.) (1990), *The Family as an Asset: An International Perspective on Marriage, Parenthood and Social Policy*. Singapore: Times Academic Press.

Raddock, D. M. (1986), *Assessing Corporate Political Risk*. Totowa, N.J.: Bowman & Littlefield.

Rafferty, K. (1989), *City on the Rock*. London: Viking.

Ralston, David A., Gustafson, David J., Elsass, Priscilla M., and Cheung, Fanny (1992), "Eastern Values: A Comparison of Managers in the United States, Hong Kong, and the People's Republic of China," *Journal of Applied Psychology*, 77(5), 664–671.

Redding, S. G. (1990), *The Spirit of Chinese Capitalism*. Berlin: Walter de Gruyter.

Reynolds, P. D. (1982), *China's International Banking and Financial System*. New York: Praeger Publishers.

Riahi-Belkaoui, A. (1994), *Accounting in the Developing Countries*, 74. Westport, Connecticut: Quorum Books.

Rice, M., and Lu, Zaiming (1988), "A Content Analysis of Chinese Magazine Advertisements," *Journal of Advertising*, 4, 43–48.

Richman, B. A. (1969), *Industrial Society in Communist China*. New York: Random House.

Riley, Mary L. (1995), "Advertising with Chinese Characteristics — Censorship of Advertisements in China," *China Law & Practice*, 1 October, 13–15.

Rocca, J. L. (1994), "The New Elites," in M. Brosseau and C. K. Lo (eds.), *China Review 1994*. Hong Kong: The Chinese University Press.

Rogers, Everett M. (1962), *Diffusion of Innovations*. New York: The Free Press.

Rohwer, J. (1995), *Asia Rising*. New York: Simon and Schuster.

Root, Franklin R. (1994), *Entry Strategies for International Markets*, revised and expanded ed. Lexington, Mass.: Macmillan Inc.

Rosen, S. (1987/88), "The Private Economy," *Chinese Economic Studies*, 21, Fall and Winter.

Russel, B. (1966), *The Problem of China*. London: George Allen and Unwin.

Salaff, J. W. (1981), *Working Daughters of Hong Kong: Filial Piety or Power in the Family?*, 7. Cambridge: Cambridge University Press.

Sampson, G. P., and Snape, R. H. (1985), "Identifying the Issues of Trade in Services," *World Economy*, 8, June, 171–182.

Samuels, J. (1990), "Accounting for Development: An Alternate Approach," in R. Wallace, J. Samuels and R. Briston (eds.), *Research in Third World Accounting*, Vol. 1, 67–86. London: JAI Press Ltd.

Schary, Phil B. (1971), "Consumption and the Problem of Time," *Journal of Marketing*, 35, April, 50–55.

Schell, O. (1987), "Serving the People with Advertising," *Whole Earth Review*, Spring, 88–93.

Schell, O. (1988), *Discos and Democracy*. New York: Anchor Books Doubleday.

Schnepp, Otto, Von Glinow, Mary Ann, and Bhambri, Arvind (1990), *United States–China Technology Transfer*. Englewood Cliffs, N.J.: Prentice Hall.

Sender, Henny (1993), "Taxing Problem," *Far Eastern Economic Review*, November 25, 52.

Sha, Zhen-quan (1992), "Supermarkets in China: Opportunities, Questions and Solutions," *Hong Kong Journal of Business Management*, X (in Chinese).

Shambaugh, D. L. (1988), "Peking Fuels Expectations It Can't Meet," *Asian Bulletin*, March, 6–7.

Shao, Hanming, and Wang, Yankun (1989), "Picking out the Pieces," *Beijing Review*, January 23–29, 15–18.

Sher, Ada Elizabeth (1984), *Aging in Post-Mao China: The Politics of Veneration*. Boulder: Westview Press.

Shih, Anne, Yeung, Desmond, and Ray, Andrew (1995), "Accounting, Taxation and Foreign Exchange Control," in Jane Withey (ed.), *Doing Business in China*, 200–221. Whitby, Ont.: McGraw-Hill Ryerson.

Shively, A. N., and Shively, S. (1972), "Value Changes during a Period of Modernisation: The Case of Hong Kong," working paper. Hong Kong: Institute of Social Research, The Chinese University of Hong Kong.

Shum, Alfred (1994), "China — Developing an Effective Distribution Strategy," *Far East Focus*, Issue 7, July, 134–138.

Shum, Alfred (1995a), "China's Administrative Protection Regulations for Pharmaceuticals: A Review," *IMS China Update*, Issue 25, July, 2–4.

Shum, Alfred (1995b), "Recruiting, Training and Retaining Key Managers in China," *IMS China Update*, Issue 20, February, 11–15.

Shum, Alfred (1996), "The OTC Market in China — A Policy for Growth," *Scrip Magazine*, February, 6–8.

Sinha, Tapen (1995), "Why Western Accounting Methods Are Needed in China Now," *Management Accounting* (U.K.), May, 18–19.

Sklair, L. A. (1995), "The Culture-Ideology of Consumerism in Urban China: Some Findings from a Survey in Shanghai," in R. Belk et al. (eds.), *Consumption in Marketing Societies*. Greenwich, Conn.: JAL Press.

Soldo, B. J. (1981), "The Living Arrangements of the Elderly in the Near Future," in S. B. Kiesler, J. N. Morgan and V. K. Oppenheimer (eds.), *Aging: Social Change*. New York: Academic Press.

Solinger, Dorothy J. (1984), *Chinese Business under Socialism: The Politics of Domestic Commerce 1949–1980*. Berkeley: University of California Press.

Sorokin, P. A. (1943), *Sociocultural Causality, Space, Time*. New York: Russell & Russell.

Spence, J. T. (1985), "Achievement and Achievement Motivation: A Cultural Perspective," in J. T. Spence (ed.), *Motivation, Emotion, and Personality*. North Holland: Elsevier Science Publishers.

State Council, PRC (1992), "Decision to Accelerate Development of Tertiary Industries," in G. Luo (ed.), *Important Strategic Decision — Accelerate Development of Tertiary Industries*. Beijing: Zhongguo Zhengfa Daxue Chubanshe (in Chinese).

State Council, PRC (1996), *Notice on Straightening the Order of Accounting and Further Enhancing the Quality of Accounting Practice*, April 19.

State Statistical Bureau, PRC (various issues), *China Statistical Yearbook*. Beijing: China Statistical Publishing House.

Stewart, Sally, and Keown, Charles F. (1989), "Talking with the Dragon: Negotiating in the People's Republic of China," *Columbia Journal of World Business*, 24(3), 68–72.

Stross, R. (1990), "The Return of Advertising in China: A Survey of the Ideological Reversal," *The China Quarterly*, 123, 485–502.

Sullivan, Roger W. (1992), "Trade, Investment, and the Fear of 'Fearful Evolution,'" *Issues and Studies*, 28(2), 51–66.

Sung, Hai-peng (1995), "A Review of China's Reform of Foreign Exchange System," *Hong Kong Economic Journal*, 28 April.

Survey Asia: Special Studies Series (1991) "The Prospects of Financial Market Developments in China," October/November, No. 16.

Survey Data (1996), *The Chain Stores Association of Guangdong, China*.

Svensson, B. (1984), *Acquisition of Technology through Licensing in Small Firms*. Linkoping, Sweden: Linkoping University.

Swanson, Mitzi (1995), *Healthcare in Shanghai.* Hong Kong: Asian Strategies Limited.

Swanz, D. (1995), "Doing Business in China," *The CPA Journal*, March, 42–49.

Tai, Hung-chao (1989), "The Oriental Alternative: A Hypothesis of East Asian Culture and Economy," *Issues & Studies*, 25(3), 10–36.

Tang, Xu, and Li, Kui-Wai (1997), "Money and Banking in China," in Kui-Wai Li (ed.), *Financing China Trade and Investment.* Westport: Praeger Publishers.

Tang, Y. W., Chow L. and Cooper, B. (1994), *Accounting and Finance in China*, 2nd ed., 24. Hong Kong: Longman Asia Limited.

Tellis, Gerard J., and Golder, Peter N. (1996), "First to Market, First to Fail? Real Causes of Enduring Market Leadership," *Sloan Management Review*, 2, Winter, 65–75.

Terpstra, V., and Yu, C. M. (1988), "Determinants of Foreign Investment of U.S. Advertising Agencies," *Journal of International Business Studies*, 19(1), 33–46.

Thoburn, H. B., et al. (1989), "The Middle Class and the Market Place: The PRC, Overseas Chinese and Thailand," *Advances in International Marketing*, 1, 143–178.

Thorelli, H. B. (1982), "China: Consumer Voice and Exit," in R. L. Day and H. K. Hunt (eds.), *International Fare in Consumer Satisfaction and Complaining*, 105–110. Knoxville, Tennessee: University of Tennessee.

Thornton, A., Chang, M. C., and Sun, T. H. (1984), "Social and Economic Change, Intergenerational Relationships, and Family Formation in Taiwan," *Demography*, 21(4), 475–499.

Thurwachter, T. (1990), "Japan in China: The Guangdong Example," *The China Business Review*, January/February, 7–17.

Tian, Ruixin, and Wang, Guixiang (1992), "Jishu yinjin chenggong yaosu (Critical Success Factors of Technology Import)," *Gongye jingji* (Journal of Industrial Economics), December, 79–81 (in Chinese).

Time (1995), October 16.

Ting, Wenlee (1988), *Multinational Risk Assessment and Management Strategies for Investment and Marketing Decisions.* New York: Quorum Books.

Toffler, Alvin (1980), *The Third Wave.* London: Pan in association with Collins.

Tong, Kung Leung (1996), "The Reform of the State Financial Policy," in *The Economic Trend of China — 1996*, Chapter 7.3, 224–229. Hong Kong: Commercial Press (in Chinese).

Tong, Louis (1995), "The Rapidly Changing Lifestyles in Asia Pacific Region: China," presentation at the Asia Pacific Marketing Conference, Marketing Association of Thailand, Bangkok, Thailand, 19–21 April.

Trade Watch (various issues), Hong Kong Trade Development Council.

Treas, J., and Wang, W. (1993), "Of Deeds and Contracts: Filial Piety Perceived in Contemporary Shanghai," in V. L. Bengtson and W. A. Achenbaum (eds.), *The Changing Contract Across Generations*, 87–98. New York: Aldine De Gruyter.

Tsang, Eric W. K. (1994), "Strategies for Transferring Technology to China," *Long Range Planning*, 27(3), June, 98–107.

Tsang, S. K., and Ma, Y. (1995), *An Open-Economy Macroeconometric Model of China: The Impacts of Foreign Capital*, BRC Papers on China. Hong Kong: School of Business, Business Research Centre, Hong Kong Baptist University.

Tse, K. K. (1985), *Marks & Spencer: Anatomy of Britain's Most Efficiently Managed Company*. Oxford: Pergamon Press.

Tseng, C. S., Kwan, P., and Cheung, F., (1995), "Distribution in China: A Guide Through the Maze," *Long Range Planning*, 28(1), 81–95.

Tseng, Ho-jen (1993), "Peasant, State and Democracy: The Chinese Case," *Issues and Studies*, 29(4), 34–50.

Tsui, M. (1989), "Changes in Chinese Urban Family Structure," *Journal of Marriage and the Family*, 51, 737–747.

Tuan, C., Wong, S. N., & Ye, C. S. (1986), *Chinese Entrepreneurship under Capitalism and Socialism — Hong Kong and Guangzhou Cases*. Hong Kong: Centre of Asian Studies, University of Hong Kong.

U.S. Congress, Office of Technology Assessment (1993), *Pharmaceutical R&D: Costs, Risks and Rewards*, OTA-H-522. Washington, D.C.: U.S. Government Printing Office.

U.S. Foreign and Commercial Service in Beijing (1994), "Franchising in China," *East Asian Executive Reports*, April, 6–13.

Usunier, Jean-Claude, and Valetta-Florence, Pierre (1994), "Perceptual Time Patterns (Time Styles)," *A Psychometric Scale Time and Society*, 3(2), 219–241.

Van Oort, H. A. (1970), "Chinese Culture — Values Past and Present," *Chinese Culture*, 11(1).

Venkatesan, M., and Anderson, Beverlee B. (1985a), "Time and Consumer Behaviour: A Historical Perspective," in C. T. Tan and Jagdish N. Sheth (eds.), *Historical Perspectives in Consumer Research: National and International Perspectives*. Provo, Utah: Association for Consumer Research.

Venkatesan, M., and Anderson, Beverlee B. (1985b), "Time Budgets and Consumer Services," in Thomas Bloch, G. D. Upah and Valarie A. Zeithaml (eds.), *Services Marketing in a Changing Environment*. Chicago: American Marketing Association.

Venkatesan, M., Anderson, Beverlee B., Wong, John K., and Chebat, Jean Charles

(1991), "Temporal Patterns in the Consuming of Services," *Third Symposium on Cross-Cultural Consumer and Business Studies Proceedings, Hawaii*, 58–59.

Wada, Kazuo (1990), *From Zero to Billions*. Beijing: China Economics Publishing (in Chinese).

Waldie, K. F. (1981), "Management — Western Ways and Eastern Needs — A Cultural Comparison," *The Hong Kong Manager*, June, 19.

Wallace, R. (1990), "Accounting in Developing Countries: A Review of the Literature," in R. Wallace, J. Samuels and R. Briston (eds.), *Research in Third World Accounting*, Vol. 1, 3–54. London: JAI Press.

Wang, Guiguo (1993), *Business Law of China: Cases, Texts and Commentary*, 12. Hong Kong: Butterworths Asia.

Wang, Guiguo, and Tomasic, Roman (1994), *China's Company Law: An Annotation*, commentary, 68. Singapore: Butterworths.

Wang, Huijiong (1993), "Technology Management in a Dual World," *International Journal of Technology Management*, 8(1/2), 108–120.

Wang, Huijiong (1994), "Technology Innovation and Enterprise Management, and a Case Study in China," *International Journal of Technology Management*, 9(5/6/7), 564–574.

Wang, N. T. (1984a), *China's Modernization and Transnational Corporations*. Lexington, Mass.: Lexington Books.

Wang, N. T. (1984b), "Reforms in Foreign Trade and Investment in China," *Hong Kong Economic Papers*, No. 15, 87–91.

Wang, S., and Qian, J. (1987), "Financial Accounting and Reporting," in *Accounting and Auditing in the People's Republic of China: A Review of its Practices, Systems Education and Developments*, 9–92. Richardson, Texas: The University of Texas at Dallas.

Wang, Shun (1993), "Confucian Culture and the Initiation of Economic Modernization," *Shehui kexue zhanxian*, No. 2, 134–137.

Wang, Wallace Wen-Yew (1992), "Reforming State Enterprises in China: The Case for Redefining Enterprise Operating Rights," *Journal of Chinese Law*, 6(2), Fall, 101.

Watanabe, Masumi (1993), "Some Thoughts on Technology Transfer," *China Newsletter*, 103, 7–12.

Waterhouse, B. (1990), "Japanese Giants Roll across Asia," *Asian Business*, Spring/Summer, 64–65.

Wei, C. T. (1980), *The Wisdom of China*. Taipei: Cowboy Publishing Co.

Weinrauch, J. D., and Langlois, A. (1987), "Reducing Conflict between Licensors and Licensees in International Licensing," *Journal of International Management*, 4, 381–390.

Welch, L. S. (1985), "The International Marketing of Technology: An Interaction Perspective," *International Marketing Review*, 2(1), 41–53.

Wheatley, J. (1996), "Seminar on Healthcare Reform," *IMS China Update*, Issue 27, February, 2–4.

White, J. M. (1991), *Dynamics of Family Development*. London: The Guilford Press.

Whiting, B. B. (1964), *Six Cultures, Studies of Child-Rearing*. New York: John Wiley and Sons, Inc.

Whyte, M. K., and Parish, W. (1984), *Urban Life in Contemporary China*. Chicago: The University of Chicago Press.

Williamson, O. (1975), *Markets and Hierarchies: Analysis and Antitrust Implications*. New York: The Free Press.

Wilson, R. W., and Pusey, A. W. (1982), "Achievement Motivation and Small-Business Relationship Patterns in Chinese Society," in S. L. Greenblatt et al. (eds.), *Social Interaction in Chinese Society*, 195–208. New York: Praeger.

Wilson, Richard (1981), "Moral Behavior in Chinese Society: A Theoretical Perspective," in Richard W. Wilson, Sidney L. Greenblatt and Amy Auerbacher Wilson (eds.), *Moral Behavior in Chinese Society*. New York: Praeger.

Wind, Y., and Mahajan, V. (1988), "New Product Development: A Perspective for Re-examination," *Journal of Product Innovation Management*, 5(4), 304–310.

Wokutch, R. E. (1990), "Corporate Social Responsibility Japanese Style," *Academy of Management Executive*, May, 56–74.

Wolf, M. (1985), "Marriage, Family and the State in Contemporary China," in D. Kingsley (ed.), *Contemporary Marriage*. New York: Russell Sage Foundation.

Wolken, L. C. W. (1990), "The Restructuring of China's Banking System under the Economic Reforms 1979–1989," *Columbia Journal of World Business*, Spring/Summer, 53–63.

Wong, A. K., and Kuo, E. L. Y. (eds.) (1979), *The Contemporary Family in Singapore*. Singapore: Singapore University Press.

Wong, Christine (1995), "Fiscal Reform in 1994," in *China Review 1995*, Chapter 20. Hong Kong: The Chinese University Press.

Wong, Clement Yuk-pang, and Lo, Kenneth (1997), "Foreign Exchange Markets in China: Evolution and Performance," in Kui-Wai Li (ed.), *Financing China Trade and Investment*. Westport: Praeger.

Wong, L., and Mok, K. K. (1995), "Dynamism and Development: The Economic Reform and Social Change in Post-Mao China," paper presented at the VI International Conference of the Asian Sociology, Beijing, November, 1–6.

Wong, Po Kwong (1996), "The Reform of Customs System," in *The Economic*

Trend of China — 1996, Chapter 7.5, 234–237. Hong Kong: Commercial Press (in Chinese).

Woodard, K. (1986), "Political Risk in China," in D. M. Raddock (ed.), *Assessing Corporate Political Risk*. Totowa, N.J.: Rowman & Littlefield.

The World Bank (1990), *China: Between Plan and Market*, World Bank Country Study, 59–78. Washington, D.C.: Author.

The World Bank (1992), *China: Reform and the Role of the Plan in the 1990s*, World Bank Country Study, 70–73. Washington, D.C.: Author.

Wu, Cuilan (1989), "China's Reform of the Financial and Tax System," in Christine Kessides et al. (eds.), *Financial Reform in Socialist Economies*, 62–74. Washington D.C.: The World Bank.

Wu, Joseph S. (1972), "Western Philosophy and the Search for Chinese Wisdom," in Arne Naess and Alastair Hannay (eds.), *Invitation to Chinese Philosophy: Eight Studies*. Oslo: Universitetsforlaget.

Wu, Lawrence C. (1986), *Fundamentals of Chinese Philosophy*. Lanham: University Press of America.

Wu, Z. M. (1993), "Basic Trend and Problems in China's Modernization," *Social Science Front*, 62(2), 14–21.

Wu, Zhenquan (1996), "China's Technology Transfer Grows Obviously in 1995," in *Almanac of China's Foreign Economic Relations and Trade 1996/97*. Beijing: China Social Publishing.

Wuster, Thomas S. (1987), "The Leading Brands 1925–1985," in *Perspectives*. The Boston Consulting Group.

Xinmin wanbao (1995), 20 August (in Chinese).

Xing, Wei (1995), "An Account of China's Technology Import and Export in 1994," in *Almanac of China's Foreign Economic Relations and Trade 1995/96*. Beijing: China Social Publishing.

Xinhua General Overseas News Service (1992), "China to Adopt New Financial Accounting Standards," December 3.

Yabuuchi, Masaki (1986a), "Technology Transfer and Technological Reform of Existing Enterprises in China," *China Newsletter*, 64, Sept–Oct, 7–10.

Yabuuchi, Masaki (1986b), "Japanese Technology Transfer and China's Technological Reform," *China Newsletter*, 65, Nov–Dec, 10–12.

Yang, C. K. (1966), *Chinese Community Society: The Family and the Village*, 2nd ed. Cambridge, Mass.: MIT Press.

Yang, C. K. (1974), "The Chinese Family: The Young and the Old," in R. L. Coser (ed.), *The Family: Its Structure and Functions*. New York: St. Martin's Press.

Yang, K. S. (1979), "Research on Chinese National Character in Modern Psychology," in C. I. Wen et al. (eds.), *Modernization and Change of Value*. Taipei: Thought and Word Association (in Chinese).

Yang, K. S. (1981), "Social Orientation and Individual Modernity among Chinese Students in Taiwan," *Journal of Social Psychology*, 113, 159–170.

Yang, Z. (1987), "Friendly Cooperation between Chinese and Japanese Banks and Development of Sino-Japanese Financial Relations," *Foreign Bankers in China*, Vol. 2, 126–129. Hong Kong: Kong Yuen Publishing Co.

Yau, Oliver H. M. (1986), *Consumer Satisfaction and Cultural Values*, PhD thesis, University of Bradford, England.

Yau, Oliver H. M. (1988), "Chinese Cultural Values: Their Dimensions and Marketing Implications," *European Journal of Marketing*, 22(5), 44–57.

Yau, Oliver H. M., Li, Y. J., and Lo, Thamis (1986), "Marketing and Marketing Research in China: Some Observations on the Distribution System and the Problems of Marketing Research," *Journal of International Marketing and Marketing Research*, 11(1), 3–18.

Yeung, Y. M., and Chu, D. K. Y. (eds.) (1994), *Guangdong: Survey of a Province Undergoing Rapid Change*. Hong Kong: The Chinese University Press.

Yin, J. Z. (1992), "Technological Capabilities as Determinants of the Success of Technology Transfer Projects," *Technological Forecasting and Social Change*, 42, 17–29.

Yokata, Takaaki (1987), "Joint Ventures and Technology Transfer to China — The Realities," *China Newsletter*, 71, 9–12.

Yu, Maozhang, and Chen, Bi (eds.) (1996), *The Chinese Pharmaceutical Market Guide 1996*, 3 Volumes, Scrip Reports. PJB Publication Ltd. and SPAC Information Center.

Zee, Winston K. (ed.) (1992), *Investing in China: B Shares*. London: Euromoney Books and Asia Law & Practice Ltd.

Zeng, Dao-xian (1992), "On the Problems of Absorption and Diffusion of Acquired Technologies," *Keji daobao*, No. 1 (in Chinese).

Zeng, Dao-xian (1993), "Setting a Foothold on National Conditions: Search for the Effective Path for Technology Imports," *Keji daobao*, No. 11 (in Chinese).

Zerubavel, Eviatar (1982), "The Standardization of Time: A Socio-historical Perspective," *American Journal of Sociology*, 88, 1–23.

Zhai, Linyu (1992), "Current Situation and Problems of China's State Enterprises," *China Newsletter*, 98, 8–12.

Zhang, Ed (1993), "Income Gap Threatens Development Growth," *Window*, December 3, 30.

Zhang, Wenxiu (1992), "A Summary of Symposium on Confucianism," *Social Sciences in China*, 13(3), 124–133.

Zhao, Chunhua (1992), "An Account on Technology Import and Export in China in 1991," in *Almanac of China's Foreign Economic Relations and Trade 1992/93*. Beijing: China Social Publishing.

Zhu, Xiaohua (1994), "Exchange Rate and Capital Flows: China's Experience in a

High Growth Period," in *Monetary and Exchange Rate Management with International Capital Mobility*. Hong Kong: Hong Kong Monetary Authority.

Zimmerman, S. L. (1992), *Family Policies and Family Well-Being*. London: Sage Publications.

Zu, Q. (1994), "Renmin shenghuo wenbu zhengzhang, Dan wujia shangzheng tupo jingjiexian" (People's Livelihood Is Increasing Steadily but Price Rises Have Exceeded the Warning Level), in Liu Jiang et al. (eds.), *1993–1994 nian Zhongguo: Shehui xingshi fenxi yu yuce* (China in 1993–1994: Analysis of Social Situation and Forecast). Beijing: Zhongguo Shehui Kexue Chubanshe.

Zwisler, Eric V. (1995), "China's New Leap Forward," *Zuellig Pharma Review*, No. 1, 2–5.

Contributors

ATUAHENE-GIMA, Kwaku	PhD (Wollongong), Head and Associate Professor, Department of Management, City University of Hong Kong, Hong Kong
BRUCHE, Gert	Professor of International Management, Berlin School of Business, Fachhochschule für Wirtschaft, Germany
CHAN, David Yee-kai	MBA (UCLA), Associate Professor, Department of Finance and Decision Sciences, Hong Kong Baptist University, Hong Kong
CHAN, H. L.	PhD (HKU), Associate Professor, Department of Marketing, City University of Hong Kong, Hong Kong
CHOW, Raymond P. M.	MSc (London), Department of Marketing, City University of Hong Kong, Hong Kong
DeCELLES, Michael D.	College of Commerce, Sultan Qaboos University
HO, John D.	PhD (Minnesota), Associate Professor, Department of Law, City University of Hong Kong, Hong Kong
KO, Anthony	MBA (HKU), Associate Head and Associate Professor, Department of Management, City University of Hong Kong, Hong Kong
LAU, Stephen Shek-lam	PhD (Lourain), Associate Professor, School of General Education, Lingnan College, Hong Kong
LEUNG, T. K. P.	MComm (NSW), Assistant Professor, Department of Business Studies, Hong Kong Polytechnic University, Hong Kong
LI, Daniel Kam-tong	MBA (East Asia), Assistant Professor, Department of Accounting and Finance, Lingnan College, Hong Kong
LI, Kui-Wai	PhD (City University of London), Associate Professor, Department of Economics and Finance, City University of Hong Kong, Hong Kong

LI, Yi-jing — Professor, Faculty of Business Administration, South China University of Technology, Guangzhou, China

LO, Thamis W. C. — PhD (City, Lond.), Professor, Department of International Business, The Chinese University of Hong Kong, Hong Kong

MASCHMEYER, Richard A. — DBA (Kentucky), Head and Professor, Department of Accounting and Finance, Lingnan College, Hong Kong

MUN, Kin-chok — PhD (Freib.), Professor, Department of International Business, The Chinese University of Hong Kong

SHA, Zhen-quan — Associate Professor, Faculty of Business Administration, South China University of Technology, Guangzhou, China

SIN, Abby — MBA (CUHK), Insolvency Officer II, Official Receiver's Office, Hong Kong Government

STEELE, Henry C. — MA (Lancester), Head and Associate Professor, Department of Marketing and International Business, Lingnan College, Hong Kong

TSENG, C. S. — MSc (London), Associate Professor, Department of Marketing, City University of Hong Kong, Hong Kong

WALKER, Gordon R. — Senior Lecturer, School of Law, Canterbury University, New Zealand

YAU, Oliver H. M. — PhD (Bradford), Associate Dean (Graduate Programmes), Faculty of Business, and Professor of Marketing, Department of Marketing, City University of Hong Kong, Hong Kong

YU, Eddie — MSc (Durham), Associate Professor, Department of Management, City University of Hong Kong, Hong Kong

ZENG, Dao-xian — Professor, Faculty of Economics and Management, Tsinghua University, Beijing, China